AF515916

The Shaping of Modern Calcutta

The Shaping of Modern Calcutta

The Lottery Committee Years, 1817–1830

RANABIR RAY CHOUDHURY

Published by
NIYOGI BOOKS
Block D, Building No. 77,
Okhla Industrial Area, Phase-I,
New Delhi-110 020, INDIA
Tel: 91-11-26816301, 26818960
Email: niyogibooks@gmail.com
Website: www.niyogibooksindia.com

Editor: Sucharita Ghosh
Design: Shashi Bhushan Prasad

ISBN: 978-93-91125-30-1
Publication: 2022

Printed at: Niyogi Offset Pvt. Ltd., New Delhi, India

For
Shipra, Ayana, Sushovona,
Aurobindo and Ranadev

CONTENTS

INTRODUCTION

In 1901, A.K. Ray wrote in the *Census of India*: 'It may be truly said that it was under the direction of the Lottery Committee that the work of reconstructing chaotic Calcutta into the decent shape of a modern town was not only inaugurated but pushed on with vigour'.[1] This book attempts to shed some light on how the work was accomplished. The present volume is, in fact, a supplement to the author's earlier work, *A City in the Making: Aspects of Calcutta's Early Growth*,[2] which dealt with the spatial growth of Calcutta (Kolkata) from the time of Job Charnock (1690) till the setting up in October 1817 of the Committee to Superintend the Effective Use of the Lottery Funds, known as the Lottery Committee. In this book, the story is taken up to 1830 when, for all practical purposes, the committee's effective work was over, the East India Company in London asking its Government in Calcutta that it be 'abolished'.[3]

The book is rooted in the official records of the committee's work spread over thirteen years which, essentially, comprise a collection of disparate events and themes, all of them tied to the main thread of the city's spatial development. The central effort has been to segregate the diverse individual threads and form each into a consistent account, all the separate strands taken together yielding (hopefully) a depiction of how the city of Calcutta acquired the rudiments of its present road-grid. To mention just a handful of the separate items which make up the story, Strand Road along the river was conceived and built by the committee as was also the arterial thoroughfare stretching from Shyambazar in the north to Park Street (now Mother Teresa Sarani) in the south comprising Bidhan Sarani, College Street, Nirmal Chunder Street, and Rafi Ahmed Kidwai Road. Amherst Street (Raja Rammohun Sarani) was built along with Cornwallis Street (Bidhan Sarani), Colootala Street (partly Maulana Shaukat Ali Street, Acharya Brojen Sil Street and Angarika Dharmapala Street) and Mirzapur Street (Surya Sen Street) being constructed linking Chitpur Road (Rabindra Sarani) in the west to Circular Road (Upper Circular Road was renamed Acharya Prafulla Chandra Road) in the east. To the west and south-west of today's BBD Bagh (then Tank Square), Koila Ghat Street (Babu Tarapada Mukherjee Sarani), Hare Street and Hastings Street (Kiron Shankar Roy Road) were opened up. Bankshall Street was created from an open space in front of the Governor's house in the early 18th century, and Church Lane, to the west of St John's churchyard, was given the consolidated shape of a street. Two 'ancient' roads, Clive Street (Netaji Subhas Road) and Chitpur Road, were widened while the entire area of Garden Reach behind the row of garden houses on the southern bank of the Hooghly was developed with roads and drainage being built resulting in an influx of native residents.

Another feather in the committee's cap was the clearing up of the vast tract of low-lying ground between Theatre Road (Shakespeare Sarani) and Circular Road (Lower Circular Road was renamed Acharya Jagadish Chandra Bose Road), a large part of which was not only known as *dhankhet* (rice field) at the time and earlier but which was also a hotbed of pestilence because of its marshy nature. As far as the aesthetic aspect is concerned, it was the Lottery Committee which introduced to the city the brick-and-mortar balustrade which today lines both sides of Red Road (Indira Gandhi Sarani) and the western side of Chowringhee Road (the northern part of which, till Park Street, has been renamed Jawaharlal Nehru Road).[4]

While it is true that the Lottery Committee did seminal work for the spatial development of Calcutta, what it achieved in reality was not much more than just scratching the surface as it were if the work left undone is considered. James Ranald Martin's *Notes on the Medical Topography of Calcutta*[5] indicates clearly the unsatisfactory state the city was in at the time the committee folded up. A similar picture is portrayed by F.P. Strong at around the same time.[6] Even so, the question arises: why were the measures taken by the committee to improve the city not taken earlier? After all, the Earl of Moira (created the Marquess of Hastings in late 1816), under whose aegis the Lottery Committee was set up, had assumed the Governor-Generalship in 1813, which means that he waited for nearly four years before the committee was appointed and began its work. Before the committee's appointment, and since the departure of Lord Minto (Moira's predecessor), water tanks had been dug and deepened and important roads such as Chitpur Road had been widened. During the Minto years (1807-13), drainage projects had been taken up, some in the native parts of the town.[7] Baithakkhanah Road (Bowbazar Street, later Bepin Behary Ganguly Street) had been extended to make the crucial connexion with Chitpur Road at Lalbazar, streets in the native areas had been paved with brick, and an important canal had been constructed towards the east (Beliaghata Canal). At the time the Lottery Committee took over, the 'great Simleah drain' was in the process of being implemented. These projects had been planned and implemented by the Committee for the Improvement of the Town and later by the Board of Conservancy which was made up of the city magistrates. As far as the provision of funds was concerned, they were generated by the lottery proceeds since the first drawing in 1809.[8]

It was argued in *A City in the Making* that the era of planning for the spatial development of Calcutta (the effective regulation of space) had begun with Lord Wellesley's appointment of his Committee for the Improvement of the Town in 1803. There were more reasons than one why Wellesley (1798-1805) penned his 1803 minute and appointed the committee, both steps taken together representing a quantum shift in the story of Calcutta's growth. In its essence, however, both steps were nothing more than the decision of a single individual, the contemporary records holding no indication whatever of a collective realisation that the need for tackling the city's spatial drawbacks had reached a critical point. It was different with the Lottery Committee's appointment in 1817, the step being more in the nature of a *systemic* response transcending the wishes of any one individual. Briefly, since in particular 1815, the working of the prevailing 'system' of planning and implementing city development projects had revealed clearly the weak links in the 'process' then current, to the point that they could not be allowed to continue to exist any longer. Consequently, everything, so to speak, inevitably pointed to the next stage of 'progress', that is, the introduction of a new system which would be more effective in attaining the objective. Unlike Wellesley, the Governor-General of the time, Lord Hastings merely played the role of a catalyst, the 'process' culminating in the appointment of the new committee.

During the Minto years, and the early period of Hastings's ten-year reign (1813-23), the magistrates of the town played a critical role in the proceedings which focussed on the city's spatial growth. When the Board of Conservancy took over the responsibilities of the Committee for Improvement of the Town,[9] the shift really meant that the magistrates were once again taking over the superintendence of such activity. But, as hindsight shows, time for the old system was fast running out, the shift to the Board of Conservancy representing nothing more than the last flicker of a candle which was on the point of being extinguished.[10] Within a couple of years the new Lottery Committee would be appointed in which the role of the magistrates would be curtailed effectively. Admittedly, John Eliot, Judge and Magistrate of the Suburbs of Calcutta, would be designated 'president' of the new committee, but this was more the reflection of his seniority in the service than anything else. In fact, the composition of the new committee would be influenced strongly by officials like the Acting Chief Secretary to the Government, William Butterworth Bayley (who was junior to Eliot in the service), and non-official heavyweights like George James Gordon, Arthur Jacob Macan and A. Colvin, Jr., not to speak of other civilians like Henry Wood and Charles Trower (another official, Henry Shakespear, was to join the committee later as also Lieutenant Charles Paton). There is little doubt that Eliot's presence, in the position he held, would be something to contend with, but he passed away barely a few months after the committee was appointed, snapping the links of the new committee with the old magistracy.

If merely the dilution of the role of the city magistrates in determining the spatial growth of the city was to lead, eventually, to the shaping of a new Calcutta, the point can be made that the attributes of the 'new system' were directly responsible for the change. What, then, was this 'new system' which Lord Hastings introduced into the core of the city's spatial planning? Seen in a broader perspective, the Governor-General was merely treading in the footsteps of Warren Hastings who was, effectually, the East India Company's first administrator to realise that there existed a wholly different aspect of the Company's territorial control other than just maximising commercial profit. Basically, it involved the fundamental transition of the Company's India administration from the mindset of a trader fixated on making the highest profit in given circumstances to that of a responsible, even conscientious, political manager who had to keep in mind, among other things, the 'welfare of subjects'. Peter Robb has summarised the transition thus:[11]

> The East India Company was developing its own notions of public service from the 1760s to the 1840s…Contrary to common opinion and despite the excesses of interest groups and of many individuals, Company servants recognised from their first exercise of political power that the Company needed to take a long view rather than a quick profit. Amidst public and private greed, they conceded that it had a duty of care to its Indian subjects…[Warren Hastings'] or his contemporaries' concerns with landed property, legal rights, education, and scholarly or geographical explorations all fitted some idea or other of the proper conduct of states.
>
> Historians began to recognise this with the reintroduction of ideology into what had been largely Namierite accounts of East India Company politics. Noted also, at the institutional level, were the Company's increasing regularity of process, its concern for legality, and its more systematic records. The Company began to profess rationality and benevolence. It sought to govern on the basis of information and analysis, as in the surveys, measurements, and reports required of the Blechyndens.[12] Thus it generated expectations, including ethical conduct and an *esprit de corps*. In practice, the Company's structure, procedures, and terms of employment were still quite some way from the ideal of a modern government or corporation; but they had started to approach that ideal, in order to meet the challenges of administering vast territories and to rehabilitate the Company with the British elite.

The Lottery Committee's records throw light on the difference in the norms of governance between the old school of the Calcutta magistrates and the new breed of Company administrators, the latter not merely being 'achievers' in the sense that projects had to be conceived and completed on time but who were also disinclined to follow in the footsteps of their predecessors in the way they went about their work generally. One example which showed up the sharp contrast between the 'professional' work ethics of the new administrators and those of the old school was the performance of Charles Trower, Collector of 24-Parganas and a very senior member of the 'civil service' who was a member of the Lottery Committee from its inception till the very end. Being appointed a writer in March 1796, by 1842 he had become the fourth 'seniormost' officer by length of service in the Bengal establishment; yet, in terms of responsibility, he was just Civil Auditor. This is comment enough on his 'utility' to the Governor-General in Council. In fact, one has to read the resonating innuendoes in the letters written by the Government to the committee to gauge the true depth of the annoyance with which the former viewed the 'misdeeds' of the Collector, the message sometimes being as direct as it could be in the circumstances (for instance, when a project estimate prepared by Trower was overridden by that of a much junior member of the committee).[13]

It would, of course, be naïve to suggest that the Lottery Committee alone put an end to the 'corrupt' practices of the magistrates by stripping the latter of their powers in matters connected with the development of the city (in fact, they were still responsible for the repair of roads and drains, watering the streets, etc.). The influence of the magistrates had been reined in, but what of the entire body of employees under them (native, Eurasian and European) who had become accustomed to a way of functioning where profiteering was the norm? The new breed of senior Company officers had to rely on such people to get work done being fully aware that they would always be prone to corrupt behaviour. The story of Rupnarayan Ghoshal, a native employee initially attached to John

Eliot in the pre-Lottery Committee days and who later became an important cog in the wheel of the committee's extensive operations regarding the purchase of native property for the purpose of making roads, etc., is a case in point. What may appear surprising is that even after being punished by the authorities for impropriety which cast a shadow on his financial integrity, important committee members (such as Henry Shakespear) who excelled in their contribution to Calcutta's growth did not hesitate to back Ghoshal's case for a pay rise not to speak of the praise showered on him for the quality and quantum of his work. The stigma of corrupt behaviour and commendation for good work coexisted easily, which was perhaps inevitable at a time when the old order was passing and new norms of work and probity were being introduced.

In fact, it was the suggestion on the part of the Committee for Excavation of Tanks (chaired by John Eliot and the members of which were magistrates) to supervise more effectively the utilisation of the lottery funds at the disposal of the authorities for the improvement of the city (which in effect meant plugging the leakage points in the use of public money) which led directly to the establishment of the Lottery Committee itself.[14] The sheer animus of the Court of Directors against the magistracy of Calcutta[15] was rooted in the belief – amply supported by the diaries of Richard Blechynden who had perforce to work with them closely – that this was a group of people to whom the responsibility of spending large sums of money on account of the city's development should never have been entrusted. The fault lay in the system itself which facilitated those who were out to make a pile for themselves.

The roots of 'corrupt' behaviour in the first hundred years of Company rule, no doubt officially encouraged by the system of private trade in which Company staff was allowed to participate, extended to the innards of the Government, not excluding those who occupied the highest positions in it. What this means is that the official records of the Government, too, were infected with the ailment which makes it imperative for the researcher to be careful with the interpretation of the records. The following is an example of this pitfall.

Fig. 1. The tomb of the police magistrate W.C. Blaquiere at the Circular Road cemetery

On 14 June 1814 the Committee for Improving the Town of Calcutta (by July the committee had been dissolved) wrote to the Earl of Moira that the implementation of its plan submitted on 13 February 1811 'for the provision of bricks and *coah* for the repair and construction of roads' had resulted in a 'considerable saving' in expenditure and also an improvement in the quality of the 'materials'. Consequently, it felt that it would be sensible to consider 'in what manner the plan might be rendered still more efficient and beneficial', although that responsibility would now 'devolve to the magistrates, in the capacity of constructors of the roads and other public works'. Enclosed with the committee's missive was a copy of William Cotes Blaquiere's[16] 28-paragraph letter of 1 June 1814 in which the magistrate said that he had been asked by the Governor-General in Council (on 25 February 1811) to take charge of 'the department of materials used in the construction and repair of roads in and about the town of Calcutta for the purpose of ascertaining what improvements could be made in the manufacture of bricks and supply of materials'.

Apart from informing the committee that during the period 16 February 1811 till 30 April 1814 he had spent Rs 9,045-2-3 on the 'enquiries and experiments', which was due to him,[17] Blaquiere added that since the committee had found the provision of the materials through the contract system to be 'objectionable and liable to abuse' the existing contracts had been 'abolished' and that he had 'commenced the manufacture of bricks'.

Commenting on the subject, George Dowdeswell, the Chief Secretary to the Government who was to be elevated to the Supreme Council in six months' time, had written on 13 June that till the adoption of the Blaquiere plan of production of bricks and *coah* 'the materials used in the ordinary repair of the roads were so bad [in] quality that it was nearly an absolute loss of money and time so to employ them'.[18] He then added:

> …it is almost superfluous to observe that I consider the particular acknowledgements of the committee to be due to Mr Blaquiere for the trouble which he has voluntarily and gratuitously taken in the superintendence of the provision of bricks and *coah*, on the footing above noticed. But I am particularly anxious to express my own sense with respect to that point, as it was chiefly at my suggestion that this troublesome business was undertaken by Mr Blaquiere.

Other members of the committee commended the magistrate for the work he had done and Blaquiere was paid the amount due to him, the Government noting that 'the plan which should be in future adopted for the provision of bricks or *coah* or other materials for the repair and construction of roads will of course engage your (the magistrates') attention at an early period of time'.

The important point to note here is that the burst of commendation did not occur in a vacuum. Peter Robb has written[19] that in the early years of the 19th century the Justices of the Peace (magistrates) began to withdraw aspects of work from Richard Blechynden, the Superintendent of Roads, on the plea of 'trying to remedy problems of cost and supply and...relieving the superintendent of tasks he was too busy to perform. They were acting, they claimed, in the public interest.' But, in the event, magistrates like C.F. Martyn and Blaquiere benefitted immensely from the change. While the former looked after the supply of bullocks and human labour, Blaquiere 'supplied the bricks and gravel for the roads, a corrupt connection that caused comment *but no action from his superiors* [emphasis added]. He had promised an improvement in quality, but what he supplied was worse than before, often so bad as to be unusable.' Robb's narrative is based on the diaries of Blechynden who, given the nature of his official duties, was intimately connected at the grassroots level with the development work going on at the time in Calcutta. Importantly, the impression one gets from Robb's account of Blechynden's diaries is that the superintendent was not someone who would have had recourse to spreading falsehood to run a person down.

Richard Blechynden's views, as expressed in his diaries, are not supportive of Dowdeswell's commendation. Both cannot be correct unless Dowdeswell had a special interest in protecting Blaquiere, the inference being that the corruption chain extended upwards to the highest levels of the Government. The question arises: was the pressure on Blaquiere so severe in 1814 that Dowdeswell had to come out in open support of the magistrate, even if such support could not be justified? Clearly, the internal contradictions of the old system of the Company's administrative functioning were about to reach a crisis point.

The Government was aware of the inclination on the part of the magistrates to flout the rules to line their own pockets, which is probably why in 1815 they were asked to furnish regularly a statement of receipts and disbursements (on 1 November and 1 May) regarding funds used for the improvement of the town and its environs. In 1817, when the Lottery Committee was set up, fresh guidelines were laid down which stipulated that the committee would have to depute at least two of its members who, aided by the surveyor, were 'to survey and report upon all works' executed with the help of lottery funds. A half-yearly account of receipts and disbursements was also to be 'regularly submitted' to the Government.[20] What stands out in the records is that not once during the life of the Lottery Committee was a shadow of doubt cast on the accounts submitted by its members for projects implemented (apart from the one occasion cited above where Charles Trower's estimate for a project was not accepted). But while the Government in Calcutta was satisfied with this aspect of the committee's work, the Directors in London were not: in fact, to such an extent that on one occasion the Court told the Government that it would have applied the axe on the committee had it not been for the high esteem in which it was held by the Governor-General.[21]

So varied were the pitfalls of the old system of governance followed by the Company in Bengal that specific guidelines controlling expenditure, on the one hand, and the broad delivery system of the administration of justice on the other often got entwined enabling the corrupt in the administration to take advantage of a fluid situation. Essentially, this was the result of a system of financial administration evolving in bits and pieces over the decades instead of following a well-thought-out plan of progressive policy and action. The resultant anomalies were mentioned by the Court of Directors in February 1817;[22] they had, in fact, already been brought to the notice of the Government in Calcutta in November 1814 and January 1816. The Court pointed to 'certain irregularities in the manner of making up the accounts of the Judicial Department: we mean the insertion of many and even larger items of expense which are merely by some [the MS is illegible here] circumstance connected with the administration of justice'. Some examples were given such as the cost of watering of roads near Government House (Rs 5,849), the repair of roads in Khidirpur, Alipur, Garden Reach and Dum Dum, and the construction of a road to the Russapaglah jail. The Court said that these, 'and probably other items included under the head of contingent or miscellaneous charges may, perhaps, be connected with the Judicial Department by the fortuitous circumstance of their being defrayed by the local magistrates who proposed or superintended the several works, and reimbursed themselves in their contingent bills'.[23]

The Court directed that all disbursements not essentially connected with the administration of justice be entered under a separate head of 'public contingencies' in the books of the judicial accountant, to be transferred every six months to the accountant-general's books as 'charges general' upon the Public Department, for which the judicial accountant would have to take full responsibility. Copies of these 'detailed accounts' of public contingencies were to be sent to London separately along with the judicial accounts. Some light is thrown on whether these reforms in the preparation of accounts ordered by the Directors were being followed in Calcutta by the Court's letter of 17 November 1819 (paragraph 27) where the point was made that although London had no objection to approving charges on the repair of 'judicial buildings' and certain roads and on the building of bridges which had been submitted by the Government, the 'injunction' had to be repeated that 'such only as relate to the Judicial Department be inserted in the judicial accounts'.

The records indicate that the new breed of officials who took over the responsibility of improving the city in 1817 was far more cohesive than were the magistrates, a trait which showed up clearly in the way some major projects were planned and implemented. To take an example, in 1815, the magistrates, to start with, could not put up a united front on the subject of the extension of the aqueducts in the city although later they agreed to a common course of action (we are not told as to what led to the change in view).[24] On the other hand, the Lottery Committee's functioning was far more transparent, individual members going to great lengths to argue their standpoints in cases where there was disagreement. An example of this was the changes suggested in the system governing the sale of lottery tickets, whether the entire lottery was to be sold to a single buyer or whether the existing system of selling tickets to a number of agents and dealers would be continued.[25] A careful reading of the records enables the unravelling of the links individual members had with investors in lotteries (dealers as well as single buyers), reflecting in the process not merely the relationship between the social categories involved in the Calcutta society of the time but also the interpersonal links which existed among specific individuals, both members of the Lottery Committee and others.

Teamwork marked the working of the committee which was, for the most part, missing among the magistrates, which probably was to be expected in view of the competing interests of the individuals concerned in amassing private fortunes. The committee also dealt with far larger sums of money than did the magistrates, in one case the investment being as high as Rs 6 lakhs, which did not escape the Court's notice.[26] Given the past experience with the magistrates where, essentially, a group of Company servants was acting supposedly in the best traditions of probity – the result, however, often turning out to be unsatisfactory – the Directors could not be blamed for not being confident that a new body of officials engaged in the same work would not repeat the misadventure. This perhaps explains the Court's view in December 1820 that what the Lottery Committee was doing could have been done better by a single officer 'whose whole time and attention could be devoted to its superintendence', the members of the committee 'scarcely (having) the leisure to attend sufficiently to the duty'.[27]

It is often said that the spatial development of Calcutta was skewed deliberately in the interests of the European population, the inference being that the geographical areas populated by natives were discriminated against. This was certainly the case, the reason being that the rulers of Calcutta at this point of time were the sahibs whose own interests were in the normal course given a higher priority than those of the ruled. It would be difficult to find an example from anywhere, especially in colonial times, of the prevalence of a different behavioural matrix governing the relations between the ruled and their rulers. This specific relationship governing the development of a colonial city flows from the primordial truth permeating human social ties that the 'ruled' will always be exploited by the 'ruler', even if the two belong to the same race.[28] The Lottery Committee performed within this steel frame of reference as it were, which leads to the suggestion that the focus of study should be on what, and how much, the committee did to improve the condition of the native areas of the city the topographical features of which in the early years of the 19th century had not altered much since the time of Charnock. This inevitably slow transformation of the city's shape is suggested by the records which tell us that in areas such as Chitpur Road and Clive Street, Hastings Street, Bankshall Street, Church Lane and Mangoe Lane, as also Fenwick's Bazar (New Market) and Burial Ground Road (Park Street), houses abutted on streets which were described as 'narrow'. What this specific configuration between houses and roads means is that when the houses were built the roads were narrower, the inference being that at the time of their construction the houses did not encroach on them at all. With the expansion of human habitation and an increase in the daily movement of traffic the roads became more crowded with the result that the houses, which were once located on the side, now began to abut on them.

The Government was aware that the predominantly native areas of Calcutta were in an unacceptable state in terms of hygiene and health. In January 1820, Henry Shakespear wrote a minute in which he said that the sorry condition of the town, especially the native part of it, was not the result of a lack of projects but the Government's inability to implement plans and schemes which had been drawn up over the years. The Chief Magistrate of the town said that the past efforts had failed 'for want of adequate funds', the inference being that an interest in improving these areas had not been absent.[29]

Shortage of funds may have been one reason which itself may have been the result of a racial attitude prioritizing the development process. But, this apart, there was another reason which had held back the authorities from freely pursuing improvement projects in the native areas. During Wellesley's time, the Committee for Improvement of the Town had drawn up a plan under which principal streets to be constructed would include 'quadrangular spaces' where 'tanks shall be dug and...small avenues...made in a direction parallel to the great roads at the distance of 150 or 200 feet'. The Government had no problem with this because it would improve the spatial attributes and topography of the town. The obstacle lay elsewhere and concerned the (at the time) nebulous phenomenon of the property rights of the native inhabitants which, for his own reasons, the imperious Wellesley was not prepared to ignore and dismiss. The Government described the suggested plan as being 'impracticable', arguing:

> The ground is the property of different individuals who *cannot be compelled* [emphasis added] to allot their estates for

> building according to any prescribed plan, and the purchase of the whole, with the houses now standing thereon, would require the expenditure of a sum of money too considerable to admit of any attempt for that purpose.[30]

In 1822, the same sentiment was foremost in the mind of Lord Hastings when he shot down an option suggested by the Lottery Committee to widen Banstala Lane (Sir Hariram Goenka Street) between Chitpur Road and Clive Street, because the step would '(interfere extensively) in the private property in the most ancient part of the city'. Apart from private property rights, religious considerations too played an important role in the decision-making process.[31]

The benefit of hindsight suggests that, since 1690, no other city improvement committee in the history of Calcutta has done so much in terms of building roads and developing virgin areas for 'modern' human habitation as did the Lottery Committee. This includes the work done by the Calcutta Improvement Trust which was set up in 1912. What, however, remains unknown and unsung is the quality of work put in by some members of the committee, such as Henry Shakespear and Henry Wood, without which it would have been difficult for the group to have attained so much in the course of just a decade. Wood, the Civil Auditor, was, in fact, the 'father of Garden Reach', a vast area which began to be filled up rapidly by natives between its opening up (by Wood) in the second and third decades of the 19th century till the arrival of the Lucknow 'prisoners' post-1857. Wood was also an innovator as far as building of roads was concerned, his ideas being at first accepted by the committee on an experimental basis. He was also a pioneer in involving natives in the development of Garden Reach a partnership which produced significant results. The only other noteworthy effort at native cooperation was that which involved the construction of Colootala Street in the northern part of Calcutta which, however, failed to work out resulting in financial problems for the committee and the Government.[32] However, not all natives were as malleable as the Nawab of Murshidabad in their response to the committee's demand for ground. Gopimohun Deb and Rammohun Dutt did not hesitate to take the Government to court to settle disputes.[33]

In the writing of the book, the author (who is not a historian, trained or otherwise) has faced the constant struggle to avoid getting enmeshed in detail and to refocus attention on the broad current of policy and the effects of its implementation. It is up to the reader to decide whether he has been successful in maintaining a balance between the two aspects of historical inquiry. There is one school of thought which holds that the minutiae of history, particularly those involving individual projects, are less important than matters of overarching policy and the general impact such projects have on various segments of the population. While the latter are no doubt critical to the understanding of the basic impulses behind the evolution of any given society, attention to the specific problems faced in the day-to-day execution of projects (which forms a large part of this book) also does help to throw light on the precise nature of the hurdles encountered at the grassroots level. Such an approach also tends to add a human dimension to the narration of larger events, making it easier for the reader to relate to the subject being written about. The basic premise here is that, human nature being what it is, there are some aspects of life and behaviour which are universal in their reach, both temporally and spatially.

A COMMITTEE IS SET UP

The 'Lottery Committee' was not the first committee to have undertaken work for the development of Calcutta. The first such committee was set up by Lord Wellesley on 2 July 1804. Curiously, the primary objective of the Governor-General was not to build broad avenues, dig tanks, establish parks and squares, and cut down the excess foliage. It was limited to tackling the ever-present danger of fires breaking out, during the summer months in particular, which affected the lives of natives much more than those of Europeans. In Wellesley's time the problem had reached critical proportions because of the rapidly growing native population of the town and the unplanned nature of their habitation, the growth in numbers following an exponential path after the Maratha scare of the early 1740s and the growing realisation on the part of the natives that the security of life and property provided by the East India Company was, in relative terms, the most acceptable law-and-order arrangement ever imposed on them or their forefathers.[1]

Wellesley thought big, which is why he appointed his committee for the improvement of the town in the first place. Piecemeal development schemes, such as the building of the Circular Road immediately after his arrival, were no doubt important but his mindset transcended that of the 'nation of shopkeepers' and he was, in fact, the quintessential 'Sultanised Englishman'.[2] His main problem, however, was to garner resources for the development schemes identified by his own committee, a hurdle which assumed serious proportions after he fell out with the Court of Directors of the East India Company following, among other things, his unilateral, almost-surreptitious, decision to build the Government House.[3] To top it all, after appointing his committee he had just a year left as Governor-General (he left at the end of July 1805) which was too short a time for him, or anyone else for that matter, to make a mark by way of implementation of the development plans for the fast-growing city.

The shortage of funds continued after his departure the problem being tackled better by Wellesley's successor Lord Minto when, specifically, the latter took up the 8 October 1807 suggestion of George Dowdeswell, the Superintendent-General of Police and Secretary to Government, to utilise lottery funds to finance the development effort.[4] Despite the initial hesitation of the Court of Directors to accept the proposal, Minto got his way by presenting the option as a *fait accompli*. When he wrote to London on 30 January 1808, Minto told the Directors that Dowdeswell's suggestion to use lottery funds to finance development schemes *had been adopted* by his Government. In the early years of the 19th century it took more than a year for a letter from Calcutta to elicit a reply from London, if the reply was sent immediately, which was rarely the case. In this particular instance, while the Governor-General had written to the Court on 30 January 1808, steps were taken within a year to institute a system of lotteries which would have as one of its objectives the improvement of the town. The records tell us that on 14 January 1809 the commissioners for superintending the lottery informed the Government that the drawing of the 'present Town Hall lottery being nearly completed', they were submitting the draft of a scheme 'for the first lottery established by Government for the improvement of the city of Calcutta', to be drawn on 1 July 1809.[5] What this means is that work on the first lottery for the improvement of Calcutta had begun before the Court of Directors' response to the Governor-General's 30 January 1808 proposal could reach Bengal.

The Directors, in fact, took five long years to respond to the Governor-General's missive – almost certainly after being informed by their private channels of information that the Governor-General had gone ahead with implementing the proposal. On 14 February 1812 the Court informed Calcutta that '...though we are not friendly to lotteries in general, we are not aware that, under the circumstances of the case and the limited extent of your powers as to assessing the inhabitants of Calcutta, any [more] preferable mode of providing for the expence could have been resorted to'. Two years later, in October 1814, after Minto had left India, the Directors once again repeated their general objections to the encouragement of lotteries *'by which we still abide'* (emphasis added) but adding that they were 'glad to find (that) the community will in any way derive a benefit from (the lottery funds) having existed'.[6]

The January 1809 scheme for the first lottery was drawn up by John Adam, the Superintendent of Lotteries, who eventually rose to become officiating Governor-General in early 1823.[7] The proposed lottery would incorporate some changes compared to the existing Town Hall lottery in view of 'the difficulty experienced' and also in view of 'a similar difficulty having been experienced by a person who speculated largely in the purchase of tickets in the late lottery'.[8] The commissioners (J. Fombelle, G. Dowdeswell and J. Thornhill)[9] proposed limiting the first lottery to 6,000 tickets, or *sicca* Rs 6 lakhs (all figures in rupees hereafter relate to *sicca* rupees unless stated otherwise), 'instead of continuing the amount at Rs 7,50,000, the standard of the past lotteries'. Quite sensibly, the commissioners were feeling their way for they said that, if required, changes would be made after their experience with the first lottery.[10] The proposal was accepted by the Governor-General in Council and orders were issued to the effect that the lotteries were to be conducted by 'a superintendent, aided by a register[11] and examiner under the immediate control of commissioners appointed by Government'. J. Fombelle, G. Dowdeswell, J. Thornhill, C. Buller, H. Stone and J.W. Sherer were appointed commissioners 'for the control of the business of the lotteries', J. Adam being named Superintendent and A.C. Seymour Registrar and Examiner.

Since the upkeep of the Town Hall was already a charge on the lottery funds, the new Lottery Committee was asked to continue looking after it. The Government ordered that

> ...the whole of the funds which may be realised by (the lottery) will be applied to the improvement of the town of Calcutta and its vicinity *after* [emphasis added] defraying the necessary expenses of the lotteries and any deficiency [that] may [arise] in the funds required for the completion of the Town Hall.

In other words, although development of the town was a far more important objective than the upkeep of the Town Hall, the first call on the lottery funds (besides the administrative expenses) was to be made by the requirements of the Town Hall. This was bureaucratic finesse at work necessary in view of the sacrosanct position held by the principle of continuity in the East India Company's system of governance. In later years, however, a concerted effort was made to reduce expenditure on the Town Hall.

The last of the 'town-improvement committees' to be set up before the Lottery Committee was that appointed on 28 March 1817 by Lord Hastings, which was asked 'to ascertain the best means of excavating tanks at convenient places in the town of Calcutta for

Fig. 2. Francis Chantrey's statue of Lord Hastings at Tank Square. A hand-coloured print by Frederick Fiebig, 1851

the accommodation of the inhabitants'.[12] Nearly seven months later, on 25 September, the committee (hereafter referred to as the Tank-Excavation Committee), presided over by John Eliot, brought to the Government's notice 'the frequent application of the lottery funds to purposes foreign to the objects to which they should be appropriated'.[13] Apart from giving a full account of the plans for the Baparitala Square and tank (Raja Subodh Mullick Square), the committee felt that the establishment cost for drawing the lotteries (Rs 652 per month, excluding the salary of the superintendent 'and other sums under the head of lottery contingencies') was 'out of all proportion to the duties connected with the responsibility of drawing it'. Consequently, it wanted a 'revision of the whole of the establishment' chargeable to the lottery fund. The Government was also informed that till then there were 'no rules…for checking the estimates on which disbursements from the lottery fund' were being made, or for obtaining 'the usual survey reports on works which have been constructed at the expense of the funds'. In view of this, it was suggested that the public works on which lottery funds were being spent be placed under 'the same, wholesome checks which all other public works of the civil department are now subject to, and that the works when finished may be properly surveyed'.

In the middle of October, the Government informed the Tank-Excavation Committee that 'an arrangement' was being considered 'for bringing the receipts and disbursements of the lottery funds under the immediate management of a committee to be specially appointed for that purpose'. A week later the Lottery Committee was appointed. Writing to London at the end of the month, the Government said that it had passed resolutions on 'the suggestions offered by the [tank-excavation] committee', one of which related to the appointment of 'a new committee to superintend the receipts and disbursements of the lottery funds, and generally for the purposes connected with the improvement of the town of Calcutta and its vicinity'.[14] It is, therefore, clear that the appointment of the Lottery Committee was the direct result of the suggestion made by the Eliot committee on excavation of tanks.

The committee 'to superintend the receipts and disbursements of the lottery funds and generally for purposes connected with the improvement of the town of Calcutta and its vicinity' (henceforth referred to as the Lottery Committee) was set up by Lord Hastings on 21 October 1817.[15] Its members were John Eliot, Charles Trower, Collector of 24-Parganas, William Butterworth Bayley, Secretary to the Government in the Judicial Department, Henry Wood, Civil Auditor, Captain H.S. Montague, Fort Adjutant, G.J. Gordon, a Commissioner of the Court of Requests, A. Macan and Alexander Colvin, Junior.[16] Archibald Trotter, who had taken over from John Adam as Superintendent of the Lotteries, was appointed Secretary of the committee, and the Civil Auditor (Wood) the *ex*

Fig. 3. The memorial to Alexander Colvin, Sr, at St John's Church, Calcutta

officio Accountant and Auditor. Arthur Blechynden was 'specially attached' to the committee as Surveyor.[17] The first procedural point made by the Government dealt with the transition from the old to the new arrangement. The functions and duties of the existing Commissioners of the Lotteries were transferred to the new committee. Secondly, 'the construction of the tank, square and road' at Baparitala (the area to the north of Dharamtala Street) – approved on 14 October 1817[18] on the recommendation of the

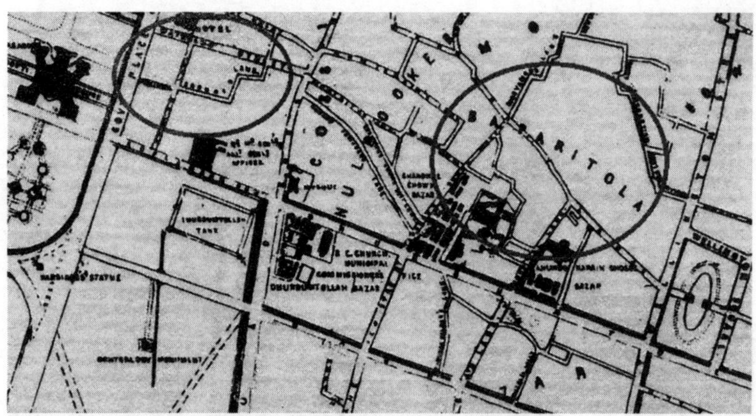

Fig. 4. Map, based on F.W. Simms' map of 1847-49, showing the Baparitala area. Also Waterloo Street and Crooked Lane

Tank-Excavation Committee comprising Eliot, Trower, Wood and James Wier Hogg – 'as well as the duties confided to those gentlemen by the orders of the Government of the 28th of March last' were brought under the superintendence of the new committee.[19] The Baparitala project, therefore, was the first major development scheme to be taken up by the Lottery Committee. The Government also made it clear that, as far as the eastern (Beliaghata) canal was concerned, since the investment on the canal had been made from the lottery funds the net profits 'which have been or may be realised from the tolls [should] be considered as applicable to the same ends as the lottery funds'. In other words, it would be appropriate if the net profits from the canal were credited to the lottery funds. Alternatively, the total investment on the making of the canal would have to be credited to the lottery account. Arguably, till the formation of the Lottery Committee, the canal was perhaps the most important project taken up by the authorities for the planned improvement of the city.[20]

Listing the specific responsibilities of the new committee, the Government resolved that the lottery funds could be used to '(excavate) new tanks and filling up old ones, of opening new streets or roads, of constructing aqueducts, bridges, ghauts, and other similar works, calculated to improve the health, convenience and comfort of the inhabitants of the city and suburbs'. However, the point was underscored that the committee was *not* to involve itself in the '*repair (of) streets, roads, drains or other works above alluded to when finished*, and that, generally speaking, *no expense be charged to those funds which can properly be included in the assessment department*' (emphasis added). The committee was asked to recommend projects it considered essential for the improvement of the town, the expense for which was to be defrayed from the lottery funds. Projects falling under the description of repair work were to be charged to the Assessment Department 'to be conducted by the magistrates'.[21]

The new committee did not lose any time and at its first meeting, on 24 November, steps were taken to set the work agenda for the period ahead. The last paragraph of the Government's 21 October resolutions had laid down explicitly that the 'duties' of the Tank-Excavation Committee would be conducted by the Lottery Committee and that the 'functions' of that committee 'as a separate committee are to cease from the present date'. The new committee, therefore, was just ensuring continuity when it resolved to appoint Eliot, Trower and Wood to 'take upon themselves the execution of the works recently authorised by Government'.

At the 24 November meeting, attended by Bayley, Wood, Gordon and Colvin, the first resolution stated simply that, 'in the absence of the president', the 'senior' member was to take the chair. In its 21 October order, the Government had not named any member of the new committee as 'president', the position being given by the new committee to John Eliot in view of his seniority in terms of his appointment as a writer in 1781. Providing an idea of the bureaucratic maze officials worked in, William Bayley, who had been appointed a writer seventeen years later in 1798, had already become Secretary to the Judicial Department in November

1817 while Eliot was Magistrate of the Suburbs and the Town of Calcutta. Although Bayley continued to hold the position of Secretary to the Judicial Department, by the end of December that year he had been appointed Acting Chief Secretary to the Government. The upshot of this was that while the Lottery Committee reported to the Government of which Bayley was Acting Chief Secretary, in the committee's pecking order Eliot took formal precedence over Bayley.[22] This apparent anomaly was also to be found in the case of Bayley and Charles Trower, Collector of 24-Parganas, who was appointed a writer two years earlier than Bayley.[23]

The Government's 21 October resolutions show that the committee's responsibilities were not sequenced, that is, there was no definite order in which projects were to be taken up for implementation; they were to be tackled as and when they cropped up. There was no sectoral prioritisation either. Within two months, Gordon, a member of the committee, tried to fill this gap, setting out in a minute a scheme of prioritisation.[24] Listing the 'relative importance' of the sectors which the committee had been asked to handle by the Government, Gordon wanted a resolution to be adopted which would form a guideline for the committee's future course of action. In his view, the health of the inhabitants would have to be given topmost priority, which meant that the committee's funds would have to be applied in the first place to the 'filling up altogether, or deepening, and cleaning, (dirty) tanks and *jheels*, several of which exist at present in the most populous parts of the town'.[25] Secondly, the accumulation of filth would have to be tackled by means of 'new drains, common sewers or kennels'; and thirdly, 'ventilation [had to be promoted] as far as can be effected by cutting down high and spreading trees, and by increasing as much as possible the number and size of streets or roads running in a straight line from south to north', a pet theme of Gordon regarding town development.[26]

As Gordon saw it, after health, the safety aspect of foot 'passengers' in the streets would have to be strengthened. An effort would have to be made to 'widen the narrow parts of the most frequented streets where a more commodious road in a parallel direction cannot be opened, and particularly to round off sharp angles'. The received wisdom here is that the growing town had no footpaths at the time, and earlier. H.E.A. Cotton writes[27] that the first footpath in Calcutta was built in Chowringhee in 1858 'by the filling up of an open drain'. This, however, may not be correct because in 1818 not only was there correspondence on the subject of paths being made for foot passengers on the esplanade (*maidan*),[28] the committee also attached importance 'to making a separate footpath on the side of some of the principal roads and streets in which foot passengers are peculiarly exposed to accidents from Horses and Carriages'. In fact, Gordon suggested that such a pathway be made for foot travellers 'wherever the width of the old streets may admit of this, and in all the new roads (to be made) by the committee'.[29]

Thirdly, Gordon said that though it was 'desirable' to focus on 'convenience and ornaments' as objects of improvement, the committee should not spend funds on these aspects 'where these are the *only* [emphasis in original] objects proposed until all the foregoing objects have been accomplished as far as may [lie] in the power of the committee'.

The last point made by Gordon was that, as a general rule, the committee should give preference to development plans which would 'combine the greatest number of important objects at the smallest expense'.

Gordon's proposal initiated a debate in the committee on the subject of prioritising development. Bayley and Trower agreed with the need for a resolution on the subject but felt that there was no need to 'fetter…ourselves' with one because the Government had already issued clear instructions on the subject. Instead, 'mutual understanding' among members of the committee would be of greater help.[30] Bayley said the building of footpaths was more the job of the magistrates than the Lottery Committee, but he agreed with Gordon on the two other points.

Wood took a more independent line when he said that 'some general plan of improvement for our future guidance' should be drawn up which should take into account the ideas suggested by Gordon. But he was clear in his mind that the first task to be taken up would have to be the 'draining perfectly (of) every part of the town',[31] the second being the opening of good roads, and the third 'constructing good tanks and filling up bad ones with the earth dug out of the new ones'. He said the police had it in their power

> …to fill up most of the unhealthy…filthy pools of water by directing the filth of the town being thrown into them, and if the owners object to their being filled up they should either be obliged to keep them clean or be subject to a prosecution on account of a nuisance.

Wood preferred to see 'a portion of the town perfected in every respect' with regard to 'the draining, the opening of streets and roads, the construction of tanks, and the filling up of low, unhealthy pools, than that the whole town should be only partially improved in any particular way'.

If Wood's view was adopted, the European part of the town would probably have been the focus of development and not the congested native parts. This, however, did not turn out to be the case which had beneficial results for the future development of native Calcutta. Colvin was the only member who felt that Gordon was on the right path and that a resolution along the lines suggested by him would serve 'as a sort of record of our intentions, which may be useful in guiding us hereafter, and are yet sufficiently general [so as] not to confine us from the attainment of any desirable object'.

In order to get an overview of the financial assets and liabilities of the committee, the committee secretary, Archibald Trotter, was asked to submit a detailed statement showing the fixed establishment cost and 'expenses at present charged on the lottery fund' as well as a statement 'showing the balance now in the treasury in favour of the fund and the demands upon that balance for sums which have been authorised by Government'. These figures, laid before the committee at its 11 December 1817 meeting, showed that the balance of funds with the committee on 27 November was Rs 1,67,280-8-11, the expected addition of Rs 72,000 from the 17th lottery taking the total to Rs 2,39,280-8-11.

The records contain a list of projects for which the Government had sanctioned funds from the lottery account from 1807-8 to 1817-18, which indicates the major works undertaken during this period.[32] The ongoing project at the time of the formation

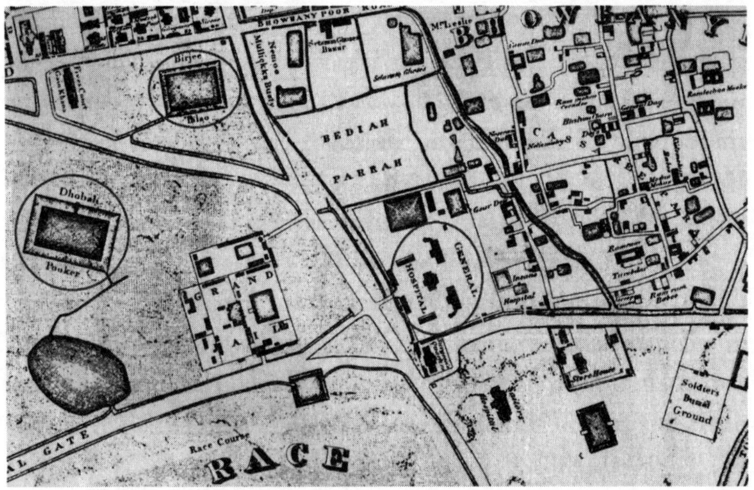

Fig. 5. J.A. Schalch's map showing Dhoba Pooker, Birjee Talao and the General Hospital (site of SSKM Hospital)

Fig. 6. The Dharamtala tank in 1865 with the Government House in the background (left). Photograph by Samuel Bourne

of the Lottery Committee was, of course, the tank and square at Baparitala and the associated new road from Dharamtala Street to Bowbazar, for which Rs 2,26,222-6-10 had been set aside. During 1813-14 Rs 1,526 had been spent on digging a tank to the north of the 'great jail' on the *maidan*, which is easily identifiable in the maps of the time.[33] In the same year Rs 972 was spent on deepening the tank at Dharamtala[34] at the south-east corner of Esplanade Row East (renamed Sido-Kanho Dahar). A year earlier, in 1812-13, Rs 14,789-8-0 was disbursed for a new tank 'proposed to be dug at Chowringhee'. This was Eliot's tank opposite today's Ho Chi Minh Sarani (erstwhile Harrington Street) and was marked as such in Schalch's map (see Fig. 7).[35] Without specifying any particular project, the list also includes Government disbursements of Rs 24,905-13-3 for 1813-14, Rs 10,990-9-1 (1812-13) and Rs 32,790-10-0 (1807-8).

❦

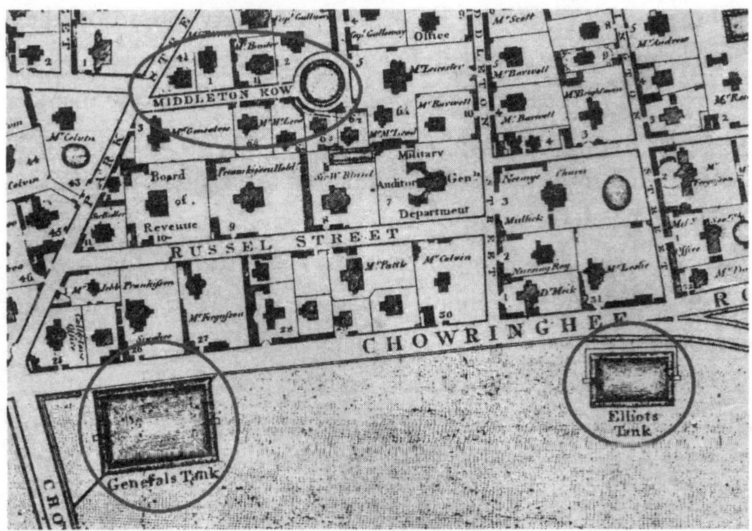

Fig. 7. Schalch's map showing Eliot's Tank, General's Tank (opposite Park Street) and Middleton Row

Four establishments depended on the lottery funds for their monthly budgets. The first was the lottery establishment itself the total monthly outgo on which was Rs 1,652, the Superintendent of the Lotteries (at this time the civilian Archibald Trotter) accounting for as much as Rs 1,000. The second financially dependent set-up was the Conservancy Department which accounted for Rs 2,177 every month. The establishment for the Town Hall cost Rs 371 a month of which the Keeper of the hall, William Hastie, accounted for Rs 250. The remaining Rs 121 was distributed among 13 native employees. The fourth establishment was that attached to the Tank Square which cost Rs 48 a month. All this apart, a contingent amount was set aside for the drawing of each lottery, that for the 14th lottery being Rs 2,373-2-0. Of this amount, Rs 1,000 went to meet the allowances of the 'sub-commissioners' and Rs 200 was given 'to the Free School boys'.

The subject of the four establishments being brought under the umbrella of the Lottery Committee was discussed in

February 1818.[36] Of the Rs 4,248 spent every month on these establishments, nearly half financed the fixed expenses of the Conservancy Department run by the magistrates. Every member of the committee without exception wanted this department to be excluded from the responsibilities of the Lottery Committee. Captain Montague wrote that since the Lottery Committee did not have any 'control' over the department, 'the revising of its establishment cannot belong to us'. Wood felt that the establishment cost of the department should be 'entirely charged to the Assessment Department.' Another official, C.R. Barwell,[37] also agreed with the transfer of the department's establishment cost liability to the Assessment Department, his argument being that the 'useful application of the proceeds of the lottery...should not be directed into other channels or expended for purposes less urgent'.

The Acting Chief Secretary, William Bayley, agreed with the need to transfer the liability to the Assessment Department but pointed out that certain heads of expenditure could not be charged 'legally' to the latter department such as the employment of *malis* at the Mohamedan burying ground, esplanade and Tank Square.

The committee members had their way. In June 1819 the magistrates were informed that the 'establishment' of the Conservancy Department which was under them would 'from the commencement of the present official year (1819-1820)', cease to be a charge on the lottery funds and was to be paid 'either from the assessment funds or from the ordinary resources of Government'.[38]

On the utility of the office of the Superintendent of the Lotteries, most of the committee members took a guarded stance. Even if it was felt that costs should be reduced, most of them felt that the existing arrangement should not be disturbed and that whatever changes were to be effected would have to be introduced at the time the existing incumbent (Archibald Trotter) left in the normal course. Captain Montague suggested that any reduction in the superintendent's establishment be 'suspended', holding out the hope that Trotter himself 'may perhaps suggest some on his return'.[39] Wood agreed that a change was required but cautioned that nothing should be done to the superintendent's office 'till the individuals now holding the situations are otherwise provided for, either by an increase of their salaries in the offices they may hold in addition to the salaries they draw from the superintendent's office, or from any other source'. The important consideration for Wood was that those appointed in place of the old staff 'should not be allowed to hold any other situation [so that] their whole time may be devoted to the duties of the lotteries', a view also held by the Court of Directors.[40]

The Acting Chief Secretary took a different line on the usefulness of the superintendent's office underscoring more heavily than any other member the importance of the office. He wrote: 'I doubt whether any member of our committee possesses sufficient information of the nature of the duties performed by the superintendent of lotteries and his establishment to enable him to judge whether that establishment is more than adequate or the expense greater than is necessary'. In his view, 'the labour and responsibility and irksomeness of the duty [are] much greater than is conceived, and that the establishment is neither too large nor too expensive'. Bayley added that even if he had held a different view, he would still hesitate to recommend any change 'of the arrangements under which 22 lotteries involving the receipt and disbursement of 150 lacs of rupees have been conducted without any error or inaccuracy to the great advantage of the public'.

As regards the Tank Square establishment, while some of the members wanted it to be taken out of the ambit of the lottery funds Wood argued that it would have to remain with the lottery funds because the house tax 'was never intended to meet its expenses'. If the proceeds from the house tax were to be used for such improvements, those living

> …at too great a distance to partake of the recreation, which a walk within the enclosure affords, might justly complain of the partial appropriation of their money, and particularly when the filth of the drains is allowed to remain untouched and many of them are driven from their houses to avoid the nuisance.[41]

As one method of increasing the funds at the disposal of the Lottery Committee, Charles Lushington, Secretary to the Government, suggested in April 1819 that the Governor-General in Council had decided to carry over to the credit of the committee 'the whole amount [Rs 29,385-7-5] arising from unclaimed prizes both in the Town Hall lotteries and in the lotteries established for the improvement of the city', the general funds of the committee being responsible for all demands that were liable to arise from the unclaimed prizes.[42] The Town Hall expenses were to continue to remain the responsibility of the committee the point being made that 'the future expense of the occasional repairs' of the Town Hall would be defrayed from the consolidated funds thus transferred to the committee. This stipulation was cited as an 'additional reason for observing the strictest economy possible in providing furniture for the building'.

If the financial responsibility for the Town Hall was to fall on its shoulders, it was but inevitable that the committee would at some point of time suggest that management control of the institution should be handled by it. Responding more than a month later to the Lushington suggestion of 30 April, the committee wrote[43] that two of the members of the Town Hall Committee were already its members and they 'would cheerfully undertake all the duties now performed by the Town Hall Committee if it were deemed advisable'. The effort to take over management control was clothed in formal bureaucratic garb when the committee clarified that the 'immediate object' of the suggestion was that the Government 'may consider the expediency of providing that timely information, regarding all disbursements which may be authorized by Government as chargeable to the lottery funds, be communicated to the Lottery Committee'.

The effort was successful and the committee began exercising its management powers over the Town Hall without wasting any time. Among other things, the records contain an undated letter from Charles Trower suggesting that 'the grand entrance on the south side' of the edifice looking out on to the *maidan* (which is still there) be thrown open as the 'inconvenience of [there being only] one access for carriages to the door of the Town Hall' on the north side had assumed serious proportions.[44] The Collector of 24-Parganas felt that the cost of the additional entrance would be 'trifling…as it will only be necessary to cover over the drain in front of the steps and to remove the present railing'. Trower was asked to submit an estimate for the project, a procedural request which drew a response from the Town Hall Committee (23 January 1821), signed by Major-General Thomas Hardwicke, Captain P.A. Cobbe and Trower, which included not only the estimate required (Rs 2,274) but also a more substantial request for the switch in the entrance.[45] The Town Hall Committee said that it had received 'several representations' regarding 'the inconvenience experienced by the public in their access to, and leaving, the Town Hall in carriages from the present confined space under the northern porch on the nights of large public entertainments' and that, as a result, it had thought of a plan to throw open the southern entrance of the Town Hall 'by removing the present railing and making such other alterations as to admit carriages to draw up close to the entrance steps'. The Lottery Committee approved of the project and sent it to the Government in the middle of 15 February 1821, the approval coming through two weeks later.[46]

Apart from the increased convenience to the public, the Town Hall Committee said that the proposed change would greatly improve the southern appearance 'of this splendid building'. At the time, the southern facade of the edifice faced the expanse of the *maidan*, and it is easy to agree with the committee why, at the time, the building's frontage in that direction would appear to have been nothing short of striking. But, why in the first place was the entrance to the Town Hall located on the northern side of the building? The only reason for this seems to be that the northern entrance was of greater convenience to the public at the time because of its easier access from the heart of the English town than would have been the case if it was located in the south.

In October 1817, the Government had made its stand clear on the Lottery Committee's future financial involvement with the Beliaghata canal which had enabled the committee to get a clear picture of the financial involvement of the lottery funds in the project since its inception. Charles Trower was given the job of 'showing the actual amount of the cost of the eastern canal as charged to the lottery funds, the gross amount of the collections and charges in each year since the excavation of the canal, and the total net profit realised since the collection of tolls commenced'. The figures were needed for the committee to judge for itself whether it would be advisable to get back from the Government the sums spent from the lottery fund on making the canal and disassociate itself completely from the project, or whether it would be more sensible to 'receive the net balance of past and future (toll) collections', in which case the liability of bearing the canal's future repair and other costs would have to be borne by the committee.

Trower sent the details sought in early December 1817.[47] The receipts from the tolls were computed from May 1810 to April 1817, the annual collections increasing from Rs 2,902 to Rs 14,633-11-12 over the period, the total collections over the seven years being Rs 71,749. The disbursements from April 1809 till April 1817 were Rs 47,216 (of which Rs 32,534 was spent on acquiring land), leaving a surplus of Rs 24,533. The committee, however, did not take a decision on whether to associate itself with the canal or sever links with it based on these figures. It wanted to consult 'the several statements in regard to the canal and the receipts and disbursements of the Calcutta lotteries' furnished to the Government by the late Tank-Excavation Committee, which the committee felt would be necessary for a decision on 'the expediency or otherwise of taking the canal into their own hands'. Since the data was not before it, discussion on the subject was suspended.

At the committee's meeting of 15 January 1818 Trower was asked 'to furnish in detail' his views 'on the relative expediency of accepting the net profits which have been, or may be, realised from the tolls on the canal or receiving back from Government the amount paid from the lottery funds' for the canal's construction.[48] For some reason or the other the Collector of 24-Parganas did not get back to the committee on the subject even a year after he was asked to do so. A reminder was sent to him on 15 April 1819, asking him to send his views on the subject 'at your earliest convenience'.[49] Again, Trower did not oblige, an omission on which the records are silent.

Clearly, something was amiss. Trower could have been unwell or out of station, but this would have been registered in the proceedings in some form or the other, which was not the case. The reminder to Trower had been sent on 15 April, the previous meeting of the committee attended by the collector being held about five weeks earlier, on 4 March 1819. On the face of it, one gets the impression that Trower had lost interest in the proceedings of the Lottery Committee. The collector, in fact, stayed away from committee meetings for the next eight months – till 4 November

Fig. 8. The nameless grave (foreground) of Charles Trower, died 1842, a senior member of the Lottery Committee, at the Circular Road Cemetery

1819 – and then again during the first five months of 1820.[50] The Lottery Committee went ahead with the task of gathering the facts required on the Beliaghata canal from sources other than the Collector of 24-Parganas. Six months after the April 1819 reminder to Trower, the committee took up the issue of the eastern canal at its meeting in the middle of October, the members considering a statement of accounts dated 20 July covering the period 'from its origins in 1808-1809' to 30 April 1819 prepared 'under the orders of the committee' by the accountant-general.[51]

Without wasting further time the committee wrote to the Government that it had found that the total disbursement made from lottery funds, 'with interest at 6 per cent per annum to 30 April last (1819)', amounted to Rs 73,679-12-7 whereas the surplus from the tolls totalled Rs 34,442-3-5. In view of this, the committee concluded that, whatever the future advantages that could be derived from the tolls on the canal, 'the public interest and convenience' would be more effectively promoted 'by their receiving, instead of the past and future profits of the canal, repayment of the advances made from the lottery funds with interest' as calculated by the accountant-general.[52]

On 25 September 1817, John Eliot, Charles Trower and Henry Wood, the three senior members of the Lottery Committee (formed in October of that year) who had been named earlier as members of the committee looking after the construction of the square and tank at Baparitala and the new road being built from Dharamtala Road to Bowbazar, submitted a statement of the receipts and disbursements of the lottery fund till 30 April 1817.[53] They had been asked to do so by the Government on 6 September, that is, about six weeks before the committee was appointed. At the time, Eliot and Trower were among the senior-most members of the Government by appointment as a writer and Wood was the Civil Auditor, which perhaps explains substantially why they were given this responsibility.

In their statement, Eliot, Trower and Wood said that Rs 55,526-6-6, which had been charged to the lottery funds on account of the Beliaghata canal should have been made chargeable on the General Department since the Government had levied a toll on all boats which passed through it. The principle involved was that if the income from a project was to be enjoyed by the Government, the cost of its construction should also be borne by it. Secondly, Rs 72,502-14-4 spent on 'materials and repair of roads' were 'properly chargeable' to the Assessment Department and not to the lottery funds.[54] Together with the balance in the hands of the committee, the quantum of appropriable funds till 30 April 1817 totalled Rs 2,32,884-8-8 (which did not include Rs 8,177-13-3 lying with the magistrates).

In their letter, Eliot, Trower and Wood made the important point that a proper audit was needed for the lottery funds beginning from the stage at which project estimates were drawn up. They wrote that there were 'no rules…for checking the estimates on which disbursements from the lottery fund have been authorised, or for obtaining the usual survey reports on works which have been constructed at the expense of these funds'. Since the magistrates were involved in town development work prior to the formation of the Lottery Committee, the responsibility for this lapse lay with them. The committee suggested that the public works to be financed by the lottery fund be placed 'under the same wholesome checks' applicable to all other public works of the civil department, and that the works 'when finished may be properly surveyed'. This requirement was fulfilled three years later (on 24 May 1821) when a permanent subcommittee of accounts was set up by the Lottery Committee comprising G.J. Gordon, George Ballard and A. Colvin 'for the future examination and audit of all accounts connected with the receipt and disbursement of sums on account of the lottery funds'.[55]

The Conservancy Department under the magistrates came in for pointed criticism when the committee urged that the department be 'directed to furnish regular accounts of their receipts and disbursements supported by vouchers, and that advances for works may be only paid in proportion to the progress made in their erection'. The letter revealed that the department at times withdrew from the general treasury 'a larger sum than [was] actually required by the officer to enable him to carry on the work' when the proper procedure would have been for the officer concerned to issue receipts for the funds received, the final receipt not only mentioning the money received at different periods but also 'the sum total received under the original order for executing the work'. Citing an example, the committee said that owing to the prevailing unsatisfactory state of affairs, Rs 5,088-13 had been lying with the Conservancy Department since December 1815 'on account of work undertaken by a member of a committee[56] who has long since finished as much of the original work as he intended to carry on'. Such a situation, the committee said, would never have come to pass 'had it been the duty of a public accountant to check the accounts of the Conservancy Department'.[57]

Within two years of the formation of the Lottery Committee, the Government initiated a periodic audit exercise so as to keep the finances in order, no doubt being prodded in that direction by the Court of Directors in London.[58] In early May 1820 James Barwell, Sub-Treasurer at the general treasury, wrote to the Lottery Committee that 'in compliance with the instructions of Government under date the 2nd July 1819' he was submitting 'a detailed account of the receipts and disbursements at the general treasury on account of the lottery fund', which indicated that a monthly interest had been allowed on the net balance of the fund at the general treasury at the rate of six per cent 'on even thousands, from 1st November 1819 to 30 April 1820, inclusive' as ordered by the Government.[59] The next day (4 May) John Trotter, the committee secretary, asked Charles Trower that, as the committee was keen on submitting to the Government 'a report on the exact state of their funds' till 30 April 1820, he would have to submit a statement 'of the several balances' standing to the committee's credit 'on account of money authorised but not yet drawn…in full'.[60] The Collector of 24-Parganas was also asked to provide descriptions of projects for which the funds had been specifically authorised as well as the date and extent of the original credit.[61] Trower submitted the information required more than a month later (on 9 June), the committee writing back a week later seeking clarifications regarding the figures submitted relating to the Hastings Street and Bankshall improvements and the setting up of the insane hospital.[62]

The questions sent to the collector regarding the two subjects were of a procedural nature, but that regarding the insane hospital went a bit further. Replying in late July,[63] Trower wrote that the sale proceeds of the ground intended for the hospital (Rs 15,130) had been credited 'in my treasury accounts to the lottery fund' because on the date of submission of the report to the committee (9 June) the sale of the land had not been confirmed by the Board of Revenue. He, therefore, had to exclude the transaction from the 'account current'. The Lottery Committee wrote back on 3 August saying that since it was 'entirely ignorant of the principle' on which Rs 11,372-12-0 had been charged originally to the lottery fund on the above account (in other words, the committee was unaware of the initial purchase of the land in question for the insane hospital), it wanted to know on what 'authority…the said debit was made as also whether the lottery funds have further been charged with any of the expenses which may eventually have attended the improvement of the ground in question previous to [its] resale'. Clearly, this was a case of the Government not being kept informed by its officers about what projects were being paid for from the treasury funds.

The committee was, however, fully aware of the position since January 1819. At its meeting on 28 January that year, the point was made that, in the statement submitted by the Collector of 24-Parganas on the disbursements made from the lottery fund till 31 October 1818, a sum of Rs 11,243-12-0 had been set down as payment 'made under a communication from the late Mr Eliot and Dr Leny[64] for lands appropriated to the new hospital at Balloogunge'. An explanation was sought immediately from the collector regarding 'the particulars connected with the communication from Mr Eliot and Dr Leny'. It is unclear whether Trower sent in a reply for the records till August the following year (1820) do not contain anything to that effect. It is more than likely that Trower did not produce an explanation at all which may be why the Lottery Committee brought up the subject again on 3 August underscoring the point that, at least officially, it was still in the dark about the project and the associated expenditure.

This time around the committee was successful for nearly three weeks later (21 August 1820), Trower sent 'the original letter and enclosures' which constituted his authority for disbursing the funds for the purchase of the insane hospital ground, making it clear that the expenditure was charged to the lottery fund 'in consequence of a *verbal communication* [emphasis added] with the late Mr Eliot'.[65] He said that the entire amount spent on the purchase and clearing of the land, totalling Rs 11,372-12, was charged to the fund, the sale proceeds of the land in question, namely, Rs 15,130, being also credited to it. But was the credit entry made for on 7 June the following year (1821) the Lottery Committee was writing to Trower that 'no credit is yet established in the account of the committee with the general treasury for the proceed realised by you on the resale of the ground at Ballygunge originally intended for the construction of an insane hospital', adding pointedly, 'a circumstance which it appears difficult to account for as the committee are debited with the advances made by you during a corresponding period'.[66] Trower wrote back on 30 June sticking to his earlier stand, namely, that 'in the month of December 1820 this transfer was made in my treasury accounts I carried to the credit of the committee'.[67] Considering the fact that an officer as senior as Trower was involved, the Lottery Committee closed the subject with the terse response to the collector's 30 June reply that it was satisfied that the land had been sold at a profit.[68]

On 18 May 1820 a major stock-taking was effected when letters were sent to all the subcommittees set up since the committee's formation in 1817 asking them to provide an account of their functions and performance during the preceding three years.[69] The reason cited by the committee for the step was that it would be submitting to the Government a report on the progress made till the end of the following June 'in the several improvements and works intrusted to their management in Calcutta and its vicinity since the original constitution of the committee in 1817'. It is not clear from the records whether the Government wanted such a three-year progress report or whether the committee was taking the initiative on its own. It is possible that, in May 1820, the committee members, perhaps encouraged by senior Government officials who were aware of the critical attitude adopted by the Court of Directors,[70] wanted to have a clear idea themselves of what precisely had been done by the committee since the time it was set up.

For us, two centuries later, the exercise provides information on the projects being implemented at the time (since 1817), and who specifically were responsible for them. There was, for example, the subcommittee 'for conducting the improvements of Beopareetuloa (Baparitala)' comprising Trower, Henry Shakespear and Barwell (those who looked after the project originally in 1817 were the late John Eliot, Trower and Henry Wood), the subcommittee 'for the improvement at the Bankshall' comprising G. Gordon and A. Colvin (the works probably included the development of the western end of Hastings Street as well), and another subcommittee 'for the improvement at Dingah Bungah (Dingabhanga)' comprising Bayley, Shakespear, Lt Charles Paton and Lt J.A. Schalch. The 18 May letter was also sent to Shakespear and Paton who were looking after 'widening the road on the south side of Tank Square and the experiment of surface draining in the Chitpore Road', to Shakespear for the works which 'from time to time has been confided to your immediate superintendence in the Durrumtollah, at Ruth Ghaut, the Free School and Colingah', and to Barwell, the Magistrate of the Suburbs, for 'the new drain at Simleah and the balustrade and road along the Course to Chandpaul Ghaut'. The latter was also asked to shed light on 'whether the road inscription stones and drain undertaken originally by the late Mr Eliot have been all erected and constructed conformably to the intention of (the) committee'.[71] Schalch was asked to provide a report on the progress made on the survey of Calcutta. However, the Birjeetala subcommittee comprising Shakespear, Barwell, Ballard and Paton was not asked for any progress report because the work it was engaged in had just begun, the Government's sanction being obtained just a couple of weeks before Trotter's letter. Also excluded was work on Strand Road (north of the Old Fort Ghat) probably because no expenditure on the part of the Lottery Committee was involved.

In its letter the committee had asked for:

> 1. Particulars of all works and improvements which have been authorised by the Lottery Committee to be conducted under your control affixing to each the sum originally appropriated for its completion and the date on which authority was granted to you for executing the same; 2. The sums which have actually been drawn…and from what treasury on account of each work, the progress already made and particulars of the disbursements on which these sums have been expended; 3. The balances continuing still at your disposal on account of the said works, respectively, and the particulars of the improvements still incompleted conformably to original estimates; 4. The sufficiency or insufficiency of the above balances to meet the presently anticipated expense of completing the contemplated objects;

> 5. The causes, nature and extent of any difference which you may at present foresee as being likely to result between the original estimates and the expected expenses of actually completing the respective works; 6. The periods at which you anticipate the probability of being able to finish each work now in progress under your superintendence; and 7. Whether the works in question, so far as they have been completed, do severally promise to be still productive of the advantages contemplated on their original commencement.

The scope and extent of the audit was, therefore, quite thorough, the exercise being identical for all the projects undertaken by the committee.

The Lottery Committee kept a tight control over expenditure and made no exception to demands even from senior officials. Thus, when Trower wrote to the committee on 11 February 1820 that he would need Rs 400 'for erecting two buildings on the north-east corner of the Loll Dighee for the accommodation of the gardeners and the convicts employed in the garden', he was asked to provide a 'detailed estimate' of the projected cost submitted by him.[72] In his letter the collector had given just two sets of details: the buildings would be 30 ft in length and 10 ft wide, and they would be built with 'the best *pucka* materials, bricks only being supplied from those under charge of the committee at Beparry Tullah' (that is, bricks which had been recovered from the buildings demolished for the project). True to form, Trower took about three weeks to provide the figures sought by the committee, the details including items such as Rs 2 for 'carpenter's work' and Re 1 for transporting rafters by hackery, the cost adding up to Rs 405-6-8.[73]

❦

REFORMING THE LOTTERY SYSTEM

Indications of a new awareness regarding audit of the lottery system are to be found in the report of the Superintendent of the Lotteries of 12 March 1818 when discussing the contingency expenses relating to the 15th and 16th Lotteries.[1] The expenditure on the two lotteries was Rs 2,434-11-0 and Rs 2,405-7-0, respectively, the Superintendent of the Lotteries, Archibald Trotter, pointing out that the figure for the 15th Lottery was Rs 6-8-0 less than the average expense incurred on the five preceding lotteries. What this suggests is that the contingency expenses of the lotteries were well under control.[2] The committee sent the superintendent's report to its auditor, Henry Wood, telling him that under the 'present [new] system' the committee thought it proper to send the report to the auditor who, after satisfying himself on the appropriateness of the statement, would send it to the Government. Under the old system, the lottery commissioners themselves checked the accounts before sending them to the Government for approval.

Trotter must have felt some satisfaction in sending these figures to the Government in view of the suggestions which Wood as Civil Auditor had made sometime earlier.[3] The suggestions had, in fact, not shown up the superintendent in a favourable light. In a first effort at substantive reform of the existing procedure relating to the selling of lottery tickets, the drawing of the lotteries, etc., Wood had written to the committee on 17 January 1818 that since the Government was 'responsible to the public for the payment of the prize tickets and for the lottery being drawn on correct principles, and being in every respect the [guarantor] to the public for the lottery being drawn in conformity with the official notification', the superintendent should prepare an account of his receipts and disbursements 'for record with the general accounts of the presidency, the same as all other officers intrusted (intrusted) with the receipts and disbursements of the public property'.[4]

With this in view, the auditor had suggested that the sale of tickets be conducted by the Bank of Bengal and that all tickets be sent to the bank 'and brought to account through the bank's books'. The new system would ensure that there would be no need for the superintendent to keep any other account of the cash transactions of the lottery connected with the sale of the tickets than what the bank accounts would furnish. This method, the auditor felt, would 'simplify' the accounts and render the 'keeping of the details easy to the officer more immediately responsible' for the holding of the lotteries. The plan also entailed a greater involvement of the auditor right from the stage of publication of the notification for the lottery concerned till the close of the drawing, which would enable the auditor 'to check the receipts and disbursements…as far as the same is connected with the sale of the tickets and payment of the prizes'. As far as disbursements from the lottery fund for town improvement were concerned, they were to be submitted in a quarterly bill to the auditor 'in the same way as contingent bills of the revenue and judicial departments, and, till passed by the Government, may remain in the inefficient balance'.

Trotter had taken three months to reply to Wood's suggestions. Wood had clothed his recommendations in the garb of 'simplification' of accounts which would enable the superintendent to keep them more easily. Trotter saw the issue differently. Writing to the committee on 22 April,[5] the superintendent listed the three objectives of the committee thus: to make sure that the full proceeds of the lotteries were regularly realised; to ascertain that the sum so realised was duly accounted for; and to make sure that no sums were charged to the lottery fund without proper authority and vouchers. Trotter described in some detail the existing system under which the lottery proceeds were realised, making the point that 'the check…over the superintendent appears to be complete'. Regarding disbursements made at the bank, the superintendent said that they were made 'on the presentation of prize tickets duly certified by the register and examiner *without any interference whatever on the part of the superintendent*, and the expenditure of the commission accruing to Government…is made *under its orders without even the knowledge of the superintendent*' (emphasis in original).

Trotter wrote that the Bank of Bengal and the Superintendent of the Lotteries served as a check on each other, adding that the bank would, 'if required, cheerfully furnish an account of their receipts and disbursements on account of the lotteries'. As for the suggestion that the superintendent draw up an account 'of his receipts and disbursements', Trotter did not consider it sensible. He argued that,

> Having neither to receive nor to disburse monies, he (the superintendent) would not keep a real cash account. And with respect to the fictitious one proposed, he must be entirely dependent on the Government, the bank, the Collector of the 24 Parganas, and the sub-treasurer for the materials of which it is to be composed, as well as for such vouchers as he might be able to procure.

As for the attainment of the first and second objectives – namely, that the full proceeds of the lotteries should be regularly realised and that the sum so realised should be duly accounted for – Trotter wrote that the arrangement suggested by Wood, 'in as far as it could be carried into effect, would apparently, and I speak with deference to his greater experience in matters of accounts,[6] involve the superintendent in a fictitious responsibility which might be attended with the greatest annoyance'. He added, 'It would to all appearance be far from rendering the business clear and, after all, I cannot see that it would be attended with any public benefit'. As for the third objective – that no sums were to be charged to the lottery funds without proper authority and vouchers – the superintendent said that, under the existing system, the civil auditor was

> …regularly informed of the authority granted for such disbursements, that the collector must regularly furnish him with a voucher for the money when paid, and that he (the auditor) has thus the means in his own office of charging the lottery account of these orders or disbursements either as an efficient balance or as sums actually paid.

Since Wood was not in Calcutta on 21 May 1818 – the day the committee considered Trotter's letter – no action was taken on the issue. But it is clear that the committee was placed in a difficult situation because when it met again two weeks later, on 4 June, when Wood was in fact present, it again failed to make up its mind.[7]

Henry Wood had suggested the reforms within eight months of the establishment of the Lottery Committee. That they were not accepted was a result of the views held by the authorities at the time the suggestions were made. But it was inevitable that with time the entire operational aspect of the different facets of the existing lottery system would be put to the test in the process highlighting its inadequacies and leading to suggestions to improve the general efficiency of the huge exercise.

In fact, Wood had made another suggestion, also in early 1818, for improved functioning of the Lottery Committee as a tool to facilitate the improvement of Calcutta, which was accepted by the Government quickly. On 21 February 1818, he had focussed attention on the nodal position of the Lottery Committee in the development process when he suggested that, 'Conceiving that the committee for the improvement of the town are interested in the appropriation of any land, the property of Government, within the Mahratta ditch, and immediately beyond it,' an order should be issued stating that

> ...all applications on the part of the public officers, and of private individuals, for the sale and purchase of any land, the property of Government, situated within the limits of the town and immediately beyond the Mahratta Ditch, may be referred to the committee for report, previous to any final decision being passed thereon by the orders of the Government.

The request was backed by the committee, the Government accepting the proposal on 24 March.[8]

John Trotter had taken over as Superintendent of the Lotteries in the last week of December 1818 and was – in an *ex officio* capacity – Secretary of the Lottery Committee as well.[9] After getting to know the ropes for three months, he proposed certain changes in the functioning of the lottery which would in essence constitute a break with the past. In January 1818 Henry Wood had suggested that the Bank of Bengal be given a more important role to play in the lottery process than previously, which would have had the impact of turning the office of the superintendent into not much more than a post office (see above). More than a year later, in March 1819, the new superintendent advanced a proposal relating to the financial operations of the lottery funds which aimed at a substantial reduction of the role played by the bank. Perhaps, the new superintendent, a civilian, was acting like one in that he was merely playing out the habit of protecting his turf. His predecessor, Archibald Trotter, too, had wanted to prevent the Bank of Bengal from playing a more active role in the lottery operations.

The burden of Trotter's 2 March proposal was that the existing procedure of the entire lottery sale proceeds being parked in the bank without earning any financial benefits for the lottery led to a sizable financial wastage for the entire lottery scheme.[10] Illustrating the point, Trotter wrote that at the beginning of the 1818-19 'official year' the balance was a healthy Rs 2,04,944-8-4, the sum being reduced to Rs 1,88,093-14-4 on 16 February 'without ever intermediately being diminished below that sum'. Taking an average value of Rs 1,96,519-3-4 and an interest rate of 10 per cent over 10 months, the superintendent calculated the nominal addition to the lottery funds at Rs 15,721-8-7. The reform suggested here was to make idle funds lying with the Bank of Bengal earn a return through judicious investment.

Trotter questioned the specific usefulness of yet another aspect of the existing arrangement involving the Bank of Bengal when he wrote that 'a much larger source of profit would accrue by an exercise [on the part of the committee] over the *entire* [emphasis in original] management of the lottery concerns as connected with the sale and proceeds of tickets'. Under the existing system, the bank sold the tickets and it was 'only accountable to Government' for payment into the general treasury of the funds remaining after the provision of the prize money, which then formed 'the capital at the disposal of the committee for promoting the objects of its establishment'. Neither the Government nor the committee 'interfered' with the sale proceeds of the tickets which '[continued] to the benefit of the bank'. The superintendent's submission was that the existing system deprived the lottery funds of 'considerable revenue which ought justly to accrue *to them exclusively* [emphasis in original] upon the principle that they are constituted solely for the avowed purpose of contributing to the convenience and healthiness of Calcutta...'[11]

He pointed out that the sale of tickets for a new lottery began on the payment of prize money relating to the preceding lottery, that is, three months before the drawing for the next lottery (fixed for 1 January). It could 'reasonably be assumed that, in general, with the exception of the tickets transferred to Fort St George and Bombay, the proceeds on the sales at this presidency are realised at the bank by the 1st of December'. This fund remained with the Bank of Bengal – 'uncalled for on the lottery account' – till around 1 April when the prize money would become payable. For about four months, therefore, 'the very large sum of Sicca Rs 5,20,000 continues to the exclusive benefit of the bank, and is convertible by it to the general objects of its constitution'. Trotter's point was that this was a financially inefficient exercise because, 'by a proper adoption of that sum on behalf of the lottery funds', a sum as large as Rs 17,333 (the rate of interest being 10 per cent per annum) could be earned for the lottery during the December-March period. Since there were two lotteries in a year, the total accrual would be Rs 34,666. Compounding this improper state of affairs was the fact that 'no adjustment takes place with the bank' till the ticket-sale accounts were received from Bombay and Madras, which took their own time.

The superintendent noted that this was the precise reason why, despite the 20th Lottery having been concluded, the net proceeds from the 18th and 19th Lotteries (Rs 73,040 and Rs 74,980, respectively) were yet to materialise. Quantifying the possible gain to the lottery funds, Trotter said that, taking the actual balance of Rs 1,78,381-7-11 as on 1 November 1817 and adding to it the net proceeds of the 18th and 19th Lotteries, an additional inflow ranging from Rs 58,841-1-9 (at 8 per cent interest rate) to Rs 67,301-5-

11 (10 per cent) could have resulted. The superintendent told the committee that the investment measures proposed by him 'would produce the contemplated advantages and upon the moderate calculation of even 8 per cent [interest rate] they would afford, subsequent to the defrayment of all the expenses, a net annual gain of 46,000 rupees or, at 10 per cent, of sicca rupees 56,000'.

John Trotter's suggestions were placed before the committee meeting in early March 1819 which led to a subcommittee being formed comprising Gordon, Macan and Colvin (none of whom was a Government officer). The new group was asked to study Trotter's suggestion regarding the 'advantages' which would accrue to the lottery fund if the committee took under its 'immediate management the entire conduct of the business connected with the lotteries with a view to the employment of the resting capital on loans or the discounting of private securities under the proposed terms' and make its own recommendations. The subcommittee took just two days to finalise its proposals: it backed Trotter's suggestions to extend control over the lottery funds lying with the Bank of Bengal. The loss of time meant losing additional funds and one can detect a note of urgency in the proceedings when the subcommittee informed the committee that it entirely approved 'of the general principle of Mr Trotter's proposition', recommending that it should be 'immediately submitted for the sanction of Government with the view of its being applied to the disposal of the large balance of cash now in hand, as well as to the proceeds of the future lotteries'.[12]

Having approved in principle the superintendent's proposal, Gordon, Macan and Colvin proposed that the Lottery Committee's Secretary (who was also Superintendent of the Lotteries) would be appointed 'accountant to the lottery committee', in which capacity, under the control of at least two committee members, he would invest the available funds 'in loans bearing interest'. This subcommittee would have to ensure that there would always be available to the lottery committee 'a sufficient sum to meet the payment of prizes and of other demands on the funds from time to time'. Other points were made regarding the rules governing investment of the funds, etc., the Gordon subcommittee stating that the profits that would accrue to the lottery fund following the adoption of the new plan would depend 'on the two contingencies of the balance of cash in hand and the ever-fluctuating state of the money market, neither of which it is easy to estimate'. It declared confidently that the profits would never fall short of Rs 20,000 'while they may considerably exceed 60,000 rupees a year'. The last point which the subcommittee made related to a 10 per cent commission on the net profits for the accountant (the Superintendent of the Lotteries) as recompense for 'all the trouble and responsibility whatever' he would have to take to get the new arrangement working properly.

The Lottery Committee found the proposals useful and sought permission from the Government to alter the system of flow of funds to itself. Hitherto, the funds were released by the general treasury or the Collector of 24-Parganas[13] but now the committee wanted 'the whole of the fixed establishments and contingencies chargeable to the lottery funds as well as the sums required for public improvements in the city and suburbs' to be paid from the Bank of Bengal *directly* 'to the persons entitled to receive them' following authorisation by any two members of the committee. As regards the need to keep the Government informed of such withdrawals from the lottery fund kept with the bank, the accounts would be 'periodically submitted' to the Government which would 'place the receipts and disbursements and the actual state of the lottery funds…in a clear and comprehensive point of view'. Another important change sought, which would facilitate daily operations, related to the disbursement without the Government's sanction of 'small sums not exceeding an amount to be specified… especially on occasions in which the delay attending the reference might be inconvenient'.

Since the proposal constituted a major reform of procedure governing the lottery fund, the Government took time (more than two months) to get back to the Lottery Committee.[14] After due deliberation it decided not to repose full control of the surplus lottery funds in the committee which included the process of investing the funds in the money market to generate interest income. By the end of the month (30 June) the Accountant-General, J.W. Sherer had approved the new rules describing them as being 'in every respect well-calculated to secure the attainment of the object in view'.

The Government argued that as long as the Governor-General in Council considered the surplus proceeds of the lottery 'to be applicable exclusively to the improvement of the city and not to the ordinary purposes of Government, it appears to be a just and reasonable indulgence that interest should be granted on the balance of those funds, which may be in deposit in the general treasury.' Under the system then prevalent, the surplus lottery funds remained with the Bank of Bengal. Under the new rules, while the bank would continue to be involved in the sale of tickets and the payment of prizes it would have nothing to do with other payments. Further, the bank would have to transfer the net surplus funds to the general treasury. The Lottery Committee, too, would have to transfer to the general treasury 'such sums as may be realised by them (from) the sale of ground or of old materials, or from other sources'.

On the debit side, all expenditure on projects for the improvement of the city and suburbs would be paid from the general treasury on the signature of two committee members and the secretary. The Lottery Committee had sought the authority to spend small sums of money associated with the improvement projects without the sanction of Government. The point was conceded the new guideline being that every month 'a credit on the treasury (would) be given to the committee to a certain limited amount, say 1,000 rupees, for petty current disbursements', the drafts to be signed by two committee members and the secretary. Further, instead of investing the surplus funds in the money market at annual interest rates varying from 8 to 10 per cent, the sub-treasurer was asked 'to allow and to carry to the credit of the lottery funds interest at the rate of six per cent on the net balance of those funds in the treasury at the end of each month, calculating the interest on each thousand'.

With the lottery striking deep roots in Calcutta society, attention was now directed to the need to reduce uncertainty and risk.

The records of early March 1820 carry the routine correspondence on the results of the 22nd Lottery and preparations for the 23rd, John Trotter, the Superintendent of the Lotteries, suggesting that, basing himself on the success attained by 'the scheme of the late lotteries', the scheme be followed again for the 23rd Lottery.[15] Following procedure, the committee forwarded the superintendent's letter to the Government with its stamp of approval. However, in the course of doing so, the committee proposed a major change for the 23rd Lottery when it asked the Government to allow it to 'receive tenders for the purchase of the *whole* lottery on the same plan as that adopted in the disposal of Government lotteries in England' (emphasis added). It was felt that no risk would be incurred by inviting 'speculators' to come forward with offers 'as none will of course be accepted without ample security by a deposit of Government notes to a sufficient amount'.[16] If no such offer was forthcoming within ten days of the lottery advertisement, the existing rules for the sale of tickets would be followed.

In past years private individuals had come forward to lift tickets in bulk which, at the time, had been a source of major relief for the Government. But the change suggested now by the committee would be a major one in that such individuals, among others, would be extended a formal invitation to buy up all the tickets before drawing began for the lottery, leaving the general public out in the cold. Expectedly, the Government proceeded with caution in formulating its response. On 10 March, that is, the day after receiving the committee's suggestion, the Chief Secretary, who was also a member of the Lottery Committee, wrote to the committee on behalf of the Government shooting down the proposal to float tenders on the ground of impracticability rather than principle. The official stand was that

> …as the ordinary period of notifying to the public the terms and conditions of the 23rd Lottery is close at hand, as the nature of the provisions which should be contained in the notification to be issued for inviting tenders for the purchase of the whole lottery would require careful consideration, and as some delay would necessarily occur in deciding upon the acceptance of any tenders which might be made under such notification, he [the Governor General in Council] does not consider it expedient to apply to the next, or 23rd, Lottery, the suggestions of the committee…[17]

The Government did not have any objections to the proposal in principle and asked the committee to submit to it 'at an early period' a 'complete draft' of the notification to be issued vis-a-vis the new scheme so that there would be ample time to study it before releasing it for use in 'the 24th or subsequent lotteries'. On 23 March the Superintendent of the Lotteries was asked to submit a report on the proposed scheme, including the provisions which would form part of the altered notification to be issued 'for inviting tenders for the purchase of the whole of the tickets in the 24th Lottery'.[18] Since he had some time before the 24th Lottery was launched, John Trotter took a couple of months to put together his note, in the event sending in a lengthy one in the third week of May.[19]

John Trotter first focussed on the legal moorings of the principles contained in Act LIV of George III 'which now regulate the disposal of the state lotteries in England',[20] the subject matter being 'that *several* [emphasis in original unless otherwise stated] persons in books opened at the Bank of England have subscribed *together* the whole of the sum to be raised by the lotteries of the year, and made the necessary deposits with the cashier of the bank'. The Act made the operation lawful by enabling the investors to pay the remaining amount due on the ticket charge by a particular date, or even in instalments 'if more convenient'.

The Superintendent of the Lotteries then discussed how far the principles applicable to the English lotteries could be extended, 'with the prospect of permanent benefit, to the lotteries in India under the modifications which local circumstances may require'. He drew attention to a number of specific issues, namely: whether the temptation to speculate was equal in Indian and English lotteries; the best mode of encouraging the sale of tickets in India; whether the inducement to, and opportunity for, investors to buy up all tickets in a lottery were the same in India as in England; whether any, and what, premium could be allowed on such bulk purchase of tickets 'allowing the longest possible credit for the ultimate payment'; and how the lotteries were affected by the 'circumstance of society in each country'.

Trotter was one of those who were against allowing investors to buy up all 6,000 tickets offered by a lottery. He argued that central to the success of the lotteries was a situation where there would be strong competition for tickets, and 'without a greater accession of contributors from amongst the native population competition could never be excited in India to the extent which exists in the purchase of the state lotteries in England'. Further, in England, the success attending royal lotteries was partly the result of 'estimating too highly the chances of gain', which led 'adventurers' to invest heavily in the purchase of tickets. He argued that

> …the proportion of tickets in an Indian lottery, with reference to the number of adventurers, is…I think much larger than at home, and therefore no prospect of gain in an inaffluent market would compensate for the loss which an adventurer would be exposed to in the purchase of an entire lottery.

The superintendent felt that the larger the number of tickets in a lottery the greater would be the element of risk to an intending investor. Further, there could be

> …no substantial grounds to expect that the lottery funds can ever be permanently benefited so much by the encouragement of monopoly…as by consulting at once the prejudice and demands of the great body of the people with a view to the extension of tickets, and the dissemination of the principles by which the lotteries are governed.

In other words, Trotter wanted the native population to be made more aware of the entire lottery system. The system, too, had to be extended beyond 'the stations in the vicinity of Calcutta' which would enable 'every person in India…to contribute upon the terms at which tickets are tendered by Government'. Spelling out the details, the superintendent said the extended populace should be

> …allowed the opportunity of purchasing their necessary tickets *before* an additional price is demanded by a market forestalled by adventurers, who do so *only* upon the payment of earnest [money] to the exclusion of a large body of the people willing to allow at once the full value of their intended purchase money.

This large market for lottery tickets comprised 'the *intending* contributors at distant stations' who, Trotter felt, were 'constantly disappointed in supplies of tickets on this account and the absence of any agent at the presidency to make timely application on their behalf'. To the superintendent, increasing the demand for tickets was the most important requirement for the success of the Indian lottery exercise. He wrote:

> With all (diffidence) I submit that the risk inseparable from the purchase of a *whole* Calcutta lottery could *never* admit of a premium being tendered. The object in the disposal of Indian lotteries should, I conceive, in the first instance be directed to the promotion of sales to the *actual consumers*, on the principle of [according] the whole public an opportunity to subscribe for their necessary supplies at the lowest possible price. And *when* these subscriptions are closed a premium upon the sale of any tickets which remain may *then* be reasonably be looked for.

Seen from the point of view of the investor, Trotter felt that, given the past experience with regard to the demand for tickets, no 'one person could tender for the purchase of a whole lottery without certain loss, [be] the conditions of purchase...ever so favourable'. To him the state of the 'money market' was an important input for the decision to make such an investment, and he saw no possibility that the chance of profit would be strong enough to make an investor take the risk involved in such speculation. Elucidating, he wrote that,

> The fluctuations...to which the money market is susceptible in India when compared with England is discouraging to speculation in an *entire lottery*, for though the low rate of money may be in favour of the adventurer *on purchase*, yet the payment at a distant period might...probably be productive of, at all events, embarrassment to the adventurer, if not loss.

In England, such 'fluctuations' in the money market were less likely to occur because of the 'usury laws (which) control the interest of the country within certain rates'. Even if the Lottery Committee were to extend concessions to investors by lengthening the period of repayment of credit, the assistance would not be effective because the real problem would still remain unresolved. Trotter wrote that only *after* (emphasis added) the subscription was closed could the committee 'very advantageously promise to contractors an extended credit'. He suggested that the concession be granted only to those investors who had bought 'the *whole unsold tickets* and not to those who may be disposed only to tender for a *partial* number'. In the event the concessions were extended to all investors, it would 'entice *petty* adventurers, and their competition would make the profits of those who contracted upon a *larger scale* (with a view to command the market) insufficient to compensate so great a risk'.

Trotter felt that the attraction of big prizes fuelled a large part of the demand, and in India he did not '...conceive the measure of temptation to be near so great as at home, nor is speculation here followed up for that reason with the same avidity as in England, where also, as I before observed, the number of tickets is less in proportion to the number of adventurers'.

The number of big prizes in the Indian lotteries was 'necessarily diminished by the extent of the 125-rupees prizes'. But nothing could be done about it because the lotteries 'could not be supported upon the present scale by any reduction' in the number of such prizes. On whether investors could be offered all tickets in a lottery or only a part, the superintendent said that, after considering 'the constitution of Indian lotteries and…all the local circumstances by which they are affected and governed', investors would much rather prefer to buy up the available supply of tickets '*after a certain period*'. If, say, 2,000 tickets were left unsold at the close of subscription, the prospect of success after a large portion of the consumers are already supplied with their tickets 'is then much in favour of adventurers, and a premium upon such sale would, I think, be certain to the extent of at least 4 per cent upon 2,000 tickets, which would be equal to a gain of 16,000 rupees upon the two lotteries in the year'.

Having painted a complex picture, Trotter proposed a plan for an Indian lottery which would include investment by speculators but after incorporating changes keeping the English scenario in mind. He wrote:

> In planning the scheme of an Indian lottery and in estimating the number of the tickets, the circumstances of society should also be considered to be totally different from the bulk of the society in England. The European part of the community, who are considered to have been hitherto the chief supporters of Calcutta lotteries, are more competent to the valuation of chances than the classes of the people in England amongst whom the demand does there principally exist. The natives, however, are unable to

> appreciate a lottery in the above way, though of late years I am credibly informed that they have greatly advanced in a knowledge of its general principles.

Taking into account the twin bases of the carefulness with which speculators evaluate the risk of buying up all lottery tickets and the 'efficiency of the market to the necessary consumption of 6,000 tickets', Trotter argued against 'making an entire sale to contractors *before* a great body of the consumers have had the opportunity of supplying their requisite tickets'. He wrote that no investor could be expected to bid for an entire lottery 'except under the prospect of (a) premium on his *average sales*, but general observation convinces me that an enhancement of price beyond the *even sum of 1,000 rupees* (before 4,000 tickets are sold) would ultimately entail certain loss on any contractor'. The superintendent emphasised the point that no advantage that the Lottery Committee would gain from the 'early sale of a single lottery' to speculators would compensate 'for probable loss on some future occasion'. He wrote,

> Should adventurers on the purchase of a whole lottery experience disappointment or loss in such a speculation, the value of subsequent lotteries would not, I think, be likely to improve in general estimation. Their value, on the contrary, would I think be more likely to fall in the opinion of the public.

John Trotter said that it was only because of this reason that he felt that the 'permanent interest' of the lotteries would be safeguarded if they looked after 'their own risk in the disposal of tickets'. If, on the other hand, they shifted this 'risk' to investors, the moment 'the efficiency of the market is in any way questioned, the probable consequence would be productive of injury at a future period'.

The Superintendent of the Lotteries had gone against the wishes of the committee when he opposed the proposal to hand over the lotteries to investors. For, it was the Lottery Committee itself which had wanted the 23rd Lottery to be conducted on the new lines, a suggestion the Government had turned down on the ground of shortage of time. Trotter's entire exercise was, in fact, the outcome of the Government's suggestion that the issue be examined in detail before any decision was taken to introduce the new system. Considering this, it is not surprising that the committee members directed a fusillade of criticism at the superintendent's proposals.[21]

Gordon took the lead basing his argument on observed fact instead of theory. He wrote that the fact that

> …a speculator has repeatedly bought up the whole lottery, and at a loss to himself without any injury to the insuing (insuing) lotteries, weighs more forcibly with me than all the ingenious arguments of Mr Trotter, and impresses me with a conviction that there are particular occasions when the whole lottery may be advantageously disposed of by public sale.

Tucked away in a lengthy minute[22] on the subject was the precise reason which, in the first instance, had led the Lottery Committee to propose the scheme for intending investors to be allowed to buy up an entire lottery. The trigger appears to have been a struggle between existing lottery ticket-dealers and 'private adventurers' with regard to the sale of tickets for the 23rd Lottery, which had led the former to '(forestall) the market and (raise) the price of tickets from the day that their sale was first announced', upsetting the calculations of the investors. On being informed by the Superintendent of the Lotteries that all the tickets for the 23rd Lottery had been 'prematurely' picked up, the committee recommended that 'the whole lottery should be offered to the highest bidder who would then acquire an equitable right to put such a price upon the tickets as his own prudence might direct'.

Gordon outlined a scheme for running a lottery under the new dispensation, which was agreed to by Bayley who wrote that there should be no objection to tickets being sold at a premium by investors because, at the end of the process, with the committee accepting the highest offer on ticket prices, 'we might increase the disposable funds of the lottery committee 6,000 or 12,000 rupees, or probably more, per annum without incurring any risk or forfeiting any advantage which we now possess'. Bayley said he would opt for the new scheme only if the entire lottery was put up for sale; if not, he would 'revert to the former plans, or rather rules hitherto published'. The Chief Secretary to the Government put Gordon in the driver's seat when he suggested that the latter draw up 'a [note] such as he may think we should submit to Government, including the plan, rules and conditions which he would propose to be published for general information' adding that both the Lottery Committee and the Government 'would thus have the question before them in a distinct and intelligible shape'.

Although John Trotter had argued against the new system of holding lotteries proposed by the committee, his proposals being shot down by the committee, he had a suggestion to offer regarding the new bidding process by investors. He said that, in case the new system was adopted, it would mean the disposal of future lotteries 'at the highest offer which can be obtained beyond Sicca Rs 6,00,000 instead of requiring the advance to be made on the value of each ticket at 100 rupees'. The best method of doing so would be to 'sell' the lottery by 'public auction' – under the supervision of the superintendent – which 'would be best calculated to ensure the realignment of the highest premium'. This method of disposal would also lead to no expense being incurred for the exercise 'excepting a mere gold-*mohur* to defray the crier's charge of attendance at the superintendent's office'. Gordon agreed with Trotter that it would be better to let the bidding be done in 'round sums than by a percentage on the price'.

Having been directed to draw up a scheme on the 'principles' suggested by Gordon, the superintendent submitted a detailed notification for the 24th Lottery on 15 June 1820 which was approved by the committee and subsequently the Government. The notification was sent to the Government on the same day along with the committee's suggestions on the new lottery scheme which could be adopted in India. The committee stuck to its 9 March position (see above) but kicked off its 15 June letter to the Government by underscoring its agreement with the Superintendent of the Lotteries on at least one point, namely, the strength of speculation in England and India. The committee said that it 'entirely [concurred] with the superintendent…that the want of excitement to speculate is greatly attributable to the limited sphere within which lottery speculation is known to an Indian society compared with the mass of population to whom the subject is familiar in England'. This was why while in India the value of tickets was 'unknown to advance to any extent until the latter days of drawing', in England lottery tickets 'generally produced a very high premium to Government on their original sale, and as the period approached for the commencement of the drawings prices further advanced in the hands of the contractors from 50 to 100 per cent'.

However, the committee took the inherent weakness in speculation in India as given and, unlike Trotter, made no effort to suggest ways to alter the situation. No importance was given to the reorganisation of the prize profile which would have protected the interest of the local. On the other hand, that of the investors was considered citing the prevailing situation in England. The committee said that, when compared to the English lotteries, smaller prizes abounded in the Calcutta lotteries the apparent objective of which was to extend 'protection' to the dealers. But, in fact, the prizes were 'too large to save risk to the dealers, and too small to benefit private speculators effectually'. The Government was told that 'the great objects of attraction are multiplied in the British lotteries', the committee having no doubt that an adoption of the same plan 'in this country would have a very striking effect in adding to the popularity of any lottery scheme'. The question was then posed whether a lottery in which 'prizes below ten thousand rupees in value formed the capitals would entice a single adventurer to risk 100 rupees' even if no deductions were to be made for expenses. Gordon's scheme, adopted for the 24th Lottery, had the following prize profile: one prize of 10,000 gold *mohur*s (Rs 1,60,000), one of a lakh of rupees, one of Rs 50,000, two of Rs 20,000, two of Rs 10,000, ten of Rs 1,000, 40 of Rs 500, 200 of Rs 250, 1,200 of Rs 125 yielding all together a total prize kitty of Rs 6,00,000. Altogether 1,457 tickets would bear prize values while 4,543 would be blanks yielding a total of 6,000 tickets.

The Government approved the new scheme at the end of June, its cautious approach being reflected by the sentiment that since 'the modified scheme' recommended by the Lottery Committee 'appears to have been prepared in communication with those who are best qualified to judge of the probability of its success', it had no hesitation in allowing its adoption.[23] The point was made that 'the disposal of the whole lottery by public auction to the highest bidder offering not less than 6,00,000 rupees' appeared to be preferable to the measure originally suggested by the committee 'of receiving tenders for the purchase of the whole lottery'.

The stage being set, the 24th Lottery was put up for auction on 15 September 1820 and was bought by the highest bidder, Alexander and Company, for Rs 6,16,500.

From the very first lottery drawn in 1809, the number of tickets on offer for each draw was 6,000. Was this number sufficient to meet the demand, or did it represent an excess of supply? At the conclusion of the 19th Lottery, the superintendent, Archibald Trotter, had written to the Lottery Committee (3 September 1818)[24] that a 'considerable number' of tickets had remained unsold till 4 August 'when the remaining ones were purchased on speculation'. Trotter wrote that this was being interpreted as 'proof that the number of tickets in the lottery is too great'. He, however, felt that this was not the case because in past lotteries, which had had the same number of tickets on offer, the supply was exhausted 'as rapidly as could well be expected'. As far as the 19th Lottery was concerned, Trotter wrote that the military officers 'have not become purchasers in the past season to the extent which they generally do'. Secondly, there was a shortage of money in circulation, 'as was once before the case'. The superintendent argued that the conditions would not be repeated in the ensuing year the inference being that the plan for the 19th Lottery could be used for the drawing of the 20th, which was agreed to by the Government at the time.[25]

In fact, the set pattern of 6,000 tickets for each lottery yielding a return of Rs 72,000 lasted well into the 1820s.[26] The lottery proceeds, in fact, increased to a lakh of rupees in the mid-1820s. In 1825 the committee reported that the actual net profit of the first lottery for the year had amounted to only Rs 45,300, which was ascribed to the 'large proportion of blanks drawn amongst the tickets which it had been found impracticable to dispose of prior to the drawing'.[27] In an effort to rectify the situation, the committee submitted a new scheme aimed at securing 'as far as practicable a profit of a lakh of rupees upon each lottery'. The scheme was accepted and implemented with the result that the second lottery of 1825 produced a lakh of rupees, the first lottery of 1826 Rs 98,200, and the second lottery of that year a lakh of rupees again.[28]

The principal reason why the arrangement was not disturbed was that, barring special requirements such as the building of Strand Road, etc., there was no pressing need at any time to increase the volume of funds needed for the city's improvement. When such a need did arise, the collection canvas was extended to include the town duties.[29] Alternatively, there were no firm indications during this period that the 6,000 tickets drawn for each lottery twice every year were in excess of the number which would satisfy the hunger for risk of those interested in playing the lottery wheel in Calcutta, Madras and Bombay. But, of course, the situation could not last indefinitely. With the progressive decline in the importance of the lottery funds for the improvement of Calcutta, seven years later the number of tickets had been reduced to 5,000 priced at Rs 100 each, the expected profit being Rs 60,000.[30]

In the intervening years, however, efforts were made by the authorities to increase the proceeds from the lotteries. The first such move was made by John Trotter, Superintendent of the Lotteries, early in 1821 when he informed the committee that the coffers were in a bad shape compared to the demands that were about to be made on the funds in the next few years.[31] As he saw it, the pressure on financial resources being exerted by 'the works which the committee are now employed in upon the banks of the river' was such that, unless an effort was made to increase the kitty, 'a suspension (of) the other works upon which the committee are presently employed or the abandonment of the other plans now under contemplation for the further improvement of the city' was inevitable. In the circumstances, Trotter proposed a scheme which would allow the development of the riverfront to continue without affecting the other projects on the anvil.

Trotter estimated that around Rs 3 lakhs would be needed to 'complete' the works on the riverside while the funds at the disposal of the committee (as on 31 December 1820) totalled just Rs 49,314. Taking into account the demands on these funds of 'the works in progress', the superintendent drove home the point that 'with even the usual assistance from the two lotteries in each of the next two years' (yielding Rs 2,88,000 at Rs 72,000 per lottery), there was no possibility of meeting 'the current requisite expenses for finishing the projected quay and road within the period at which the works can easily be completed with adequate funds'. The superintendent's remedy was to hold an additional lottery annually during the 'present and ensuing year' which would yield the additional resources necessary for the projects in question. He said he had 'the pleasure to state that the result of the inquiries I have made upon this subject holds forth every reason to look for certain success'.

Elucidating, Trotter said that the success of the 'present' lottery (the 24th),[32] along with the 'intermediate circumstance' of a drying up of sources offering capital a handsome return, though temporary, were two important reasons behind the proposal for an extra annual lottery. A third reason was the declared use to which the funds generated by the extra lottery would be put, namely, the building of the riverfront road and quay. Also adding value to the exercise would be the fact that the projects would be 'of more general benefit to the interests of Calcutta inhabitants and to natives in particular than any improvement which has hitherto been completed under the management of the committee'. He pointed to 'the wonderful premium of 50 per cent at which the tickets in the present lottery are known to have been sold…by contractors before the commencement of the first day's drawing', arguing that this was 'almost a guarantee in itself' for the success of the scheme proposed by him. There had also been a 'great increase' in the demand for tickets in Bombay and Madras 'this last half-year through the high temptation offered from the capital prizes in this lottery' as also in the Bengal drawings, especially since the institution of the 10,000 gold-*mohur* first prize, which showed that, under the existing scheme on which the lotteries were run, the sale of 6,000 tickets in each of the three lotteries would be '(guaranteed)...*at this present time*' (emphasis in original).

Trotter, however, was aware of the problems the contractors would have to face if three lotteries were to be held every year. The first was the fact that the holding of three lotteries would shorten the period for which the contractors would get credit compared to the previous system, which would affect the premium they would be prepared to pay.

Secondly, it was possible that the holding of three lotteries 'in such close succession as every 4 months [would] decrease the avidity with which tickets are now purchased'. Even so, Trotter felt that despite the problems, which could lead to a 'considerable' reduction in the profits of the contractors, they would still be able to expect a premium from each lottery 'at all times (which) would be ample to meet such a contingency'.

Just in case the committee did not agree to increase the number of lotteries, Trotter said the objective of increasing the lottery proceeds could be met by increasing the *size* of each of the two lotteries to, say, 8,000 tickets in place of the existing 6,000. In Trotter's view, the contractors would then 'continue to enjoy the same credit as exists under the present system whilst perhaps adventurers might possibly be induced...to offer at first a higher premium on the purchase of 2 lotteries of 8,000 tickets than on 3 of 6,000 each'. In order to increase the demand for tickets, Trotter suggested that the prizes on offer could be increased by one of Rs 1,00,000, one of Rs 50,000, and 400 of Rs 125.

John Trotter had made his suggestions on 3 January 1821 which were discussed by the committee at its meeting the next day. As on an earlier occasion, his views were again shot down by some of his colleagues on the committee. Gordon proposed in a minute a scheme radically different to that of the superintendent, arguing that, given the prevailing market conditions at the time, it would be improper to disturb the existing scheme of the lotteries. He felt that the prevailing investment mood would 'prove a strong encouragement to (investors) to venture on the next lottery a much larger premium than they deemed it prudent to hazard on the last provided all essential circumstances and conditions are allowed to remain as they then were'.[33] Any alteration, whether in the number of lotteries to be held in a year or their size, would lead to 'a new risk...the extent of which is not to be calculated with precision and difficult even to be estimated within any degree of approximation'. Gordon felt that the changes suggested by the superintendent would, therefore, have to be set aside on this general ground.

On the three-lotteries proposal, Gordon said that there would be 'so many disadvantages' that even if each lottery in the new arrangement were to contain just 4,000 tickets 'few would venture to offer any premium on the purchase, and still fewer if each lottery were to consist of 5,000 tickets'. In the latter case (5,000 tickets), no premium would be offered whatever so that the net gain to the development fund compared to the proceeds generated by the existing scheme of the lotteries would be just the 12 per cent of the additional Rs 3 lakhs, or Rs 36,000, in a full year whereas, if the lottery was held on the existing principles 'without any essential change', the committee 'may safely calculate on getting at least that sum in the form of premium on one lottery'. He, however, felt that investors would find a lottery comprising 7,000 tickets and held twice a year more acceptable than three 5,000-ticket lotteries held over the same period.

Gordon agreed with Trotter's observation that the market had improved but said there were a number of reasons why 'foreign' sales were less important than the Bengal market, which was under 'the immediate eye of the speculator', such as 'uncertainty of the sale of the whole number of tickets sent to be disposed of, the difficulty of controlling the price from time to time according to circumstances, the risks of exchange, etc'. What this meant was that, keeping the interest of the investor in mind, any decision to increase the number of lottery tickets had to be based on the 'extent of the Bengal market' much more than that in Bombay and Madras.

Having rejected the two changes in the lottery system proposed by Trotter, Gordon then moved on to an aspect which was not mentioned by the former but which was closely connected to the prevailing state of the money market. He said that since too much money was floating around with too few opportunities for investment, the next lottery (25th) should be bid for in 'sealed tenders' instead of being put up for public auction. The 'sealed tender' approach would induce some amount of investment discipline in the bidding which would 'leave a *wide margin* [emphasis in original] for profit and thus give an opportunity of going with safety beyond their single bid'. Given the state of the money market, the public sale approach would encourage very high bids from selected investors 'to the full value of the lottery', which would have the effect of discouraging others 'from offering competition, for who would take the trouble of bidding with the certainty of not succeeding unless they overbid those who know the value of the subject of competition'. Gordon concluded that if the new speculators were to have their way, there would of course be 'a better chance' of the committee getting 'a proper share of the profit in subsequent lotteries'. This would, however, be the lesser of two evils because 'any change in extent or frequency would produce a degree of uncertainty as discouraging to speculating, moneyed men as it would be to a seaman to be set adrift in the midst of the [ocean] and in cloudy weather too without chart or compass'.

Gordon maintained that, in the event of the other conditions of holding the lotteries (periodicity and size) remaining unchanged, the prize profile needed to be altered. As he saw it, in the existing lottery scheme there were just seven prizes that could be considered to be of some value: 'there are very few purchasers of whole tickets to whom a prize of 1,000 Rs or under is of any material consideration'. He, therefore, proposed that two more sizable prizes be offered and 'all the 500 and 250 Rs prizes [be included] into the mass of the lowest denomination', which he proposed to be 10 gold *mohurs*. The new prize-list would be: one of 10,000 gold *mohurs* – Rs 1,60,000; one of 5,000 – Rs 80,000; one of 2,500 – Rs 40,000; two of 1,000 – Rs 32,000; four of 500 – Rs 32,000; 12 of 100 – Rs 19,200; 1,480 of 10 – Rs 2,36,800. There would be a total of 1,501 prizes valued at Rs 6,00,000 with 4,499 blank tickets.[34]

The committee took ideas from both the Superintendent of the Lotteries as well as from Gordon when it proposed to the Government that the existing lottery scheme should be changed.[35] It accepted the fact that there was an excess of investible funds floating around in the money market and also the need to enhance the resources with the Lottery Committee. However, it refused to tinker with the periodicity of the lottery drawings because it would increase the risk to intending investors. Trotter's suggestion to raise the size of each lottery and Gordon's proposal to increase the number of big prizes so as to make the exercise more attractive to investors were accepted. Trotter had suggested that the size of the lottery be enhanced to Rs 8 lakhs; the committee opted for Rs 7 lakhs, a figure which Gordon had mentioned. The latter had also preferred two extra-big prizes: the committee increased the number to five. The new prize profile it proposed was as follows: one of 10,000 gold *mohurs* – Rs 1,60,000; one of 6,000 – Rs 96,000; one of 3,000 – Rs 48,000; one of 2,000 – Rs 32,000; three of 1,000 – Rs 48,000; five of 500 – Rs 40,000; 12 of 100 – Rs 19,200; and 1,712 of 150 – Rs 2,56,800. In all there would be 1,736 prize-bearing tickets yielding Rs 7,00,000, and 5,264 blank tickets, the total number of tickets being 7,000. The proposal was accepted by the Government three weeks later, the 25th Lottery being bought at open auction on 15 March by a native outfit Punchanund Mitter and Company for Rs 7,38,000.[36]

THE FIRST PLANNED SQUARE

For more than a hundred years after Charnock landed in Calcutta, and stayed on, there was only one 'square' in the fast-expanding town, namely, Tank Square (presently BBD Bagh). The square was not planned; it had evolved around the Laldighi (the waterbody in the square) the history of which is buried deep in the past. With the advent of the Lottery Committee in October 1817 the scenario was to change. Within a span of a decade there would come into being four squares with tanks, all of them located along one arterial road stretching from north to south. These were Cornwallis Square, College Square, Wellington Square and Wellesley Square, all four of which sport new names today. The first to be constructed was Wellington Square (Raja Subodh Mullick Square) and, along with it, the road to the west of it – from Dharamtala Street (Lenin Sarani) in the south to Bowbazar Street (Bepin Behari Ganguly Street) in the north. The project, implemented by the Lottery Committee, was conceived some years before the committee was appointed, the seed being sown by Henry Wood, Civil Auditor, in a letter written on 29 August 1814 to John Eliot and members of the Committee for the Improvement of the Town of Calcutta.[1]

Wood had focussed attention generally on waterbodies, or tanks, pointing out that, owing to the high price of ground 'within the Mahrattah Ditch' (ranging between Rs 100 and Rs 3,000 a *katha*) and the continuing rise in its value, many landowners had been persuaded to fill up tanks on their premises which had formerly supplied water to the people. As Wood saw it, the problem was that, in the course of 'a few years', the remaining tanks would be filled up 'when the inconvenience now experienced by the poorer classes of inhabitants for a supply of water in the months of May and June…will be greatly increased if they are not allowed to resort to the river for drinking water'. In fact, so severe was the problem that the tanks had to be 'guarded by peons and the water served out with a sparing hand, the *bheesties* of the opulent classes being allowed to carry away a few *mussucks* daily when the poorer classes are only permitted to quench their thirst on the spot without carrying any away'. At the time Wood was busy making an aqueduct[2] and he wrote that since the water channel, if extended, would not be able to 'do away entirely the serious inconvenience' of a shortage of drinking water for the natives, 'the propriety of immediately purchasing ground in the most centrical situation within the town, as well as at convenient distances around the Circular Road, to be laid out in tanks for the public use,' be considered. If the idea was accepted, the tanks could be filled with the help of an expanded network of the aqueduct.[3]

The Government's response to Wood's suggestions led directly to the setting up of the committee for excavation of tanks by the magistrates.[4] On 14 March 1815, the Vice-President in Council, N.B. Edmonstone, wrote that Wood's August 1814 letter had contained 'very important suggestions calculated to promote in an eminent degree the health and convenience of the inhabitants of this populous city'. In view of this, the magistrates were to furnish the Government

> …with very little delay as possible…a report of your sentiments on those subjects [the aqueduct and tanks] together with estimates of expense which will be incurred

> in carrying into effect such part of those suggestions as may appear to you to be expedient, and of a nature to admit of their being immediately adopted.

Nothing much seems to have happened regarding tank-excavation for the next couple of years. The subject cropped up again on 12 March 1817 when Wood, while informing the Government that the work on the aqueduct along Chowringhee had been completed from Dharamtala in the north to Park Street in the south, said that he was not aware of 'any progress' having being made regarding the measures recommended by him in the 29 August 1814 letter 'although I am given to understand that the want of water in the month of May had been severely felt by the different classes of inhabitants'.[5] Since 'nothing can so essentially add to the health, comfort and convenience of the population of a great city in a hot climate as a plentiful supply of good, wholesome water', he was 'induced to press the subject again…from a persuasion that the Government must ever indulgently give its attention to a subject so intimately connected with the comforts of the increasing population of this great city'. He said that on an earlier occasion he had marked out on a map of Calcutta the possible sites where tanks could be dug and 'open spaces' (possibly squares and parks) could be set up, which he was now submitting to the Government for further consideration and action. In case there was any objection on the ground that the cost of purchasing the plots needed to implement the plan was too high, the Civil Auditor focussed on a point of principle, namely, that

> …in the execution of a plan which has for its object the supply of good water to the inhabitants, and the opening of spaces to admit a free circulation of air into the centre of the

> town, the price of the ground should not be allowed to be an obstacle in the way of so essential an improvement.

He wrote that 'if the ground is valuable for building on, it is still more so for the purposes which I propose it should be purchased'. If the lottery funds were not enough to finance the 'full completion of the works recommended', Wood suggested that the inhabitants be allowed to subscribe to a loan the interest on which at the rate of six per cent was to be charged to the lottery funds and the principal 'to be liquidated by half-yearly payments out of the surplus proceeds of the lottery'. Not wasting any time, in late March 1817 the Government ordered that 'estimates of the expense attending such parts of those suggestions as might appear to be expedient…be made with as little delay as possible'.

On the same day that Wood's letter was considered by the Government, the magistrates were informed of the changes sought by the Civil Auditor in the plan to construct the aqueduct and also of the drain suggested by him on the northern side of Dharamtala Street.[6] They were told that the Government had already approved of the alterations suggested by Wood which left the magistrates with little scope to come up with their own ideas. On the same day, the Tank-Excavation Committee, comprising John Eliot, Charles Trower, Henry Wood and James Weir Hogg, was set up to commence 'arrangements for the excavation of one or more tanks in that part of the town where they may appear to be most urgently required'. The committee was asked initially 'to exercise… discretion' in selecting projects, and that as soon as they identified one they were to report 'the same to Government, submitting a plan and an estimate of the expense of purchasing the necessary ground and digging the tank'.[7] The committee reported back in the first week of June stating, without providing any details, that it had 'fixed on the centre of the Dhurm Tollah as the spot where a tank is most urgently required' and that the 'probable expence of purchasing ground, buildings, etc, and excavating the tank will not exceed 1,80,000 rupees'. The final cost, it added, would be considerably less than the estimate consequent on the resale 'of part of the ground' bought for the project. An amendment was sought to the 28 October 1814 bye-law which would introduce the word 'tanks' and thereby facilitate the authorities to purchase ground for digging waterbodies.[8]

The Government sent the report back to the committee asking for 'much more detailed information' before the Governor-General in Council could approve the project estimate.[9] A plan was sought which would show the

> ...actual situation and extent of the whole quantity of ground proposed to be purchased in the first instance, the dimensions of the tank itself, and of any roads or other public objects to which the ground is intended to be appropriated and, lastly, the quantity and situation of the ground of which the resale is contemplated by you.

The Government wanted to know the price of the land needed for the project, the number and estimated value of the houses which would have to be demolished for which compensation to the owners would have to be arranged, the amount expected to be realised from resale of a part of the ground, and the net cost of the project. The committee was asked to list the advantages which would result from the completion of the project.

More than three months passed before the Tank-Excavation Committee produced its second report on 25 September 1817.[10] Signed by Eliot, Trower and Wood,[11] it laid out a detailed plan of the square and tank and the expected expenditure on it. The project would provide 'good water' to the inhabitants, fill up 'swamps and low places in its vicinity with the earth excavated from the tank', open a space for the 'free circulation of air and recreation of the inhabitants', and improve 'the appearance of the town by affording the speculator in buildings an opportunity of obtaining portions of ground suitable to his purposes'.

As regards the new road (there was no mention of it in the initial report), the committee said it

> ...would offer to the public wishing to proceed from the center of the Dhurrumtollah to the centre of the Bow Bazar the means of so doing in 1/3rd of the time it can at present, for instead of going over a space of 300 feet, a space of 243.3 feet will only (have) to be passed over.

According to the Eliot committee's second report, the intended square, within the area marked ABCD, would have sides 500 ft long which would have a tank at its core (IJKL) surrounded by a 20-ft walk (EFGH) to be enclosed by a 'wall or railing'. The tank itself would not be a square because '400 feet by 450 feet [would be left] for the water'. Schalch's map shows an oval tank with a

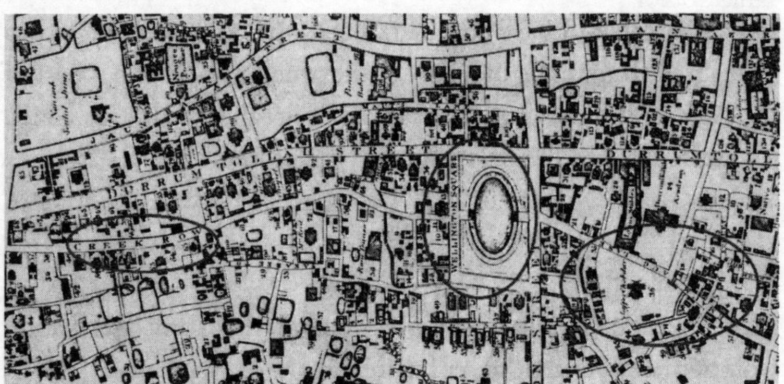

Fig. 9. Schalch's map showing Oval Tank at Baparitala, Creek Row and Imambagh Lane to the west

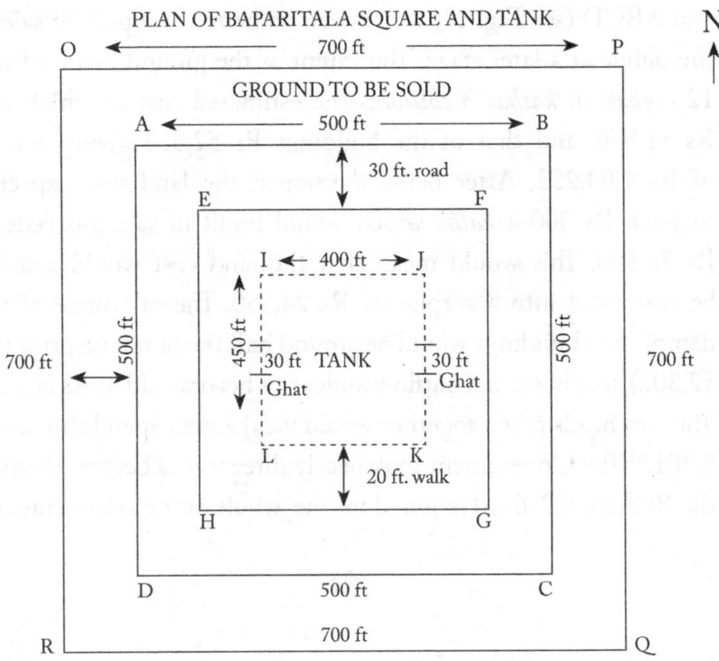

Fig. 10. Plan of the tank at Baparitala

north-south alignment of the elongated sides with two 30-ft-wide ghats to the east and west of it. Beyond the wall or railing of the tank would be a 30-ft road on all four sides. The square (ABCD) would be enclosed by another square (OPQR) with 700-ft-long sides, the committee proposing to buy the ground between the two squares 'for the purpose of reselling'.

The cost of making the square and tank would together add up to Rs 1,04,348-6-10 and the new road to Bowbazar Rs 17,592, making a total of Rs 1,21,940-6-10. From this sum Rs 17,844-9-5 would have to be deducted as the sale proceeds of the 'building materials' of the demolished houses, which would result in the 'net probable cost' to the Government of the proposed tank, square and road being Rs 1,04,095-13-5. To this would have to be added the money spent on the ground and buildings between OPQR and ABCD (see Fig. 10) which were to be redeveloped for sale to the public at a later stage. The extent of the ground involved was 12 *bighas* 16 *kathas* 3 *chittacks* the estimated cost of which was Rs 51,950, and that of the buildings Rs 52,302 giving a total of Rs 1,04,252. After being developed the land was expected to fetch Rs 300 a *katha* which would result in sale proceeds of Rs 76,800. This would mean that the land cost would actually be converted into a surplus of Rs 24,850. The sale price of the demolished buildings would be around half the purchase price (Rs 52,302), that is, the net outflow under this head would be Rs 26,151. The two heads taken together would yield a net expenditure of Rs 1,301.[12] The Government took nearly three weeks before releasing the Rs 2,26,222-6-10 required for the 'whole of the arrangements'.

John Eliot, president of the Lottery Committee and a member of the subcommittee looking after the Baparitala project, passed away on 19 January 1818.[13] His place on the main committee was taken by C.R. Barwell, the Acting Magistrate of the Suburbs of Calcutta and a Justice of the Peace of the town, who was also included in the subcommittee looking after the Baparitala project.[14] Since Eliot was a workhorse who did not quite abide by the civilities of genteel behaviour, his removal from the scene was likely to have an impact on the pace of work on the improvement of the town generally.

That the Baparitala project was progressing at a fast clip is suggested by the report of the subcommittee in early February 1818 that Rs 54,742 (out of Rs 1,04,348) had been spent with work about to begin on pulling down the buildings which had been bought.[15] However, not all was smooth sailing. As was to be anticipated, some house owners were not prepared to accept readily the price offered officially for their property. Imambaksh,[16] whose 6 *bigha*s 17 *katha*s of ground was required for the project, was named as one of those who had put up stubborn opposition to the subcommittee's plans. He had rejected the price offer of Rs 27,500 computed on the basis of Rs 200 a *katha* which was considered to be sufficient compensation 'and equal to what has been taken by others in the vicinity'. Probably, Imambaksh was able to oppose the Government's offer in view of his long experience of interacting with sahibs, which, among other things, had generated a familiarity with the rulers – as well as, perhaps, a degree of contempt. The subcommittee wrote that this local native luminary had 'refused to come to any accommodation notwithstanding the utmost endeavours of the committee to afford him every reasonable indulgence and satisfaction'. In view of this, it was proposed that Imambaksh be compelled to come to a settlement by applying Section 7 to 14 of the Jury Act of October 1814.[17]

A similar course of action was suggested with regard to the case of Black[18] and Meer Jaun who owned, respectively, a lower-roomed and upper-roomed house for which Rs 11,500 and Rs 3,032 had been offered. The committee passed on the request to the Government in the second week of February 1818 the magistrates being asked in early March 1818 to invoke the Jury Act 'to value the property of the individuals named…[Imambaksh, Black and Meer Jaun], and to tender to them, respectively, such sums as may appear an equitable and just valuation of their property'. If the property owners concerned failed to accept the valuation made by the magistrates, the latter were to 'adopt the legal measures which may be necessary for summoning a jury'. Since this would be the first instance of a jury being formed under the 1814 bye-law to settle a dispute of this sort, the Government asked the magistrates to tread with caution.[19]

Progress along the Jury Act road was slow. Even seven months later nothing appears to have moved on the Imambaksh front. As the committee found to its discomfiture, the jury method could not be employed because the provisions of the 1814 bye-law 'were considered to be confined strictly to sewers and streets' and not to squares and tanks as in the present case and that, therefore, the premises could not be obtained by forming a jury.[20] For this specific hurdle, the Government had only itself to blame because the problem was foreseen in June 1817 by the Tank-Excavation Committee which, in fact, had asked for a suitable amendment of the 1814 law.

The situation had become pressing for the Lottery Committee because by October 1818 as much as Rs 76,676 had already been spent on buying up 'numerous, small *pucka* built houses and huts and premises occupying the greater portion of the ground required for the intended improvements'. Further, the buildings bought had been demolished and the ground cleared. As the authorities viewed the problem, it was only the 'obstinacy and perverseness' of Imambaksh that was standing in the way of progress.[21] On the last day of September the Government was told that the former *thanadar* had 'hitherto resisted every overture' which the committee had made 'to induce him to consent to the transfer of the property in question'.[22] Further, the 'real extent and value' of the ground belonging to him had turned out to be greater than that estimated earlier. On its part, the committee was prepared to foot the higher bill but the owner was averse to receiving 'a pecuniary compensation'. Faced with such intransigence, and perhaps more in desperation than anything else, the committee members approached Imambaksh individually for a solution, the latter eventually agreeing 'to receive in lieu of his premises in the Durrumtollah Street an estate [garden] offered for sale at 36,000 rupees belonging to a Mr Smith near Chandnee Choke together with 3,000 rupees in lieu of another separate spot of ground included within the limits of the proposed square'.[23] The helplessness of the authorities in the case suggests that, at least in this instance, even though the East India Company was the supreme power in the land, it had to act within the confines of the law to get its way and that, at times, the law which (on the face of it, at least) could not easily be tampered with was not on its side.

The Lottery Committee was fully aware that the total investment of Rs 39,000 to acquire the property of Imambaksh exceeded its real value. Even so, it recommended (on 30 September) to the Government payment of the sum, the point being made that if the present hurdle was crossed the committee did 'not anticipate any further difficulties in the speedy completion of this highly useful work'. Nine days later, the Government approved the purchase of Smith's property at Chandney Chowk and Imambaksh's ground at Baparitala and directed the company's attorney to prepare the deeds, etc., – which, in course of time, was to lead to yet another, though minor, problem between the Lottery Committee and the redoubtable Imambaksh.[24]

Imambaksh's name does not appear in the records for the next four-and-a-half months. In late February 1819, the Collector of 24-Parganas, Charles Trower, passed on to the committee a petition in which the former *thanadar* alleged that he was being asked to foot the cost of the paperwork necessary to effect the agreement between the committee and himself the agreement being that no such cost would devolve on him.[25] That this was indeed the case was testified to by Trower himself who told the committee that the 'understanding' between him and Imambaksh 'when negotiating for the ground in Beparrytollah' was that the latter was to be delivered Smith's premises 'free of all expenses'. Imambaksh had petitioned Trower that he could not execute the agreement with the company attorney, Robert Waller Poe, on 15 February because the latter had demanded Rs 400 as 'his costs'. The burden of Imambaksh's case was that Trower should settle with Poe the costs issue, and Imambaksh would in turn have 'no objection to execute the papers at any time you desire, without being charged any costs whatsoever'. Within a week the committee wrote to Poe telling him that Imambaksh was to be 'exonerated from any expense arising out of the conveyance (made) over to him of the property recently purchased from Mr Smith'. The process, however, took another three months to complete with the Government instructing the committee (on 2 June 1819) to 'cause the immediate payment' of Rs 3,000 to the sheikh so as to complete the proceedings.[26]

With Imambaksh out of the way, the principal hurdles holding up the construction of the square and the tank had been removed. But problems were piling up as far as the new street being built from Dharamtala Street to Bowbazar was concerned. On 9 December 1819 the Lottery Committee was once again writing to the Government seeking the appointment of a jury so that the ground needed for the road in question could be acquired 'in the manner prescribed in the 9th section' of the 1814 bye-law.[27]

In particular, two landowners, Yarro Kussye (Kasai) and Rajnarain Nundee (Nandi), posed a major problem, the former's land and building being situated to the west of the new tank, a 'considerable portion of it (lying) immediately on the line of the new road'. The extent of the ground involved was 13 ¼ *katha*s which, at Rs 176 a *katha*, was valued at Rs 2,318-12-0. The value of the building on the ground was estimated at Rs 1,726-14-0, the total coming to Rs 4,045-10-0. Since Kasai thought the price was a bit too low for him and did not agree to part with his property for this amount, with a view 'to (saving) time and (avoiding) the expense of summoning a jury' the committee had offered a higher price, 'one very considerably above the real value of the premises'. But the revised offer was turned down. Rajnarain Nandi's ground measured 12 *katha*s and, at Rs 200 a *katha*, was valued at Rs 2,400, the 'compensation for removing huts' being Rs 82, the total coming to Rs 2,482. The committee said that here, too, the price offered was 'more than the real value' of the premises but Nandi wanted 'the very exorbitant price' of Rs 500 a *katha* which would have fetched him Rs 6,000 for the land in question. In June that year (1819) Imambaksh had wangled as much as Rs 39,000 from the Government for his property required for the project. It is possible that the example of Imambaksh was foremost in the minds of both Kasai and Nandi.

But if they were thinking of repeating the Imambaksh case, they were making a mistake. In Imambaksh's case a jury could not be formed because the 1814 bye-law was not applicable to the construction of squares and tanks. But the road issue was different in that the 1814 law was fully applicable. Within a week of the committee's request, orders were issued to set up a jury.[28] Nandi had put up a brave front when he had set the price for his property, but immediately after the move to set up the jury became known he realised he could not have his way and was sensible enough to climb down from the Imambaksh-horse. On 3 January 1820, Henry Shakespear wrote that Nandi had agreed to the committee's valuation of his property (Rs 2,482) which meant that the jury would now only have to deal with Kasai, who too fell into line three months later.[29]

More than two months later, the jury route was chosen once again to settle problems which had emerged to the north of the square. In March the committee informed the Government that it could not get on with building a road to the north of the tank because of the unhelpful attitude on the part of some landowners.[30] The services of a jury were sought (the request being granted on 1 April 1820), the magistrates being asked to purchase 'the several spots' under the 1814 law.[31] Five 'errant' land-owners were named among whom Rajnarain Nandi figured once again. Nandi was agreeable to parting with his ground provided the others parted with theirs, but the latter's objections rendered Nandi's conditional acquiescence 'nugatory'. Among the other landowners in the area who were involved were Ramcunder Dutt (Ramchandra Dutt), Kistnomohun Ghose (Krishnamohun Ghose), Treelochun Mittur (Trilochan Mitra) and Brindabun Doss (Brindaban Das), Dutt being the only one who 'positively refuse(d) to sell on any terms' whatever. The others imposed conditions on parting with their property: while Ghose wanted in compensation a 'similar quantity (of ground) contiguous to his property', Mitra and Das preferred that the Government buy up 'their whole estates, including large *puckah* houses' located to the north of the ground wanted specifically by the Lottery Committee. Ghose's demand was described as being 'impossible' to meet while acceding to the wishes of the other two would lead to costs going up steeply quite apart from the fact that the additional property was not needed for the project.

Much more important than the problems affecting the development of the area immediately to the north of the square were those associated with the construction of the road from Dharamtala Street to Bowbazar to the west of it. Inevitably, the primary bone of contention was acquisition of ground, the Lottery Committee bringing some of the instances to the notice of the Government on 8 April 1820.[32] The attitude of Tillukram Puckrasee (Tilakram Pakrasi) and Collypersaud Nundee (Kaliprasad Nandi) was especially problematic their property straddling the ground which was required for the new road. As the committee saw it, the most efficient path which the road could have traversed from the new square to Bowbazar would have been along a straight line between the two points. But this path was obstructed by a Shib temple on Pakrasi's property which, the latter felt, would be 'impossible' to remove. In fact, the committee itself wrote that moving the temple 'might give dissatisfaction to the Hindoo inhabitants of the neighbourhood', in the process providing yet another example of the Lottery Committee's awareness of matters affecting native sentiment while executing major development projects. But even if the temple problem was solved, the planned path of the road would still have entailed the purchase of 'the large brick house' belonging to Pakrasi, which would have increased substantially the cost of the project. In view of this, a westwardly deviation was suggested in the road's direction which would have avoided Pakrasi's property.

While Pakrasi was not prepared to dispose of that part of his house where the temple was located, he had no objection to giving up that part of his property through which the road's revised alignment lay. This, too, was the stand of the other natives whose property was similarly affected – except for Kaliprasad Nandi whose house, 'as well as the verandah of it', lay in the road's path. Since Nandi was unwilling to relinquish the part of his house required for the project, the committee proposed that it purchase 'only the verandah' and realign the road accordingly. If Nandi's verandah was to be left untouched, the projected road would have to be narrowed down to a width of 50 ft at the spot in place of the 60 ft it would be throughout. Not only did Nandi reject the proposal, he also refused to dispose of the whole of his house, which the committee offered to purchase from him. If Nandi's house and verandah were to be left untouched, the road would have to take an eastward course, which would not be possible because there was 'another Seeb Thakoor on the opposite side of the street'.

Clearly, this was a case where the Lottery Committee was willing to alter the alignment of a major road in order to suit the convenience of natives. In its 8 April letter, the committee had told the Government that it had taken pains to show that 'conciliatory measures' had not been neglected in getting on with the project 'in which the health and convenience of the public is so much (involved)'. However, not being able to make any headway, it recommended that a jury be summoned 'to determine either the value of Kaliprasad's house and premises, or of his verandah only, leaving him the option of disposing of whichever he thinks proper'. The Government agreed with the suggestion but not before regretting the Lottery Committee's inability to get Pakrasi to change his mind so that the road could follow a straight path from the new square to Bowbazar.

The Lottery Committee took the comment to heart for subsequent events make it clear that, despite the setting up of a jury being allowed to evaluate Kaliprasad Nandi's property, fresh efforts were made to get Tilakram Pakrasi to part with his house. One probable reason for the renewed effort may have been the fact that Pakrasi had died in the meantime and the committee felt that his heir, Anundchunder Mookerjee, would agree to demolish a part of his house, which was the committee's initial demand. But this was not to be the case. Immediately after the Government approved of the setting up of a jury (on 14 April), Mookerjee petitioned the committee that if the road were to be carried through the house, it would be 'ruinous [to the petitioners who were] destitute of every means to enable them to build another house for their residence'. In view of this, Mookerjee sought a 'reconsideration' of the alignment of the new road and asked the committee, 'in conformity to a former resolution, to order the said road to be carried over your petitioners' ground preserving the building house', and that they were prepared to receive the compensation for the ground 'as fixed by the said resolution'.[33] The committee chose not to respond and set aside the petition for 'future consideration'.

In the weeks immediately following, an attempt was made to get Mookerjee to soften his stand the effort being not entirely unsuccessful. On 13 June 1820 the 'Moira Square subcommittee'[34] (comprising Trower, Shakespear and Barwell) reported that in spite of its effort 'to persuade Anundchunder…to sell the whole of his house in order to carry the road out straight from Moira Square to the Bow Bazar Road' (an alignment which the Government had preferred) he had refused to do so. Tilakram Pakrasi had objected to the removal of the temple from its existing location. Mookerjee now said that his premises 'being divided by the road, he could find room neither on one side of it nor the other for the erection of a new house, and that unless he could reside in it his patrimony would [not] be received'.[35] The Surveyor to the Lottery Committee, who was asked to take a close look at the property, reported that 'a tolerably good house might be built in the southwest corner of the ground'. Mookerjee ruled this out on the ground that such a house 'would be cut off from the remaining part of the old one, and from the use of the tank, to the destruction of his privacy and comfort'. There was, however, one bit of good news, namely, that an 'arrangement' had been arrived at under which Mookerjee would sacrifice 'a slice of his house' from which, as the subcommittee put it, he 'will suffer no small inconvenience', but one which would enable the new road to be made 'with a turn much less sudden than in the former plan'. The 'turn' could be reduced further if Nandi's verandah was acquired for which the appointment of a jury had already been ordered.

More than two years into the construction of the Baparitala square and tank project, and the new road to Bowbazar, Trower, Shakespear and Barwell provided an overview of the work drawn up in response to a request made by the Lottery Committee in the middle of May 1820.[36] The main thrust of the report (submitted on 1 July 1820) was that around Rs 20,000 would be needed to complete the entire project, light being also thrown on the various heads of expenditure already made, the areas where fresh funds would be required (see below), and why in certain cases the estimates made originally for the project had been exceeded. Among the payments made in excess of the estimate (Rs 45,972-6-10 ½), the subcommittee mentioned the purchase of 'houses and premises' on the land needed for the square.[37] According to the subcommittee, the gap between estimate and actual expenditure was the result of the original estimate not taking into account 'any actual engagements entered into with the parties'. While in some instances the property was found to have been undervalued, in others larger sums had to be paid 'to induce the proprietors to dispose of their premises'.

The subcommittee also slipped up on the projected cost of excavating the tank by having to pay an extra Rs 10,921-4-15 under the head.[38] Given the experience which members of the subcommittee already had in excavating tanks in the city, it is not a little surprising that the Baparitala tank estimate had been based only on the basis of the quantity of earth to be moved, 'no allowance (being) made for removing it, a work involving great labour and expense'. Incidentally, the excavated earth was used to fill up 'several noxious tanks and swamps' in the opening up of the new road to Bowbazar, which involved the employment of coolies to move the earth over 'a considerable distance' which added to the cost. Further, the piling up of excavated earth was bound to create problems for the subcommittee unless tackled expeditiously. In fact, a few months earlier, Shakespear had warned the committee that unless 'immediate measures for opening a communication with the eastern side of the Dingah Bangah' were taken, 'the worst consequences are to be expected from any heavy fall of rain, which will inevitably wash a part of the earth again into the tank and destroy the banks of it'.[39]

This apart, several large springs were found in the bed of the tank which 'greatly impeded' the work of excavation because water had to be emptied from the tank continually.[40] This added to the labour cost because a far larger number of native labourers than planned had to be engaged to take out the water from the tank as it was being constructed. The *Calcutta Journal* (2 February 1820) wrote:

> We learn by a Correspondent that they are beginning to make some progress in the Oval Tank in the Dhurrumtullah. About 800 *Coolies* are now employed on it, who appear to have got down to the second course, or about 13 feet deep. The soil is excellent, rich garden mould. The spot is intersected by wells, some of which are supposed to contain springs; if so the Tank will always have a good supply of water.

In fact, as Shakespear wrote to the committee later (5 September),[41] the water 'gained so fast upon the workmen from the numerous springs found at the depth of 16 or 20 feet that it was thought impracticable to complete the tank without pumps'.

Pumps had to be ordered from Calman and Company, but before they could be put to use the labourers were able 'to dig the tank to a sufficient depth by having the water baled out night and day in the mode usually adopted by the natives without the aid of pumps'. Shakespear's objective in writing to the committee was that the cast-iron pump, which cost Rs 660 to make, was now available for work elsewhere and that it could be put to use 'in the several tanks which it is proposed to dig on the grounds about to be purchased from Mr Camac in the Dhee Birjee'.[42]

Yet another reason behind the excess investment for the Baparitala tank, square and road project (to the extent of Rs 17,381-0-10) was that the width of the road to Bowbazar had been doubled to 60 ft. Consequently, there was no mention in the original estimate of the value of the larger number of buildings which would have to be acquired to build a wider road, the subcommittee being 'compelled to purchase several at a heavy expense'. This, in fact, brings us to five specific paragraphs (8 to 12) of the subcommittee's 20 July letter which highlighted the point that the original plan for the square and the road to Bowbazar – as propounded in the Lottery Committee's letter of 25 September 1817 – had not been 'strictly adhered to'. The subcommittee wrote that it was 'induced, in communication with the committee, in a very early stage of our proceedings, to attend more to the *spirit* than the *letter* of the instructions [emphasis added] by which we were authorised to carry these several improvements into execution'. This must have been a point of concern with the subcommittee since implementation of deviations from the original plan nearly always entailed additional expenditure which would have to be justified to, and approved, by the Government. It is more than likely that the subcommittee embarked on this path only after consulting the committee ('in communication with the committee'), but such consultations must have been for the most part verbal because there is no evidence of such interaction in the records. On its part, the Government not only accepted the 'modifications...in the original plan' but also described them as being 'judicious'.[43]

A critically important aspect of the financial scheme for the project, replicated in other projects on a wide scale by the Lottery Committee over the years, was to buy up ground and buildings around the square with the intention of selling them later (after developing them) at a profit, which would have the effect of reducing the net investment.[44] This part of the scheme ran into trouble because of two reasons: first, the owners of the ground and buildings sought to be purchased were just not willing to part with their property; secondly, the 1814 bye-law on which the Government banked so much to compel the sale of property only provided for 'compelling the purchase of property when required for the opening of roads and drains' and not for building squares and digging tanks. This systemic weakness of not being able to have its way was acknowledged by the Government in an August 1820 letter where it noted that the procedure adopted had led to an increase in costs ('materially augmented') and a diminishing of 'the value of the improvements themselves in some degree'.[45]

There was also a change in the original plan of buying up ground and buildings around the square with the intention of reselling them at a higher price later. The area involved was 240,000 sq. ft, the square itself being spread over 250,000 sq. ft (500 ft by 500 ft). The subcommittee reported that, except on the northern side of the square, 'little of this ground' had been bought with the result that 'the favourable results anticipated by that arrangement have failed'. It was noted that should 'a very large portion' of the ground (around four *bighas*) bought on the northern side of the square be sold (at Rs 400 a *katha*), a saving of around Rs 32,000 could be made. The subcommittee added that, if the committee approved of the sale, a stipulation could be made with every sale contract that 'handsome buildings [be] constructed on the northern border of the square by which the appearance of it would be rather improved than injured' (see below).

In its 1 July 1820 overview of the work done on the Baparitala project, the subcommittee had said that at the time of writing it had an 'actual' positive balance of Rs 2,309-14-9 ½, which was no mean achievement in view of the fact that work on the project had been continuing since 1817 and the original estimate for the entire project entailed an expenditure as much as Rs 2,37,452-6-10 (including the extra amount to be paid to Imambaksh).[46] The subcommittee, however, pointed out that there were five specific heads under which work was yet to be done for which a further Rs 22,232-14-4 would be required. These were: levelling and forming the square; making the drains around the square; levelling and paving the road from the square to Bowbazar; making drains on both sides of this road; and constructing an iron railing around the square for which Calman and Company had been roped in (the railing arrived in October 1821).

Adjusting the balance in hand (Rs 2,309-14-9 ½), the subcommittee asked the Lottery Committee for a further Rs 20,000 'to enable us to complete the above works'. The committee wrote to the Government in late July 1820 backing the request for additional funds and putting in an extra word for selling off the ground to the north of the square. It said that the construction of ornamental houses on the northern side would lead to the appearance of the square being 'greatly improved'. As regards the argument that 'reducing the size of the square' would be 'more than counterbalanced' by the saving which would result if the ornamentation was not effected, the committee asked the Government for permission to dispose of the ground 'provided that an adequate price can be obtained for it, the purchaser at the same time engaging to erect upon it handsome and substantial buildings on a plan approved by the committee'.[47]

While the Rs 20,000 sought was sanctioned a month later, the plea to construct ornamental buildings was rejected on the ground that the improvements 'actually effected…were directed rather to the removal of former nuisances and causes of unhealthiness and to the comfort and convenience of the community than to the purposes of embellishment'. The further point made was that 'any appropriation of the open space now obtained to the construction of buildings would proportionately diminish the free ventilation of a crowded part of the city'. It is intriguing why the Government took this stand because, first, implementation of this part of the plan would have brought in funds which would have reduced the burden on the lottery funds, the benefit of which the Government was fully aware. Secondly, the argument for 'embellishment' was not rejected when the Tank-Excavation Committee had made it initially on 25 September 1817.[48]

The Governor-General had other ideas regarding the beautification of the new square which he expanded upon in a minute.[49] He proposed that the square be named after the Duke of Wellington (the same Arthur Wellesley, the younger brother of Lord Wellesley, who was in Calcutta twenty years earlier) and that his statue be erected under a canopy to be brought from the ruins at Agra.

Lord Hastings added that he wanted Captain Joseph Taylor of the Bengal Engineers to supervise the work because 'his experience in the repair of the Taj [would] have taught him how those costly ornaments to which I allude may be taken down with least hazard of their receiving injury.' At the time, Taylor was engaged in constructing the lighthouse at Sagar, a work from which he was relieved and asked to proceed to Agra. He would be paid a monthly 'civil allowance' of Rs 400 and was asked to submit a note on the establishment he would require to execute the work. It is from this time that the new square, which till then carried the name Moira Square after the Earl of Moira, the Governor-General, came to be called Wellington Square formally.[50]

After completion of the square, the subcommittee turned its attention to the subject of access to it from other parts of the city. In the first half of October 1820 it wrote to the Lottery Committee focussing on the need for better access to the square from the west.[51] The existing access from that side, 'towards Cossetullah Street' (Bentinck Street), was 'narrow and inconvenient', the specific suggestion being that Imambagh Lane be widened to an average width of 30 ft for a length of 800 ft 'where it connects with a good-sized road leading into Dhurrumtollah Street', at a cost of around Rs 3,950-10-0 which would go up a bit after 'paving the new parts and making proper drains'. Ten landowners were named from whom 'buildings' and ground had to be bought for the widening of Imambagh Lane. They were: Mirja Meajaun, Moulowe Abna Alee, Massoom Mullick, Assaree Bewa, Carim Bux, Mrs Moffat, Sabany Butcher, Sarajudeen Mullick, Sheke Ayaroo Cussye and Emambux. (As we have seen, the last two were important players at the time the ground for the Baparitala project was being cleared.)

The Lottery Committee approved of the project on 26 October, agreeing to the subcommittee's suggestion that since work on Imambagh Lane was 'closely connected with the improvement of the square' the cost be defrayed 'from the funds arising from the sale of the surplus ground on the east and west side of the square'.[52] As late as on 8 March 1821, when the money had already been spent, the committee sought *ex post facto* the Government's permission to defray the expense on widening Imambagh Lane, the approval coming through a month later.[53] Schalch's map of 1824 shows the road after completion, its location being to the north of the Dharamtala Academy and Lyon's stables (see Fig. 9).

BIRTH OF THREE MORE SQUARES

The Baparitala project had created ripples of development in the immediate neighbourhood. The benefits flowing to the inhabitants of the area were numerous, the Lottery Committee detailing them in a letter initially drafted by Bayley (a member of the committee and Chief Secretary to the Government) and subsequently (in March 1821) approved by the committee for submission to the Government.[1] The first benefit was the 'facility of communication now afforded between the Dhurrumtollah Street and the Bow Bazar by a broad street running north and south, and between the Circular Road and the square by the construction of the Dinga Banga Street'.[2] The second benefit resulted from the filling up of a very deep and broad ditch known as Dingabhanga *khal* and of several offensive pools and small tanks, and from raising and levelling the ground generally.[3] A further improvement was the removal of numerous privies and public nuisances which existed on the ground occupied by the tank, square and new streets not to speak of the abundant supply of 'pure and wholesome water' now afforded by the new tank.[4] A fifth benefit of the project would be the better draining and 'more effectual ventilation of all that portion of the town in the vicinity of the tank and square and by the new roads', the sixth being the 'consequent salubrity and improved appearance of that part of the town which lies between the Dhurrumtollah and the Bow Bazar'.

The Lottery Committee cited these benefits to shift its development focus further north. The committee wrote that

> …the want of a broad street of communication from north to south throughout that extensive portion of the city was sufficiently obvious. There were numerous and offensive pools scattered throughout that space, but few tanks of large size containing pure and wholesome water for the use of the inhabitants. The population was crowded together in huts exposed to the loss of their lives and property from frequent conflagrations.

The absence of wide roads and the difficulty in getting adequate water supplies prevented the existing fire-fighting arrangements from being effective. The committee added that, apart from 'promoting the salubrity of the town and the personal safety and comforts of the people', the improvements it had in mind would also 'facilitate the watching of the town and the prevention of robberies'. The committee was confident of attaining these ends because the 'experiment' carried out in the part of the town 'between the Dhurrumtollah and the Bow Bazar' had 'fully realised' the 'official objects'.

COLLEGE SQUARE AND STREET

The new road which the Lottery Committee now proposed is the College Street of today. The 60-ft-wide road would be 4,420 feet long and would be a continuation (from Bowbazar) of the new road just built from Dharamtala northwards (Wellington Street, now Nirmal Chunder Street), its alignment being 'a straight line nearly due north' to 'Simleea Street situated to the northward of the Muchwa (Machua) Bazar Road'.

In theory, a major road like the one proposed would not be complete if it did not have at least one spacious square on it.

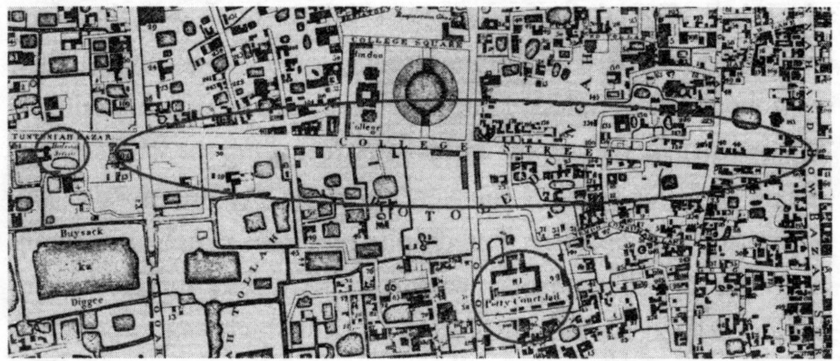

Fig. 11. Schalch's map of 1824 showing College Street, the Petty Court Jail and Balaram Sarkar's house

The committee, in fact, said that the new square and tank were not new propositions but had been mooted as early as in 1815. A 'convenient spot' measuring 27 *bigha*s had been selected 1,250 yards to the north of the new Baparitala square and tank the price of the land, which was owned by Collysunker Ghosaul (Kalishankar Ghoshal), being considered 'moderate'. The cost of digging the tank and building the square with a railing, etc., was pitched at Rs 40,000. However, the ground for the square did not come in one consolidated lot, the Surveyor to the Lottery Committee, Arthur Blechynden, informing Henry Shakespear in the second week of June 1821 that it was spread over 'three spots…belonging to Collysunker Ghosaul situate at Puttuldungah (Pataldanga) and Mirzapore'.[5] What this meant was that, instead of negotiating with one person, the Lottery Committee would have to talk to a number of land and house owners to complete the process of land acquisition. The company attorney, R.W. Poe, was asked to prepare the documents required for the transfer of ownership of the land marked out by Ghoshal at the price of Rs 150 a *katha*, which came to around Rs 80,000.

The committee applied to the College Square and road project the experience it had gathered in course of buying up land for the Baparitala project, the objective being to cut down on delay which had affected the former project adversely.[6] It was, therefore, anxious to purchase additional ground for the road project than what would be 'absolutely required' to an extent which would be 'equal to an average surplus width of 90 feet along the whole extent of one or other sides of the new street for eventual resale'. The committee felt confident that, despite problems which would crop up in the normal course, it would be able to buy sufficient extra ground needed for the purpose at a price which would permit 'a very advantageous resale' after completion of the new street. The estimate was that the sale of surplus land would ultimately bring in as much as Rs 1,10,400. Compared to the estimated Rs 150 a *katha* purchase price of the land, the selling price for the surplus land after development was put at Rs 200 a *katha*. The same arrangement of buying and reselling surplus land would have to be gone through 'as far as practicable' with regard to the projected tank and square.

The committee, however, cautioned that the purchase 'of nearly all the ground and premises required' would have to be effected *before* actual construction began of the new street and square. This was because the value of ground would go up 'in proportion to the facility of access to it, and the actual construction of a broad street along the first portion of the proposed line would greatly augment the expense to be incurred in subsequently procuring the requisite ground for the remainder'. The committee felt that priority had to be accorded to the purchase of ground related to the square and tank because the earth excavated from the site would be needed for filling 'the pools and small tanks' and for raising the ground on which the new road was to be built.

The net balance of funds with the Lottery Committee at the time was about Rs 2,26,000.[7] Since nearly all the ground and buildings required for the project had to be bought before work began (the new road and square were expected to be completed in 18 months), the committee calculated that the total volume of funds which it had to have at its disposal for 'satisfactory or economic execution' of the project was 'at least' Rs 3,50,000. In other words, before the sale of surplus ground could be effected there would be a shortfall of around Rs 1,24,000 for the new project, a gap which would have to be filled. The Lottery Committee homed in on the surplus funds lying with the Court of Requests no doubt emboldened by the 16 April 1819 order which had enabled utilisation of the surplus for 1818-19 and 1819-1820 for city improvement work. Pointing out that the Court of Requests had already piled up a neat surplus of Rs 5,57,603-8-5 from 1 May 1802-03 till 1817-18, generated by its 'commissions and fees', the committee felt that, taking into account some recent improvements effected by the Court of Requests in the jail attached to it (incidentally, the line of the new road was just about 130 yards to the east of the wall of the jail [see Fig. 11 for the location of the Petty Court Jail]), there would still be about Rs 5 lakhs left in the kitty. It was proposed that the committee be allowed to use Rs 1,30,000 from the court fund for the road project.

The Lottery Committee had sent the project to the Government on 8 March 1821. The sanction came through a month later the Governor-General in Council noting that it would have preferred a more 'specific' break-up of the estimate despite the fact that it was aware of 'the difficulties which must attend the formation of more detailed accounts of the expenditure to be incurred in extensive improvements of this nature'.[8]

The committee was empowered to resell 'any portion of the ground purchased…which may remain unappropriated after completing the street and square' and to pay to the treasury such proceeds 'after the whole of the expense connected with the improvements shall have been defrayed'. The Government commended the committee for selecting 'with care and judgement' the line of the new street and the tank and square 'in the vicinity of Puttul Danga (Pataldanga)', and empowered it to alter the plans 'if in the progress of your arrangements any partial change in the erection of the street or in the scite assigned for the tank and square should be deemed expedient'. Looking ahead, the Governor-General in Council wanted the road to be constructed as straight as possible, *not losing sight 'of the eventual extension of the street at a future period as far as the northern extremity of the city, according to the plan suggested in the year 1815'* (emphasis added). The project having been cleared by the Government a 'subcommittee for central improvements' comprising Bayley, Shakespear, Ballard and Colvin was formed to implement it, 'including the improvement in the neighbourhood of the jail of the Court of Requests'.[9]

As word got around about the new project objections began to pour in from those who feared that their property would be affected. The Lottery Committee had first written to the Government about the College Street project on 8 March 1821. Just two days later – that is, weeks before the project was sanctioned by the Government – Chandra Sekhar Mitra and Bholanath Mitter, two native inhabitants of the area through which the road was to pass, sent a petition stating that the demolition of their house and tank was unacceptable because, as they argued, if they shifted from their house which was ancestral property, they would lose their caste in the Hindu social hierarchy. The petitioners wrote[10] that 'the house together with its tank has been hereditary property of your petitioners' family in which they have resided for successive generations from time immemorial past' and that 'according to the established custom of the Hindoo religion, which strictly injoins that a person's hereditary property, which they call *bhadrason* or the happy seat, should be guarded against every invasion, they cannot, in consequence, dispose any part of their [abode] without a dereliction of principle'. The point was also made that they also had to provide for 'the numerous relations…which, under the above injunction, must all reside under the same roof' and that since the extended family was growing they required 'an increase of room for their convenience and accommodation'. This apart, the water in the tank was 'highly useful to the inhabitants of the neighbourhood as a wholesome beverage and also as the readiest means of extinguishing dreadful conflagrations which [have] occurred in more than one instance' thus making it 'a permanent blessing to all within its vicinity' (see below).

A number of families in the Simleah area had been relocated from Gobindapur when the new fort had begun to be built half a century earlier, the Mitras being one of them.[11] They wrote:

> The house in which your petitioners reside was originally conceded by Government as an exchange for [their] seat [at] 'Govindpore' where the present Fort William is erected – by which arrangement this city is now become so impregnable that it bids defiance to the most formidable foe. Under such peculiar circumstances your petitioners felt themselves perfectly secure forever in the full and peaceable enjoyment of their property, and now, at this lapse of time, to suffer or experience any molestation, your petitioners cannot but think [it] extremely unexpected and equally oppressive.

The Mitras proposed an alternative when they referred to 'the road which runs adjoining to the west side of your petitioners' house, where other tenements and waste land are available', which could be 'easily obtained as the owner of such property will cheerfully embrace the opportunity of parting with them for certain advantages'.

Following due procedure, the committee sent the petition to the subcommittee and, after a further exchange of correspondence, it was decided (in May 1822) that a jury would have to be called 'to assess the property' and that its decision 'should be deemed conclusive'.[12] In July the petitioners approached the Governor-General stating that, 'to prevent any unnecessary obstacle to the progress of the road,' they had 'taken the precaution to represent the circumstances to the Lottery Committee before they began to cut the road from Bow Bazar, and long previously to their purchasing any ground for the purpose...'[13] They said they had even pointed out to the committee an alternative route which the road could take 'so as to render all encroachments unnecessary' on their own premises, which would involve '(buying) one of the old unfinished outoffices attached to the house of one Bulloram (Balaram) Sircar' (see Fig. 11 for the location of Sircar's house in Thantania Bazar). It was also pointed out that, in similar circumstances, the Government had accepted the pleas of other native petitioners, the example of Tilakram Pakrasi being cited specifically.[14]

As with their initial petition to the Lottery Committee, in their appeal to the Governor-General in Council Chandra Sekhar Mitra and Bholanath Mitter focussed on the religious aspect of the issue. They wrote:

> Your lordship's petitioners are Hindoos, and the religion they profess most solemnly prohibits tanks from being sacrificed to any end whatever as they are religiously dedicated and made sacred, and as the sin of such action is so great as to be considered equivalent to the heinous sin of selling a man's own child and wife.

Hindu scriptures were quoted to support the point. A practical reason for not doing away with the tank was that its water had been 'an excellent beverage to the inhabitants in that neighbourhood', at least '2,000 men, women and children' using it daily 'as also your lordship's petitioners and their families who are numerous and who have from childhood been used to it, and a change might probably be attended with material injury to their health if they are unfortunately deprived of their tank of salvation'. The petitioners concluded their appeal by saying that they were 'exempt' from the application of the Jury Act because 'there is nothing mentioned in [the 1814 rules and ordinance] of religious places and tanks that are religiously dedicated'.

In early August the Government sent the petition to the Lottery Committee requesting it to provide 'a report upon the circumstances set forth in the petition and to offer such suggestions as they may deem proper'. The committee stood firm, writing back on 12 August that it was 'completely satisfied' with the stand taken by the subcommittee, namely, that the Mitras 'do not furnish any reasonable objection to the prosecution of the Central Road in the line originally projected by the committee and from which no deviation could be made without incurring a very heavy additional expense'. Consequently, the proposal for a jury was fully backed by the committee.[15]

The subcommittee had written to the committee two days earlier (10 August) justifying its stand, namely, that 'it was not for any slight difficulty that they (the Mitras) were exposed to the inconvenience of which they complain'. The point was made that there was no means of avoiding the line of the road it had decided on 'but by destroying the...road altogether and by incurring a very heavy additional expence'. Of interest is the subcommittee's revelation that the line of road was 'originally fixed by the situation of a *musjeed* near the Bow Bazar and a Hindoo place of worship of considerable resort near the petitioners' house,[16] to escape interfering with which we were forced upon their tank'. Chandra Sekhar Mitra and Bholanath Mitter were then charged with 'wrongfully accusing us of turning the road (which is a straight line) for their annoyance' and also of 'improperly [making] use of false plans to mislead the European friends who have interested themselves in their behalf'. As regards the religious point made by the petitioners, the subcommittee dismissed it with the observation that this 'is not a case on which any well-founded religious scruple can exist'. The subcommittee's comment on the Tilakram Pakrasi case stands out because it indicated a contriteness on the part of the authorities which was not a common occurrence in the records of the time. The point was made that the case, 'though greatly stronger than their (the Mitras') own, in as much as it involved the destruction of an idol house, is one which many of the committee have always regretted having submitted to, and for which they have often been found fault with, both by natives and Europeans'.

On 22 August 1822 the Government wrote back to the Lottery Committee agreeing with the stand taken by it and rejecting the plea of the Mitras. Substantively, it was argued that 'a sufficiency of space for the road does not exist between the large house occupied by Bulram Sirkar and the tank, which is the subject of the present representation'. An encroachment on one or the other was, therefore, indispensable, the committee doing 'wisely in resolving to take the space required from the tank in preference to destroying the house'. Further, the preservation of the line of road already selected and 'avoiding the public places of Hindoo worship situated at the corner of Simlea' were two additional reasons for adopting the stand taken. The magistrates were asked to summon a jury to assess the value of the 'space of ground and tank' belonging to the Mitras which was required 'for the new road constructing to Simlea'. A month later the proceedings were completed with the jury valuing the property at Rs 4,340 (at Rs 250 a *katha*).[17] By this time, the new road had been opened 'to the Mutchua Bazar Street', that is, within a year and four months of the project being sanctioned in early April 1821.

❦

During the time the Mitra issue was being played out, the Lottery Committee considered another (undated) petition from Gokool Chunder Mistry on 21 June 1821.[18] The plea in this case was less complex its main thrust being that Mistry be given a plot of land specifically identified by him ('a piece of empty ground that belongs to the Honorable Company' to the south of the existing premises) in exchange for the ground taken from him for the new road and that the cost of building a new house on it be reimbursed to him. As with the Mitras, Mistry harped on the theme that the premises needed for the new road had been the family's abode for four generations the land being given to it by the Government itself after the earlier house located in Gobindapur had been taken over for the building of the new fort.

What is of interest is the fact that a number of those living in the area who had been affected by the new project chose the line of confrontation, which led the Lottery Committee to seek the services of a jury.[19] Among them were those living to the east of the proposed square whose property was located 'immediately in the line of the projected road' on that side of the square. The committee told the Government three months later that the 'aggrieved' inhabitants – Ramtunoo and Cossinaut Dutt, Ramjee Dutt, Joynarain and Kurzeenarain Dutt, Bykul Doss, Bhujun Doss, Poihub Doss, Ram Doss and Kepon Doss – had 'pertinaciously' refused to agree to the 'very liberal terms' offered them their stand being that they would part with their property only 'at a price more than double its value' and 'far exceeding' what the committee had paid for other land purchases in the vicinity.[20] The Government was told that the work had to be done with expedition 'on account of the approach of the cold weather' and, consequently, an early decision on the setting up of a jury to value the property in question was needed. The request was approved the very next day (28 September) but the magistrates were told that till the value of the property in question was ascertained by the jury and the property itself transferred to the Lottery Committee, 'the commencement of the important works…must be suspended'.[21] In other words, due process had to be followed even if it meant that in doing so the project could get delayed.

In mid-January 1826 the Lottery Committee reported that the iron railing around 'College Square' had been completed and that the square 'delivered over to the charge of the magistrates in the Conservancy Department'.[22] Meanwhile, some delay had occurred 'in finishing the new tunnel[23] [carryied] on by the magistrates under the authority of Government', which had prevented the sale of small parcels of ground to the south of the square, but the committee felt that this would 'in all probability be speedily effected'. A year later, in early February 1827, the committee (then comprising Shakespear, Barwell, Wood, J. Master, Colvin and Hogg) reported that the total expenditure incurred on the project was Rs 3,35,811-15-3 and that Rs 1,09,010 had been repaid into the treasury at various periods leaving 'the actual expence' to the lottery funds at Rs 2,26,801-15-0, which was 'an excess of only Rs 5,161-15-0 beyond the amount estimated in the subcommittee's report dated 31 October 1823 submitted to Government on 28 November 1823, but still within the original estimate to the amount of Rs 12,799'. Given the size of the project, this was, by any reckoning, a creditable performance.[24]

WELLESLEY STREET AND SQUARE

The third section of the arterial north-south link, Wellesley Street, was to be taken up only after 'the early expected completion of that part of the Central Road which is carried from Bow Bazar to Mookteram Baboo's Street' (College Street). In its proposal submitted to the Lottery Committee in early 1823,[25] the subcommittee, comprising Henry Shakespear and Alexander

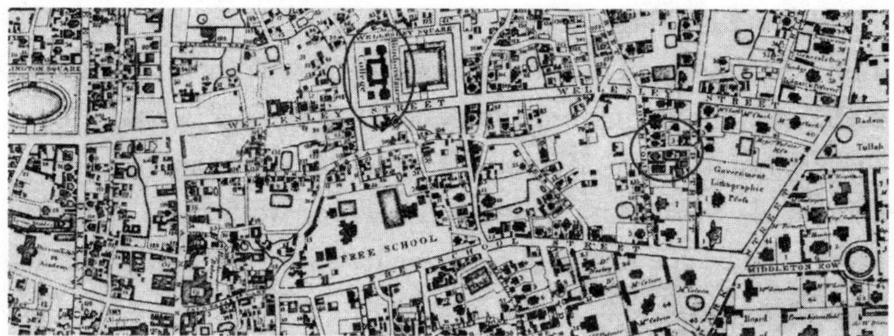

Fig. 12. Wellesley Street in Schalch's 1824 map; also the Madrassa in Wellesley Square and the road linking Royds Street and South Colinga Street

Colvin which was looking after the project, wrote that it was now considered expedient to propose the opening of 'a further portion of that line of communication through the city; and the part which it appears desirable to proceed first with is that extending from the Dhurrumtolah opposite Wellington Street to the recently effected improvement in Colingah leading to Park Street'.[26] Essentially, therefore, the project was to fill the gap between the southern end of Wellington Street and the northern end of 'that portion of the same line of road which has been recently constructed from Park Street to Colingah'. Shakespear and Colvin wrote that, when completed, 'the [new] communication which we should propose to name Wellesley Street will be opened nearly *in a direct line from Wellington Street to Park Street*' (emphasis added).

The subcommittee wanted to build a square with a tank on the proposed road, its justification being that, 'In no part of the city is a good tank and an extensive square more required than on the line of the road now proposed to be opened.' The inhabitants of Colinga had, in fact, petitioned the Lottery Committee on the subject, Shakespear and Colvin expressing the hope that the Government would approve of the project if only 'for the sake of the health and comfort' of the people of the locality. The proposed tank would be 300-ft square with an open space of 60 ft and 40 ft roads 'on each side of it'. The estimated cost of buying the ground and buildings 'required merely for the road' would be Rs 1,00,000, the cost of making the road, 65 ft wide and 3,300 ft long, Rs 12,000, the drains and bridges Rs 8,000, Rs 1,00,000 for the six-*bigha* tank, Rs 15,000 for the associated roads and ghats, and another Rs 15,000 for digging and levelling work. To be added to this would be the purchase price (at Rs 250 a *katha*) of a surplus 20 *bigha*s of land to be resold later, which would cost Rs 1,00,000. The Lottery Committee would, therefore, require a total credit of Rs 3,50,000. The subsequent resale of the surplus ground (at an expected Rs 375 a *katha*) would fetch Rs 1,50,000 leaving the net expenditure at Rs 2,00,000.

The scale of the financial requirement was considered to be comfortable enough to be met 'from the resources at the disposal of the Lottery Committee', resale of surplus ground in the neighbourhood of King's Bench Walk on the riverside (to the west of the Supreme Court)[27] and in College Street providing around Rs 1,70,000. While this amount would be 'immediately realised', the disbursements on the new project would have to be made gradually, the subcommittee adding the comforting thought that 'as we can do little more before the end of the ensuing rains than conclude the necessary bargains for the purchase of the ground required, the proceeds of the 29th and 30th Lotteries will be available before the work can be completed'.[28] Work began following the transfer of Rs 3,50,000 from the treasury but progress was not as smooth as expected. On 1 December 1824, Shakespear and Colvin wrote to the Lottery Committee that during the rainy season of 1823 steps had been taken to acquire the ground required for the project, but they were unable to obtain the 'whole quantity which we had reckoned upon for resale'. As the subcommittee put it, the delay had 'materially affected our calculations'.[29]

During the 1823-24 working season, the ground had been cleared and the tank excavated with the road being opened northward from South Colinga Street to Jaun Bazar Road (S.N.

Banerjee Road). Providing a picture of what the lay of the land was like in the area further north in the early years of the 19th century, the subcommittee wrote:

> The difficulties of obtaining the premises of [the late] Colonel Wray,[30] in the hands of the Master in Equity, and of those belonging to Mr Chew[31] who demanded an exorbitant price for them prevented us from completing the remainder of the street between the Jaun Bazar and Dhurmtullah Roads, and at our recommendation the magistrates were directed to obtain possession of those premises by the assessment of a jury.[32]

The jury award upset the subcommittee's estimates. The jury considering the land price at Rs 800 a *katha* compared to the subcommittee's Rs 500 a *katha,* Chew was awarded Rs 24,000 the estimate being Rs 16,820. Further, the jury valued the buildings at their present cost, the subcommittee taking their actual cost of construction, which was much lower. The premises of Colonel Wray, for which the subcommittee had provisionally set aside Rs 10,000 (based on its expectation of the award), was yet to be obtained, the independent estimate for the property being Rs 7,182. A result of this was that while the estimated expenditure on the ground and buildings required just for the road had been put at Rs 1,00,000, the actual expenditure under the head had shot up to Rs 1,30,156-13-2. Included in this sum was the cost of buying ground and constructing a road 'from the southwest corner of the square to Colingah Street' which, as the subcommittee explained, 'though not provided for in the estimate appeared to us indispensably necessary to the convenience of the neighbourhood'.

In some cases, the subcommittee itself was responsible for the actual cost exceeding the estimate. For example, it admitted that there were cases where it was found 'upon more accurate surveys' that the estimate for ground and buildings 'fell below what the proprietors were justly entitled to', and in others, 'to avoid the trouble and expence of appealing to the decision of a jury, we were induced to pay something more than [what] the premises were actually worth'.[33] Though the estimate for making the road till Dharamtala had been put at Rs 12,000, the actual expenditure till Jaun Bazar had reached Rs 11,464-9-16, the remaining part till Dharamtala costing another Rs 5,000 adding up to a total of Rs 16,464-9-16. The subcommittee explained the difference thus:

> The estimate was calculated on the measurement of the length and breadth of the road at the usual rate of 6 rupees per 100 feet, but omitted to provide for the pulling down and removing buildings, filling up a tank which intersected the road, and clearing and levelling the ground, in all of which operations, though they could not have been accurately estimated at the time, a considerable sum was expended.

The actual expenditure on 'drains and bridges' came to Rs 9,915-10-9 while the estimate had been pitched at Rs 8,000. The excess here was the result of making drains on the road 'leading from the south-west corner of the square to the Free School', which were not included in the estimate. Further, the tank covered 16 *bigha*s the cost of which had been put at Rs 1,00,000. The actual expenditure, however, including the cost of removing huts (Rs 840) came to Rs 1,17,836-11-11 the excess being the result mainly of the higher price paid for the buildings 'which could not be procured eventually by the interference of a jury, and we were consequently compelled to make the best bargains we could'. The actual expenditure on the roads, ghats and drains within the square was within the estimate of Rs 15,000. Throwing light on the existing drainage arrangement in the area, the subcommittee wrote: 'The drain on the south side of the square connects the drainage of nearly the whole of Colingah with the main drain running eastward to the Circular Road. It was necessary to construct it of large dimensions, and safety required that it should be covered in,' which entailed a 'heavy' cost. The subcommittee felt that the 'improvement which had thereby been effected in draining a low and populous part of the city has been highly beneficial, and was essentially necessary to the full accomplishment of the objects contemplated by the committee'.

The estimate for digging and levelling the tank had been put at Rs 15,000 the actual expenditure being Rs 17,785-3-0. The subcommittee's note on this aspect of the work is of some interest because it applied to all other tank projects which the Lottery Committee had engaged in in the course of its work. It wrote:

> Experience has taught us that it is not practicable to excavate tanks in the city with as much economy as similar work may be performed in other situations. If left to be dug by contract (the usual plan) the work would be protracted to the great inconvenience and annoyance of the surrounding inhabitants. It is necessary that the excavations should be completed and the tank finished in one working season, that is, between the 1st of December and the end of April, and we had frequently more than 2,000 men employed at one time in the work. The result was that the banks were secured before the commencement of the rains, and the least possible inconvenience occasioned by the throwing up and removal of the earth.

As regards surplus land, the plan was to buy 20 *bigha*s at Rs 250 a *katha* at a total cost of Rs 1,00,000 for resale later at a higher price (Rs 375 a *katha*) which would have yielded an extra Rs 50,000. The subcommittee reported that the actual cost of buying just 12 *bigha*s 14 *katha*s 8 *chittack*s (including buildings) had come to as much as

Rs 91,350-15-12. Winding up its report, the subcommittee noted that till 30 November 1824 actual expenditure had totalled Rs 3,97,519-0-16 and receipts Rs 3,82,557-13-0 leaving a gap of Rs 14,961-13-16.

At the time the College Street and Square project was being mooted, the Lottery Committee had expressly said that, generally, in the implementation of projects where purchase of land from the public was involved, the purchase had to be made at the commencement of the work (that is, before development) so that the sale of ground was not made later at 'extortionist' rates. It is against this background that the Wellesley Street subcommittee's comments on the excess of actual expenditure under this specific head should be seen, pointing to its culpability for the mismatch between estimate and actual expenditure. The subcommittee wrote that, despite its best efforts, it was 'unable to procure the quantity of ground originally calculated upon' a result of which was that 'the set-off against the expense of this undertaking has been proportionately reduced'. It wrote:

> The people are now so fully aware of the advantage arising from the opening of roads and squares near their premises that it has become a matter of great difficulty to induce them to part with more of their ground than is actually required for a public road, which they are aware can alone be taken from them by recourse to the provisions of the bye-law.

This apart, some of the surplus land had come with buildings, the subcommittee regretting that it had not included the value of the buildings in the cost estimate for such land. However, the silver lining was that the resale of surplus ground had been effected at a price between Rs 400 and Rs 500 a *katha*, which was much in excess of the expected rate of return at Rs 375 a *katha*. It was hoped that 'the remainder of the ground' (around 5 *bigha*s 14 *katha*s 6 *chittack*s) would fetch the same price, which would bring in Rs 19,750-11-10 and reduce to that extent the total cost of the project. In the event, this hope was belied. Although the square and the road had been completed and had been opened for public use, the Lottery Committee was reporting in the middle of 1826 that, after accounting for all receipts and expenditure heads, there was left a negative balance of Rs 23,539-0-1.[34] On the credit side, nearly two *bighas* of ground had remained unsold the sale proceeds of which were expected to meet the deficit. The committee apprehended that because demand for property of 'this kind' had fallen the price of the ground would have to be reduced 'in order to effect a more rapid sale'. In March 1827 the committee was writing to the Government once again that problems continued to face the Wellesley Street project regarding the sale of surplus land. At the end of December 1826 the committee had sought permission to sell the land on the best terms obtainable, which was sanctioned, but in fact only 'a small portion' of the ground had been sold.[35]

The Lottery Committee sent the subcommittee's report to the Government a week after receiving it, the latter accepting the reasons cited for the excess expenditure under several heads. It wrote that the explanation 'appeared to be perfectly satisfactory' the excess payments being the result of

> ...circumstances which they could not control such as the decisions of juries in some cases, the necessity of purchasing in others at prices fixed by the proprietors where the bylaw did not apply, and in several more [instances] from a wish to avoid that reference to a compulsory mode of adjustment which it has always been a principal object with the committee to make use of as seldom as possible.

Fig. 13. An 1851 salt print by Frederick Fiebig of the Mahomedan College (Madrassa) in Wellesley Square

The committee held that the 'chief defect in the estimate' was the 'insufficient sums allotted by the subcommittee for the purchase of buildings'. Alternatively, 'the chief cause of the excess of expenses [arose] from its having been found impossible to procure the expected quantity of ground for resale unencumbered with buildings', particularly the land which was bought 'for the use of the Mussulman College [which] had many houses on it'.[36] In fact, the ground set aside for the madrassa 'would readily have sold to individuals at [Rs 500 a *katha*]'.

The Government sanctioned the disbursement in late January 1825 stating that though the inability to stick to the original cost of Rs 2,00,000 was to be 'regretted', the 'failure and disappointment of that expectation' could not be the result of 'any want of zeal or exertion' either on the part of the Lottery Committee or those to whom the work had been entrusted.[37]

However, the committee would have to bear the cross for the 'omission to include the value of buildings on the ground required for the square...[an] error which they could have effectually guarded against'. The Government made it clear that the extra expenditure of Rs 88,344 on the project would 'proportionately... retard the progress of further improvements'.

CORNWALLIS STREET, SQUARE AND AMHERST STREET

At the end of October 1823, Shakespear and Colvin – forming the subcommittee for the Central Road improvements informed the Lottery Committee that the Central Road, 'from Bow Bazar to Mookteram Baboo's Street' (College Street), had been completed (except for the square's iron railing) and that 'nearly the whole of the surplus ground'had been resold.[38] The subcommittee took pleasure in stating that the 'valuable improvement (would) be effected for about Sicca Rs 18,000 less than the original estimate which amounted to Sicca Rs 2,39,600'. This, it was felt, was to a large extent the result of 'the command of funds' afforded by the surplus fees of the Court of Requests. As for the improvements' utility to the people, the subcommittee pointed to 'the crowded appearance of the street' which was 'the best proof of the benefit that this liberality has been the means of conferring on the public'. Regarding sale of surplus ground, it was pointed out that while the average purchase price was between Rs 168 and 225 a *katha*, that of the sale price lay between Rs 322 and Rs 665. This, the subcommittee affirmed, provided 'full and fresh confirmation of the soundness of the principle on which the committee have recently acted, in their recommendations to the Government, and holds out a satisfactory prospect for the success of their labours'. (As we have seen, the principle ran into trouble in the course of construction of the road southwards to Colinga.)

In the same letter, the continuation of the road northwards (Cornwallis Street, today's Bidhan Sarani) was proposed, linking

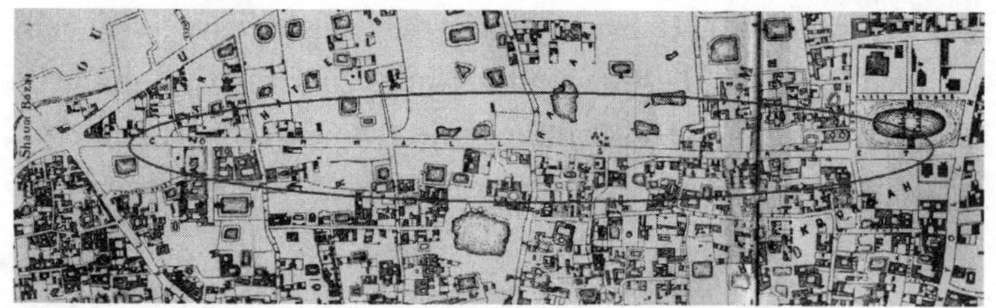

Fig. 14. W. Heysham's 1856 map showing Cornwallis Street

it with Circular Road 'near Shyambazar bridge' which would enable it to become 'the direct thoroughfare to Barrackpore and Dum Dum for a large portion of the city'. On funding of the project, the subcommittee said that 'the additional funds lately placed at the disposal of the committee' would be needed for the 'various other improvements on which they are at present engaged'. In particular, 'the extension of the Strand during the ensuing season' would be provided for by the sale of the Camac estate. What this meant was that the extension of College Street northward would depend for its financing 'on the future growth of the lottery funds' unless the Government was 'disposed to afford their aid to the undertaking'. This is precisely what the subcommittee proposed when it wrote that the

> ...experience of the benefit that has always attended the extensive purchase of land for the purposes of improvement and resale may, perhaps, induce Government to make a fresh advance to the committee for the specific purpose of purchasing ground easily procurable, and advantageously situated in those parts of the town through which it is intended to open roads.

For the proposed project, not only was the land required cheap, there was also the added advantage of an 'almost total absence of buildings'. The subcommittee made bold to declare that 'no part

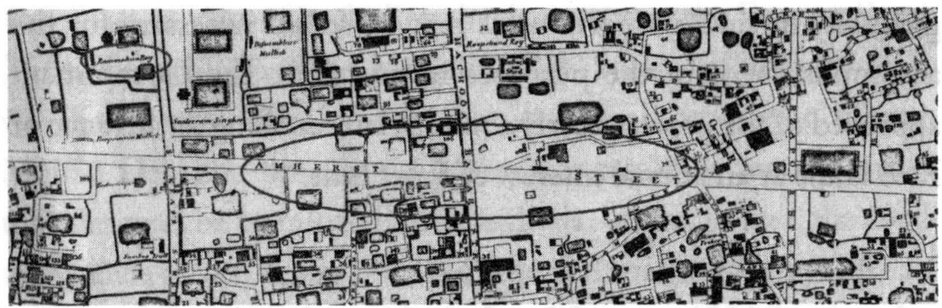

Fig. 15. Amherst Street, from Schalch's map of 1824. The map also shows Rammohun Roy's house

of the city [was] so favourable for such purchases as that of the intended line of the Central Road, including the space eastward between it and the Circular Road'.

Apart from the extension northwards of the Central Road, the subcommittee proposed that another road be built to the east of it halfway between it and the Circular Road, 'in a parallel direction with the Central Road from St James' Street in the Bow Bazar, to near the Hilsah [Halsi] Bagan on the Circular Road'. This, then, was the genesis of Amherst Street (Raja Rammohun Sarani). Work would be taken up first on the extension northward of the Central Road, and only after its completion would construction of 'the other line' be taken up. However, the land for the second road would be bought along with the purchases made for the Central Road, which would ensure that the price would be 'much lower... than we shall in all probability be able to obtain it hereafter when the intention of opening a road in that direction may become more generally known'. An estimated Rs 5,65,000 would be required to buy the ground needed for the two roads (90 *bigha*s for the Central Road and 72 *bigha*s – without tank or square – for the eastern road), and if this sum was advanced by the Government 'at a low rate of interest' the whole of it could be 'restored to the treasury' once the project was completed. Writing to the Government at the end of November 1823, the Lottery Committee backed the proposal and sought an advance of Rs 6 lakhs 'to be drawn...

basis of that, apply 'for a credit for the whole sum at once'. Since implementation would be 'gradual', the committee felt that a credit of Rs 2 lakhs would be sufficient to continue work 'during the present year' without putting a stop 'to other works of minor importance'. On 9 June the Government sanctioned an advance of Rs 2 lakhs sought by the committee but made it clear that

> …no new works involving any considerable expence are to be undertaken by the Lottery Committee until the Central Roads, tanks and squares…shall have been completed and the advance of Rs 6 lakhs sanctioned…on the 23rd December 1823 shall have been repaid into the treasury.

By the end of March 1827 the committee was writing to the Government that Cornwallis Square 'and the smaller one on the Mirzapore Road' had been completed and could be handed over to the magistrates. Cornwallis Street had been completed as well.[43] As for Amherst Street, the committee expected its commissioning 'in the course of the present season [1827]' there being a 'difficulty' involving Ruplal Mullick, the owner of the ground through which the road was to pass into Bowbazar, and also with Ramtanu Mukherjee 'at the opposite end on Mannicktollah Street', both of whom were refusing to part with their ground 'at what appears to be a fair price'. Consequently, the Government was asked to set up a jury, which was ordered in the last week of May. On the last day of March 1828 the subcommittee informed the Lottery Committee that Amherst Street was 'now open to the public' and that 'it be made over to the charge of the magistrates'.[44]

The financial arrangement governing the entire project ran into trouble when George Money,[45] who had agreed to buy up the whole of the surplus land, reneged on his commitment. Faced with Money's unwillingness, or inability, to implement the scheme, the Lottery Committee suggested to the Government that the previous commitment of Money be scrapped and be replaced with an arrangement under which he 'should retain the land purchased by him in the Central Road and be relieved from that which he engaged to purchase in Amherst Street or the Eastern Road'.[46] This would leave a balance of Rs 1,22,787 which Money would have to pay to the Government. In November 1828 the Government approved of the arrangement and Money was asked to pay the amount due from him 'in four equal instalments of 2, 4, 6 and 8 months from 1 January 1829 with an interest at the rate of 6 per cent per annum'. If Money declined to accept the amended offer, the Government wanted steps to be taken 'to enforce the fulfilment of the whole of his engagements with the subcommittee'.[47] On his part, Money had recourse to 'technical objections to the completion of his contract [by] alleging mainly that the conveyances proposed to be granted by the committee on account of the land sold to him are insufficient'. In view of this, the Lottery Committee asked the Government to 'cancel' the 7 November arrangement and explore the path of a legal resolution of the problem.

Financially, the Cornwallis Street-Amherst Street project had turned out to be problematic the main reason being the inability to sell the surplus ground at a profit. The pressure on the committee was immense the Government having made it clear (on 7 November 1828) that as much as Rs 5,99,077-6-0 had been withdrawn from the funds (Rs 6 lakhs) given as loan for the project on 23 December 1823 and that Rs 1,45,542-2-4 had been returned to the treasury at the time of writing leaving a balance of Rs 4,53,575-3-8. The committee was asked to make every effort to dispose of the surplus ground although it was acknowledged that it would be difficult to get a good price for the land in question.

The Government of Lord Bentinck (the latter had succeeded Lord Amherst as Governor-General earlier in 1828), however, had a comforting word for the Lottery Committee when it said that there was no doubt that the loan had 'considerably facilitated' the work of the committee 'and have in great measure accomplished the object for which it was granted, by enabling the committee to improve, at a comparative small expense, the most insalubrious parts of the town and to [add] materially to the comfort and convenience of the inhabitants'.

'FILTHY STATE OF THE DRAINS'

Writing to the Government in September 1814, John Eliot, Magistrate of the Suburbs of Calcutta, who had just been relieved 'from the *zillah* duty', underscored the sea change brought about in the drainage situation of the town area falling under his jurisdiction.[1] The rains that year had been the 'most incessant and heavy ever known' and yet the impact of the downpour was said to have had been minimal in some of the areas under his charge. Eliot wrote that

> ...nothing can be more beautiful than the present state of the Esplanade [*maidan*] and Course[2] where not a drop of water now lies, though before these improvements were commenced it was a perfect marsh and a serious nuisance to all Chowringhee and, in particular, around the Supreme Court Jail [then located where the Victoria Memorial Hall now stands].

He said that all the tanks had been filled with water 'which scarce occurred in any former season, to the universal benefit of the inhabitants of Chowringhee, Bhowannypore, the suburbs and in particular to the unfortunate people confined in the Supreme Court Jail, as also the sick in the hospitals, general and insane'. In any other year the streets would have been flooded by 'some feet of water', but in 1814 they were free of water 'entirely'. The magistrate further wrote that 'the complete state of the draining system is shewn by the roads undergoing less destruction than ever, being freed from that lodgement of water so very injurious to that substance of which the roads in this country are formed'. The Maratha Ditch too was 'drier than it ever was known in seasons of the greatest drought'.

Perhaps John Eliot was blowing his own trumpet louder than what was warranted by the state of the existing drainage facilities, perhaps not.[3] The fact of the matter, however, is that he did have a lot of experience in handling the drainage issues related to the city.[4] In fact, it was he who had mooted one of the early, and major, drainage projects undertaken by the Lottery Committee – the 'great Simleah drain' running west to east from Chitpur Road to Circular Road – giving it practical shape at the initial stage.

On 11 December 1817 Eliot wrote in a minute that the sketch of the drain submitted to the Lottery Committee (not to be found in the records) – which the magistrate said was 'executed by a native' – described certain spots as 'water' which, however, was 'the very reverse of that element and most desirable to be removed'. He wrote that he had employed the most expeditious method of getting rid of 'all this filth in the very centre of the native part of the town', which led him to do the job 'without submitting a full statement of the expense to be incurred'. Clearly, this was a transgression of official procedure (but was it, in the early days?) which, perhaps, only Eliot could get away with. The justification which Eliot cited for the 'impropriety' was that he wanted to accomplish the work as quickly as possible, 'whatever the charge may be', in the interests of 'not only promoting cleanliness in the town but…ultimately (completing) a system of draining where it is most required'.

Eliot's minute was the result of 'enquiries' he had made on his own regarding 'some old water courses that originally were in a direct line east and west of the town from the Chitpore Road to the Circular Road', channels which in some places had been 'usurped' by individuals and in others 'stopped or changed as suited each person's convenience in arrangement of their buildings or other purposes'.[5] In Eliot's view, this had a serious impact on the 'cleanliness and healthiness of the town' and he took it on himself to 'restore' the water courses and also remove 'all useless trees from the borders of the several water courses of the town and suburbs and (also) all such trees as generally existed in the town'. The inference here is that, in the second decade of the 19th century when the town was in the middle of a consistent growth surge, traces of the earlier, primeval, verdant cover of the region still remained, spread across the town to such an extent that a concerted effort had to be made to cut it down to make way for a new Calcutta.[6] Eliot took the help of natives to accomplish his task. He called a meeting of 'all the leading natives of Calcutta at my residence in Clive Street to endeavour to prevail on them to aid and promote so very desirable an object'. The result was helpful. As he wrote, he was 'promised their cordial cooperation to aid my endeavours in this essential of effectually draining some of the worst and most shocking places of the whole town'.

A week after Eliot submitted his minute to the Lottery Committee, the committee wrote to the Government (18 December) that its president had 'discovered an old water course extending from the Chitpore Road through Simleea Bazar to the Circular Road, the route of which has in some places been changed and in others entirely stopped'.[7] Since 'systematic measures' had to be adopted to drain the town effectively (see below) and since a proper plan to implement the project would take some time, it suggested that 'the opening of the water course pointed out by Mr Eliot, and which has been carefully inspected by other members of the committee',

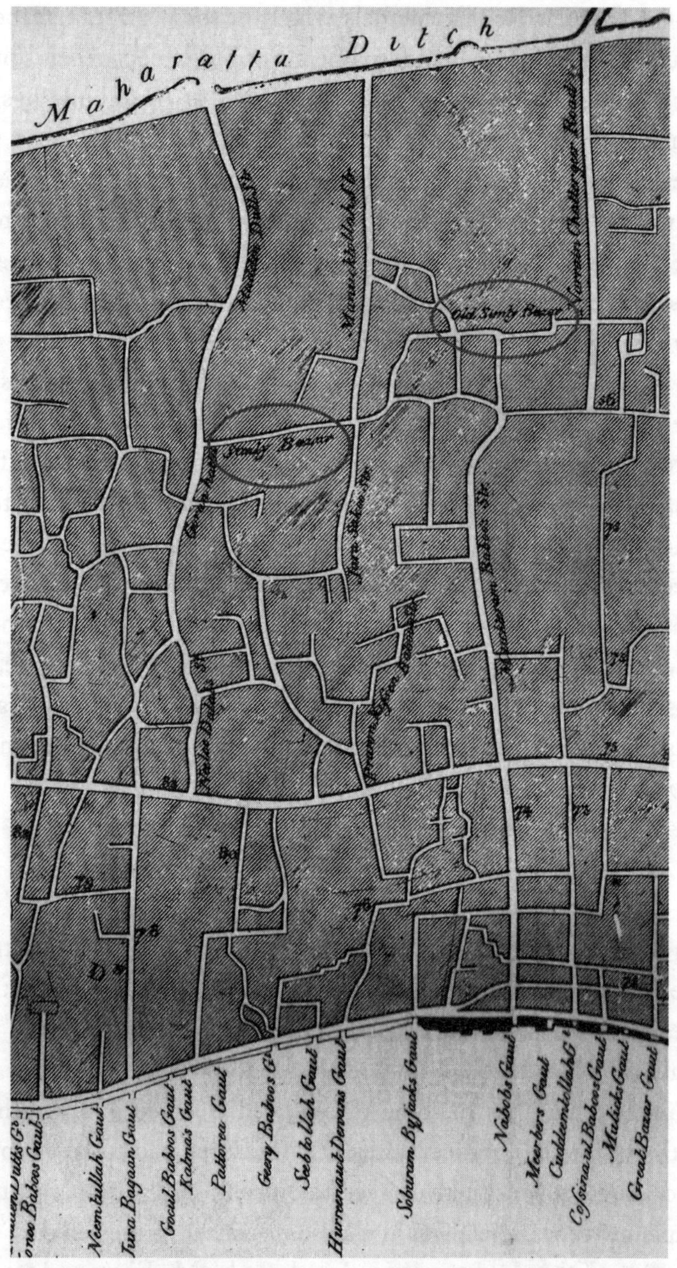

Fig. 16. Detail of Mark Wood's map (1784-85) showing the location of Simleah (Simly) Bazar

would be 'of the utmost consequence'. This apart, the reopening of the old watercourse would be 'the means of draining one of the most filthy and unhealthy parts of the city' at a 'comparatively trifling expense'. Echoing Eliot, the committee wrote that the natives had generally shown 'every disposition to give up such ground as may be required for the undertaking'. However, since those proprietors who would have to give up their property would have to be paid an 'equitable compensation', the committee felt that Eliot be given 'a discretionary authority to disburse such sums as may be necessary for that purpose, not exceeding in the aggregate Sicca Rs 5,000 chargeable on the lottery funds'. The Government sanctioned the project in the first week of the new year.

Eliot began work on the drain for which he says he found a lot of support among the 'lower orders' of the natives. The reference here to the 'lower order' of the natives is of interest because the proceedings carry a number of complaints from natives better placed in life who felt they had been given a rough deal by the magistrate in the course of the project's implementation. Eliot now approached the Lottery Committee for funds which were required for compensating those affected by the project. He wrote: 'It is of material consequence to the effectual attainment of this measure that I should be authorised to settle with the several occupants for straw and tiled houses to be removed, and some *kutcha* walls with a few mortar-brick buildings.' He added that, given the length of time these huts and other constructions had been in existence, 'it is but just to render the owners some indemnification for removing their residences as they agree and can be settled with to prevent any loss of time'. The compensation exercise would be an ongoing process which would 'not admit of the least delay without being attended ultimately with much inconvenience from the intrigues of designing and interested natives'. At some places, where 'more considerable (sums)' would be required 'than I should consider myself authorised to pay', the magistrate wrote that he would take members of the committee to such spots to ascertain for themselves the scale of the funds needed.

The Lottery Committee president then raised the question of whether the funds so taken would be charged to the lottery funds or to the Assessment Department, a point that was to crop up in the years ahead with respect to projects big and small. Eliot's view stands out because of its lack of clarity. He said that the project was essentially 'a *new* [emphasis added] undertaking from the length of time that the several occupants have been in undisturbed possession of the land', which would mean that the Lottery Committee would be within its rights (under its charter of functions) to foot the bill. But he also added that 'the sums now required are merely for the removal of the numerous buildings, as the land is *readily relinquished*' (emphasis added), which would imply that the project was not a new one and paying for it would, properly, be the responsibility of the Assessment/Conservancy Department and not that of the committee. Eliot went out of his way to bring to the notice of the committee the munificence of a native, Kosaul (Kushal) Dutt, who had given up as much as a *bigha* of land for the opening of the Simleah 'water course' or drain 'of the width of ten feet', asking in return for the earth excavated from the drain to be used to fill up 'a filthy tank he wishes to be filled'. The magistrate portrayed the exchange as having, on the one hand, resulted in 'a large saving in (the) purchase of the land', to the tune of Rs 8,000 (Rs 400 a *katha*), and, on the other, securing 'the removal of a nuisance'.

All members of the committee except for Henry Wood extended support to the magistrate's scheme.[8] Wood wrote that if the cost of the project exceeded Rs 5,000 he would consider it more sensible to have

> ...the work...done well at once, and instead of opening an old drain I would recommend the construction of a new

> *puckah* drain to run down the middle of any of the adjoining streets, with openings into it, so as to admit the water from any low places to the north and south of it.

Gordon gave qualified support when he wrote that there was little doubt that the principal benefit flowing from Eliot's project when completed would be the removal of 'unhealthiness in the quarter of the town where it is to be executed'. However, if ever there was a need for the committee to spend its resources 'limited as they are... to remove a similar *but more extensive nuisance* [emphasis added] in any other quarter, the future security in point of healthiness that will be afforded by (the) draining effected on Mr Eliot's plan must give that a decided preference'. Colvin, Bayley and Trower supported Eliot's plan, the first two taking the trouble of paying a visit to the site of the proposed drain.

Bayley, who was about to be made Acting Chief Secretary to the Government, was most persuasive when he wrote that he had

> ...inspected the whole course of the proposed drain [and had found that the] existence of an old drain of considerable dimensions is traceable at intervals throughout the whole line, but it has in many places been stopped up and encroached upon. That the reopening and enlarging this drain would be of the greatest public benefit must be obvious to anyone who will examine that part of the town. The nearest drain of any real use is in Monicktola Street. [The] part of the town through which the drain is proposed to be carried is...the most filthy in Calcutta, and from the number of dirty tanks, public privies and various receptacles of filth and putrid matter with which it abounds the atmosphere must be...most unwholesome at all times of the year, and the improvement which would result from opening a wide drain proportionately great.

Bayley said that the drain 'would run nearly in a straight line from the Chitpore Road through the Simleea bazaar to the Circular Road; and I do not know that a more solid or real improvement could be effected than that which would result from Mr Eliot's plan being fully executed'. As regards the cost, he said that compensation for those affected would add up to quite a pile but 'certainly much less than would be incurred if an old drain had not formerly existed'.

Of the six members who commented on Eliot's project, only H.S. Montague referred to the by now well-established view that all the old drainage schemes of the town had been constructed on the faulty proposition that the slope of the land was towards the river when in fact it was towards the salt lake in the east. He wrote that although the implementation of Eliot's project would be 'productive of the most beneficial effects to a part of the town which one cannot survey without wondering how human beings can inhale the exhalations of such filth with impunity', the fact was that the reopening of the old drain was proposed at a time when the town 'was erroneously drained towards the river' and this could possibly mean that it 'would not entirely answer the object in view'. Montague said that the pathetic state of the drain was probably 'in a great measure attributable to the original defect in its construction'. Curiously, although he must have been aware of it, in his minute Eliot did not refer to this built-in physical drawback of the defunct drain explicitly. The Lottery Committee's 18 December 1817 letter to the Government recommending Eliot's plan lifts the veil on this apparent incongruity, namely, the members avoiding comment on the faulty principle of drainage followed in Calcutta in the early days when it had been underscored officially as being the basic reason for the failure of the town not being drained effectively till that time.[9] The letter made it clear that 'the complete accomplishment' of the effective drainage of the town could be effected only if the drains were made 'on a very different plan from those which are usually to be found in Calcutta'. Specifically, the point was made that the reopening of old water courses 'would not be consistent with the more comprehensive arrangements which the committee have under their consideration'. However, since 'much time' would be needed before forming 'a conclusive judgement of the practicability or expediency of those arrangements or submit the details of the plan to the Government', in the intervening period projects like Eliot's Simleah drain could be taken up because it would mean draining – at a 'comparatively trifling expense' – 'one of the most filthy and unhealthy parts of the city'.[10]

John Eliot died on 19 January 1818, that is, just about five weeks after he had begun work on the Simleah drain.[11] Three days later, Henry Wood proposed that as a means

> ...of recording our sentiments of the great loss we have sustained by the lamented death of our late president Mr Eliot, and at the same time of transmitting down to posterity the usefulness of his labours, and of preventing their ever hereafter being rendered unavailable by the encroachment of the natives, I would beg to propose that we recommend to Government our being permitted [to] erect stones at the head of every water course and road made by him, with a written inscription declarating of its length and width and the place to which it leads, and that each written inscription be headed by the name of Mr Eliot and state the year in which the work was performed by him.[12]

This was nothing but hero worship pointing to the exalted position which John Eliot had carved out for himself amongst his colleagues and peers. Needless to say, the Government sanctioned the expenditure early in February, C.R. Barwell, Magistrate of 24-Parganas, being asked to look after the drain project.

A year later, on 19 February 1819, Barwell submitted to the committee a full account of the expenditure made on the project[13] the list of payees revealing that 58 individuals were compensated of whom just 9 received Rs 100 or more. Barring a handful of people who had to part with walls, houses and *postahs*, 15 of those affected had to give up their huts for which they were offered a price ranging from Re 1 to Rs 8. The expedition with which Eliot went about his job is indicated by Barwell's report which stated that Rs 1,956 had been spent by the late magistrate in about five weeks (9 December 1817 to 14 January 1818) while Barwell took more than ten months to disburse Rs 1,895-11-11 (12 March 1818 to 18 January 1819).

The 21 October 1817 guidelines had stipulated that the Lottery Committee was not to repair or maintain old drains, a stipulation which with the passage of time was bound to be questioned not only because the drainage issue was central to the spatial expansion of Calcutta but also because effective drainage meant the proper working of the *entire* network of drains, old and new.[14] Clearly, from an administrative point of view, the committee ought to have been in charge of *all* drains instead of only the new ones. The theme had been underscored during the Wellesley years and it was only a matter of time before the issue cropped up again following the formation of the Lottery Committee.[15]

Four months after the committee was set up, on 13 February 1818 Henry Wood shot off a letter describing the horrific state the town's drains were in and suggesting a change in the system followed till then of cleaning them.[16]

The situation, Wood wrote, could not be worse. What is more important, and revealing, is that

> ...the houses erected at Chowringhee and on the grounds in the vicinity of the Government House do not pay towards the establishment so large a sum in proportion as the houses, shops, and buildings of the Burrah Bazar, China Bazar and the other parts of the town at present totally neglected.

Wood's main point was that while the drains were, indeed, cleared of filth, the dirt removed was not taken away but allowed to pile up 'in the drains on the sides of the public ways, to the annoyance of the residents, as well as the passengers passing on the roads'. He said that a 'large establishment was paid at the expense of the householders and tenants without their reaping any proportionate advantage to the outlay'.

He suggested a change in the establishment responsible for cleaning the drains. He felt that in place of hired labourers superintended by overseers, the contract system should be employed with a schedule of penalties being worked into the contract if the work was not completed on time. As he wrote, 'The system of contract will probably meet with much opposition in as much as its adoption will necessarily throw out of employ very many individuals who at present receive salaries without performing any adequate duty for the same'. An effort would be made to emphasise the indispensability of overseers, but Wood wrote that 'the best overseers of a duty to be performed are those most interested in its being performed well, and who suffer inconvenience by the non-performance of it'. If the terms of the contract were written down, 'and the forfeit for non-performance clearly defined', it would only require prompt attention on the part of the magistrates to the complaints of the inhabitants 'and an establishment to point out the contractors to the complaining individuals, and others to proceed to the spot...to ensure the duty being well-performed'.

Wood referred to the existing system of the collection of filth from drains and elsewhere which was 'carried to tanks and low places requiring to be filled up by the owners'. For this an 'expensive cart establishment' had been retained, the earth removed being sold 'for a large sum of money'. The Civil Auditor said that he had information that 'part of the cart establishment hired for the removal of the filth had rehired itself at low wages in the service of private individuals'.[17] Under the system proposed, by making the removal of the filth a part of the contract, the money paid would go to 'the cleaner of the drain and the remover of it', which would act as an 'additional stimulus to exertion on the part of the individuals on whom the inhabitants are dependent for cleaning the town'. Admittedly, the existing system of removing the filth could also be amended by transporting the dirt to a more distant place, which would be healthier for the town. But, as Wood argued, this would lead to the level of the town not been raised gradually, which was desirable from the point of view of general healthiness.

Henry Wood's February 1818 initiative to alter the system of cleaning drains in the town did not get very far although he was successful in drawing attention to the state of the town's drainage which was in a shambles and needed immediate attention if the healthiness of the town was to be improved. The records indicate that, apart from specific projects, there was no further discussion on the subject, which was revisited in late April 1819 when Henry Shakespear, the Officiating Chief Magistrate of the town who had just been made a member of the Lottery Committee (26 March 1819), brought it up once more.[18] Shakespear suggested that the committee set aside funds for cleaning the existing drains before the commencement of the rains. The Chief Magistrate was a hands-on man who knew the inner workings of the magistracy, especially whether it would be able to meet the demands of policy implementation which the Lottery Committee was bound to impose upon it. He said that he was induced to make the proposal 'from a conviction of the inadequacy of the establishment under the magistracy for the purposes required, so long as the drains in the town remain in their present state'. The existing establishment would possibly be sufficient

> ...when a general cleaning has taken place, but the drains in the interior of the town are choked up with dirt and rubbish, the accumulation of years since Calcutta has been a town, and four times the conservancy establishment would not serve to clear them in the next two months.

The impact of the existing drainage situation on the health of the people of the town was nothing short of disastrous. Shakespear explained that, in the absence of a general cleaning,

> ...half the drains in Calcutta are worse than useless – water and filth, which would otherwise be carried off, remains stagnant, and hence proceeds no doubt much of that sickness which prevails amongst all classes, but particularly amongst the lower order of people, towards the close of the rains, and which has occasioned such a dreadful mortality in the last few years.

He argued that since the Lottery Committee's goal was to improve 'the health and comfort' of the inhabitants, the lottery funds could be used to clean the drains. In fact, the construction of new drains had already contributed towards that end, and here Shakespear took the opportunity to focus on the *integrated* nature of the drainage system as a whole, making the point that either the entire network functioned efficiently or nothing worked at all. He said that it would be 'superfluous to show that those improvements (the construction of new drains) are deprived of half their utility unless the whole of the drains connected with the new ones are rendered efficient'. He suggested that each member of the committee take charge of the cleaning 'of those parts which cannot conveniently be looked after by others'.

Though he could not be faulted on his argument, Shakespear too failed in his effort to bend the guidelines. Perhaps, other members of the committee thought the same way too, but the rules were sacrosanct and the committee maintained blandly that the suggestions could not 'be complied with consistently with the orders under which the application of the lottery funds is limited to new works'. The Officiating Chief Magistrate was, however, nothing if not tenacious. Towards the end of the year he made another effort to improve the drainage facilities of the town. The cold weather was just setting in and Shakespear wrote in early November 1819[19] that he wished to bring up the subject 'in the hope that the present season may not be allowed to pass away without something being done towards improving the state of the drains in the interior of the town'. He said that 'the magnitude of the labour and expence of new-draining (sic) Calcutta seems to have...prevented the work from being commenced upon' and no steps had been taken 'to correct the present defects because the whole cannot be undertaken at once upon a grand systematic plan'. He, however, felt that the problem could be tackled piecemeal in that 'many bad drains' could be got rid of and improved 'at no great expence (and) without interfering with any general system of draining which may be adopted hereafter with reference to the levels of the town should the state of our funds ever enable us to commence such an undertaking'. Shakespear's specific proposal was that the drains of all roads running north and south should be

Fig. 17. Schalch's map (1824) showing the area where Shakespear's drainage experiment was carried out; also the stretch of Chitpur Road along which a drain was made

filled up 'and surface-drained to empty themselves into the deep drains running east or west to the salt water lake or the river'. As a pilot project, he suggested that all the roads 'connecting Cotton Street and Burtollah' be taken up 'where several of these crossroads are to be found'.

Taking note of the proposal, the Lottery Committee set up a 'subcommittee for surface-draining' comprising Shakespear and Lt Charles Paton, the latter being asked to attend all committee meetings as an honorary member in the absence of his senior, Captain P. Phipps, who was on his annual tours for the inspection of buildings in the Lower Provinces.[20] The subcommittee was to carry into effect an 'experiment' of the sort proposed by Shakespear, who was given a free hand in selecting any part of the town 'as may appear most expedient to you and Lieut Paton'. An expenditure of Rs 400 was allowed for the experiment, the committee asking Shakespear to report to it on the 'practical advantages which may be found to result from the adoption of your proposition'. In April 1820 the subcommittee declared that its experiment, costing Rs 370-2-7, had been successful the proposal being made to extend the surface-draining project to a new stretch of Chitpur Road which would, among other things, be widened.[21] The proposal was accepted and a further Rs 400 allocated for the additional work. Even though the Court of Directors was not happy with Shakespear's 'experiment', there is little doubt that it constituted a big step forward in making roads cleaner, if for no other reason than the fact that it began implementation of the principle of effective draining of the city from the west to the east generally.[22]

A critical part of the drainage work was ascertaining the slope of the land over which Calcutta had spread itself. The subject had been discussed earlier but not by the Lottery Committee which had just been set up. Since no comprehensive effort at tackling the drainage problem could be made without first settling the 'level of land' issue, the committee set the ball rolling on 11 December 1817 by asking Arthur Blechynden, its surveyor, to report on the lay of the land in an area enclosed by Dharamtala, Circular Road, Bowbazar and Cossitala.[23] Blechynden wrote back at the end of the month saying that he had measured two sections instead of the three suggested by the committee, 'there not being a third direct communication from the Cossitullah to the Circular Road, as a reference to Upjohn's map will shew'. Providing us with an idea of what these lines of communication were from today's Bentinck Street in the west to Circular Road in the east, the surveyor wrote that the first one commenced 'at Emaumbarry Lane, and passes through Emaumbaug, Beparrytollah and Creek Row into the Circular Road, where there is a fall of 3 ft 5 inches'. The second line of communication commenced 'at Grant's Lane and, passing through Meery Jaun Gully, Copollytollah, Hyderam Bannarjeah's

Lane, Punchanund-tollah Lane and Gowconnah Lane, enters the Circular Road through Chapadoleah-parah Lane, south of the Boitaconnah bazaar', the fall in this section being 3 ft 8 inches. The fall along Bowbazar Road was 3 ft 7 inches and that along Dharamtala Road 3 ft 9 inches.

Blechynden was then asked to report on the slope of the ground in the north-south direction between Dharamtala and Bowbazar, his finding being submitted in February 1818.[24] The three sections studied were: (a) along Kenderdine's Lane, Gurriah Mha Lane, entering the Dharamtala Road through Chandney Chowk, where there was a fall of half an inch to the south; (b) from Durga Churn Peethoory's Lane, through Kanzketchypooker Lane, Bancharam Unkoor's Gully and Emaumbaug Lane, joining Dharamtala Road through Baparrytollah Lane, showing a rise of 2 ½ inches to the south; (c) along Scavenger's Lane, through Puddoopooker and Neembotollah (Nebutala) Lanes, entering Dharamtala Road through Sankarrytollah Lane, where there was a fall of 10 inches to the south.[25]

For the next two years work on studying the slope of the land continued although not under the auspices of the Lottery Committee. Lt William N. Forbes of the Bengal Engineers was given the responsibility his work being interrupted by his having to leave for Europe whereupon, in December 1819, J.A. Schalch, the Deputy Assistant Quarter-Master General, was asked to complete the 'Calcutta levels' in addition to the ongoing survey work he was engaged in.[26] Four months later, in April 1820, Schalch informed the committee that he had completed 'the levelling operations' and would resume 'the survey of the town' his hope being that he would be able 'to deliver them in' soon.[27] 'Soon' stretched to four months, Schalch explaining in a letter to the committee the reasons for the delay and also what his empirical findings were as far as the 'height' of the town was concerned with respect to the river on the west and the salt lake in the east.[28]

Schalch discovered that the findings of Forbes were 'unsatisfactory'. Schalch did not lay the blame at the door of his service colleague arguing instead that the circumstance in which Lt Forbes found himself was responsible for the errors. The upshot was that Schalch had to begin the work of collecting data '*de novo*' (on 21 February 1820) after completing the work he was engaged in on the Dum Dum cantonment. By late April he had completed the work of data collection, the next four months being taken up 'in the calculations and in finishing off the plans, etc'. Throwing light on his *modus operandi*, Schalch wrote that knowing full well the main objective of the exercise, namely, the 'most effectual mode of draining the town', he made sure he omitted nothing 'in the construction of the plans and sections which I thought could afford information on that head; and to render the whole as connected as possible, such information is inserted on the parts of the plan to which it more immediately refers'. Indicating the level of detail involved, Schalch wrote that an index map had also been added for

> ...the sake of more ready reference, shewing the streets up which the sections have been carried, and with a separate sheet, containing an abstract of the levels; and a few appropriate remarks accompany the plans and the sections, which thus speak for themselves and render any further explanation here unnecessary.

Schalch wrote that 'the highest ground is near the river, sloping gradually towards the Circular Road, and continuing so to the salt lake'.[29] This was not a new finding: in 1799 Richard Blechynden had told the authorities the same thing.[30] In fact, Schalch's summary of his findings referred to the levels taken in 1783-84 and 1803-04, saying that he had 'every reason to believe' that they were correct. The problem with these early exercises lay elsewhere, namely, that there were 'no plans with the tables, and no reference made in the latter to the precise spots from which the calculations were deduced', thus reducing their utility greatly. Since 'great changes must no doubt have taken place in the state of the roads since these tables were constructed', Schalch wrote that he could not vouch for their accuracy which is why he had drawn attention to the

> ...expediency of placing stones, embedded in masonry, in certain parts of the town to register their relative heights (so) that, in the event of the construction of aqueducts, drains, etc, they may serve to prove the correctness or otherwise of any levels that it may then be found necessary to make.

Fifteen such stones had already been put up, and the remaining ones would be installed 'in the course of another fortnight'.

The mean height of 'the surface of the town (was) about two feet below the river at its greatest height in the rains, or 12 feet above the salt lake at the same season'. Most of the streets were on this level. Clive Street was

> ...the highest, and Muchwa (Mechua) Bazar Street the lowest. The former, near Meerbhurs [(Mirbahar] Ghaut, is 8 feet above, and the latter, near its center, is 6 feet below the top of Chandpaul Ghaut, which is commonly between 2 & 3 feet higher than the river in the rains, at spring tides.

Describing the slope of the land from the north, Schalch wrote that 'Parallel to the river, there was a gentle slope towards Muchwa Bazar Street, from Chitpore-bridge on the one side, and a line drawn half-way between the Bowbazar and the Dhurrumtollah on the other,' and that to the south of this line there was 'a gentle declivity towards Brijootollah'.[31] Schalch felt that 'the great difference in the relative heights of the river and salt lake in the rains' made it imperative that one or the other had to become the receptacle of rainwater during the rainy season.

It was towards the salt lake that the town's drains had to be aligned because of the following reasons:

> In the months of July, August and September, the tides in the river rise at an average to 11 feet above the salt lake, and only fall to 2 feet below it. But on some days the river does not descend to within a foot of the level of the salt lake, whereas at a high spring tide the river attains a height of between 13 and 14 feet above it.

On the other hand, the salt lake constituted a body of water which remained 'at a uniform height throughout the rainy season, uninfluenced either by freshes or tides'. There was simply no danger of the water flowing back into the drains even if the latter's mouths were located at its level 'half a mile beyond the Circular Road', their gradient being 5 ½ feet to the mile, 'or about 1 inch and a quarter in 100 feet'. Given the physical attribute of the two waterbodies, the conclusion was that 'if the water which descends on the surface of the town during a heavy fall of rain be equally distributed by cross drains into the great sewers, and these were made of a sufficient capacity and slope, no obstacle will be opposed to its free passage into the lake'.

Schalch had written to the Lottery Committee on 2 August 1820. The very next day the committee sent the report to the Government with a request – granted on 1 September – that an extra copy of the measurements be made by Andrews, Schalch's assistant, which would cost Rs 800. The copy was completed and sent to the Government on 10 May 1821.[32] The map, which Schalch suggested be engraved in sections and cover 'a part of the suburbs' as well (a suggestion which was accepted by the Government), quickly established itself as an important point of reference. Four years later the Government set aside Rs 2,512 from the Lottery Committee funds for buying 50 copies of it at Rs 40 a copy, the number of copies to be made being determined by Schalch himself.[33]

The Government was appreciative of the labours of Schalch generally. It wrote back in the beginning of 1 September to say that the work 'appears to have been completed with skill, care and diligence and the drawings are executed with great neatness while the general remarks contained in Lieutenant's Schalch's report cannot fail to prove highly useful in the practical regulation and improvement of the drains of Calcutta and its vicinity'.[34] Being a hard taskmaster, the Government asked Schalch to resume work on the survey of the fast-expanding town 'as soon as the state of the season will admit' the hope being expressed that it would be completed 'with as little delay as may be consistent with its accurate and satisfactory execution'.

To Schalch the 'levels' work was an addition to his principal task, namely, completing the survey, to which, as he said, he stood 'more immediately appointed'. The work, in fact, was an offshoot of the map project mooted by the Lottery Committee at its meeting on 14 October 1819[35] where it was pointed out that the absence of such a cartographic aide was 'impeding' improvement work. The committee offered to 'superintend its prosecution' and said that it was prepared to point out to the officer entrusted with the job 'the principal objects to which his attention should be directed, and… could communicate with him on all points during the progress of the work'. Apart from the help such a map would provide for its own work, the committee felt that the city's magistrates too stood to gain from such a venture because it would 'facilitate the assessment and collection of the house tax'. It would also be 'a desirable record in many of the public offices at the presidency'.

The Lottery Committee laid down the broad guidelines of what the preliminary survey of the city should contain, which indicates the great detail the exercise involved.[36] Among other things, the work had to be drawn on a sufficiently large scale to show distinctly the following particulars:

> Every street, road, lane and alley, distinguishing by a different colour those which are *pucka* from those which are *cutcha*; all reservoirs, tanks, *jheels*, aqueducts, sewers and drains with the direction of the course of the latter; all buildings and spots of ground the property of Government, as well as public offices, and all other buildings of a public nature, religious edifices, hospitals, schools, bazaars, public and private, ghauts, the stations of police guards or custom house officers, fire engines, etc; the boundaries of large estates or premises, and the number of all houses, as far as practicable; sections of the levels of the town to be annexed in the margin.

Following the completion of the survey, a map would be 'engraved on a scale corresponding with the accompanying sketch'.[37] The committee was not far wrong when it said that the demand for engraved maps of Calcutta 'would more than suffice to defray the expense of the engraving, and that individuals would be ready to undertake the risk if it were not thought more advisable to leave it to the Lottery Committee'. The cost of the establishment associated with the exercise would not be considerable and would be defrayed from the funds of the committee.

Bayley, the Chief Secretary to the Government and a member of the Lottery Committee, wrote to the committee the very next day (15 October) that before the Government could respond to the proposal it would like to know the time required for the survey to be completed and, secondly, the total expense involved, including the establishment 'to be attached to the officer who may be employed, and other contingencies'.[38] Five days later, the committee told the Government that the survey would take three years to complete 'if conducted by an intelligent and experienced officer with the aid of two native surveyors and with the occasional assistance which might be rendered by Mr Blechynden, who is already attached to the establishment of the committee'. As regards the cost of the survey, the committee said that around Rs 16,000 would be required for the three years, the break-up being Rs 7,200 for two 'intelligent native assistants, a *tindal*, *clashees*, etc' at Rs 200 a month, including contingencies, and, at Rs 250 a month, Rs 9,000 as 'staff allowance of the officer who might be employed on the duty'. Even if the entire amount was to be paid from its own funds, the committee said it would not be 'disproportionate to the importance of the objects in view'. However, a hint was dropped that the survey could be financed from other sources as well when the committee said that, in view of the benefits which would result for 'several branches of the public service', the Government would have to decide whether the entire amount would be met by the lottery funds, a nudge that was ignored the total outgo being drawn from the lottery funds.

The survey was sanctioned at the end of October 1819 the committee being informed that Lt Schalch, an honorary member of the committee, had been appointed to implement it. Arthur Blechynden was to assist Schalch 'in the prosecution of the survey as far as may be consistent with Mr Blechynden's other duties'.[39] The Government wanted the committee to report on the survey work in October the following year (1820) and 'at the same period in subsequent years'.

In May 1820 Schalch was asked to submit a progress report on the work done till the forthcoming 1 July, which he did three days later (4 July).[40] Among other things, he said that work had been completed in the part of the town lying to the south of Burying Ground Road (Park Street) 'and the road leading from it to the fort (Outram Road), including the jail'. The final drawing of the survey depended on how much 'the largest-sized antiquarian paper' available could accommodate, which led Schalch to tell the committee that as much of the survey as could be fitted into the paper on an appropriate scale had been 'completed'. As far as the remaining part of the work was concerned, he said he would have to delay 'finishing off until I have done a portion sufficient to fill another sheet, as constant exposure to the atmosphere, particularly at this season, renders the paper soon unfit to receive the necessary colouring'. He added that he had also completed, 'on loose sheets', the survey of the area bounded by Bowbazar Road in the north, Dharamtala in the south, Circular Road in the east and Old Court House Street in the west with the exception of 'a small part in the south-west corner'. The survey was completed by July 1824 the Lottery Committee informing the Government in the middle of January 1825 that the work was over and that 'the copies required by Government' had been furnished by Schalch (who had become a Major by then).[41]

Schalch's survey was undertaken with the objective of finalising an effective drainage plan for the city. But the Deputy Assistant Quarter-Master General did not think too highly of the efforts that were being made at the time to solve the drainage problems. This is made abundantly clear in an appendix to a report (dated June 1821) written by Schalch focussing on making

> ...a grand...water communication between the Upper Provinces and the eastern side of Bengal and Calcutta, open and secure for every description of boat by forming a

> junction between the Gurroy (Gurroy) and Hoogly rivers by means of canals at the head of the Sunderbunds, lessening the expense by taking advantage of such *nullahs* as flow in a suitable direction, thus avoiding the large rivers and the inconveniences of the present route.[42]

Schalch felt that, as far as the drainage plans for the city were concerned, 'the more beneficial improvements [were] giving way to the more splendid and dazzling'. He wrote:

> It is only by consulting the peculiar localities of a town, and by taking advantage of them as far as they will admit, that any improvement in its atmosphere can be expected. Those of Calcutta are too apparent to escape the notice of the most unobservant, and it need scarcely be mentioned that they consist in the lowness of its site, numerous swamps in the most central parts, the great height to which the floods of the river rise, the existence of an extensive morass bounding one-third of its circumference, together with a damp, heated atmosphere favourable to every description of putrefaction, and the absence of rain except in a few occasional showers for more than seven months in the year.

He hoped that 'many of the evils arising from these causes may...be lessened by adopting a more effectual mode of draining the town and by removing more speedily the filth and offensive matter'. As he put it, 'An ill-drained town in a low situation may be compared to an ill-flued house which, the more beautiful the superstructure, the greater the regret that so much labour and expense should have been exhausted in pleasing the eye while the health and comfort of the tenant have been neglected'.

Schalch tried to weave his thoughts on drainage of the city into the scheme of canals which he had drawn up to improve the transport prospects between the Upper Provinces and eastern Bengal. He wrote:

> The first [step] is the construction of sewers of a large capacity, from the Hoogly river to the circular canal, parallel with the principal streets [and] running in that direction, of such depth that the tide may enter them washing out the contents of the drains into the canal. The whole will afterwards be carried to a distance of nine miles from the town, and ultimately by the numerous outlets from the Salt Lake into the Sunderbunds. It is intended that these drains shall run behind the principal large streets where the small number of *pucka* buildings will permit, otherwise under the streets themselves. In retired parts the public privies might be placed over openings in the top. By this plan, the town would be cleared of filth every twelve hours without any annoyance to the population which will obviate the present offensive practice of its being carried openly and disgustingly through the streets.

There were bound to be many objections to the plan, but Schalch maintained that

> …none…upon deliberate investigation will be found to create a despair for its ultimate success; and when we consider the numerous advantages that will result from its adoption, we surely will not put in competition with them either a few temporary objections or the expense which at the utmost will not exceed 50,000 rupees a mile.

He said it was unnecessary to dwell 'on the evils of the present system of removing the ardure of the inhabitants. Indeed, they are well known and too disgustingly familiar to the inhabitants in general while they are particularly offensive to those residing near Jackson's and Umratullah Ghaut and to the shipping in the river.' He felt that the adoption of the plan would 'bring down on its promoters the blessings of the most considerable class of inhabitants in point of numbers who can then perform their ablutions as sacredly enjoined by their religion without having their feelings and prejudices daily outraged and wounded'.

The Lottery Committee had nothing to do with Schalch's report on opening a waterlink between the Upper Provinces and the eastern side of Bengal and Calcutta. But since the city's drainage figured in it the report was sent to the committee for its 'information and guidance'. Focussing on the city drainage issue, the Government said that there was a proposal to cut a canal and, although there was necessarily no link between the canal proposed by Schalch and the city's drainage, the Lottery Committee could extend its investigations to include 'the probable influence of the proposed work [the canal] on the health and cleanliness of the city, [which was] as obvious a point of enquiry as the degree in which it may be calculated to facilitate commercial intercourse'.[43]

A committee comprising Shakespear, Gordon, Ballard and Captain H. Morrieson was formed to study Schalch's plans relating to the drainage of the city, the report being submitted in late October 1822.[44] Among other things, the committee said that the

> ...excavation of the proposed canal [by Schalch] through the salt water lake to join the eastern canal, and the continuation of the line of canal from thence to join the Hooghly at Chitpore, seem to us to be essential to the general success of the scheme and to promise advantages of the highest importance to the comfort and accommodation of the city.

However, the committee felt that Schalch's plan for conveying 'the filth and ordure of Calcutta through tunnels to the new [eastern] canal would not in our opinion [be the] answer'. It wrote that the objections made by the Lottery Committee, Blechynden and others had 'induced the conclusion that the experiment ought not to be tried'. However, the construction, 'at proper intervals of tunnels, described by Mr Blechynden, from the Chitpore Road to the new canal is considered highly desirable, as they would tend greatly to improve the drainage of that part of the town'. The committee suggested that the magistrates be asked

> ...to undertake the construction of one tunnel of that description on the side of the Mutchwa Bazar Road, or between that and the Loll Bazar, as an experiment calculated to show how far the advantages of such a system of drainage would counterbalance its expence ['estimated by Mr Kyd[45] at 50,000 Rs per mile'].

In a report (dated 26 January 1822) on Schalch's plan, Richard Blechynden[46] wrote:

> Calcutta stands upon the bank of a noble river, and it becomes of consequence to open the drains at once into it rather than let the water dribble 3 miles to the salt water lake, and thence through the Sunderbunds to the sea. The main drain south of the Loll Diggee is very deep, yet who has seen that quarter of the city inundated at the highest tides.
>
> An extremely heavy shower of rain of long continuance might lay a street under water owing to more water falling than the drains could deliver during that period. But this would equally happen in any town however high it stood. If no injury occurs from the drain at the Bankshall, why

> should it in the northern parts of Calcutta which are higher? The surface of the river water will be the same before each station; only where the land is higher the drain must be proportionately deeper.
>
> I would therefore propose that a large tunnel (similar to that at the Bankshall)[47] be made across the city at every 2,000 feet or as near to that more or less as the situation of the streets would permit – the chamber of this tunnel to ascend gradually from the river until it is only 3 feet below the surface of the ground; this aperture (aperture) being with the arch as little as could be allowed for people to descend to clean it. Thence the slope should turn the other way and that portion of the city (which I believe would not be very large) drained towards the Mahratta Ditch, so that should a heavy fall of rain happen at the very top of high water still there would be a vent to the east for what the river did not receive, and a free course when desired would be left to the tide to wash out the tunnel and collateral drains.
>
> When I made the tunnel (in 1807) to fill the Loll Diggie from the river, I added a valve a short distance to the east of the tunnel to prevent the escape of any of the water and to throw the whole into the Loll Diggie. This valve, of course, precludes any water passing into the Loll Bazar and Boitaconnah Street drains although it admits drainage from them. But if this valve is raised the water will pass freely through the city to the Mahrattah Ditch, and without the slightest damage to any drain or house whatever. The rate would not exceed half a mile per hour.

The committee had, in fact, recommended that a tunnel be constructed from Chitpur Road to the Circular Road and eventually to the new canal, as described by Blechynden. But where was it to be located? Would it be to the north of Mechua

Bazar Street or to the south of it, an issue on which the magistrates had to take a decision? On 20 March 1823 Holt Mackenzie, Secretary to the Government in the Territorial Department, had asked the magistrates of the Conservancy Department to report on 'the utility of constructing a tunnel as proposed by the late Mr Blechynden' and also send a 'detailed estimate' of such a project.[48] Henry Shakespear, Chief Magistrate of the town, had written:

> With the exception of a small space north of the Bow Bazar Road, which is drained to the southward, the whole of the drains of this quarter run northward to the sides of the Mutchua Bazar Road and thence in an easterly direction to the Circular Road. By intersecting these drains with the tunnel, the water and filth from the Tarretta Bazar, Champtollah, Chunam Gully and the streets south of the petty court jail (see Fig. 11), one of the dirtiest parts of the town, will be arrested in its course and be carried off in a direct line to the Circular Road, and ultimately to the new canal.

The Chief Magistrate wrote that instead of buying up ground just for the sake of constructing the tunnel it would be 'so much better [to link it up] with the opening of a road from the Chitpore Road to the Circular Road' that he would suggest writing to the Lottery Committee 'how far it may suit their plan to open such a road halfway between the Bow Bazar and Mutchua Bazar Roads, stating our intention in the event of the committee undertaking the road to propose to Government the adoption of that line for the projected tunnel'. Shakespear added that he was aware that a road was in the contemplation of the Lottery Committee extending from Chitpur Road to the College Square and that, 'in furtherance of the object proposed, they may be induced to carry it on the Circular Road'.[49]

On behalf of the magistrates in the Conservancy Department, Shakespear and Charles Trower wrote on 19 September 1823 that 'it will tend essentially to the salubrity of that part of the town lying between the Bow Bazar and Mutchwa Bazar Roads if a tunnel is constructed midway between those roads from the Chitpore Road to the Circular Road', adding that 'this quarter of the town is particularly low and the drains run in a northerly direction for a considerable distance before they turn to the eastward to which the fall in the soil naturally inclines'.[50] In the same letter, the magistrates said that work on the tunnel could begin as soon as the ground for the new road in contemplation of the Lottery Committee (Colootala Street and Mirzapur Street) 'in the direction in which it should be carried' was cleared. Three weeks later, in October, the Government authorised the magistrates to build a tunnel 'or covered drain' along the new road being built by the Lottery Committee at an estimated cost of Rs 33,996-14-0 'under the superintendence of your own officers'.[51]

Fig. 18. A view of the aqueduct in front of the Town Hall. In the distance can be seen Chandpal Ghat. By Frederick Fiebig, 1847

RIVER WATER FOR THE TOWN

The construction of elevated roadside brick-and-mortar channels to convey water from the river to interior areas of the city was first mooted by Lord Minto's Committee for the Improvement of the Town, the proposer being Henry Wood.[1] In the first week of May 1813 he had suggested a plan to extend 'river water supply to the tanks in the event of the rains failing' to the 'part of the town extending from Chandpaul Ghaut to the south-east gate of the Government House, from thence to the east end of Writers' Buildings and the west end of the Durrumtollah'. Wood, of course, had a much larger project in mind the total estimate submitted by him for the entire project, which included the building of a number of roads, adding up to Rs 60,000. Instead of taking up the whole project as suggested by Wood, the committee proposed that only a part be implemented immediately, the option being there to extend the scheme to other parts of the town based on the results of the initial implementation.

The curtailed plan involved building a 'channel', or conduit,[2] 'on the side of the principal streets [through] which the water is to be conveyed from Chandpaul Ghaut'. The committee said that the channel would be built 'much upon the principle of that *already constructed* [emphasis added] on the side of the Course road', the inference here clearly being that the first aqueduct in Calcutta was built on the *maidan* and not along any street. The alignment of the *maidan* channel followed that of the present Red Road and perhaps a part of the road to Khidirpur, but this is not certain. There was a railing to the west of the channel, from Government House to the Chowringhee Gate of the fort, which was removed in March 1815 at the instance of John Eliot.[3] An immediate economic benefit of the project would be the saving in wages paid to the *bheesties* which, it was felt, would 'induce the proprietors of the houses, who now water only a small portion of the streets, to keep the streets well-watered at their own expense'.[4] The committee also said that when the 'drain' (the word used by the committee for the aqueduct) was completed it would afford 'a ready supply of water to the engines for the purpose of extinguishing fires which [in view of] the late conflagrations has been much wanted'.

Since Wood's estimate for the building of the aqueduct (Rs 15,000) was 'on the lowest scale such as only to cover the actual expense attending the construction of masonry', the committee asked the Government to advance the amount, which was done a week later. Wood himself (he had volunteered to superintend the work 'free of expense') was allowed an establishment costing Rs 70 a month which would be chargeable to the funds of the Committee for Improving the Town.[5] Importantly, at this point of time, the central purpose of Wood's 'conduit' was restricted to watering 'the principal streets' of the town.

The aqueduct was completed in 15 months Wood writing to John Eliot and members of the Committee for the Improvement of the Town on 29 August 1814 that 'the whole of the experimental part of the aqueduct [is] finished [along] with the waterwheel[6] and its masonry and the requisite masonry for two complete sets of china pumps', in the process 'fully (answering) the expectations I held out to your committee as an inducement to undertake the work'.[7] He wrote that initially the aqueduct had been planned with the following specifications: the retaining wall being 1 ½ ft thick, 1 ½ ft in height, the waterway 1 ft by 1 ½ ft, the foundation 1 ½

Fig. 19. A view of the aqueduct near Chandpal Ghat. On the left is the Supreme Court building. By James Baillie Fraser, 1826

ft in depth (see later for the measurements of aqueducts built five years later). The entire aqueduct was to have been built 'on a level or a little below the level of the roads'. However, before beginning the work he had checked the level of the roads 'with reference to the bank of the river at Chandpaul Ghaut' and had found that, in order not to disturb the operation of the existing drains 'running between the river and east side of the Government House, as well as to preserve the water from being fouled by the drainings of the roads', the aqueducts had to be constructed *above the ground* 'so as to admit of the aqueduct passing over…the drains, and the drainings of the roads passing under instead of over the aqueduct as originally intended'. In view of this, the construction plan of the aqueduct had to be altered (the depth of the foundation had to be increased 'in proportion to the unevenness of the roads') and as this in some places was 'very considerable' the cost estimate was likely to be affected seriously. Consequently, in an effort to control costs, the dimensions of the aqueduct were revised. The thickness of the retaining wall was reduced from 1 ½ ft, which enabled Wood to increase the breadth of the waterway and reduce the breadth of the foundation, all of which led to the cost being reduced to Rs 15,772-9-8 2/5, which was Rs 772-9-8 2/5 more than the estimate of Rs 15,000.

Wood then focussed on the benefits which could flow to the people generally from an expansion in the aqueduct network. He wrote:

> From the height of the aqueduct at the west end of the Durrumtollah and Bow Bazar, the water may be conveyed to the most distant parts of Chowringhee, the east ends of the above streets, and through many of the adjoining streets, should it be deemed an object worth the consideration of Government. The use now made of the water by all classes of people…induces me to state – the Lottery funds cannot be better expended than in prolonging the aqueduct, and by its means furnishing every class of inhabitants with the first necessity of life in this hot climate, or a supply of water.

The Government asked the magistrates to report back on Wood's suggestion to extend the aqueduct network, which they did a year later,[8] recommending 'a continuation of the aqueduct down the Durrumtollah, Bow Bazar, and to Beerjee Tullow' in the south. In a minute dated 30 August 1815, John Eliot, the president of the Board of Conservancy,[9] wrote that the usefulness of the aqueduct built from Chandpal Ghat was already evident from the response it had elicited from the native inhabitants of the city.[10]

Eliot proposed an establishment to look after the aqueduct already made, which would cost Rs 72 a month (a serjeant for Rs 40

Fig. 20. Natives using the aqueduct at Tank Square. Also seen is the balustrade. By James Baillie Fraser, 1826

and 8 peons for Rs 32), because 'the natives are now converting the aqueduct to the convenience of a resting seat, and loaded baskets are now put upon it to its serious injury, and without such guards it will soon be destroyed, and it is indispensable that every means should be adopted for its preservation'. He suggested that special regulations be drafted so that the police could assist the peons to seize people causing 'injury' to the aqueduct. The two other members of the Board of Conservancy, William Rumbold and C.F. Martyn, agreed with the view to extend the aqueduct along Dharamtala and Bowbazar Streets and to Birjee Talao 'provided the expense do not amount more than 25,000 Rs in each street'.

In the middle of October, the magistrates of the town (Eliot, W.C. Blaquiere, J.B. East, J.B. Birch and R.C. Fergusson) wrote to the Government that they were not 'fully prepared' to back the Board of Conservancy's view regarding the utility of the aqueduct but were subsequently 'persuaded' that 'in addition to the supply of water which it affords for watering the roads, the water is a great public benefit to the inhabitants of the town in general'.

They, therefore, had no hesitation in recommending an extension of the aqueduct along Bowbazar and Dharamtala Streets and to Birjee Talao. In fact, they wanted the stretch to Birjee Talao to be undertaken 'immediately' which would cost the lottery funds Rs 13,545, which was sanctioned a week later.[11] In December, the magistrates told the Government that the construction of the aqueduct from 'the corner of Durrumtulla to Birjee Tullow' had been entrusted to Wood and that steps had been taken to begin the work.

The Government was also informed of the

> ...expediency of removing the railing which at present stands on the eastern side of the Esplanade, on the site of the proposed aqueduct from Durrumtulla to Park Street, and that a parapet wall be erected on the inner wall of the aqueduct and a balustrade fixed thereon *similar to the balustrade round the Loll Diggy* [emphasis added].[12]

The inference here is that when the esplanade was formed half a century earlier, a wooden railing separated it from the Chowringhee Road to the east. The magistrates' letter indicates that the railing was still there in 1815, certainly along the stretch from Dharamtala to Park Street and probably extending southwards till the Birjee Talao as well, marking out the land under the control of the military authorities. The second point to note is that, in December 1815, the tank at BBD Bagh already had a balustrade, which means that the ornamental brick-and-mortar railing in Tank Square was perhaps the earliest such railing to adorn Calcutta's streets (see Fig. 20).[13] The magistrates said that the balustrade project, costing Rs 3,024, would be sensible to undertake because the removal and repair of the existing railing would cost 'nearly what the balustrade can be constructed for' and a balustrade would always be 'an ornament to the Esplanade...(and) be durable and

Fig. 21. The stretch of the Chowringhee Road balustrade between Dharamtala and Park Street in 1865. Photograph by Samuel Bourne

not require the constant repair which a wooden railing calls for'. The balustrade was sanctioned on 22 December, the magistrates being asked to build an aqueduct and balustrade from Dharamtala for a total investment of Rs 16,569. The project, however, had to be curtailed, the decision being taken subsequently 'to extend it no further' than Park Street (see below), the cost being Rs 8,456.[14]

The use of aqueducts represented a quantum shift in the technology used to get water from the river to wash the streets, especially during the summer and winter months when rain was scarce and dust storms were frequent. At its very first meeting on 24 November 1817, the Lottery Committee resolved that 'early measures be adopted for carrying on the aqueduct from the west angle of the Dhurrumtollah to the Circular Road' in the east.[15]

Fig. 22. The aqueduct in front of Government House, around 1865. The building on the left is still standing, sporting a wooden verandah across its frontage. Photograph by Samuel Bourne

In fact, the project had been mooted earlier, in August 1814 (see above), but, as the records indicate, the Government had not authorised its construction as it had done in the case of the tank at Baparitala, the new road from the Dharamtala Street to Bowbazar, the excavation of a tank 'to the north of the great jail', or the deepening of the tank at Dharamtala.[16]

The ball was set rolling at the Lottery Committee's 11 December 1817 meeting when it was resolved that Wood, who had 'fully considered the best means to be adopted' to build the aqueduct in question, be asked to submit 'such observations and suggestions as may appear to him to be useful to the committee on deciding on this point [the aqueduct's extension]'.[17] Wood did so at the end of the month,[18] the committee being told that the Dharamtala Street aqueduct would be much more useful to the community than one along Chowringhee (from the Dharamtala crossing to Park Street and beyond). As he saw it, the extension of

Fig. 23. A painting of the aqueduct in front of the south-east gate of Government House on Old Court House Street by James Baillie Fraser, 1826

the aqueduct to Birjee Talao (that is, till the crossing with Circular Road in the south) would no doubt facilitate the watering of the road in that direction but the benefit arising from it would be confined 'to the few individuals occupying the houses erected to the east of the road, which do not exceed 12 in number'.[19]

This apart, the water available in the tanks on the esplanade to the west of Chowringhee Road was 'amply sufficient to supply every drinkable or culinary purpose to the inhabitants residing to the south of the Burying Ground Road'.[20] Wood said that the number of houses along Chowringhee bore 'no proportion to the number [down Dharamtala Street] and, consequently, the number of individuals likely to benefit from it must be proportionately greater' in the latter locality. Secondly, Wood said that the want of water during the dry season was 'more severely felt in the direction of the Dhurrumtollah than (in) almost any other part of the town', and the aqueduct – the most important function of which was to convey water to the community – would, therefore, be of much greater use in this part of the city. The income profile of people living in the Dharamtala area was also important for the aqueduct to be extended down the street. Wood wrote that the Dharamtala area was 'studded with houses' belonging to Europeans and natives alike, most of whom hailed from 'the middling and poorest classes of countrymen (who) can least afford to pay the expense attending the conveyance of water from the tanks in the Esplanade, at times when the owners of private tanks refuse the public permission to convey any water from them'.

Linked to the proposal for an aqueduct down Dharamtala Street was Wood's suggestion to build a 'new *puckah* drain' on the northern side of the road, the aqueduct being built 'on its retaining wall which would serve the purpose of preventing carriages from falling into the drain and [would] lighten the expense of the two works'.[21] The proposal for a *pucka* drain on the northern side of the road had, in fact, been made by Wood in his 29 August 1814 letter to the Committee for the Improvement of the Town in which he had argued that the drain was 'very much wanted to carry off the immense body of water which flows down [the street], sweeping away in its course the foundations of the walls and houses owing to the defective principles in which the present earthen drains are constructed'. When completed, the drain would 'effectually prevent any future encroachments on [this public road] as well as tend to keep [it] clear of water during the heaviest fall of rain'. Wood had said that the cost of the project would be 'greatly' reduced because the foundation and retaining wall of the aqueduct along the road would form part of the retaining wall of the drain. The drain would have a waterway of 3 ft by 3 ft in the west increasing to 6 ft by 6 ft in the east and would cost an estimated Rs 25,000.[22]

Three years later, writing on 30 December 1817 to the Lottery Committee, Wood reiterated that a drain along Dharamtala Street had been a long-felt need because, while the gradual incline of the ground in the area was towards the salt lake in the east, the existing drain was 'much too narrow' to carry off the water in that direction.[23] Further, instead of the width of the drain gradually increasing 'so as to meet the accumulated body of water in its progress to the eastward', it was constricted at a number of places 'forcing the water out of its natural direction, which on a heavy fall of rain tends to flood the street, and it at all times prevents the drain from being kept in the cleanly state it ought to be (in)'. Not surprisingly, Dharamtala Street was flooded regularly after 'every heavy fall of rain'.[24] In order to prevent such problems in future, Wood said that the bed of the new drain would have 'a gradual slope from the south-east gate of the Government House (which is the highest part of the town) to the Circular Road', its width increasing 'in proportion to its distance from the same point'. Wood wrote that the 'new drain' built on the southern side of the road had been based on faulty principles, its bed being constructed 'with a view (to) conveying part of the water up the natural level of the ground towards the Government House'. This had led to an accumulation of filth in it 'as the water is prevented (from) flowing till such time as a sufficiency has fallen to surmount the artificial level given to the drain, when it flows in its natural direction'. He suggested a reconstruction of the drain's bed which would impart to it a slope in the right direction, that is, from west to east. To be built of masonry comprising the 'very best materials', Wood estimated the cost of the aqueduct-drain project at Rs 26,985. To this would have to be added the monthly salary of a European overseer which 'may amount to 1,200 rupees in the whole [year]'.

The Lottery Committee put off further discussion on the subject till it was 'more accurately informed' about the funds position.[25] At its next meeting held in late January, the committee wrote to the Government backing Wood's project and seeking sanction for the proposed expenditure (Rs 26,986 plus the cost of engaging an European overseer at Rs 100 a month).[26] The approval came through a month later, a subcommittee comprising Bayley, Captain Montague and Wood being formed to implement the project. The composition of the subcommittee underwent change over the next two years, in fact to such an extent that it resulted in the project being delayed much more 'than could have been anticipated'.[27] The project took more than two years to complete, the subcommittee informing the committee on the last day of August 1820 that the total expenditure incurred had been about Rs 500 less than the projected cost of Rs 26,986. The expenditure on the European overseer had overshot the original estimate of Rs 1,200 by Rs 900 because of delays over which the subcommittee had no control.[28]

Bayley and his colleagues on the subcommittee said that the results were good, the

> ...experience of the present rains fully [justifying] the expectations that were entertained of the benefit to be derived from the construction of the drain, which is sufficiently large for the greatest quantity of water that can be collected in it, and however small the quantity none ever remains stagnant in it.

During the dry months, some accumulation of filth would no doubt take place but it would 'be easily removed by the scavengers without any risk of the level being injured as is frequently the case in drains that are not constructed of masonry'. As regards the aqueduct, the subcommittee said that it had not yet started functioning because water had not yet begun to flow into it, but it was hoped that it would 'equally be found to answer the purposes for which it was intended' (see below).[29] Five months later in February

1821, the teething problems of the aqueduct led to Shakespear's proposal that the sides of the reservoir 'at Chaundpaul ghaut' be raised by two feet so that it could hold the extra water required to supply the Dharamtala aqueduct.[30] The Lottery Committee was also told that the new water conduit had been reported to be 'leaky' and that steps would have to be taken to set the problem right. Paton was asked to submit an estimate for the reservoir work and to implement it 'with the least possible delay', the work finally costing Rs 162-8-6 ¼.[31]

During the making of the drain and the aqueduct, a large part of the western section of the Dharamtala Street must have been turned into a busy zone of construction activity. The records indicate that payments for the work being done had begun to flow from the last week of April 1818, work on both the projects having been taken up simultaneously.[32] Among myriad other problems, the disruption of traffic along the road must have been severe, more so along the northern side of the road where both the new drain and the aqueduct were coming up. Inevitably, reports of the disruption found their way into the official records of the time. On 3 May 1819 Shakespear, the Officiating Chief Magistrate of Calcutta, wrote to the Lottery Committee that the 'head scavenger of the south division', J. Stear, had reported the accumulation of a huge amount of earth on Dharamtala Street owing to the building of the aqueduct which had led to some of those living on the street threatening to complain if the rubbish was not removed. A couple of days earlier, Stear had written that 'there is an immense quantity of earth taken out of the new drain in Dhurrumtollah, and are daily taking out more. I suppose upwards of 1,000 loads is now laying [sic] in the road which I am not able to take away with the present establishment of hackeries'. Shakespear suggested that, 'if not otherwise required, the earth may be thrown down at the west end of the Dhurumtollah near the tank where it will be of use in raising the side of the road'. The Lottery Committee agreed with the suggestion and asked Shakespear to go ahead with the work provided the expense was not charged to the lottery funds.

Two months later, in the second week of July 1819, Shakespear drew attention to the state of Dharamtala Road 'in consequence of the building of the new aqueduct and drain'.[33] As he saw it, the main cause of the problem lay in the fact that the aqueduct, being constructed on the north side of the road, was above ground level with the result that those living on that side of the road had been 'forced to throw up mounds of earth to enable them to enter their houses or gateways'. These mounds were '1 or 2 feet high and project 5 or 6 feet into the road, not only rendering it dangerous to approach that side of it but destroying the appearance of the finest road in the town'.[34] There was also an associated drainage problem. The existing drainage channels had a north-south alignment, the water flowing through drains under the aqueduct towards the southern side of the road. Shakespear pointed out that the drain openings were left 'considerably below the level of the road even as it is at present' with the result that they were bound to get 'choked up, as indeed they already are'. He suggested that the northern side of the road be raised sufficiently 'to throw water off from it into the drain on the south side'. This, he felt, was the 'only way left of restoring the beauty of the road and may be done by laying down the *soorkee* rubbish now [lying] in Beparee Tullah'.

The Lottery Committee asked the surveyor to send a report on the subject on the same day (8 July), which Arthur Blechynden did a fortnight later, in which he supported Shakespear's proposal to slope the road from north to south.[35] He said he had found around 33 passages through mounds of earth on the side of the road 'to enable the proprietors of houses to enter their premises'. These heaps 'were not only dangerous as well as unsightly, but by throwing the water towards the centre of the road materially tend to destroy it'. He had also taken levels of the road eastward till the point the aqueduct had been constructed (that is, 'near' Baparitala) – and had found that it was 'consistently' higher than the drain on the southern side of the road.[36] The aqueduct being so much higher than the road, consequently leaving a gap between it and the road surface, 'apertures 18 ½ inches square' had been made 'at regular distances to convey the water off the road under the aqueduct into the public drain north of it'. But in many places these receptacles, being a foot to 1 ½ ft deep, had become 'choked up with *koah* and *surkey* from the road'. This apart, the aqueduct had been sunk into the road at five spots, '3 inches near the Cossitollah, then 6 inches each time at different places, making a fall of 2 ft 3 inches near Beopareetollah'. In other words, at these places there was no gap between the road surface and the aqueduct. In view of his finding that the aqueduct was consistently higher than the drain on the south side of the road and the blockages in the openings leading to the north drain, Blechynden had no difficulty in agreeing with the remedy suggested by Shakespear, namely, sloping the road from north to south 'so that all the water may be conveyed into the drain on the south side'.

The surveyor lamented that the aqueduct was positioned where it was, that is, to the south of the north drain and not between the line of houses and the north drain itself – which would have left the drainage channels from the road into the north drain undisturbed. This would have tackled 'some of the evils pointed out by Mr Shakespear…as the road could then be sloped from the centre to the sides' for effective drainage. However, it is clear that even if the position of the aqueduct was shifted northward, the problem of easy access to the road from the houses to the north of the road would have remained because of the aqueduct itself. Even so, the surveyor suggested that in the remaining stretch of Dharamtala Street eastward, the aqueduct 'be constructed close to the houses, and the public drain be made between it and the road'.

Blechynden's letter to the committee was dated 26 July. In early September the committee asked Shakespear to take on the job of sloping Dharamtala Street from north to south utilising in the process 'the necessary materials from the buildings pulled down at Beopareetollah'.[37] However, the committee did not comment on the surveyor's proposal to position the aqueduct between the line of houses and the north drain on the stretch of Dharamtala Street to the east of the new square.[38] The work was completed in three months. In the middle of December Shakespear submitted the consolidated statement of expenditure on the project, the committee being informed that 'raising and levelling' the north side of the road 'as far as the new square' had reduced 'the inconvenience to which passengers and persons residing in the street were subjected by the mode adopted in the construction of the aqueduct'.[39]

Five months later, in May 1820, Shakespear suggested – a proposal which was accepted by the committee – that the raising and levelling work he had just done be extended to the eastern part of Dharamtala Street 'as far as the aqueduct is carried'. This work would take about two to three months to complete in which time the aqueduct would also be finished. The investment would not exceed that incurred on the western part of the road, or Rs 900. Shakespear was true to his word for he reported to the committee in the middle of August that the job had been completed.[40] The cost, however, had exceeded the estimate by Rs 90-5-10 because the surface area of the road which had to be raised and made 'puckah', extending from the new square to Circular Road in the east, was larger than the corresponding area in the western part of the road. This was because the road east of the square was 'much wider' than its western section, a feature which has not changed over the past two centuries.

Though the aqueduct along Dharamtala Street was completed in 1820, the benefits promised by its construction took some time to materialise because of the inability to direct enough water into it. In early February 1821, the *Hurkaru* was writing[41]

> ...in the studious desire to accomplish much, it may happen that measures, calculated to give full effect to what has been fortunately completed, with the object of increasing public comfort, may be occasionally overlooked. We should imagine that from some such cause the capacious aqueduct, that has been carried along the Durrumtollah, has failed as yet to yield that grateful benefit to the inhabitants of the street, and to those who have occasion to pass through it, which they had been anxiously looking for. The complaints, indeed, that we have heard lately respecting the clouds of dust suffered to sweep along the Durrumtollah, while the means of preventing their rise or accumulation appear to be accessible, have been very numerous, and as far as we have seen from casually passing in that direction, have been very just.

It was just a matter of time before a suggestion was made to extend the aqueduct network to other areas of the city. Chowringhee Road (till Park Street), and Dharamtala Street had been covered, and it was not just a coincidence that Europeans resided in both areas. Cossitala and the road to Chitpur – the other important thoroughfare at the time – were important candidates but the native population in these areas far outnumbered the European complement. Burying Ground Road (Park Street) was gradually taking shape, but it was far from Chandpal Ghat, as was also Chitpur Road. This, however, was not the case with the neighbourhood of Tank Square where, incidentally, the first concentration of Europeans had been located in the immediate aftermath of Charnock's arrival. The locality was not only the original sahib locality, so to speak, but was also close to Chandpal Ghat from where the river's water was being sourced for the budding aqueduct network.

The initial move to get river water to this area was made in February 1819 – more than a year after the Government had sanctioned the Dharamtala aqueduct – by Charles Trower, the Collector of 24-Parganas and a senior member of the Lottery Committee, who wrote that 'numerous representations' had been made to him by 'residents in the streets commencing at the south-west corner of Government House, and the treasury, and continuing in a direct line to the north up to Clive street' about the 'clouds of dust which are constantly flying in these streets' because of a scarcity of water.[42] Trower suggested that the aqueduct 'be continued from the most convenient part of its present course through the streets above alluded to'. The area was home to 'public offices and principal places of resort' which, the Collector felt, could persuade the Lottery Committee to agree with his proposal.

A couple of weeks later, in early March, John Trotter, Secretary to the Lottery Committee, asked the Surveyor, Arthur Blechynden, for information on 'the distance and rate per hundred feet which it might be reasonable to allow for continuing the present aqueduct from the south-west corner of the Government House down to the residence of the late Mr [John] Eliot in Clive Street'.[43] The committee also explored the feasibility of extending the water channel along Bowbazar when it asked the surveyor to find out the distance between 'the eastern extremity of the Loll Bazar and the point in Tank Square whither the aqueduct is now carried'. Blechynden informed the committee that the distance 'from near the south-west corner of the Government House' to the house of the late John Eliot was 3,691 ft and the cost would 'average about 196 Rs per 100 lineal feet of the best *pucka*, including in that sum the expence of syphon drains across streets and the entrance to some of the houses and also of small drains under the aqueduct to carry off the water from the street'.[44] This was a rough calculation because, as the surveyor wrote, no 'regular estimate' of the expense of the project could be formed without taking the 'levels' of the aqueduct from its point of commencement to its termination 'as also the plan of the streets through which it is to pass'. The committee was also told that the distance 'from the Circular Road through the Bow Bazar to the north-east corner of the Loll Dhiggy where the aqueduct terminates' was 6,563 ft. The surveyor was asked to send a 'regular estimate', which he did within the next fortnight, which was forwarded to Captain Phipps, the Superintendent of Buildings, Lower Provinces, for his comments.

Three weeks later, Phipps placed a spoke in the wheel when he wrote that his assistant, Paton, had been able to 'build at 14 rupees instead of 16, which is 1/8th less [than Blechynden's estimate], and if the drain can be taken at the same rate, which I think it may, the expence would only be 6,000 rupees', the surveyor's estimate being Rs 6,865-9-7¼ .[45] The plan of the aqueduct enclosed in Paton's letter is of some interest because it contains construction details which can be compared with Wood's 1814 specifications (see above). The '*pucka* aqueduct' in question was to be 3,691 ft in length, 1,000 ft of which was to be 3-ft high, including foundation, 1 ft 6 inches broad and 1 ft 6 inches deep with 'walls' a foot thick. Another 1,691 ft was to be 3 ft 6 inches high, including foundation, 1 ft 6 inches broad and 1 ft 6 inches deep with walls also a foot thick. The remaining 1,000 ft was to be a 'syphon drain' 4-ft high, including foundation, 3 ft deep, 2 ft broad with 'walls and arch' 1 ft 6 inches thick. At this juncture (29 April), quite abruptly, the committee put off considering the project 'until some general system can be adopted for carrying on and supplying the aqueducts'.

Fig. 24. Thomas Daniell's view of new buildings in Chowringhee in 1787

Even till the middle of the last century, a common sight in Calcutta at daybreak was the watering of its principal streets, the water being sourced from the hydrants by the side of the roads. In the 19th century, the water was brought by *bheesties* first from the numerous tanks and the river itself and then from the aqueducts which had been constructed on some of the main roads of the city. Washing the roads and keeping them clean was an important function of the authorities, but which arm of the Government was to do the job? Should the watering of roads be the financial responsibility of the Lottery Committee or the city magistrates? The subject had cropped up at the beginning of the 19th century with Lord Wellesley crossing swords with the Court of Directors in 1803. While the Governor-General had wanted the Government to take on the responsibility, distant Leadenhall Street had preferred that, instead of the burden being borne by the Government exclusively, 'all European inhabitants of the town as well as the more substantial of the Asian inhabitants of every description' should contribute towards the effort. In 1808, the Court had specifically prohibited the cost of watering the streets to be borne by the authorities. Subsequently, the Committee for the Improvement of the Town had suggested that houseowners in a street contribute towards the cost of watering the street, a proposal which was shot down by the Directors.[46] In later years, the magistrates had begun to water some of the streets once again.

During the Lottery Committee years, the subject cropped up when, in early January 1820, Henry Shakespear informed his colleagues on the committee that he had tried in vain to get residents 'on the east side of Chowringhee Road from Dhurrumtollah Road to Park Street' to subscribe to a scheme of watering the contiguous stretch of the road.[47] The magistrate wrote, 'Some have agreed to do so but many have objected, and the houses indeed are so much detached from each other [as indicated by contemporary paintings of Chowringhee Road (see Fig. 24)] that it would be difficult to realise a sufficient sum for the purpose by [just the] subscriptions of individuals'. He said that this would result in the aqueduct 'constructed at the expense of the committee chiefly for this object [watering of the streets]' being 'rendered in a great measure useless'. The Officiating Chief Magistrate argued:

> As the keeping of the roads in question free from dust during the months of January, February, March, April and May will tend to the comfort of a large portion of the inhabitants of Calcutta, and as I conceive the committee are especially called upon not to allow the aqueduct they have constructed to remain useless, I strongly recommend that the watering of the road be undertaken at the expense of the committee.

Shakespear did not stop at making the suggestion; he offered his services to superintend the establishment to be set up for the work. Working on the assumption that one *bheesti* could water 10,000 square feet of road, he calculated the probable monthly expense of the proposed watering establishment thus: a *sarkar* or *jemedar*, at Rs 10 per month; a *naib* at Rs 6; and 45 *bheesties*, at Rs 4 a month each, totalling a monthly expenditure of Rs 196.

A week later, on 13 January, the committee wrote[48] that while it fully agreed with the magistrate on the importance of the subject of watering roads, under the rules laid down it did not feel 'warranted in suggesting to Government the appropriation of any part of the lottery funds to the purpose of watering the roads'. But since it agreed with Shakespear's view that individual subscriptions would not be able to generate adequate funds for the purpose in question and that the subject was one 'conducive to the health and convenience of the public', it felt that the Government could ask the magistrates to water Chowringhee Road, as far as the aqueduct extended, 'at an expence not exceeding 196 rupees per mensem'. For good measure, the committee added that the scale of expenditure could be reduced to the extent of the subscriptions made by 'those persons occupying houses in the vicinity of the road'. The Government agreed with the suggestion to set up an establishment to water Chowringhee Road, from Dharamtala Street to Park Street, at a cost not exceeding Rs 196 per month 'until the commencement of the rains', the magistrates being asked 'to entertain an establishment of *bheesties* for the purpose'.[49] In effect, therefore, the Government accepted Shakespear's idea of an establishment being set up to water the stretch of road concerned at a maximum cost suggested by him and also took into consideration the Lottery Committee's stand that it would be unable to bear the cost of such work.

The aqueducts made watering of the streets more 'efficient' in that the *bheesties* did not have to carry the water in their *mussacks* all

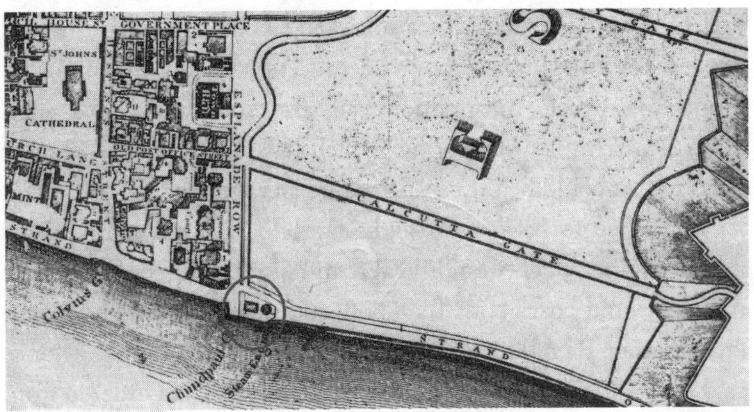

Fig. 25. Schalch's map (1824) showing the location of the reservoir at Chandpal Ghat from which water was supplied to the aqueducts

the way from the tanks, or even the river, to the spot to be watered but had just to fill their sacks from the roadside masonry channels. Before piped water began to be supplied throughout the town,[50] the water in the aqueducts came from the 'reservoir' located at Chandpal Ghat, to the south of the Supreme Court (where the Calcutta High Court stands today). Before steam power was used to fill the reservoir with water raised from the river, 'china' (or suction) pumps were used to do the job.[51] The *bheesties* were also used to raise water which is reflected in the contemporary expenditure accounts of the Government.[52]

It was but a matter of time before the next 'jump' in technology presented itself to help raise water from the river.[53] The committee had come to know in the middle of July 1818 from one of its members, Arthur Macan, that William Jones, 'an intelligent architect and mechanic', had ideas about the erection of a steam engine at Chandpal Ghat for raising water from the river and that he had in fact 'commissioned' such an engine from England.[54] The committee asked Jones about the cost of a 10 horse-power steam engine and the 'probable expense of the additional machinery and buildings which it will be necessary to construct to raise the water for the aqueduct'. He was also asked about the establishment needed for 'the management of the engine' and the probable monthly expense. Information was also sought on how soon after the arrival of the engine, 'which it is understood is shortly expected', it could be set up and made operational.

Jones wrote back a fortnight later to say that a 10 horse-power engine which would be able to raise 4 ½ tons of water per minute would cost about Rs 8,000, additional machinery, house, etc., another Rs 6,000, adding up to a total of Rs 14,000.[55] Jones said that if the committee wanted the engine he had ordered from England he would gladly hand it over and 'forego any little profit I might have upon the sale of it provided the public were better served'. However, he passed on the information that J Calman and Company had ordered two other engines of 8 horse-power strength which 'were particularly ordered for raising water 30 feet, which is the greatest height of your reservoir'. If both were installed, the cost of operating them would be a little more than working a 10 horse-power engine 'as one house with a partition and one chimney with double flues would do for them'. Further, both engines would be able to work at the same time 'with little more attendance than would be necessary for one and they would possess the advantage of never being [totally] idle, as one would work while the other underwent repairs'.

Jones's letter made the Calman steam engines (which were meant to pump out water from docks and operate at 'large indigo works') look attractive, which led the committee to enquire whether the company was prepared to sell the engines to it and at what price. Jones had written that the Calman engines were scheduled to arrive in June of that year, but for three-and-a-half months there was no response from the company to the committee's letter. When it did respond in late November, it apologised for not being able to provide 'a definite answer' on the price of the engines 'as their invoices have not yet arrived' because of delay in the arrival of the consignment. As regards the 'necessary buildings' and the cost of working the engines, the point was made that Jones's estimate would not be exceeded.[56] Another interminably long period of silence ensued, the company finally writing to the committee on 19 January 1820 that the two 'pumping engines' of 6 horse-power each (not 8 horse-power, as Jones had informed the committee) had indeed arrived, and that they would be able to handle 'a quantity of water fully equal to what the present brick aqueducts from Chandpaul Ghaut are capable of conveying and are made on the most simple principles to obviate any difficulty in keeping them always in perfect repair'. Each engine was capable of pushing about 34,650 gallons of water every hour which,

> ...if conveyed by pipes to any elevated part of the city, can be distributed to the lower parts by small brick aqueducts, the importance of which when fires are prevalent and the convenience and comfort of watering the roads at all times are too obvious to need further recommendation to your notice.

The total cost of the two engines would be Rs 28,000, the monthly recurring expenditure for one being Rs 300, which the company felt was 'very considerably less than the monthly expenses at present incurred at Chandpaul Ghaut while the quantity of water will be increased on a three-fold proportion'.

The letter also threw light on a problem being faced by the authorities in disposing of accumulated filth on the banks of the river. Extolling the virtues of one of the two engines, the company wrote that the equipment was 'particularly adapted' to assist the members of the committee

> ...in removing the nuisance so generally complained of at Jackson's Ghaut,[57] by supplying the reservoir with water, to

> force the filth through a culvert into that part of the current of the river which would convey it away without offence to the inhabitants and those living on board the different vessels at moorings in the manner that has been suggested.

The sales pitch, however, had little effect for in early February the committee wrote just one sentence to the company stating that 'no immediate prospect' existed of acquiring either of the steam engines offered by it.[58]

The dismissive nature of the Lottery Committee's communication to Calman and Company may be explained partly by the fact that, in the meantime, things had started moving on the William Jones front. On 25 March 1819, Jones had informed the committee that the engine ('of 10 horses double power') made by Butterly Iron Works of Derbyshire, which he was offering, had 'at last arrived with as many extra articles as will last fifty years and all necessary tools for an engine house'. The equipment had been tested in England and had 'proved to be an excellent one'.[59] Providing a clue as to why he had promoted the virtues of the Calman engines, Jones wrote that he had an alternative use for the engine he had ordered, but since he had given the committee the first right of refusal it was now at the committee's service. The total cost of the engine, including transport, was £917-7 shillings, the engine itself being worth £600.[60]

Opinion within the committee on Jones's engine was divided. Bayley said that while the price seemed 'moderate enough' the purchase could be effected only if the committee could show 'when, where and for what purpose we want it'. Colvin and Macan said that Jones should be asked if he could keep the engine with him for some time ('without much inconvenience') till 'we can come to a decision about it, say for a fortnight from this time', which did not turn out to be the case. Gordon was more positive and said that the engine should be bought as it would be '[a good] buy for the cheapest and most effectual mode of raising water'. He suggested that it could be set up at one of the ghats in Clive Street and that the committee could pay '30 per cent on the invoice price, or say 10,000 rupees, which will do little more than (look after) the expence of bringing it out, etc'. Trower, the Collector of 24-Parganas, advocated purchase 'if we are sure we can get people to manage it properly'. Looking at the subject differently, Barwell said the engine could be 'quite useless if, as at present, there be no receptacle for the water that would be thereby raised', implying that a new reservoir would have to be made since the engine would be 'sufficient…for the supply for the present reservoir'. Referring to Gordon's suggestion, he felt that another reservoir would have to be built 'before we lay out 10,000 Rs for what will be useless to us until that shall have been done'.[61]

The committee asked Macan to find out from Jones 'what precise sum he would require for the engine', the cost of erecting it and getting it working, and also the quantity of water that would be raised to a height of 24 ft 'in a stated time'. Jones replied in early April stating that he would sell the engine 'with all spare articles and tools' for Rs 9,000, set up the 'pump building and other machinery' for Rs 6,000, build a new reservoir twice the extent of the old one for Rs 1,600, and provide 'European labour and instruction to the people who are to work the engine, for six months after it starts' for another Rs 1,600, all adding up to Rs 18,200. This figure would not include 'filling in low ground or other troublesome occurrences'.[62] Jones offered to undertake to 'erect the works perfect and complete' and also to superintend 'the works for six months after they are furnished' for a consolidated Rs 20,000. Alternatively, he would superintend the business 'for 10 per cent on the outlay, whichever is most agreeable'. The 'probable cost' of working the engine night and day would be Rs 440 per month, the engine being capable of raising about 5 tons of water per minute to a height of 24 ft.

On 15 April, the committee wrote to the Government recommending that the engine be procured for the town, the step representing substantive progress in the effort to develop the healthiness and cleanliness of Calcutta. It said that the engine was required 'more immediately...for the purpose of raising water to supply the aqueducts already constructed or in progress, and those which it may hereafter be found necessary or expedient to construct for the convenience and comfort of the community'. At the same time, the committee wanted to 'combine with that object the means of cleansing some of the principal drains' of the town. It wrote that the 'large body of water which the engine is capable of raising, namely 5 tons a minute from the height of 24 feet, is abundantly sufficient for these purposes'. The price of the engine, at Rs 9,000, was considered to be 'extremely reasonable' there being no problem in building the facility which would house the engine or in providing for its 'proper and safe superintendence'. Its operational cost would not exceed whatever was being incurred for raising water at Chandpal Ghat.

As regards location of the engine and the new reservoir, the Government was told that since expert advice was needed on the subject the committee would not proffer a definitive suggestion. Even so, it stuck its neck out when it wrote that 'the vicinity of the new office for the collection of the town duties in Clive Street will be found best adapted for the purpose'.

However, since the basis for the suggestion was not foolproof, the committee suggested the appointment of 'an engineer officer (who) may be permitted by Government (to) verify the levels now in the possession of the committee, to take such further levels as may appear necessary, and to furnish the committee with his advice and opinion' on a number of points. These were: the best location for the engine and the reservoir and the size of the latter; the construction of a main aqueduct which would be connected 'with the present aqueducts, and of its supplying such smaller aqueducts as may be hereafter required, to furnish a sufficient quantity of water for the convenience of the community in all the most populous parts of this city'; combining the scheme of aqueducts with 'a plan for cleansing some of the principal drains by throwing into them a large body of water from the main aqueduct'; and the 'probable expense which the completion of these several objects would involve'. The agenda suggests that the authorities were now prepared to use the network of aqueducts not just to supply water for watering the roads (which was Henry Wood's initial justification for setting up aqueducts) but to promote generally the healthiness and cleanliness of the town.

The committee wrote that without the aid of an experienced and 'scientific engineer' it could not 'judge of (the engine's) practicability, of its probable expense, or of the best means of eventually carrying it into effect'. The 'greatest accuracy' would be needed to determine 'the best direction for the main aqueduct, and in securing its proper elevation with reference to the general load of other parts of the town'. Two weeks later, on 30 April, the proposal for the steam engine was approved and an expenditure of Rs 9,000 sanctioned. Lt William Forbes was deputed to look after the engine's operations 'to the extent which his other official avocations may conveniently allow'.[63] A week later (6 May), the committee asked Jones to 'retain charge of the engine and the other articles' till a site was found for the construction of the reservoir'. Jones agreed to the proposal reassuring the committee that 'the most particular parts of the engine being packed in leaden cases can take no harm, nor are they liable to be lost'. He asked the committee to pay him the amount due to him for the engine 'to keep him harmless', which was agreed to. As he put it, his friends would be of little help because they were 'circumscribed and engaged in speculations not likely to be speedily productive'. He had borrowed funds from Alexander and Company to pay for the engine and if the committee paid the value of the engine 'to those gentlemen, it will save me interest and enable me to invest the amount in another engine which I shall shortly want'.[64]

Seven months later, in the first half of December, the committee stirred itself into action once again when it felt the need to ascertain 'whether the apparatus attached to the steam engine bought from Mr W Jones is complete in every respect to admit of its being immediately used'.[65] Perhaps it was the death of Macan three months earlier which led the committee to revisit the subject. A letter was despatched to Jones who wrote back to say that his steam engine was 'complete in all points' and had 'spare articles sufficient to repair any injury it may sustain for many years, with the tools and implements necessary for the engine-keeper'.[66] However, he said he had made it clear in past correspondence that there was 'no machinery beyond the fly-wheel shaft, and still requires all the pumps and machinery belonging to them' which he proposed to furnish with the engine-house and reservoir for Rs 11,000 in addition to the price of the engine, 'being in all sicca Rs 20,000'. Jones said that he proposed 'to instruct a person to manage it and see that it worked well for six months without any further charge for my attendance'. Should the committee appoint anyone else to run the engine, Jones said that he had enclosed 'a list of articles that I expect by the first ship, some of which would be useful in erecting the works and can be had from me at a moderate price'. The committee took no action on the proposal and let the letter 'lie for future consideration'.

Nine months later, things moved decisively on the steam engine front. On 21 September 1820 a subcommittee was formed comprising Trower, Shakespear, Wood and Schalch which would have to consider and report 'on the place which may appear most eligible on the banks of the river for erecting and establishing the steam engine'.[67] Schalch was included in the subcommittee in view of his work on ascertaining the levels in different parts of the city, which would be important in determining the spot where the reservoir would have to be located from where the water would flow through the main aqueduct into the town's drains.

Even in the early 19th century, pollution was an issue of public comment and debate in Calcutta.[68] In early December the Lottery Committee wanted to know specifically whether the use of wood instead of coal as fuel for the engine would 'materially or entirely' remove the 'inconvenience' resulting from the smoke generated by the project.[69] A letter was written 'to several gentlemen who are known to use fire engines in and near Calcutta', among whom were the Serampore missionaries Joshua Marshman and William Carey, the committee's request to them being that they use wood as fuel for their engines for 'two or three days' and then report back on whether 'the smoke from the engine is so materially diminished as no longer to be inconvenient or offensive to the immediate vicinity', and whether the use of wood 'considerably enhances the expense of fuel for the engine and in what portion as compared with coal'.[70]

The subcommittee took four long months to report back on both the subjects, namely, the location of the steam engine and the pollution aspect. On 6 April 1821 it wrote that, considering the levels at the different points of the city, the highest point was 'the top of Meerbuhr Ghaut' (Mirbahar Ghat) and that, 'supposing there (was) sufficient space to admit of aqueducts being constructed on the sides of the roads', water could be conveyed from that point on the riverbank 'to the north as far as Rath Ghat [at the foot of Shobha Bazar Street],[71] to the east as far as the Circular Road, and to the south as far as Chanpaul Ghaut'.[72] However, the subcommittee felt that it would not be possible to implement the plan because of the 'insuperable obstacles' the authorities would have to overcome, including the widening of 'the road from Clive Street to Ruth Ghaut, of Cotton Street and the Mutchooa Bazar Road, and also of Council House Street' in the south, a job which would involve 'an incalculable expense which the funds of the committee are wholly unable to meet'.

In view of this, the steam engine was proposed to be set up at a spot between Chandpal Ghat and the fort 'at the end of the Esplanade walk [the Respondentia] where the shed still stands over the works formerly erected for raising water at that place' (see Fig. 25). The selection of the spot was backed by the argument that from there it would be able to

> …command the whole of the present aqueducts which, agreeably to the levels, might be extended…down the Bow Bazar Road, and to the northward if necessary on the new Central Road[73] from the Dhurumtollah Street to the Mutchooa Bazar Road, besides being carried throughout the whole of the European part of the town lying to the south of Dhurumtollah Street, wherever the width of the streets will admit of aqueducts being constructed.

As regards the pollution aspect, the Lottery Committee was informed that the 'most satisfactory experiments' had confirmed that the use of wood would be less dirty than coal.[74] This apart, the placing of the engine by the side of the river would be an additional reason for air pollution not spreading to the city.

Some light was thrown on the construction of the city's drains at the time when it was pointed out that though the engine would help to get water into the interior of the city through the aqueducts, it would not assist much in flushing out the myriad drains. In conclusion, the subcommittee hoped that the Lottery Committee would agree to set up the steam engine 'without which…it will be impossible sufficiently to supply the existing aqueducts or to extend them'.

Two weeks later, on 19 April, the committee sought the Government's approval for the project which came through in early May after the military authorities had cleared the setting up of the steam engine and the reservoir at the locations selected by the Lottery Committee.[75] On 10 May, after a gap of 18 months, the subcommittee was asked to get in touch with Jones specifically to ask him whether he was still interested in the project on the terms he had offered two years earlier (April 1819), the only change being the cost of operating the engine which would now be run on wood instead of coal. The Government had only agreed to pay for the engine, spares and tools,[76] and the committee felt that a clear assertion of Jones's continuing interest in the project was required before the Government could be approached for the release of additional funds. In particular, the subcommittee was asked to suggest which of the two alternatives offered by Jones (see above) to superintend the working of the engine could be accepted and, more generally, the mode to be adopted for 'the permanent superintendence and conduct of the engine'.[77]

At this point, the unfolding story of the installation of the steam engine was interrupted by the death of 'Mr Jones of Seebpore' which was communicated to the Lottery Committee by G Jessop and Company in late September 1821.[78] Since the event was likely to lead to a delay in the erection of the project on the riverbank, Jessop offered his company's services 'as civil engineers to complete such works as had been taken in hand by our much regretted friend and left unfinished by his decease', on the same terms as those agreed to by Jones. The company, in fact, offered the carrot of completing the work at a lower price. Jessop said that the pumps which Jones had intended to instal were in its possession and that the committee could have them at the price agreed to

Fig. 26. William Wood's 1833 rendition of Esplanade Row (West) showing the steam engine at Chandpal Ghat

by him. The very next day (27 September) the subcommittee was asked to take a decision on the issue but was cautioned that it should use its 'discretion in the selection of a proper person for the duty in question' which should be based on 'such enquiries as you may be enabled to make into the comparative capabilities of the different engineers in Calcutta for such an undertaking'.[79]

In early February 1822 the Government sanctioned the Lottery Committee's estimate for setting up a 'substantial octagon' steam engine 'on the south side of the reservoir near Chaundpaul Ghat'.[80] The site for the engine house had been altered and the cost of the project (Rs 24,305-10-9) was higher than that estimated earlier. The subcommittee said that the new spot chosen was 'the only one where it could be erected to command the existing aqueducts'. Further, the spot would also have the advantage 'of the reservoir which, with a trifling addition to it, will be sufficient to contain a large body of water (600 tonnes) for the supply of the aqueducts during the ebb of the tide when it may not be practicable to work the pumps'. The pollution aspect would be taken care of by the fact that the chimney – seen in the paintings of the riverbank of the time – would be 62 ft high which would ensure that the smoke issuing from it would be carried 'far above the neighbouring houses'. The subcommittee, in fact, categorically gave the assurance that the 'inhabitants in the neighbourhood' would not have to face 'the smallest inconvenience or annoyance from the smoke provided wood alone [was] used for the boiler'.

HARE STREET AND ITS VICINITY

Any map of Calcutta will show that the area to the west and south-west of BBD Bagh (Tank Square) is covered by a grid of straight streets. But this was not always so. The grid we see today emerged early in the 19th century solely as a result of the Lottery Committee's work. In fact, the road layout in the area prior to the committee's work is perhaps the best proof that the early growth of the town was wholly unplanned. Yet, this was the area where the seat of the East India Company's Government in

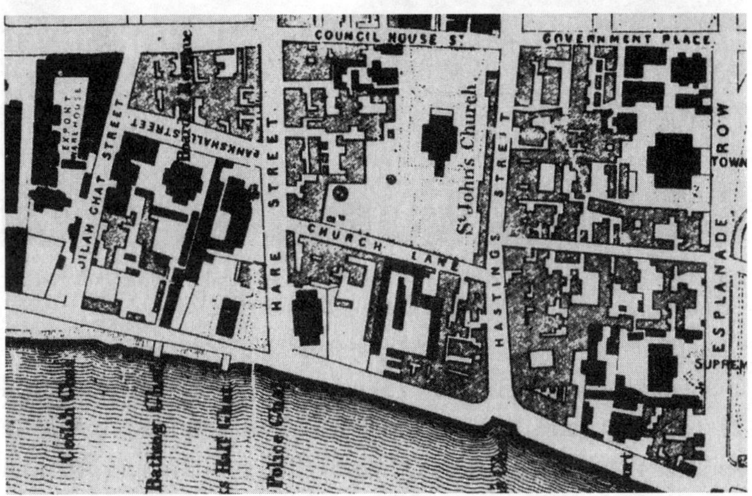

Fig. 27. W. Heysham's map of 1856 shows the Tank Square (BBD Bagh) area after the roads were straightened out

Fig. 28. The monument over the grave of Admiral Charles Watson, in St John's churchyard

Bengal was located prior to 1757 when Shiraj-ud-Daula attacked the English garrison in the first Fort William, and even more so after the recovery of the town by Robert Clive and Admiral Charles Watson. The area, in fact, had come to form the heart of the English town within a couple of decades of Job Charnock's

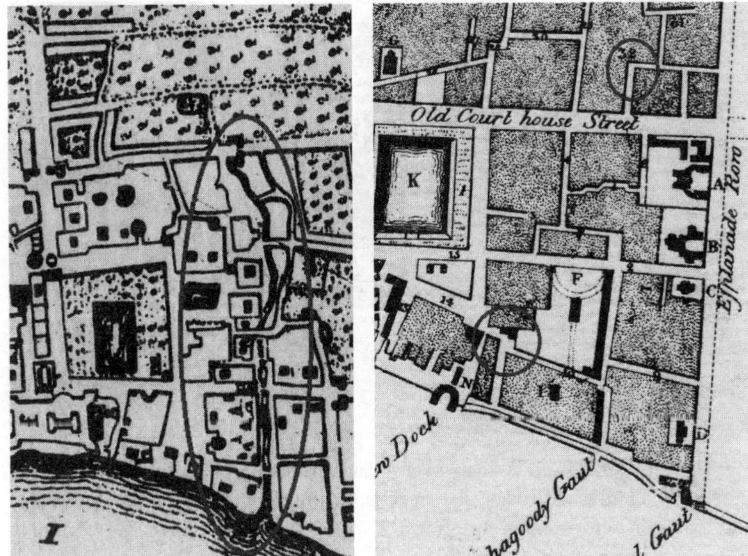

Fig. 29. Left: Detail of the 1742 map showing the creek and the first graveyard of the settlement. Charnock had arrived just 50 years earlier

Fig. 30. Right: Wood's map of 1784 showing St John's Church F, the Mint I, Bankshall Street 14, Church Lane 10, and Post Office Street 9. Also shown is the location of the constriction-spot at the northern end of Church Lane and Dacre's Lane 32 as it existed at the time

landing at Sutanati in August 1690, the gradual expansion of the English presence covering wider areas progressively, especially to the east and south.

The earliest map extant of the area is that which shows the 'territory of Calcutta marked out in the year 1742', followed by William Wells' plan of Calcutta in 1753, Mark Wood's map of 1784-85 and that by Aaron Upjohn in 1792-93. All four maps (Figs 29 to 32) show that today's Hare Street did not exist till the close of the 18th century. In 1742, the alignment of Hastings Street (Kiran Shankar Roy Road) is marked by the old creek making its way eastward from the river with a couple of bridges thrown across it; but there is no road as such. Only two roads, both of which have come down to us 270 years later, can be seen

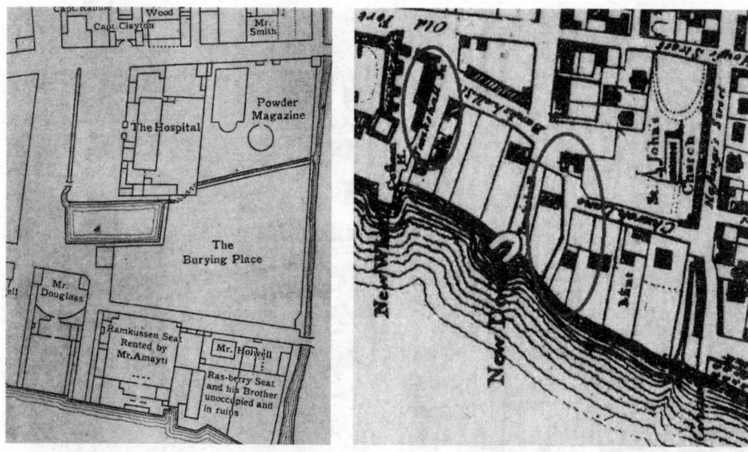

Fig. 31. Left: Detail from William Wells' plan of Calcutta, 1753. The Burying Place is St John's churchyard today; the creek is on the right. The location of the first hospital of the settlement is also shown

Fig. 32. Right: Detail from Upjohn's map of 1793 showing the Bankshall Street-Church Lane 'constriction', Tanskshall Street and Police Office Lane leading to Police Ghat

in the 1742 and 1753 maps, namely, Council House Street – previously known as 'the road to the [Holwell] monument' – and Church Lane, to the west of St John's Church.[1] But within the next 40 years, as is clear from Wood's 1784-85 map, both Hastings Street and Bankshall Street had emerged in their rudiment, the map also showing the mint[2] to the west of Church Lane and the church itself, the first cathedral of the town of Calcutta (see Fig. 35). Wood's and Upjohn's maps are very similar to each other; after all, not even a decade separated the two. The latter shows a Tankshall Street (erstwhile Koilaghat Street, today's Tarapada Mukherjee Sarani) to the south of the old fort.[3]

The only 'good' road was Church Lane, disfigured by buildings and godowns jutting out into the passage. By the time Wood drew his map in 1784-85, the eastern part of Hastings Street had taken shape – from the Council House Street end till the post office which was situated to the north of Post Office Street.[4] This was

Fig. 33. Left: The barely visible plaque indicating the house on today's Kiron Shankar Roy Road where Warren Hastings, the first Governor-General of India, resided

Fig. 34. Right: A detail of Upjohn's map showing King's Bench Walk and Vrignon's godowns which obstructed Hastings' Street

probably because Warren Hastings' family dwelling house was located at No. 7.[5] Till Church Lane the road was like any other, but beyond that point it was practically impassable because of the godowns which lined the road on the northern side. In fact, in 1805, Lord Wellesley's Committee for the Improvement of the Town described Hastings Street as 'ending' at Church Lane.[6] As regards Bankshall Street, both Wood and Upjohn identify it by name its alignment then being a bit different from what it is today. In the late 18th century, Bankshall Street was nothing more than just a broad passage (not a *road* in the conventional sense of the term) to Church Lane further to the south-west, the passage being severely obstructed by sharp bends and an assemblage of transport equipages perennially gathered there in view of the police office being located towards the river and accessed by a narrow lane. David Hare's house was situated at the point of congestion, to the north of the church grounds (see Fig. 45).

Both the problems – the obstruction caused by godowns to the continued passage of Hastings Street to the riverside and the congestion at the point where Bankshall Street met Church Lane – were severe enough to have been mentioned by the special committees set up during the time of Lord Wellesley in 1804. In fact, the special committee to improve 'the environs of the town of Calcutta' had specifically proposed that 'the range of godowns obstructing the passage from Hastings Street to the river – known as Vrignon's godowns[7] – be removed', the reason being that

> …this narrow passage is the principal thoroughfare for goods and passengers proceeding from Chandpaul Ghaut and Kootchagoody (Cutchagoody) Ghaut into the town and, consequently, carriages, hackeries and palanquins are frequently interrupted in their progress and detained, to the great inconvenience of the inhabitants, and obstruction to the commerce of the town.[8]

Nine years earlier, in 1796, the Justices of the Peace had written: 'No part of the town is more frequented than Cutch Goody Ghaut, close to which the depth of the water being sufficient to admit of large ships, many vessels of that description are continually receiving and discharging cargoes.'[9]

Available evidence suggests that the *entire* length of Hastings Street was used by traders to stock their wares and not only the part of the street near the river. As early as 17 April 1780, J.D. Pearse and John Petrie, administrators to the late Colonel John Fortnom, wrote to the Calcutta Committee of Revenue that Fortnom had 'erected a range of godowns' on land north of the drain which he had constructed from the 'great street [Council House Street] down to Cutch Godee Gaut' at his own expense.[10] In fact, both Wood's and Upjohn's maps show these godowns as being located to the south of St John's Church. As regards the congestion at the point where Bankshall Street met Church Lane, the 1804 special committee pointed out that a 'similar inconvenience' arose from the 'narrow and irregular passage between the houses occupied at present by Mr Hare, the watchmaker, and Mr Terry contiguous to the Bankshall'. The special committee wanted the road to be widened and 'a more regular direction be given to it', the Committee for the Improvement of the Town agreeing with both the suggestions.

Being contiguous to the river, this area of the town was closely tied up with commercial interests, and it was only to be expected that with the expansion of trade and commerce the situation would get worse. Consequently, it was just a matter of time before the Lottery Committee turned its attention to improving conditions there. The Governor-General himself took the initiative to clear the western end of Hastings Street, and it was only after this that the committee began to act.[11] On 12 February 1818 the Executive Officer of Fort William, Major Thomas Wood, wrote to the committee that the Governor-General, just before leaving the city on one of his tours, had asked him to enquire 'whether a range of godowns from the north end of Old Post Office Street along the north side of Hastings Street and extending down to the river' could be purchased so as to make that street 'of the same breadth from its eastern end down to the ghaut'. Wood informed the committee that Alexander Colvin, one of its members, had spoken to Vrignon, the owner of the godowns, who had agreed to sell the property for Rs 42,000.[12]

A survey of the godowns conducted by Arthur Blechynden, Surveyor to the committee, revealed that they occupied 15 *katha*s 5 *chittack*s, the stables owned by Vrignon to the east (towards Church Lane) 1 *katha* 1 ½ *chittack*s, and the ground to the west of the godowns (towards the river) 'including the stables of the house tenanted by Mr Becher'[13] 3 *katha*s 14 *chittack*s. Blechynden wrote that since the price of land in the area ranged between Rs 1,000 to Rs 1,200 a *katha*, the godowns, given 'their situation and the rents they bring in', could be worth between Rs 20,000 to Rs 25,000. He corroborated Colvin's figure of Rs 42,000 sought by Vrignon as the value of his godowns and the stabling to the west, including the price of the ground they occupied.[14]

The committee felt that the price sought by Vrignon was too high and decided to explore 'a more economical plan to obviate the inconvenience and danger resulting from the very confined nature of Hastings Street *at the east end of the godowns* [emphasis added] belonging to Mr Vrignon'.[15] The quotation above is important because it indicates the precise spot where the constriction in the passage of Hastings Street was at its worst, namely, to the west of the point where the road was met by Church Lane. Vrignon was unwilling to dispose of the stabling 'at the corner of Church Lane' and yet, as the committee saw it, acquiring the spot was essential to the effective implementation of its plans as was also 'a small part of the godown adjoining to them', and also 'a part of the ground occupied by godowns attached to the house belonging to Nilmunny (Nilmony) Chunder' on the opposite side of the road.[16] Blechynden wrote that acquiring these spots of ground would not only 'widen the street considerably in the narrowest part' but would also 'improve the appearance of this part of the town'.[17] It was hoped that Vrignon would agree to dispose of the stables at the corner of Church Lane after he was apprised of the committee's overall plan by the surveyor, the latter being also asked to find out if Nilmony Chunder would be willing to sell the ground required to the south of the road and at what price.

Vrignon, however, stood firm intimating the committee that he would 'rather keep the godowns than dispose of them, or any part of them, as the remuneration they would give me would never equal the rent I now receive for them'. However, since he would not like to offer 'any obstacle against a public benefit', which is what the widening of Hastings Street would represent, he was prepared to dispose of one godown, 'with the stables, coach house, etc to the east' (which is what the committee wanted) for not less than Rs 9,000, adding that he be allowed 'the remainder of the ground which the committee might have unemployed after the completion of the proposed improvement' on which he could build new stables, coach house, etc, for 'otherwise my house at No. 3/3rd will be entirely spoilt'. If the committee wanted to take two godowns his price would be Rs 16,000 to which would be attached the same condition applicable to the sale of one godown.[18] Blechynden felt that while the price sought by Vrignon was 'certainly high for the small quantity of ground required', it had to be kept in mind that the sale would deprive him of one of his large godowns not to speak of the cost of putting up new stables. As for Nilmony Chunder, the surveyor said that the price he was seeking for his ground was 'exhorbitant in the extreme'. Chunder was supposed to have got back to him with a firm offer 'in a day or two', which had not happened leading Blechynden to the view that he was not keen on selling the ground.[19]

Setting aside the price issue, the Lottery Committee focussed on a barter deal and asked its surveyor to find out whether Vrignon would be interested in '[taking] the spot of unoccupied ground laying to the southward of the road running from Tank Square to [Koila] Ghaut in part payment for such portion of his present property as it may eventually be resolved to purchase'.[20] The ploy failed, for nearly two weeks later Blechynden reported (on 6 May 1818) that Vrignon was not interested in the barter proposal because the property offered was 'too far from my house'.[21]

The surveyor also wrote that, in conformity with the plan of continuing the north side of Hastings Street 'in a direct line to the river', he had calculated the quantum of extra ground needed for the project at nearly 11 *katha*s the value of which would be around Rs 16,000. This, however, would exclude 'the deterioration of property which such an arrangement must occasion by taking so much ground from each house as not to leave sufficient space for rebuilding the out-offices'. Blechynden was then asked to find out whether Vrignon was willing to sell his entire property 'extending from Church Lane to the riverside' and at what price. The property was substantial, the committee being told that it comprised '4 upper-roomed houses with a range of godowns to the south' containing between 6 and 7 *bigha*s of ground valued around Rs 2,50,000.[22] This last initiative was the result of discussions among committee members some of whom had referred to the method of raising resources employed in projects like the Baparitala tank and square, namely, that if the property could be acquired on 'reasonable terms' that part of it not required for the project in hand could later be sold at a higher price thus effectively reducing the cost of widening Hastings Street to 'a comparatively trifling expense'. But this move, too, got nowhere with Vrignon pleading inability to sell the property because it was in the shape of 'bequests of my late father to me and other members of our family'. Faced with a tough roadblock on the Vrignon front, the Lottery Committee asked Blechynden to pursue the unfinished business with Nilmony Chunder who continued to play hide-and-seek with the surveyor, finally not providing the information sought by the committee.[23] Perhaps, Chunder was not taking Blechynden seriously which led the committee to ask Barwell, Magistrate of the Suburbs of Calcutta, to interact with Chunder directly. The change in stratagem worked: the very next day (19 June 1818) Chunder sent a letter to Blechynden stating that since the ground required by the committee stood 'stable, coach house and godowns' without which no tenant would take his house, he was not in a position to sell the land required for the widening of Hastings Street. But, of course, he had no objection to selling his entire property which stood on a *bigha* and 10 *katha*s provided the Government paid him a sum which would fetch him a monthly interest of Rs 500 which would be equivalent to the monthly rent for his house. For all his alacrity in responding to Blechynden's queries after being informed of the entry of Barwell on to the stage, Nilmony Chunder was a day too late: the committee chose not to respond to his letter till it had received a report from the Magistrate of the Suburbs.[24]

In early July 1818, the Lottery Committee sought to widen its focus and include in it the north end of Church Lane, that is, the end towards the bankshall. Noting that people were being put to great inconvenience because of the 'confined entrance from Bankshall Street into Church Lane' (see Wood's and Upjohn's maps Figs 30 and 32), it asked the surveyor to submit to it

> ...a plan of the street extending from Hastings Street to the Banks Hall and that he enquire and report whether the proprietors of the small houses opposite to the west end of the house belonging to Mr Hare, the watchmaker, are willing to dispose of them and, eventually, the sums required for those premises and the sums which he may consider them to be worth.[25]

Clearly, the objective was to remove the houses which would have reduced the congestion in the area.

A decade earlier, in the middle of 1809, the western part of Hare's house was in the limelight for a different reason. At the time, there was some movement regarding the ownership of property at the point where Church Lane met Bankshall Street, a kink in the alignment of the roads leading to severe congestion. On 7 July of that year David Hare wrote to the 'worshipful magistrates for superintending the police of Calcutta'[26] that he had come to know that the Government was selling off a plot 'to the westward of my house' and that he was not happy with the development. The sale, he said, would not only cause 'very considerable injury to my property by blocking me up to the westward, and closing up a door and window, which has been open in my house for these 30 years' but it would also 'hurt the public road of which it [the plot to be sold] makes a part'. Hare said that the ground put up for sale formed 'a recess in a very narrow part of the street by which alone carriages are enabled to turn or pass one another conveniently'. The space also afforded a place 'for the carriages and hackerys which come to the police office every day to stand at without interruption to the road'. He said that if the plot was sold it would render 'one of the principal avenues to the church, mint and the police office very inconvenient'. Providing a clue to the precise location of his house, Hare wrote:

> When I purchased my house[27] I considered it of more value because it was open on three sides on which I thought it could not be blocked up, two being bounded by the street and one by the churchyard. I have, however, found that a piece of the churchyard to the southward has already been sold by private contract, unknown to me, and now a piece of the road to the westward is advertised for sale.

Hare offered to buy the plot to prevent it from being taken by 'persons who would injure me and employ it for disagreeable purposes' at a price which would be 'as much or even more than any ground has been sold for in this neighbourhood for the last 12 months'.

The magistrates sent Hare's letter to the Government with a supportive covering note which said that

> Without giving any opinion on the reasonableness of Mr Hare's proposal to purchase this ground for his own use, if any sale should take place we beg leave to state that from the report and plan our surveyor has sent to us, it does appear that the appropriation of this piece of ground to any other purpose than that to which it is at present applied could be productive of considerable inconvenience to the public.

The Government suspended the sale of the plot and told the Board of Revenue that before making any such 'similar sale within the limits of the town of Calcutta, you will make it an established rule to refer the case to Government in order that the opinion of the magistrates and of the proper officers may be obtained on the subject'.[28]

Apart from the kink in the road alignment involving Church Lane and Bankshall Street, there was yet another reason of long standing for the congestion at the north end of Church Lane. This was the absence of a respectable road to the river on the west from the point where Bankshall Street 'connected' with Church Lane which, if the official correspondence of the time is any indication, was affecting the city's trade adversely. The principal 'culprit' here was the building which housed the Marine Paymaster's office. In 1804 Wellesley's special committee to improve the environs of Calcutta had stated specifically that the office in question occupied three-fourths of the ground which 'formerly constituted the approach to one of the principal ghauts of the town and that, in their judgement, the disuse into which Kuouillah (Koila) Ghauth has of late years fallen for commercial purposes may fairly be ascribed to the obstructions occasioned by the encroachment above adverted to'.[29] The committee had said that if the approach was widened 'by the removal of this house, the ghaut in question would in consequence of its local advantages become one of the most convenient and popular ghauts in Calcutta'.[30]

Nothing happened for five years (Wellesley had put in his papers at the end of July 1805). On 29 November 1809, the Committee for Improving the Town of Calcutta wrote that it would be 'a very desirable object' if the offices of the Marine Paymaster were removed 'with the view of widening the street called Bankshall Street leading to Coilah Ghaut'.[31] Since a decision such as this could not be taken on the spur of the moment, the Government said that the subject would be taken up 'on receipt of some further information which has been required…respecting the state of that building'. A fortnight later, taking note of the views of the committee which had been set up to survey the Marine Paymaster and Naval Store Keeper's premises, the demolition of the house was ordered, the decision being based on the premise that money spent on its repair would be 'manifestly a waste of the public money'.[32]

A year later, on 10 November 1810, the committee on the city's improvement wrote to the Governor-General, Lord Minto, telling him that problems had surfaced once again. The Marine Paymaster, H. Churchill, had written to it on the day he had received a notice from the committee's Surveyor Richard Blechynden (10 November) pointing out that the outhouses attached to the 'new building ordered to be erected for the marine paymaster have been constructed precisely on a part of the spot which we were so desirous of obtaining for the important purpose above noticed'.[33] Churchill argued that the new house had been built 'exactly agreeable to the plan approved and ordered by the Government', and that it had been 'placed on the only spot that it can be without an additional expence of about 1,000 rupees, as the ground to the westward [that is, towards the river] falls at once about eight feet, and in the months of September and October is overflowed by the tide'. The Marine Paymaster's point was that either the building should be allowed to stand where it had been built or that the Committee for Improvement 'should allow for the additional expence', which the committee was not prepared to do. Churchill reiterated that the new building 'is certainly no incumbrance as it is 20 feet further from the Old Road,[34] which is now 50 feet wide instead of 22'.

The sole objective of the Committee for the Improvement of the Town was to ensure that the offending outhouses were removed and that 'such part of the ground attached to the Marine Pay Office as is required for widening Bankshall Street be appropriated to that purpose'. The Government agreed to do so in the middle of November, the additional expense to be incurred on removing the outhouses being met by other departments and not the committee. The strategic importance of the 1810 development is that it ultimately paved the way for the subsequent extension of the road south of Tank Square down to the river, that is, today's Hare Street.

At its 2 July 1818 meeting, the Lottery Committee had asked its surveyor to draw up a plan for Church Lane primarily to tackle the congestion at its northern end. A fortnight later it formed a subcommittee; comprising Captain Montague and G.J. Gordon to 'talk to the [proprietors] of the houses and grounds which it may eventually be necessary to purchase with a view to widen and improve the street leading from Church Lane to the Banks Hall'.[35] Three weeks later Gordon apprised the committee of the 'measures' taken by the subcommittee to accomplish the objective which were described as 'judicious and proper'.[36] However, the point was made that it would be 'highly convenient' to combine with Gordon's plan for the north end of Church Lane the improvements suggested for Hastings Street at the lane's southern end, the committee not having been able to come to any 'definitive resolution' of the problems involved. A month later, on

6 August, a larger subcommittee was formed with the addition of Henry Wood and A. Colvin (Montague was excluded because of 'other official avocations') its job being to place before the Lottery Committee specific suggestions which would accomplish 'both the objects in contemplation'.

In the middle of October, Wood and Gordon submitted their proposals to develop the three roads, namely, the western end of Hastings Street, Church Lane and Police Office Street, the total cost of the project being put at Rs 68,000. (The cost break-up was as follows: widening Hastings Street Rs 42,000; Church Lane Rs 8,000; Police Office Street, including access to that street and Church Lane, Rs 18,000.)[37] Regarding Hastings Street, the subcommittee focussed on the impact the proposed development would have on trade and commerce when it wrote that the western end of the road was used as much as the Cutchagoody Ghat (to which it led) owing to the 'depth of water and other favourable circumstances'. The ghat, in fact, was an important 'landing place for all such goods as are not required to pass through the Customs House'. The heavy goods traffic, however, was impeded in its smooth flow into the city 'by the narrowness of the road where it forms an angle with Church Lane'. In order to remove the constriction and also enhance the appearance of the street 'in point of ornament', the subcommittee proposed that the north side of the street should 'form one straight line throughout its whole length'. For this not only would a 'range of godowns' on that side of the street have to be bought and demolished but 'a part of the offices attached to the house at the southwest corner of Church Lane, and a small slip of ground in the rear of the godowns' would also have to be bought and removed. The latter operation would cost an additional Rs 3,000 making a total expenditure of Rs 45,000 (Rs 42,000 being paid to Vrignon for the godowns). However, the net investment would be reduced by Rs 3,000 which would be the value 'of the buildings materials' disposed of.

The focus regarding Church Lane was on widening the street uniformly from the point where it met Hastings Street in the south to its linking up with Bankshall Street in the north. The godowns opposite Hare's house 'and extending in a line thence to the Police Ghaut' would have to be removed, as also 'an old godown' about the middle of the road belonging to the mint, 'which projects obliquely into the street narrowing the road at one point five or six feet'. Further, a part of a house belonging to Vrignon, 'which opens from Hastings Street but projects deeply and abruptly into Church Lane, greatly reducing the breadth of the road where it meets Hastings Street', would also have to be removed. The subcommittee estimated that the extruding part of the house could be bought for Rs 7,000 or, if the entire property were to be purchased, Rs 18,000 would have to be spent 'and that part not required disposed of', which would reduce the net expenditure. It was also suggested that the vestry of St John's be approached to 'carry back' the railing to the west of the churchyard 'far enough to leave the road of an equal breadth at the two extremities'. The cost of this alteration would be no more than Rs 500. As regards the narrowness of Church Lane in the north where it connected with Bankshall Street, the subcommittee said that the problem was an old one and that it rendered 'the access of carriages to the police office, the mint and the dwelling houses in the neighbourhood very dangerous'. If the specific proposal to give the road a new alignment was accepted, the subcommittee said that the total cost of this part of the project would be 'comparatively trifling…as a very considerable portion of the sum required to purchase the ground and building in the new line might, with the sanction of Government, be repaid by disposing of the space that would be left to Mr Hare' (see later).

Like Cutchagoody Ghat to the south, Police Ghat was also a busy landing place for goods but, unlike the former, it was also used by those who paid customs duty on their consignments. However, its potential was being stunted because of the lack of access to it. The subcommittee wrote:

> The Police Ghaut is at present almost inaccessible from the narrowness of the lane leading to it (see Fig. 32). The removal of the godowns on the right of the street would render the ghaut, from its neighbourhood of the Customs house, from the large open space attached to it, and from the depth of water close to the bank, extremely well-adapted for the landing of goods, and would thus afford a very great convenience to the mercantile community.

But implementing this part of the project would be uncertain because widening access to the ghat would have to take the legal route in view of the encroachment of privately owned buildings. If the Government considered this part of the plan for the area worth pursuing, the Advocate-General would have to be roped in to move the Supreme Court 'for permission to the guardians of an infant named Kassinath [Kashinath] Roy[38] to sell such part of his property as will be required by the committee'. The subcommittee could not provide a firm estimate of the cost of developing access to the Police Ghat because of the anticipated legal problems. However, it felt that a maximum of Rs 20,000 would be spent the cost 'in all probability' not exceeding Rs 15,000. In the event, however, these figures were grossly exceeded the house of the child raja being sold for as much as Rs 50,000.[39]

Wood and Gordon had submitted their proposals on 16 October. Without wasting any time the Lottery Committee forwarded them to the Government 'in a less mature shape than they intended' in view of the intimation received from Vrignon that his 'pecuniary interests' were being 'seriously affected by the delay which has already occurred in the negotiations [for the sale of his property]', and that unless the issue was adjusted quickly he would have to accept 'an offer which has been made to him from a private quarter for the disposal of the property required for the proposed improvements'.

The committee backed the proposals as being 'calculated to be of great advantage to the public' and sought the Government's approval to be allowed to exercise its 'discretion in the completion in the proposed investments at an expence not exceeding in the aggregate 70,000 Rs chargeable to the lottery funds'. The Government was assured that the state of the lottery funds at the time was comfortable enough to 'admit of this expenditure being made without inconvenience'.[40] The proposals were sanctioned the same day the committee being asked to talk to the church vestry regarding the pushing back of the railing to the west of the churchyard while the Government would take up with the mint people the matter of the errant godown sticking out into Church Lane.[41]

In the last week of December 1818, the subcommittee provided the Lottery Committee with a progress report of the work done on the integrated project.[42] It was a mixed bag indicating rapid progress in one sector while in the two others obstacles had held up work. Vrignon's property ('offices, godowns and ground') had come into its possession along with the deeds of transfer, and 'considerable progress' had been made 'in demolishing the buildings and in removing the rubbish'. The 'beams, doors and windows' had been sold at public auction but at a price which was 'very inadequate to their real value'. The rubbish of the 'roofs, etc' was used to fill up 'a very offensive tank on the property of Rajah Raj Kissun (Rajkrishna), situated at the back of the Esplanade Row where it joins Cossitollah'.[43] Some of the bricks recovered from the demolition work were set aside for making the foundation of the new part of the street (Hastings Street) while a part was sent to Henry Wood for constructing the footpath and railing along the Course.[44]

The subcommittee, however, was not in a position to say whether its valuation of the old materials would turn out to be correct since it had not yet been able to ascertain whether the supply of old bricks would be adequate to meet the construction needs and whether any surplus would be left to be sold in the market (the estimate of proceeds under this head was Rs 3,000). Importantly, costs were overshooting the estimate already, an example being the unexpected expenditure on 'erecting the new fronts and offices... for Mr Vrignon in consideration of the additional ground and old offices which he gave up beyond the property that was originally bargained for'. The subcommittee had drawn Rs 3,933-1-3 under this head against an estimate of Rs 3,000, which pushed up the total cost of improving Hastings Street to Rs 45,933-1-3 from Rs 45,000, an increase which was accepted by the Lottery Committee and allowed by the Government.[45]

Since Raja Rajnarain Roy's house was sold to the Government at the end of 1819, it is not surprising that, in its December 1818 report, the subcommittee reported a lack of progress on this front. In the absence of any progress being made regarding purchase of the house, it was suggested (the Lottery Committee backing the proposal) that a jury be set up to arbitrate the issue, which would be 'the most speedy mode of ascertaining the real value, and requiring possession' of the property. The Government accepted the suggestion and in the middle of January 1819 asked the magistrates to begin the process of forming a jury 'to inquire into and decide upon the amount of the compensation to be allowed for that part of the property of the late Rajah Kishenaut Roy, which is required for the intended improvements of the street leading from the Bankshall to the Police Ghaut'.[46] In the event, however, the property was sold at a price (Rs 50,000) acceptable to the Government without having recourse to a jury. Even so, some hurdles still remained to be tackled, such as the godowns at the western end of the road leading to the Police Office which were yet to be demolished because alternative arrangements had not yet been implemented 'according to a plan to be proposed by the magistrates'.

As for Church Lane, there had been no movement regarding the demolition of the godown belonging to the mint while the select vestry of St John's had said that it lacked legal authority to 'alienate any portion of the church grounds', in this case throwing back the railing which would have given the road 'an uniform width from Hastings Street to Police Office Street'. The subcommittee had written to the church vestry seeking 'very important assistance which it is in your power to render the [lottery] committee in the execution of their plans by granting your permission to appropriate to public use a small part of the ground at present included within the churchyard'. A plan was sent along with the letter (which incidentally, is not to be found in the church vestry records)[47] showing 'the additions to be made to the width of Hastings Street and Police Office Street as well as the proposed improved line of Church Lane'. The portion of ground belonging to 'the Cathedral' which the committee would need were also indicated in the plan. The subcommittee wrote:

> In order to render Church Lane of an uniform width and to connect Colvin's Ghat and Hastings Street by a safe and commodious line of road with the Customs House and its commercial neighbourhood, it is proposed by the Committee to purchase not only the whole line of godowns marked off in the plan but also a part of the dwelling house at the corner of the churchyard[48] which projects into Church Lane…

The purchase, however, could not be effected except at an expense 'disproportionate to the object', unless the Vestry gave its consent

> ...to grant to Mr Vrignon a small slip of ground in the rear of the house measuring about 16 feet in breadth and 47 in length, without which there would remain after the disposal of the west end of the house no room for the requisite offices...

The subcommittee wrote that in order to reduce the expenditure on the improvements, the Lottery Committee had planned to dispose of 'the unoccupied piece of ground' between the east side of 'the proposed new sweep of road, from the head of Police Office Street to Bankshall Street, and the premises of Mr Hare', the spot being bounded on the south by the churchyard.

The point of bringing up the subject was that, in case the sale of the plot went through, it was hoped that the vestry would have no objection to permitting Hare 'to substitute the wall of the building he may erect on that space for the present enclosing wall...which will otherwise abstract three windows of the lower apartments of [the] new house'. If the vestry agreed with the suggestions, 'every expence attending the proposed alterations' would be defrayed by the Lottery Committee.

The response of the church was sympathetic, but it said that its hands were tied. The vestry wrote that it 'might have acquiesced' to ceding 'certain portions' of the churchyard 'without a departure from the rules of law bearing upon the matter in question and without a breach of our trust to the public', but 'we...conceive that we have not the legal right to alienate any portion of the churchyard land'.[49]

Faced with this response, the subcommittee felt that the Government, 'the only representative of the public', could be asked to delegate authority to the vestry to take the step required so that the public could be benefitted by being given a better Church Lane. Alternatively, it was suggested that the Government apprise the vestry 'through the usual channels' that the committee's requirement had official support and that such action should suffice 'to remove the difficulty at present felt by the vestry in acceding to the committee's proposition'. The critical importance of the issue at hand was underscored when the subcommittee told the Lottery Committee that the purchase of Vrignon's property 'at the corner of the churchyard' could not be effected 'until the ground requisite for his offices has been procured from the vestry'.[50]

In its 15 January 1819 response[51] to the Lottery Committee's letter of 26 December, the Government placed the issue of the shifting of the churchyard railing on a pedestal, making it the fulcrum on which depended the success of the entire project. It wrote that the measures proposed for widening Church Lane

> ...as connected with the improvements now in progress or in contemplation in Hastings Street and in the street leading to the Police Ghaut, appear to Government to be of considerable importance, as well with reference to the public convenience generally as to the more commodious access which would be thus afforded to the cathedral.

This was the reason why the Governor-General in Council had asked the Lottery Committee to purchase a part of Vrignon's premises, 'situated on the southwest angle of the grounds of the cathedral, and the same motive has since induced him to accede to the suggestion of the committee with regard to the removal of a part of the buildings belonging to the mint which projects into Church Lane'.

The point was then made that the measures would not bear fruit unless the railing to the west of the church was carried back 'in the mode pointed out in the plan so as to leave the road of equal breadth at the two extremities'. The measure was 'unobjectionable in itself provided the expence of rebuilding the wall and railing

[was] defrayed from the funds of the Lottery Committee'. The vestry would be apprised of the decisions, specifically the fact that the suggestion to push back the railing had received official sanction. As regards the subcommittee's view that the vestry had to provide the ground required for Vrignon's offices before the purchase of the latter's property at the corner of Church Lane could be effected, the Government said that the issue would be 'sent to the general department' for consideration and the Lottery Committee would be kept informed of developments. In view of the official go-ahead regarding relocation of the church railing, the subcommittee was asked to get in touch with the church vestry so that the suggested improvements could be carried out 'with the least practicable delay'.

Nine months later, in October 1819, the subcommittee provided the Lottery Committee with a break-up of the expenditure on the Hastings Street-Church Lane segment of the project, the burden of the communication being that Rs 9,104-4-5 had been spent in excess compared to the estimate.[52] The cost of the Church Lane improvements had been estimated at Rs 8,000 but, as it turned out, the entire sum had to be paid for just the part of Vrignon's house which had to be pulled down at the south-east corner, the estimate for which had been put at Rs 7,000. Further adding to costs was the fact that 'the inner wall' of the house had to be pulled down and a new one built 'at a considerable expense'. The committee wrote to the Government the next day (14 October) suggesting that the excess expenditure be adjusted against the Rs 20,000 which had been 'appropriated for the improvement of the street leading to Police Ghaut', a work which had now been combined under 'the improvement contemplated in the opening of the new road between Tank Square and the river' (see below). This would leave Rs 10,895-11-7 from the fund untouched which the committee wanted 're-credited to the unappropriated funds of the Calcutta lotteries', which was allowed in early November.[53]

By early 1819, the 'whole of the improvements…in Hastings Street and Cucha Goody Ghaut' having been completed and the improvements in Church Lane being 'very nearly complete', the Lottery Committee turned its attention to the feasibility of building a ghat on the river 'in continuation of Bankshall Street with the view of affording a more commodious access to the river at that part of Calcutta'.[54] Wood, Colvin and Gordon were asked to consider the subject in February 1819, which ultimately led to construction of Hare Street (as it exists today) – from the 'great tank' in the east to the river in the west, in one straight line. This is what was proposed precisely by the subcommittee at the end of April the previous plan being to open a wide road from Bankshall Street to the Police Ghat 'through Police Office Lane', an old road alignment which had taken irregular shape within the first 50 years of Charnock's arrival in 1690 (see Upjohn's map, Fig. 32). As the subcommittee saw it, the new proposal would be 'far more commodious to the public and ornamental to the city',[55] as it, in fact, has turned out to be over the past 200 years.

The survey for the new road had opened up two options. The first was to consider whether the projected line of road could be constructed on 'public' land, which in this case was the ground attached to the Master Attendant's office. It was found that by removing 'a line of buildings which have been fitted up as stables by Commodore [John] Hayes [the Master Attendant] at his private expence, a good line of road might be carried betwixt his dwelling house, office, etc and the houses occupied by Mr [Robert] Fergusson and the Police Department'. But the potential for problems cropping up was sizable. The ground had once been conceded by the Government to the merchants of the Exchange Committee to put up their own building[56] but now there was uncertainty about the project. When the subcommittee got in touch with the merchants, it was told that their intention 'to erect an exchange on the site originally proposed [was still there], though it was liable to many objections'.

The merchants, however, declared their readiness to help out with the road project (as also did Commodore Hayes) by being willing to amend their construction plans, if required. Understandably, they were enthused by the Lottery Committee's proposed new road because, among other things, it would make the location of their own building far more attractive than it was. As the subcommittee reported, the merchants were willing to contribute 'so much towards effecting it [the new road project] as may, we hope, reduce the whole expence to the lottery fund to a sum whose amount may not appear to Government more than adequate to the importance of the object in view'.[57] The subcommittee took this opportunity to push the case for pulling down the Master Attendant's office. It argued that the ground near the riverbank was 'not calculated to afford a secure foundation for any large structure' and that, consequently, there was 'no good ground for building so large an edifice [as the exchange] within the spot assigned by Government unless the present confined and decayed building' occupied by the Master Attendant was taken down to make room for the project. It added that the proposed exchange was expected to be an 'ornamental' addition to the town and that it would 'regret' to see the objective negated, which was bound to happen if the old building remained standing because it would obstruct the view of the new exchange.[58]

The subcommittee was aware that the exchange's building project at the location cited was uncertain. Subsequent events were to show that the surmise was not incorrect.[59] In view of this, the second option was advanced which, though more expensive, was 'far more regular in appearance and (promised) much greater convenience'. The plan envisaged 'the entire removal of the old buildings' occupied by Fergusson (the house of Raja Rajnarain Roy) and the police office, which would allow 'a road of eighty feet in width being carried in a direct continuation of the south side of Tank Square to the river, terminating at the present Police Ghaut'. Sowing the seeds of the present alignment of Church Lane and Bankshall Street, the subcommittee said that 'instead of connecting Church Lane with Bankshall Street by a curved line of road, as formerly proposed, it should be continued in a straight line, so as to meet the new street nearly at right angles'. On 2 February 1820 *The Calcutta Journal* was reporting:

> The Police Office is to be removed to the house east of Mr Palmer's in the Loll Bazar, the same place where the office was held many years ago. When this change has been effected, the improvement in Bankshall Street will be resumed, and in a short time we may expect to see the road continued to the river side close to the present Police Ghaut.[60]

The subcommittee had expected that no jury would value the child raja Rajnarain Roy's property at more than Rs 30,000 and that the police office premises owned by Kashinath Bonnerjya (Banerjee) would be priced at Rs 55,000. After building the new road, 37 *katha*s of saleable ground would be left as extra ground which would fetch as much as Rs 37,000 (at Rs 1,000 a *katha*), to which sum would be added the contribution to be made by the merchants (Rs 23,000) yielding a total of Rs 60,000 'towards diminution of the expence'. Even if the acquisition of landed property added up to a lakh of rupees in the event of a jury attaching a higher value to Rajnarain Roy's property, the subcommittee said that Rs 40,000 would have to be shelled out by the lottery funds for the entire project, which would be an acceptable deal. In terms of ornamental content, the scheme would be even more impressive than the one 'just…executed in Hastings Street'.[61]

The subcommittee's report was sent to the Government at the end of April 1819 the Lottery Committee making the point that the projects sanctioned earlier for widening 'the lane leading to the river near the police office' and 'opening a more safe and easy communication between Church Lane and Bankshall Street' had not yet been taken up, and this for a good reason. In course of 'personal enquiries and communications with competent judges', it had been found that an arrangement 'more advantageous to the public than the one already sanctioned' was available in the opening of a street to the river directly 'in the immediate vicinity of Bankshall Street and the house occupied by the Master Attendant'. The project (which finally turned out to be abortive) would lead to the removal of 'several old and decayed buildings' not to speak of the erection of the projected exchange which would 'add materially to the regular and ornamental appearance of the city'.

The committee wrote to the Government that the 'ultimate expence' of the projected improvements would lie between Rs 25,000 and Rs 40,000 (see above), its hope being that the actual figure would not exceed 'the median amount of those sums, or about Rs 33,000'. From this amount would have to be deducted Rs 17,000 which had been sanctioned earlier for improvements in Police Office Lane (which had not been effected), leaving an uncovered sum of Rs 16,000 which could be 'very beneficially disbursed from the lottery funds'. The Government was asked to sanction Rs 1,00,000 (being the 'highest estimate' for the purchase of the property of Raja Rajnarain and Kashinath Banerjee), to instruct the magistrates to set up a jury to value the raja's house 'which, as belonging to the infant heir of the late Casheinaut Roy, cannot be procured without the intervention of a jury', and to remove the building occupied by the Master Attendant's office and its site, to the extent required by the proposed merchants' exchange, be handed over to the exchange committee. The Government's approval was given on 21 May for the funds sought and the setting up of a jury, but there was no word on the demolition of the Master Attendant's office which was specifically sought by the committee. The Governor-General in Council merely agreed to transfer to the exchange committee 'that portion of the ground now occupied by the office of the Master Attendant (as marked in the plan)' provided there was no 'serious objection' from the Marine Board.[62]

Hare Street is named after David Hare because his house was situated in the neighbourhood. What is not known equally widely is that but for Hare's helping hand the road may never have been built. A report drawn up by Gordon and Colvin (members of the Bankshall subcommittee) in early July 1820 revealed that the delay in finalising the design of 'building a new exchange' by the exchange committee had almost led to the project being given up but for 'the spirited conduct' of Hare who 'guaranteed us against [a] greater surplus expense for the purchase of the two houses than (the) originally estimated sum of Sicca Rs 40,000' in return for 'receiving the spare ground that might remain on both sides of the new line of road'. This apart, Hare had also committed himself not to build any houses on the spare ground 'that shall not be ornamental to the street'. Perhaps this was why Hare later insisted on the same restrictions being placed on Ramdulal Dey when the latter was gifted land in the area by the Government (see below).[63] In the event, in order to keep his commitment, Hare had to transfer to the committee Rs 68,000 because the expenditure on the two houses added up to Rs 1,08,000 (Raja Rajnarain Roy: Rs 50,000, and Kashinath Banerjee: Rs 58,000). This amount exceeded the value of the ground which Hare was given after the layout of the roads in front of his house had been altered.[64]

In 1820 itself preliminary work on Strand Road had begun a critical aspect of which was the raising and levelling of the ground, the magnitude of the task depending on the state of the riverbank which varied from spot to spot. To the west of the bankshall was a strip of land which belonged to the bankshall itself, which had already been 'prepared' by Hayes, the Master Attendant, at his own expense. According to the subcommittee, Hayes had spent a 'considerable' Rs 5,000 or Rs 6,000 on the ground which was about 60 or 70 yards from the bank. Writing to the committee in November 1820, the subcommittee felt that since 'nearly the whole extent' of the raised ground would be required for the construction 'of the new road and quay leading from the new ghaut [the Police Ghat] to Coila Ghat [further north]', Hayes should be reimbursed for his outlay 'on the principle that advantage ought not to be taken by the public of an improvement effected at the expense of a private individual without refunding the cost that would be required for the same purpose had it still remained to be accomplished for the use of the public'.[65]

At this point, David Hare made his appearance once again. As we have seen the subcommittee wanted the Government to reimburse Hayes for developing the ground concerned for the new riverside road. A method was devised which would obviate the need for the Government to pay Hayes for the work done, the payment being made by Hare for purchase of ground in the vicinity which was of no use to the authorities. To the south of the bankshall premises was located a 'narrow slip lying between the great tunnel[66] that runs through the bankshall premises and the ground that has been disposed of by the committee on the north side of the new road, or Hare Street, leading from Tank Square to the new ghaut'. The subcommittee wrote that 'the line of the street cuts off the eastern corner of Commodore Hayes' out-offices and runs so close to the back wall of the same premises for a considerable extent that no building can be interposed to screen them, forming a very offensive object if suffered to remain'. The suggestion was that if Hare was given 'the space on which these stand', located to the south of the bankshall premises, along with the slip of ground referred to earlier he would be able to put up 'more sightly structures on the spot', at the same time paying to the Government the sum which would be transferred to Hayes 'as well as build the requisite out-offices on another spot'. The Lottery Committee backed the scheme, but not before making it clear that it was granting a favour to David Hare since the two spots of ground involved were not offered for public sale, which kept the price low.

The Lottery Committee had written to the Government on 9 November 1820 for a decision on the issue, the approval coming a week later. The Government wanted the committee to ascertain the extent of Hayes's expenditure on developing the ground in question 'with as much accuracy as circumstances may admit'. Underscoring the inclusiveness of the bureaucratic approach, the committee was asked to get the Marine Board to certify officially that the latter 'was not aware of any important objections of a public nature' to the improvements contemplated, specially the transfer to Hare of the slip of ground on the bankshall's premises, north of Hare Street.[67]

Fig. 35. St John's Church, consecrated in June 1787. It stands on ground gifted to Warren Hastings by Nabakrishna Deb of the Sobhabazar family

HENRY SHAKESPEAR'S MINUTES

Henry Davenport Shakespear, who in 1820 was the Officiating Chief Magistrate of Calcutta as well as a member of the Lottery Committee (inducted in March 1819), was deeply engaged in the city's development work, as were the other members of the committee. Shakespear's involvement was, however, a shade stronger than that of the others, as is suggested by the volume of work he shouldered as also his occasional gentle, unsolicited prodding of the committee to get on with the job as expeditiously as possible.[1] Among his many important interventions was his 13 January 1820 minute which, among other things, provides an overview of the town's topographical state, from Dharamtala Street southward to Circular Road.[2]

A part of the minute dealt with the poor drainage in 'Brijeetollah and its neighbourhood' (the area south of Theatre Road) where the native population was 'small', a problem which had, in fact, already been highlighted by him at the end of the previous year. Shakespear's finding was that

> ...in the height of the rains, the tide from Tolly's Nullah comes up the drains on the south side of the Circular Road near Brigeetullah and, crossing the road, flows into the drains nearly as far northward as what is called Theatre Road, running eastward from the Circular Road to the theatre.[3]

Shakespear, however, felt that this was not an important reason for the sickness that usually prevailed in the area. The effects of the periodic flooding were 'baneful' no doubt but they probably would not occur if 'proper attention' was paid to 'the sluice gates on the north side of the nullah nearly opposite the Allypore Jail' further to the south-west. This apart, the number of people likely to be affected by the flooding was 'small'. As Shakespear saw it, the more important reason for the generally unhealthy conditions prevailing in the area was the nature of the area's topography which was low and marshy. He had discovered that the drains to the south of Circular Road were higher than those on the north with the result that water stagnated on the northern side of the road. But this happened only till the end of October 'when they begin to dry up'. He felt that a 'professional person' was needed 'to determine how much the beds of these drains may be raised so as to carry off the water to those on the south side', care being taken not to raise them to a level which would affect adversely 'the general draining of Chowringhee'. Not being someone to wait interminably for orders to begin work, Shakespear had already engaged Richard Blechynden, the Surveyor of the Town, to look into the issue.

He then focussed on general principles and said that the sorry condition of the town, especially the native part of it, was not the result of a lack of projects but the Government's inability to implement plans and schemes which had been drawn up over the years. Shakespear then hit the nail on the head when he said that the past efforts had failed 'for want of adequate funds'.

An important aspect of the issue was whether the shortage of funds affected development work equally throughout the town, or was the burden of the shortfall carried by the native parts in particular? A simple answer to this question is not possible despite the overarching a priori assumption that, in such a situation, Europeans would favour their own race where development projects were concerned. The records indicate that such an inherently biased approach to civic development was indeed to be expected, and did in fact exist, but what cannot be ignored is that there were also instances of 'errant' and maverick officers of the East India Company's administration who exhibited a keen interest in drawing up development plans for the native areas of a rapidly expanding city.[4]

As an example of projects not implemented, Shakespear delved into the past and referred to a slew of schemes listed in a 24 July 1804 communication from J. Lumsden, Chief Secretary to the Government, to Major-General W.N. Cameron, a member of the first-ever committee appointed 'for considering the means of improving the town of Calcutta'.[5] Among other things, the overarching point which Lumsden made was that while the acquiring of private property would necessarily be an essential part of the exercise, in the process the Government would not tolerate any assault on the sanctity of such property. A result of this was that the Governor-General in Council always made it a point to ask the committee concerned to get the approval of property-owners before any decision was taken to acquire ground for the construction of roads and tanks which, as experience over the past two centuries has shown, has always made the job of improving a city like Calcutta extraordinarily problematic. Of interest here is that, to start with, the development initiative was the direct result of the need to prevent fires from breaking out in parts of the town, the committee telling the Government unequivocally that it was submitting its suggestions 'to improve the construction of the several quarters of the town which have been lately burnt and to prevent the destructive effects of fire in those places in future'.[6]

In his minute, Shakespear wrote that the improvements listed in 1804 'although sanctioned by Government and intended to be defrayed from its funds were never carried into effect'.[7] The important question is: was this a direct result of the departure of Lord Wellesley in 1805, the Governor-General being under a cloud as far as the Directors of the East India Company were concerned? In fact, this phase of sluggishness in the implementation of policies for the town's development appears to have lasted till the end of Lord Minto's tenure in 1814. Being the senior official he was,[8] it is reasonable to expect that Shakespear was fully aware of all this, but his public comment was that he was unable to 'discover' the reason, or reasons, why the schemes were 'relinquished'. He, however, asserted that if the policies 'were necessary then, they are greatly more so now [1820] when the population of the town, and particularly the European part of it, has so much increased'.

The Officiating Chief Magistrate laid emphasis on the point that it was only Government expenditure on an increased scale that would be able to produce the sought-after results. In other words, the main effort to improve the town had to be financed by the Government, that is, the Governor-General in Council. As was the case with individual contributions, the Lottery Committee's funds, which were got 'from other sources', were simply not enough for the purpose in hand, especially for 'works of magnitude'. The minute concluded with the declaration that

> ...unless, therefore, the Government comes forward to rescue the inhabitants of its capital from the baneful effects of living in swamps and breathing a polluted atmosphere, the conclusion of each rainy season must bring with it a return of disease and mortality that has particularly of late years committed such ravages amongst the inhabitants of the town.

However, the point was made that although the Government was to be held responsible for the improvement schemes not being implemented over the past 15 years or so it was not as if nothing had been done. Being a magistrate himself, Shakespear protected and extolled the virtues of his tribe and what it had accomplished in the recent past.[9] He was quick to defend the drainage improvement work effected over the past two or three years, especially since the Lottery Committee had taken up development work in right earnest. He wrote in his minute that while there was the general supposition that 'much of the unhealthiness amongst the inhabitants during the last few months has proceeded from the bad state of the drains, and accumulation of dirt in the towns,' the principal factor responsible for the prevailing sickness among the population was 'the exhalation and damp of low marshy ground and stagnant pools'.

Shakespear had included in his minute two memoranda focussing on two parts of the southern division of the town. These reports are today of great value because they provide, first, a picture of the physical lay of the land as it existed at the end of the second decade of the 19th century and, secondly, an account of how development initiatives first took shape the footprints of which still mark city life at the beginning of the 21st century.

Included in the first memorandum[10] – entitled 'Memorandum on an inspection of the Upper South Division, that is the part of the town lying between Old Fort Ghaut, Writers' Buildings, Loll Bazar and Bow Bazar Road to the north and Champaul Ghaut, Esplanade Row and Dhurrumtollah Street to the south' – was

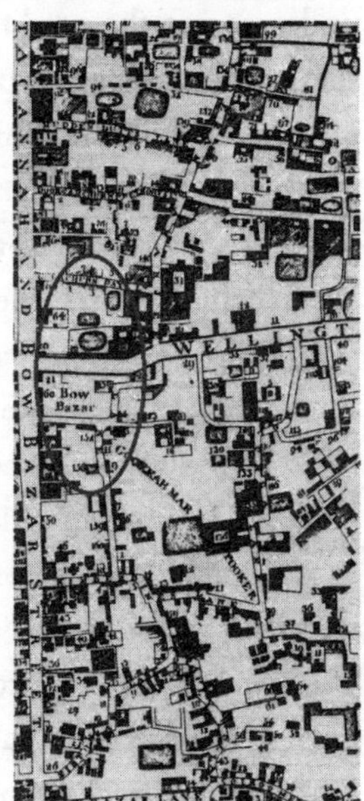

Fig. 36. The area east of Bowbazar Lane which had some dirty tanks which Henry Shakespear wanted to remove. Detail from Schalch's map

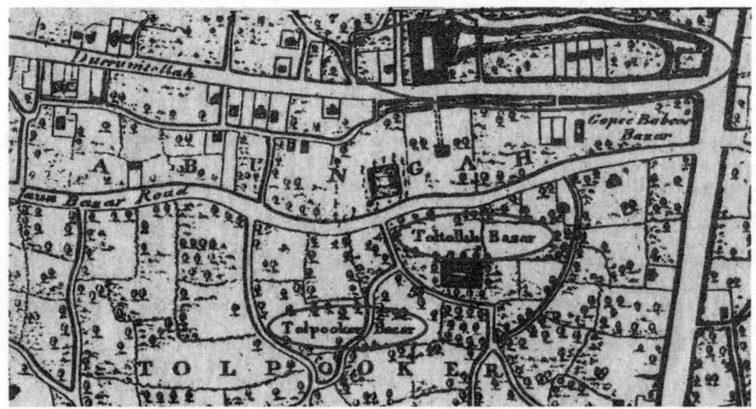

Fig. 37. Upjohn's map of 1793 shows the drain to the north of Dharamtala Road; also Talpukur and Taltala Bazars

a list of 'dirty tanks' to be filled up to the east of Bow Bazar Lane, which gives the names of the property owners as well (see Fig. 36). However, the most important part of the memorandum dealt with the drain and road to the north of Dharamtala Street, running parallel to it till Circular Road in the east (see Fig. 37), Shakespear underscoring the need to develop the area which was in many ways seminal for the future progress of the neighbourhood.

The Officiating Chief Magistrate wrote:

> Near the new tank at Bepareetollah commences an immense drain[11] which carries off a large body of water from this part of the town and empties itself into the drain on the north side of Dhurrumtollah Street whence it is conveyed to the new canal.[12] On the side of this drain there runs nearly the whole way and within 100 feet of the Circular Road a broad road of 25 or 30 feet in diameter.

The important inference to be drawn from Shakespear's statement is that there existed a road along the stretch to the north of Dharamtala Street *before* the Wellington Square tank was excavated, that is, before the building of Creek Row. Another point of interest on which little light is thrown is whether, before the making of the Wellington Square tank, the 'immense drain' also extended westwards beyond the location of the tank? Clearly, it should have, along the path of the creek which went right up to the river on the west, but of this no trace remained in the early 19th century. If traces of the creek, subsequently transformed into a drain, did exist at the time there is little doubt that it would have been mentioned in the official records, but there is no direct reference to this at all.

Shakespear had two suggestions to make: first, that the existing road to the north of Dharamtala Street be connected with the new tank to the west and to Circular Road in the east 'and that the drain be made *puckah* by which the space it occupies will be reduced and leave sufficient for a good street'; secondly, 'that a puckah tunnel be constructed in the bed of the drain and the road carried along the top of it'. This would leave some ground on both sides of the road, 'the sale of which would partly repay the Committee for the expense of making the tunnel'. Clearly, the two suggestions were alternatives. The Officiating Chief Magistrate said that at the eastern end of the road-drain complex a 'small lower-roomed house' would have to be bought by the Government to effect the connexion with Circular Road; and on the west, 'some small buildings and huts covering a space of 200 yards' would have to be bought 'to connect with the new tank'.

The memorandum[13] on the 'lower south division' of the town, that is, 'all to the south of Dhurrumtollah Road', provides a picture of the Colinga area generally (to the east of today's Mirza Ghalib Street, or erstwhile Free School Street) and the terrain further south between Theatre and Circular Roads. On the area between Dharamtala Street and today's S.N. Banerjee Road (Janbazar

Street), Shakespear does not have much to say except that to the east of Potooreetollah 'there is a nasty tank the property I believe of Government'. From this place, 'there is a deep drain running eastward almost in a straight line nearly as far as the Circular Road'. Since this 'basic infrastructure', irrespective of quality, was already in place Shakespear felt that 'nothing would be easier than the draining of this ground between the Dhurrumtollah and Jaun Bazar Roads'. He added that 'all the cross drains' running north-south between the drain to the south of Dharamtala Street and the deep drain 'might be surface drains whereas most of them are deep and consequently the receptacles of filth'.

Moving across Janbazar Road, the memorandum noted that there was 'a low swamp or pool extending two or three hundred yards on the south side of the Jaun Bazar Road near the Circular Road to the north of Mr Wilson's house'.[14] Shakespear noted some 'bad tanks' in the area – one to the east of Fenwick's Bazar (the area covered by today's New Market) – and said that 'the drain projected to be cut through Taltollah Bazar would greatly improve the draining of the northern part of Colinga and the Tulpoker Bazar' (see Fig. 37). Fenwick's Bazar itself was not only extraordinarily dirty but was 'sufficient to make the houses in Chowringhee unhealthy when the winds set from the east'. In order to facilitate the general development of the area, Shakespear said it was 'highly desirable that the road intended to have been made *puckah*, and carried through to the Jaun Bazar, should be constructed'. The road should be made 40 feet wide 'and the ground on both sides raised and levelled to induce persons to purchase and erect good houses on it'. The inference here is that neither was the ground in the area conducive to good houses being built on it (it was probably populated by huts) nor were there any *pucka* houses at the time. In other words, it was the Lottery Committee which first took up the work of 'modern' town construction in the area.

Regarding the area further south and east, Shakespear wrote:[15]

> The south-east part of Colingah as far as Colingah Street must be extremely unhealthy from the innumerable pools, swamps and tanks in it. Nothing will correct this but the purchase of a considerable space, digging a good tank and filling the low places. The whole of Colingah is intersected with winding lanes [a feature which still marks the area today], and of course drains occupying unnecessary space, and most inconvenient for the inhabitants.

The area had been 'particularly sickly this season'. The Officiating Chief Magistrate wrote that he did not know of any part of the town which was 'more deserving of the notice of the committee than this'. Moving in a still more south-easterly direction, Shakespear said that the area between Colinga Street and Burial Ground Road – the area immediately to the west of Lower Circular Road (Acharya Jagadish Bose Road) till Park Street in the south – was dotted with 'several nasty pools' but was not so bad as the part of Colinga further north. He added that there was 'a very excellent *kutcha* road [which ran] nearly through the centre part of Colingah [possibly, following the alignment of the future Wellesley Street]_which ought to be made *puckka*'.[16] Further south, from Park Street till Theatre Road, Shakespear says that the ground was 'generally speaking well-raised and free from pools'.[17] Focussing on the area to the south of Theatre Road, Shakespear wrote that located in the ground to the east of the theatre, 'between the continuation of Camac Street and Short's Bazar Road[18] is Brahmin Bustee…[which] has a fine tank in it' (see Fig. 38). The surrounding ground was high but was 'divided by a broad drain having grass and jungle on both sides which in the rainy season must render the situation unwholesome'.

He suggested that one way to get rid of the drain was to dig a tank to the east and fill it up with the earth thus excavated.[19]

❦

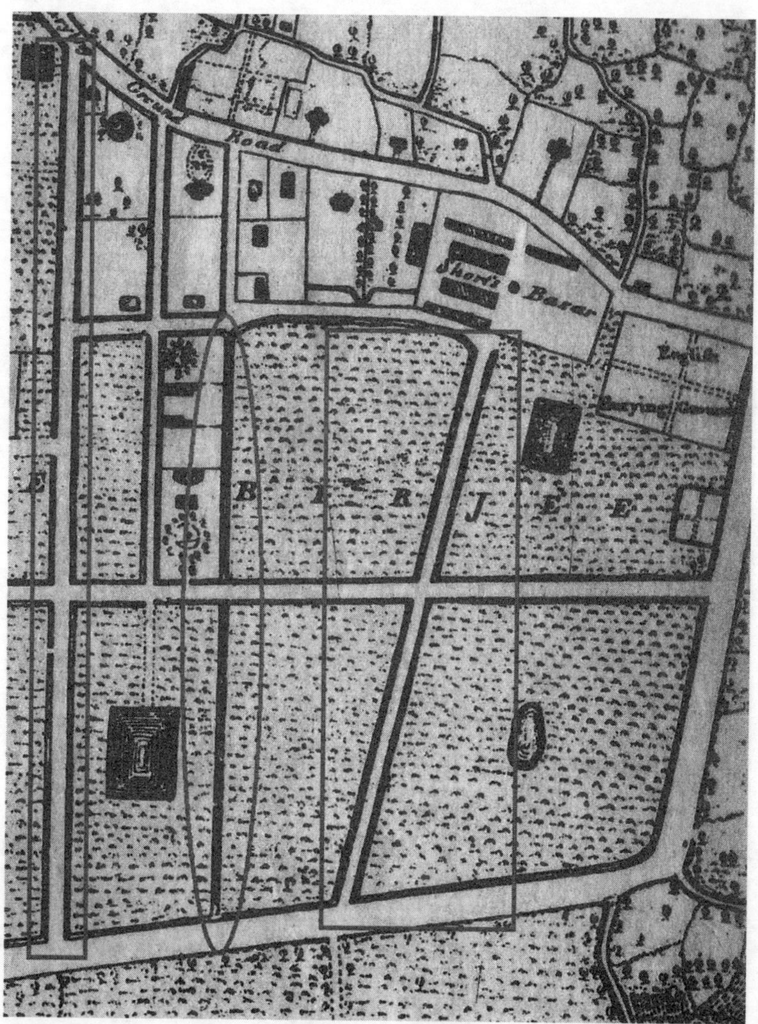

Fig. 38. Upjohn's map of 1793 showing Short's Bazar Road (right) and Camac Street (left). The map also shows the big drain (marked) running to the east of Camac Street

Henry Shakespear's minute, placed before the Lottery Committee in early February,[20] had not merely detailed the poor state of the town but had also indicated the scale of the work to be done to improve things. While the committee decided to take up the points made in the minute 'at a future period' what it did immediately was set up a subcommittee comprising Bayley, Shakespear, Paton and Schalch to attend to that part of the report devoted to the 'opening of a road from the east side of the new tank at Beopareetula and filling up the Dinga Bunga drain' (to the north of Dharamtala Street). The new panel was asked to ascertain how far the improvement at Baparitala (the new tank and square) 'would be promoted by filling up the Dinga Bunga [drain] and making a straight road over its present scite to the Circular Road, connecting it with the new tank'.[21] This was, in fact, the initiation of the idea of making Creek Row. The subcommittee was also asked to report on the project's 'expediency', the estimated cost, and also on the 'most expedient method of carrying off the water which now runs into the Dinga Banga'.

Four months later, in early June 1820 the subcommittee reported on the work already implemented and what remained to be done.[22] It said that the work of 'filling up and reversing the small drains which formerly ran to the southward and emptied themselves into the *khal*' (presumably the remnant of the old creek) had been completed under the supervision of Shakespear. The second task – 'connecting the *khal*...with the drain' which would enable 'the water formerly flowing down the *khal* (to) be carried nearly in a direct line into the new *pucka* drain now constructing on the north side of the Dhurrumtollah Road' – was in the process of being implemented, the committee's approval being required to spend funds which would facilitate the project's completion. The linking of the drain to the *khal* would entail requisitioning 'part of a *pucka* godown as well as part of the premises of Byrob Telee [Bhoirob Teli], and likewise some ground belonging to Neeboo Bustumee' (Nebu Boshtomi). The subcommittee thought it advisable to connect the new square with the road running by the side of the *khal*, for which it was necessary to purchase the whole of Teli's property as he had objected to selling the part of it required. The total expenditure under the three heads came to Rs 3,484-8-0, but this was subject to adjustments which would reduce the immediate outgo to Rs 1,704-8-0. Rupnarayan Ghoshal[23] had come forward with the offer that he would buy whatever land was not required for the project but which had to be bought because of the purchase conditions imposed on the subcommittee by the sellers concerned.

Ghoshal was a man of means even though the earnings from the work he did for the Company were relatively limited. This perhaps explains why he could make an offer to buy from the committee for Rs 1,780 the surplus land not required for the Dingabhanga drain and road project, which reduced the net cost of the project ultimately. Bayley and Shakespear were, in fact, confident that the committee would fully recover from the sale of the Dingabhanga ground 'the whole if not more than the expense which may be incurred in the purchases required to be made, and in the filling up of the *khal*'. They, therefore, sought permission to sell the land recovered after the *khal* was filled up 'and the *khamar* grounds on the sides of it'. On the same day (1 June), the Lottery Committee backed the Dingabhanga subcommittee's suggestions and sought sanction for their implementation, which materialised a month later.[24]

The construction of Creek Row was an integral part of the development of the area north of Dharamtala Street which covered both the Baparitala square and road project and the Dingabhanga plans. This was reflected in the 1 July 1820 request made by the subcommittee looking after the Baparitala project to make a 'separate application for authority to employ a sufficient number of *coolies* to carry on the improvements at the Dingabunga, which do not probably appertain to our subcommittee'. The effectiveness of the project involving the square would be evident only after the Dingabhanga work had been completed which is why, even though the Dingabhanga subcommittee was in charge of the *khal* development scheme including the associated road project, the Baparitala subcommittee sought the investment on the employment of the *coolies*. On its part, the Lottery Committee sought the Government's permission (subsequently granted) to employ 200 *coolies* per month for around four months for filling up the Dingabhanga *khal*, the estimated cost being put at Rs 750 a month, or Rs 3,000.[25]

Apart from filling up the *khal* and making the new road (Creek Row), the Dingabhanga subcommittee was also working towards improving connectivity between this road and the part of the city to the north of it. At the end of March 1821, well after the Dingabhanga project had been completed, the subcommittee informed the Lottery Committee that it had 'made *puckah*' the Nimbootollah (Nebutala) Lane 'from the Dingabungah Road to

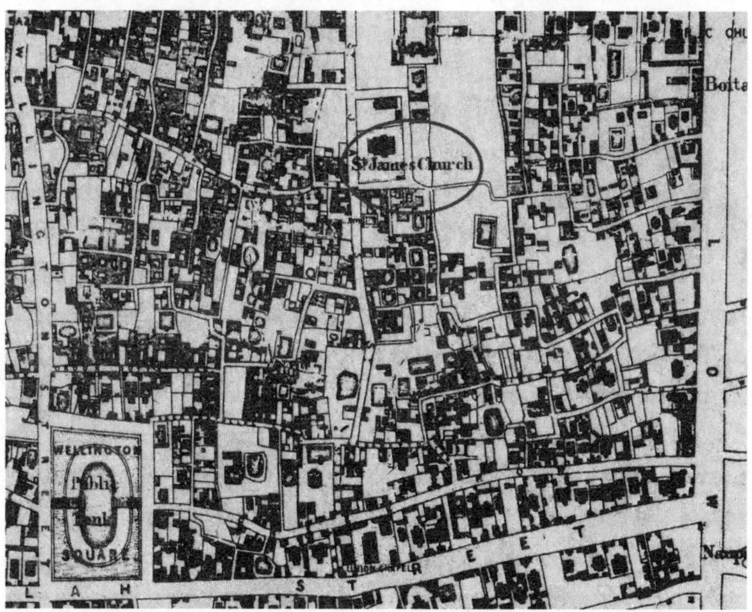

Fig. 39. Heysham's map of 1856 showing the location of St James's Church

the new chapel building[26] at the *goukhana* near the Bow Bazar Road' at a cost of Rs 245 which it wanted the committee to reimburse.[27] The specific problem faced by the subcommittee was that a plot of land, in extent 12 *chittack*s and costing Rs 225 (at Rs 300 a *katha*), at the north end of the lane had to be bought from Bissonauth Uddecary (Biswanath Adhikari) to make the connexion with the churchyard, specifically to make 'a gateway of the new church at Scavengers Lane'[28] but such an expense could not 'properly be charged to the [lottery] fund'. The remaining Rs 20 in the cost estimate related to compensation 'for pulling down and removing tiled huts'. The committee approved the expenditure but as a contingent expense so that the guidelines governing the use of the lottery funds were not violated.[29]

Nebutala Lane (Street) extended northward till the new church leaving an unbridged gap between it and Bowbazar Street. It was only a matter of time before the gap was filled up. The proposal was made by Shakespear in September 1821 who said that the 'principal object' of the exercise was to provide a 'convenient and handsome access to the new chapel now building on the site of the old *gowkhawnah*', an additional advantage being the 'opening of an almost direct communication between the Durrumtullah Road and the Bow Bazar Street'.[30] The 40-ft-wide road would cost Rs 16,603-12-0 of which Rs 12,300 would have to be paid to four individuals for land (at Rs 300 a *katha*), namely, Ramnarain Ghose (Rs 5,400 for 18 *katha*s), Parbuttee Churn Banerjee (Rs 3,000 for 10 *katha*s), Koonjoodoss Byragee (Kunjadas Boiragi, Rs 2,400 for 8 *katha*s) and Kowtook (Koutuk) Ghose (Rs 1,500 for 5 *katha*s). The Lottery Committee approved of the project, the Government's nod following shortly, facilitating easier north-south communication between Bowbazar Street in the north and Dharamtala Street in the south.[31]

The road was completed in 1822, Shakespear taking the opportunity to propose further improvements in the area costing the committee Rs 3,825, which would include widening and straightening of an 'irregular lane' on the south side of the chapel 'which is connected with opening a road eventually from the chapel to the Circular Road, which will tend to improve that part of the town, and to facilitate access to the chapel for the Christian population which inhabit it'.[32] (If later maps of the area are any guide, the road, estimated to cost Rs 22,920-11-2, was not built finally.)

The plans to improve the lane were driven by the desire to clear the immediate neighbourhood of native huts, etc., which were likely to disturb proceedings at the chapel and the adjacent school. The Chief Magistrate sought permission to be allowed to engage with Bissumbur Odikary (Biswambhar Adhikari) either to exchange or purchase his premises through which a part of the southern road would pass. This was considered essential because the ground was

> ...covered with huts occupied by natives who from their proximity to the chapel are likely to disturb divine service, whilst the shabby look of the huts indenting on the chapel yard destroys the appearance of the premises which, if surrounded entirely by a road as they would otherwise be, would have a handsome and uniform effect.

He also '[strongly recommended] that [a specific parcel of ground] may be thrown into the churchyard or kept clear for public purposes connected with the chapel or school'. The changes would cost the committee Rs 3,825 and the Government Rs 4,137-8-0 (which would be paid from the proceeds of sale of surplus land of the old *gowkhana* 'lying to the east of the chapel'). The improvement of the area was completed by the end of 1823 there being a balance of cash to the extent of Rs 477-2-11.[33]

❦

Shakespear had penned his first minute on the 'southern' part of the town on 13 January 1820. Nearly a month later, on 7 February, he laid before the committee his views on the northern part of the town, which he called the 'upper north division', comprising 'all the town lying between the Chitpur bridge and Mahrutta Ditch to the north, and Cotton Street and the Mutchooa Bazar to the south' (see Fig. 40).[34] This large area was subdivided into smaller sections, the first of which extended from Baghbazar Road in the north to Kutooah Street[35] in the south and the Shyambazar Road. Shakespear wrote that the ground in the area was 'high' and roads were 'much wanted'. There were a few of them, 'and those few, excepting the Dum Dum Road, bad'. On the road branching off east from Chitpur Road at Sobhabazar, leading to Gopimohun Deb's house and beyond, Shakespear wrote that it was incorrectly described in Upjohn's map as being 'straight (and) wide' when, in fact, 'it becomes a narrow winding lane' from Deb's house. He suggested that it would be a major improvement if the road was extended to Circular Road in the east having 'the same breadth as it is so far as Gopeemohun's'.

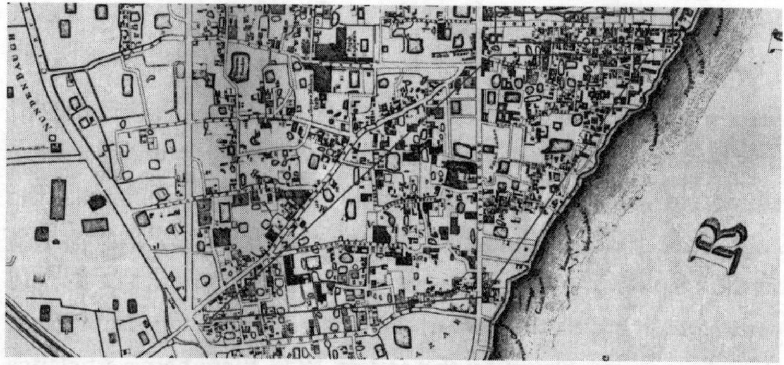

Fig. 40. In Schalch's 1824 map Kutooah Street had been renamed Sobhabazar Street. The map also shows a part (marked) of Shakespear's 'upper north division' of the town; also the location of Rath Ghat to the west of Sobhabazar Street

Rath Ghat was located at the western end of Kutooah Street.[36] Shakespear wrote to the committee on 27 February 1820 that Rs 9,113 'had been laid out in constructing a fine *puckah* ghaut and a sluice gate for the purpose of draining the vicinity, but which has never yet been completed'.[37] Work on the ghat proper, which had been 'finished', had begun under the magistrates in March 1816 and had 'ended' in May 1818, the 'incomplete' tag relating to the purchase of property to the south of it which had affected work adversely on the 'sewer and sluice gate', also located to the south of the ghat. The property to the south comprised ground on which there was a building, the considered view of Richard Blechynden, the surveyor, being that unless the ground was also bought it would not be worthwhile just to buy the house standing on it. Shakespear's point was whether the Lottery Committee was willing to lay out 800 or 1,000 rupees to purchase the house 'or whether the sluice from which much advantages might be derived to the draining of that part of the town shall remain in its present useless state'. The project needed to be completed because there were 'several bad pools on the south side of Kutooah Street which in the rains overflow, inundating the houses and rendering them damp and unhealthy, which the proposed sluice and drain would remedy by carrying off the superfluous water into the river'. The committee agreed with Shakespear's suggestion that the Rath Ghat work be completed according to the original plan and, accordingly, sanctioned Rs 1,000 for the purchase of the house concerned.

In the area to the south of Kutooah Street, till Jorabagan Road, the 'only improvement' needed was its draining into the 'south drain of Kutooah Street, and so into the river at Ruth Ghat'. In Shakespear's view, the part of the town from Jorabagan Road to Cotton Street in the south could not have been filthier. He wrote:

> From Jura Bagaun Road to Cotton Street the town is beyond description dirty and unwholesome. The quantity of

Fig. 41. Schalch's map showing the area of the city (marked) from Jorabagan Street to Cotton Street in the south

> filth collected in different parts of it is enough to occasion a plague. This is no doubt in a very great degree to be attributed to the neglect of the conservancy officers, but still more so to the construction of the roads and drains. The former are chiefly in earth; the latter have been cut so irregularly that, excepting in the rains, they can be of no service in carrying off liquid filth. Those few that have been made *puckah* are now so decayed that they tend rather to obstruct than to accelerate the passage of water. Many of the lanes are so narrow that a wheelbarrow could scarcely enter them, and to this the scavengers attribute the accumulation of dirt.

Shakespear was so taken aback by the condition of the area (see Fig. 41) that he was unable to propose any well-thought-out remedy except the construction of 'a central drain to the river and surface draining on both sides', a suggestion the feasibility of which he was yet to ascertain.[38]

❦

Shakespear then shifted his attention to the area east of Chitpur Road, between Shyambazar Street and Simleah Road, his view being that there were no 'particular observations' to make for this part of the town. He wrote: 'There are several good roads in earth which ought to be made *puckah*', but he could not recommend that they be 'laid with bricks' in view of the fact that 'there are so many [roads] in the central parts of the town…in that state'. From Simleah Road to Machuabazar Street, which too had many earth-roads 'which ought to be made *puckah*', the ground was 'pretty high', the northern part of the area being marked by the large drain[39] which the Lottery Committee had completed the previous year (1819). The southern part of this section was crisscrossed by 'numerous drains' which, however, Shakespear wrote, did not prevent the area from being 'full of pools of bad water' during the rainy months. The south-east part was 'thickly wooded' which, to the reader 200 years later, provides an idea of how this part of the town looked like at the beginning of the 19th century, and earlier. Shakespear suggested a straightening out of the Simleah Road and 'what is called Bebee Cisper's road' in a 'more direct line to the Chitpore Road', the 'entrance to them at the west end being very confined'.

In Shakespear's scheme of things, the 'lower north division' of the town extended from the Machuabazar Street-Cotton Street alignment in the north to 'Writers' Buildings, Loll Bazar and Bow Bazar Road in the south' (see Fig. 42). Regarding draining of this area, he found that the existing drains in the north-east part of this division were at 'great depth' carrying their content towards Machuabazar Street the inference from this being that 'some error' had crept into the original draining of the part of the town

> …lying on the east side of Chitpore Road in the neighbourhood of the Terethee Bazar,[40] which, instead of being drained towards the Loll Bazar Street to the south,

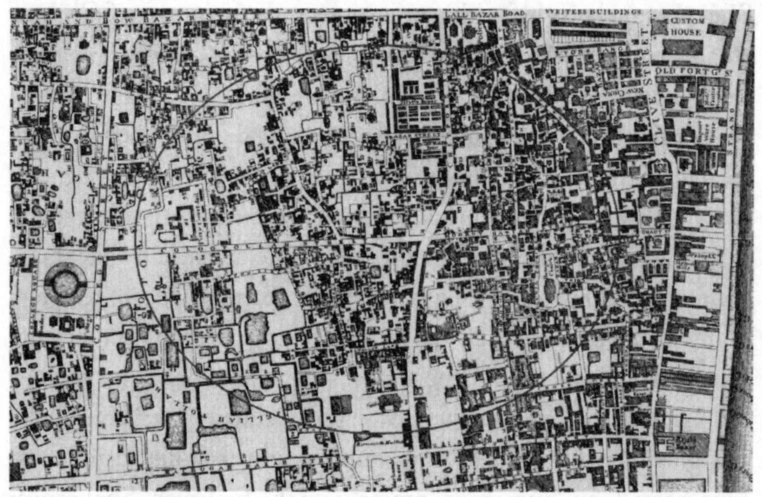

Fig. 42. Schalch's map showing a part (marked) of Henry Shakespear's 'lower north division' of the city

> or the Circular Road to the east, have been drained through the high land to the Mutchooah Bazar Road to the north.

Since Tiretta Bazar and its neighbourhood was 'perhaps the dirtiest part of the town' and an effective drainage solution perforce had to be found, he suggested that the situation could be improved 'either by cutting a sewer in a direct line from the Chitpore Road to the Circular Road', halfway between the Lalbazar and Machuabazar Roads, or 'by widening and making *puckah* the drain on the north side of the Loll Bazar on the principle adopted on the north side of the Dhurrumtullah Street', the choice between the two alternatives being left to the Lottery Committee. At the time, the drain to the north of Lalbazar Street was of little or no use 'being in some places very confined and impeded by small arches', but being enlarged it would be able to 'carry off (a) considerable body of water which must now find its way twice the distance by numerous windings before it reaches an open channel'.[41]

Having outlined the alternative 'solutions' to the drainage problems affecting the area, Shakespear looked ahead towards the possibility of drawing up a more permanent solution to the unsatisfactory drainage conditions, the Lottery Committee being urged to turn its thoughts to 'the best mode of draining this very offensive and consequently unwholesome part of the town'. He pointed out that to the west of Chitpur Road (towards the river), the existing drains throughout the year were for the most part 'full of liquid filth which…is partly absorbed and partly evaporated, which must render the air in a great degree noxious and unwholesome'. The Officiating Chief Magistrate's suggestion was to build a tunnel, 'on the principle of that near the Loll Diggee',[42] from the Foujdar's house on Chitpur Road 'down Moorghyhatta Street, crossing the Old China Bazar Street, to Jackson's Ghaut', a plan which, according to Shakespear, 'was once in the contemplation of the committee'.[43] An incidental suggestion made was that 'a range of godowns lying between the house occupied by Mr Lackersteen[44] (in front of Jackson's Ghaut) and the old China Bazar' be bought by the authorities which would enable 'a fine street (to) be opened in that direction comparatively at a small expense'. In conclusion, Shakespear appealed to the committee to draw up a 'systematic plan…for making *puckah* the streets of the town which are now in earth'. He said that he had made a list of such streets with an estimate of paving them, his specific proposal being that the committee should begin the process by taking up one street every month, five years being required to complete the entire project (see below).

The minute was discussed in the committee with members putting forward their own ideas on the subject. Gordon felt that a subcommittee should examine the proposal for a tunnel from

Chitpur Road to the river. Colvin called for a subcommittee to deal with drainage which would be 'very usefully employed on personal enquiries during the next six months assisted as they will soon be by Lt Schalch's [findings on the Calcutta levels]'. Bayley, the most senior Government functionary on the committee, argued that despite all the proposed measures appearing to be 'desirable and important', the present state of the finances of the Lottery Committee would make it difficult to decide on 'where to begin and which to choose'. His own view was to apply the resources available to only '*one* part of the town' (emphasis in original). As he saw it: 'The prevailing winds are from the south. If we remove nuisances, open new streets and squares in the southern part, we are in fact doing good to the inhabitants of the northern part also'. On Shakespear's proposal on making *kutcha* roads *pucka*, Gordon cited the resource-shortage argument to shelve it for the time being. Citing the same reason, Ballard wanted the focus of the committee's work to remain on 'the works in hand' and to attend to development imperatives 'in the vicinity of the Circular Road'. The committee as a whole did not comment on Shakespear's suggestions and kept them aside for 'future consideration'.[45]

Seven months later Shakespear brought up the subject once again citing an easing of the resource problem in the wake of the just-adopted new lottery auction system.[46] On the drainage issue, Shakespear pressed home his point by saying that the experiment tried out on the west side of Chitpur Road[47] 'sufficiently shows the practicability of surface-draining, of carrying on the plan upon a more extended scale'. Following Gordon's advice, he suggested that a subcommittee be set up and the Government's permission be sought for 'our disbursing a sufficient sum for carrying on the work in such parts of the town as may appear most to require improvement'. Such a subcommittee, he felt, should work in close coordination with the superintendent of the roads and drains so as to prevent 'mistakes which might interfere with the general draining of the town'. An investment of Rs 2,000 every month, or Rs 24,000 for a whole year, 'would enable the subcommittee to make considerable progress in the respective works within the year', a proposal which was accepted by the Government a month later (see below).

In an effort to deflect further opposition to the project, Shakespear quoted chapter and verse to impress on the Lottery Committee the point that the development of drainage and roads fell within the ambit of expenditure of the lottery funds when the Calcutta lottery was first instituted more than a decade earlier. On 12 October 1807, the Government had told the committee for improving the town that it would have to direct its

> ...attention to the following objects of public and general utility: 1st, the construction of drains or watercourses in those streets or places in which works of that description may be requisite; 2nd, the reconstruction of such of the existing drains as shall appear to have been originally formed (as is very generally the case) on erroneous principles; 3rd, the construction of the streets which have not yet been paved with bricks or other materials in those parts of the town which, from their extensive population, may appear to require it.[48]

Shakespear's wide-ranging minute on the southern section of the city had led to the construction of Creek Row to the north of Dharamtala Street. His minute on the northern part of the city had led to the formation of a subcommittee comprising Shakespear and Lt Paton to tackle problems on the drainage and road fronts.[49] Among other things, the subcommittee was asked to draw up a report on the 'progress...already been made and of the success which has resulted from the (Chitpur Road) experiment' (mentioned by Shakespear in his minute) which would enable the committee 'to form a correct judgement on the expediency of carrying on the plan of surface draining upon a more extended scale'.

Within two weeks, the subcommittee informed the committee that the Chitpur drainage experiment, conducted to the west of the road, had been a success. A 2,016-ft surface drain had been completed from Murgihata Street to Banstala Gully (see Fig. 17), which had led to the freeing up of road space measuring two to five feet, which in turn had led to a widening of Chitpur Road rendering it 'greatly more convenient and safe for carriages in this much frequented thoroughfare of the town'. The subcommittee said pointedly: 'We cannot but consider it satisfactory that the difficulty in meeting with deep drains (some of which must, of course, be left open) can so easily be overcome should the plan be introduced on a more extended scale'. There was, however, one problem specific to Chitpur Road which had led to a sharp increase in costs. The principal deep drain ran along the east side of the road with the result that 'whenever deep drains running from the westward joined the old drain, it was necessary to carry them into the deep drain on the east side of it'. This had led to the building of 'four new bridges across' Chitpur Road which placed 'a very heavy charge' on the expense of the experiment, the four *pucka* bridges together costing Rs 629-4-2 ½ (or nearly 42 per cent) of the total expenditure of Rs 1,512-0- ¼.[50]

Armed with the subcommittee's report, the committee wrote to the Government in early October backing Shakespear's Chitpur Road surface-draining 'experiment' and his proposal to pave *kutcha* roads.[51] Noting that no 'precise expense' had been estimated for the road project, the committee said that the projected investment for both the schemes 'would admit of considerable progress' being made over a period of twelve months, the funds being used 'very beneficially' for the purpose mentioned. A fortnight later, on 20 October, the Government sanctioned the funds sought but not before cautioning the Lottery Committee that, while extending the surface-draining option to 'such other parts of the town as they may select', it was to make sure that there was no interference with 'the general draining of the town'. It also approved the suggestion to convert *kutcha* roads into paved ones 'in the most populous parts of the town', leaving the selection of the roads to the committee. Funds to the extent of Rs 24,000 was released for the 'official year 1820-21' the point being made that on the exhaustion of the kitty the committee was to apply again 'for such further sum as they may judge expedient with reference to the state of their funds and other considerations'.[52] The committee formed a subcommittee six days later comprising Bayley, Shakespear and Paton tasking it with the selection of spots where the drainage and road improvement could be effected.

Chitpore
Baug Bazar
Old Powder Mill Gaut
Rogo Meeters Gaut
Cassheram Meeters Gaut
Bonomalee Sircars Gaut
Ketooah Gaut
Rutteelah Gaut
Sootalootee Hautcolah
Aree tollah Gaut
Manick Baboo's Gt.
Madden Dutts Gt.
Toonoo Baboos Gaut
Neemtullah Gaut
Jura Bagaan Gaut
H
O
O
G
S
O
T
O
T
D

STRAND ROAD – CLEARING THE TABLE

When Job Charnock landed in Calcutta in 1690, the channel of the Hooghly was located further to the east than is the case now. The bank was dotted with the stray village, interspersed with open spaces and thick vegetation. Within 70 years the scene had changed beyond recognition owing to the

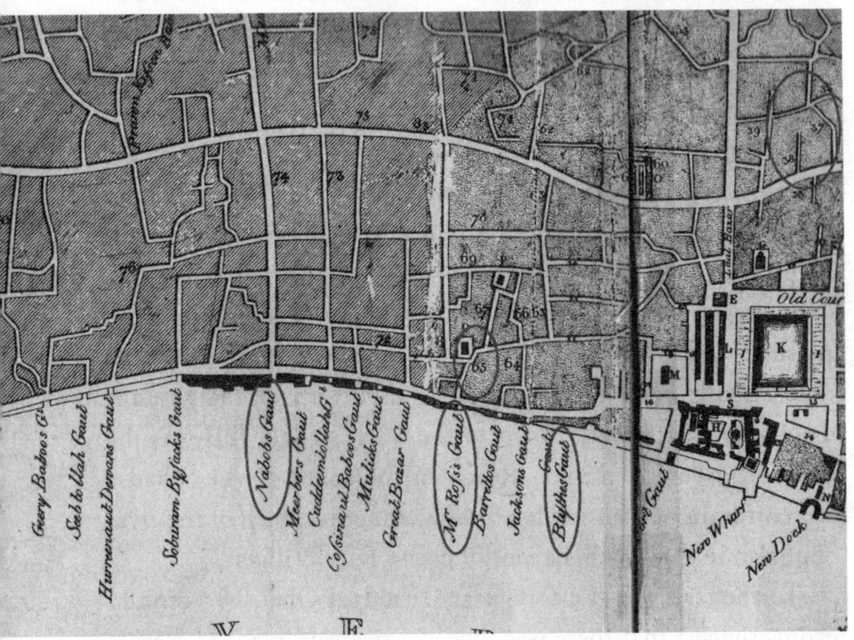

Fig. 43. Wood's map (1784) showing the street by the river; also Kutooah Street (81), Bonfield's Lane (65), Zigzag Lane (37), Weston's Lane (38); also Ross's, Nawab's, and Blythe's Ghats

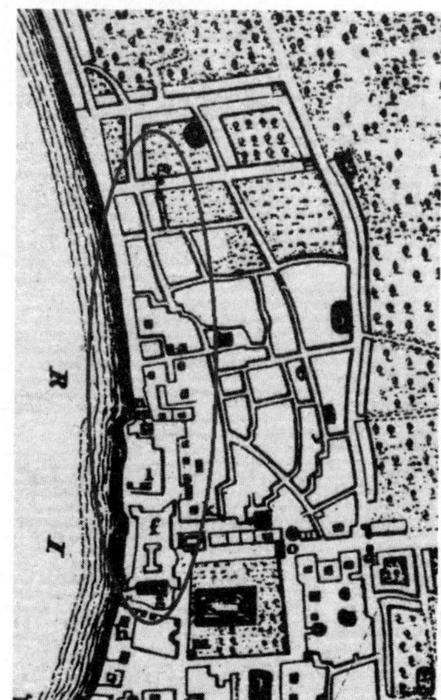
Fig. 44. The 1742 map does not show any road extending northward along the riverbank from the old Fort William

expanding trade and commerce triggered by the East India Company. In 1767 the official records were stating that 'the street by the river side to the northward of the Custom House [located where the first Fort William was situated in today's BBD Bagh] had been greatly encroached upon by a number of *golahs,* little straw huts and boutiques that have been indiscriminately reared'. The specific suggestion was that no such construction should be allowed 'to the southward of this spot' which would 'relieve the inhabitants from the apprehensions of fire, and of their houses being entirely undermined by rats'.[1] (Since Strand Road had not been built at the time, was this street [Wood's 1784 map (see Fig. 43) shows that it ran north till Kutooah Street] the precursor of the later Clive Street [Netaji Subhas Road]?) Of interest also is the fact that the 1742 map does not show any such road northward of the old fort. With the advent of the sahibs, houses came to be built along the riverbank the grounds of some of which went down to the water's edge. This was the case not just with Garden Reach in the south – which had a concentration of such garden houses along the reach of the river – but also in the north, beyond the first Fort William.

To the south of the fort, near Chandpal Ghat, 18th century records suggest that there was indeed a riverside 'road' 24 ft wide running between the water's edge and the houses to the east. Thomas Lyons, after whom the Lyons Range area in the business

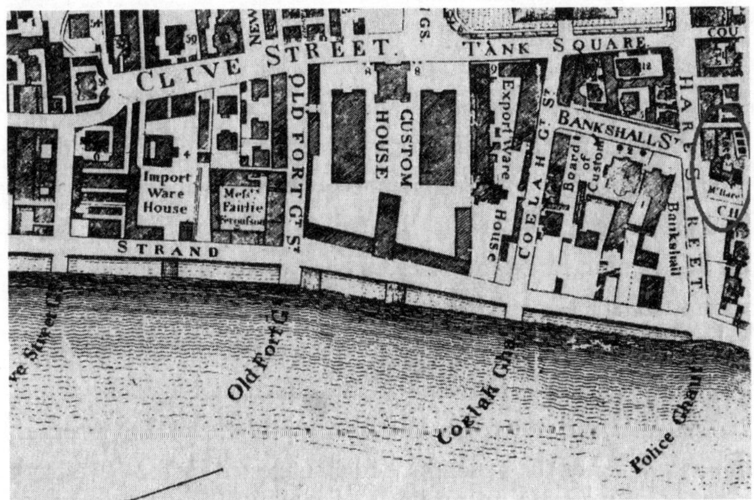

Fig. 45. Schalch's map showing the riverbank from Police to Koila Ghat, the location of the bankshall, the import warehouse & Clive Street Ghat; also David Hare's residence (marked)

district of Calcutta today is named, had plans to strengthen the embankment of the river at this point and increase the width of the road to as much as 50 ft.[2] There is, however, no clear picture of how long this road was or whether it was a road at all or, which is more likely, it was just a promenade which later developed into the Respondentia Walk.[3] However, with increasing economic activity and population pressure it was just a matter of time that a riverside road, or strand, would be developed which, among other things, would provide to the inhabitants easier access to the river, both for recreation and commerce. Perhaps, the first step towards having a north-south riverside passage – if only for a part of the riverbank – was taken when efforts were made to open a public way from Koila Ghat in the north to Police Ghat in the south. The Government pressed the case for such a passage, and thus was sowed the seed of Strand Road which sprouted within a couple of decades.[4]

❦

In the 18th century, the Hooghly was shifting its course rapidly to the west leaving space for Strand Road, as we know it today, to be built on reclaimed ground. The entire project was the brainchild of the committee 'for reporting upon the best mode of appropriating the Government lands on the banks of the river' (hitherto referred to as the Riverbank Committee), comprising H. Shakespear, H. Mackenzie, J. Hayes and G.J. Gordon, which submitted its 73-paragraph report to the Government on 1 March 1820.[5] The report based on a survey of the riverbank conducted by Henry Osborne, Surveyor in the office of the Collector of 24-Parganas, was sent to the Lottery Committee for it to ascertain 'in what manner the general scheme' suggested by the Riverbank Committee could 'best be prosecuted and to what extent [it] may be practicable to carry it [out]'.[6]

The report's value lies in the fact that it is perhaps the only contemporary source which provides a clear picture of the ownership structure of the riverbank and the uses it was put to in the early 19th century. It kicked off with the declaration that the 'boundaries of the city on the banks of the river Hooghly extend from the Marhatta Ditch (or Chitpore Bridge) on the north to the junction of Tolly's Nullah with the river on the south', adding that 'Our attention having been hitherto directed more particularly to that part of the town inhabited by Europeans, we shall confine this report to the banks of the river lying between Tolly's Nullah [in the south] and Jackson's Ghaut [in the north]...' Painting a property profile of the entire stretch of the riverbank, the report said that the bank between the junction of Tolly's Nullah and the Hooghly, where the Hastings bridge now stands, and the fort in the north ('nearly ¾th of a mile') was used mainly for military purposes, 'for the reception of garrison stores, which it would be inconvenient to keep in Fort William'. It referred to a Baloo Ghat[7] which was 'particularly convenient for the embarkation of troops, the loading and unloading of military stores, etc.' The report said

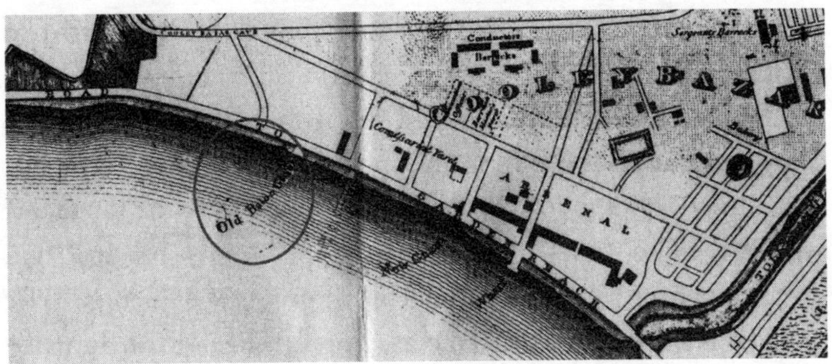

Fig. 46. Schalch's map showing the old Baloo Ghat and the 'new road to Garden Reach'

that it had already been proposed that 'the new mint be erected at the junction of the Nullah', a proposal which was not accepted.[8] The committee felt that the area could not be put to better use than 'it is at present' implying that the status quo ante be maintained.

The part of the riverbank from the 'north glacis' of the fort to Chandpal Ghat, a distance of 'nearly ½ a mile', was offlimits for 'private individuals' who were not allowed 'to have communication with the river'. Immediately to the south of Chandpal Ghat was located the reservoir and waterworks 'for supplying the aqueducts'. The space was kept clear 'and appropriated to a public promenade', probably the southern extension of the old Respondentia Walk. The report said that the entire stretch from Tolly's Nullah to Chandpal Ghat was Government property which formed 'the western boundary of the esplanade of Fort William'. The area north of Chandpal Ghat, to Cutchagoody Ghat[9] 'measuring 675 feet', was not solely Government land. It was littered with private property some of the owners being leading lights of Calcutta society. Subject to the Lottery Committee's approval, the Riverbank Committee wanted the area along the riverbank from Chandpal Ghat to Cutchagoody Ghat to be public property because this would enable the authorities to build along the entire stretch a 'public wharf, in continuation of that intended to be constructed from the Custom House [in the north] to Cutchagoody Ghaut'.

Viewed from the river today, this area is dominated by the State Bank of India's offices, the spot where the Bank of Bengal stood throughout much of the 19th century. At the time the report was drawn up (1820), the riverbank between Chandpal and Cutchagoody Ghats was occupied by the premises of George Tyler and the late Sir Robert Chambers, Chief Justice of the Supreme Court from 1791 to 1799 who had returned to England in 1799 and had died in 1803.[10] According to the report, the survey of the bank had found that the ground forming Tyler's premises contained 'a much larger quantity of ground than is specified in the *chittas* of 1197 BS' (1790). As for Sir Robert's property, the report said that his house was previously the property of Thomas Lyon, a *patta* having been granted to him in 1186 BS (1779) covering 1 *bigha* 2 *kathas* 'on condition that if he [Lyons] erected any buildings or walls upon it he would forfeit the grant'. Chambers bought the property around 1780 and within a year he had sought, and was given (on 23 August 1784), a *patta* for the ground measuring a *bigha* and a *katha* 'in which the former conditions on which the ground was granted to Mr Lyon are cancelled and taken off'.[11]

The report then focussed on the stretch of the riverbank between Cutchagoody Ghat and what it called Davidson's Ghat in the north, the two ghats being 750 ft apart.[12] Today, the ground between the two ghats lies to the west of Church Lane. In 1820, there were three buildings covering the ground: the southernmost was the property of Gabriel Vrignon, the next was the mint and the third was occupied by Palmer and Company, 'now occupied as the Marine and Registry Office' (where the Metcalfe Hall stands today). The records state that the third bit of ground measuring 1 *bigha* 3 *kathas* was occupied by Ramdoololl Sircar. The extent of Vrignon's premises corresponded to the *patta* 'granted in favour to the person of his name in the year 1206 BS [1799 AD]'. As regards the mint, the report said that a part of the ground measuring 6 *bigha*s 15 *katha*s on which the 'mint office' stood was *khamar* land, the rest being owned by Gabriel Gillet[13] and a Mr Lebong. The extent of the mint's premises appeared to have 'rather increased probably in the quantity projecting towards the river beyond the line of Mr Vrignon's wall' to the south of it. This is because the river was shifting its course westward with the result that land was being reclaimed on the eastern bank (adjacent to the mint). The same explanation may be cited for the report's finding that Palmer and Company's property had also increased compared to its original size as indicated in old land records. There were copies of two *pattas* of the Palmer property which, the report said, were granted to Colonel Samuel Hampton[14] in 1801 totalling a *bigha* and three *katha*s, an area which had been exceeded in 1820.

As regards the ground between Davidson's Ghat and Coila Ghat[15] further north (700 ft apart), the report said the space was occupied by 'the present Police Office, the Bankshall premises and part of the Marine Store Yard, and the grounds of the Marine Paymaster's office' (see Fig. 45). The police office building and grounds measuring 2 *bigha*s 14 *katha*s 15 *chittack*s was owned by a A. Hunter, the bankshall premises covered 12 *bigha*s 9 *katha*s 8 *chittack*s, and a Mr Lubjah was the former owner of the Marine Paymaster's office which stood on 16 *katha*s. Since the police office building had been purchased by the Lottery Committee to construct what is today Hare Street, the report concluded that the whole of the space between Davidson's Ghat and Coila Ghat was Government property. Describing the riverbank in the area vis-à-vis the water level, the report said that, at its height, the river overflowed 'the west end of the [marine] storeyard', there being thus the clear need to raise it by three or four feet 'to render it fit for building on'.

The next section of the riverbank (650 ft) covered was that between Coila Ghat and Old Fort Ghat, that is, the ground on which stood the first Fort William of the English settlement. In 1820 this space was occupied by the export warehouses and the Customs offices (see Fig. 45). To the north of Coila Ghat, 'a large spot' was used for the 'landing of materials for the repair of the roads in the town'. The Riverbank Committee had already suggested that a spot above Coila Ghat be appropriated for the building of offices 'for the servants of the export warehouse', which had been agreed to by the Government.[16] The space between the two ghats had 'received some addition' following the construction of the new Customs wharf.

Proceeding further north, the Riverbank Committee then turned its attention to the space between the Old Fort Ghat and Jackson's Ghat (1,125 ft).[17] This section is of more than passing interest because of the light it throws on the extent and nature of Reverend William Johnson's[18] ground located in the area, and the complex issues involved regarding proprietorship which generated some controversy. The Old Fort Ghat[19] was marked by a flight of steps (shown clearly in one of Thomas Daniell's paintings) to the north of which lay a spot of ground measuring 8 *bigha*s 15 *kathas* which was entered in the *chittas* of 1196 BS (1789 AD) as *khamar* land 'in the possession of the Reverend Mr Johnson with a godown and tiled house on it' (see Fig. 49). The report suggested that steps be taken to raise the ground 'to the north of the Old Fort

Fig. 47. Reverend William Johnson

Fig. 48. The Old Fort Ghat, by Thomas Daniell, 1787

Ghaut and west of the ground granted conditionally [to Johnson] with a view to the appropriation of it to public purposes'. In extent the ground was about 400 ft square, the report adding that 'there are some anchors and dismounted guns lying at the corner of it near the remains of the old ghaut, and in the northeast quarter is a mound on which there are two or three huts occupied by boatmen from the police guard boats'.

Probing the legitimacy of the title to the ground, the Riverbank Committee pointed out that, despite there being no reports of any claim being 'seriously maintained to this spot', there were reports of it being 'occasionally used for the deposit of old guns and anchors'. As a result of this use, 'a dubious occupancy' had been exercised over a part of the ground 'by Messrs Clarke and Company [Fergusson, Clarke and Company] on behalf of Mr Johnson' and, therefore, the need had arisen to establish the right of the Government over the ground in question. The committee said that since no *patta* for the land in question had ever been granted to anyone, it belonged to the Government in view of the 'undisputed…general proprietary right of Government to all land not granted to individuals nor occupied for such a period as to lead a Court of Justice to presume a grant'. Buttressing the argument, the report said:

> In Calcutta, indeed, Government has the *double right of sovereign and zamindar* [emphasis added]; and by established custom, even in the case of persons who have long had possession, it is the practice for them, when [an] excess is discovered, to apply for and obtain a pottah from the Collector for such excess and pay a corresponding revenue.

Further, though such applications were 'commonly, if not invariably, complied with', the very procedure 'appears to imply the option of granting or refusing a pottah, of letting the ground to any individual or of appropriating it to the use of the state'.

Dividing Johnson's 'property' into two parts, the report said that the ground to the eastward was not held by him by virtue of a *patta*: it was in fact granted to him 'under special conditions' by Warren Hastings' Government. Considering the 'origin and extent' of Johnson's tenure, it was felt that the Government would face no difficulty in exercising proprietary right over the plot in question. A further argument was advanced to back the Government's right to the plot which necessitated the unearthing of engaging details regarding Johnson's initial proposal to acquire the ground. Johnson in his 11 March 1777 letter[20] to the Governor-General and his Council wrote:

> I would propose at my own expense making an ample and commodious landing place agreeable to the accompanying plan and to keep it constantly in thorough repair for publick

> use; and in order to carry this scheme into execution I have to [solicit] of your Honorable Board a grant of the waste land lying between my house and the old Fort, with permission to erect on that side next to the river a range of godowns, and to rail in the whole being about one hundred and twenty yards in length and one hundred and eight yards in breadth with posts and chains, leaving a road to the old Fort forty feet in breadth and another road of fifty feet opposite the ghaut.

Three weeks later, in early April, the Governor-General and his Council approved of Johnson's proposal with, however, a proviso which indicated that the Government was not willing to allow Johnson to derive immediate economic benefits from his control of the ground in question. The grant[21] of the ground was to be made

> ...with the additional condition that the ground to be kept vacant, *viz.* the space bounded by the high road on the east [Clive Street], by the wall of Mr Johnson's garden on the north, *by the new range of godowns on the west* [emphasis added], and by the old Fort on the south, shall not be employed for any purpose whatsoever whether for erecting buildings or for the receipt of rubbish, lumber or

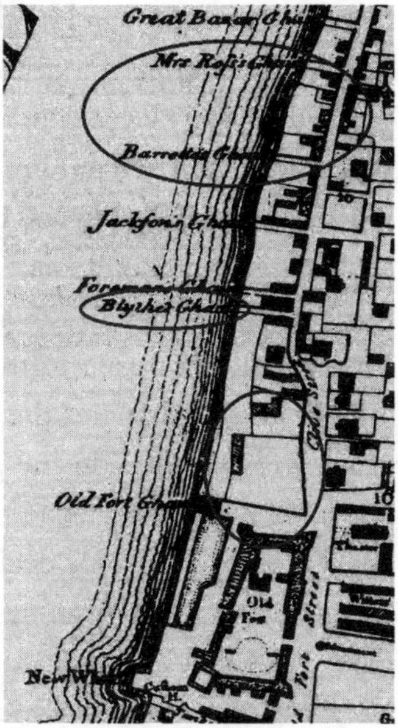

Fig. 49. Upjohn's map of 1793 showing the ground of William Johnson to the north of the old fort; also Blythe's, Mrs Ross's and Barretto's Ghats

> effects of any kind, but that it shall be kept entirely free and open at the sole charge and risk of the grantee, his heirs, executors and assignees, and that on failure of this condition the Governor and Council shall be at liberty to stop up the passage to the river and resume possession of the whole ground.

Within eight months (30 December 1777), Johnson was writing to the Government again intimating it that a 50-ft-wide ghat would not do in view of 'the great quantity of goods and merchandize continually landing [there] and the concourse of people at all times assembled for that purpose'. His proposal, accepted by the Government, was to put up at his own cost a ghat 'near the old Fort wall (a situation peculiarly advantageous from its vicinity to the Customs House godowns), making it eighty feet wide with a road of the same dimension'.

Johnson left India a decade later, in February 1788.[22] It is but natural that with time he began wondering what he was going to do with the vacant land by the river which he had taken from the East India Company a decade earlier to build a road and a ghat. He had abided by the conditions imposed on him when the land had been transferred to him, but he had also spent some money on it after the transfer. He had built a range of godowns and a railing separating the ground from the road and had expanded the ghat and road which lay to the south of the land. Just before leaving for England, he wrote to the Government that he had spent Rs 14,000 on the ghat and the road, Rs 7,000 on the railing, and as much as Rs 44,000 on the godowns, totalling Rs 65,000, which was a 'very large' sum for him.[23] This apart, the value of the ground concerned had not only declined 'much…since the year 1777 but seems to threaten becoming lower yearly for some time to come'. (Why this had happened is not explained in the letter.) Even if the value of the land had increased with time, his hands were tied owing to the terms of the grant which had ruled out sale and were applicable for an 'unlimited' period. Johnson wrote: 'The [annual] interest sicca Rs 7,800 is, therefore, constantly pressing upon me in addition to repairs while I may neither sell nor improve or make the most advantageous use of my property.' He added that these 'perplexities, however hard while on the spot, increase much to an absentee' so much so that they were '[obstructing] altogether my desire and wish to return to Europe'.

Johnson suggested two options to the authorities: taking back the ground from him on payment of the principal amount he had spent on it, or releasing him from the restrictive features of the grant by allowing him '[to use] the premises to the best advantage and to grant me a usual pottah in lieu of the present deed subject to the established rent of the ground in Calcutta'. If the first option was chosen by the Government, he would lose the accumulated interest on the capital amount and the sum spent on repairs, which he could set off by the rent received from the godowns. In case of the second option, he could, if he chose to, sell the land for a price (he said he had been offered Rs 65,000 for it 'some time ago') or develop it so as to ensure 'adequate returns' in the future. The 1787 correspondence[24] reveals that the Government explored, unsuccessfully, the possibility of buying the land from Johnson, the option of lifting the restrictions of the original grant not being considered at all.

The Riverbank Committee held that revisiting the historical background of the tenure of Johnson's ground – 'to the east of the spot which we are of opinion is the exclusive property of the Government' – was necessary because even if a claim was instituted to the spot in question on the ground of its 'contiguity to the land granted conditionally to Mr Johnson', such a claim could be

> ...met by a reference to the peculiar terms of the grant in which the land granted is specifically stated to be bounded

> on the west (i.e. on the side next to the river) by a range of godowns [see above] beyond which, therefore, neither Mr Johnson, his heirs, executors or assignees can possibly assert any just claim.[25]

To the north of the ground granted conditionally to Johnson lay two parcels of ground containing 3 *bigha*s 13 *katha*s 8 *chittack*s and 1 *bigha* 3 *katha*s 8 *chittack*s, which were held under separate *pattas* 'and granted to the trustees of Mr Johnson on May 13 1793'. To the west of 'Begum' Frances Johnson's house on the riverbank[26] was another parcel of ground measuring 1 *bigha* 13 *katha*s 2 *chittack*s granted to her in December 1794 on the condition that her *patta* would be revoked 'at the pleasure of the Government should any public inconvenience be hereafter found to result from the grant'.[27] The report said that in 1820 all these several parcels of ground, measuring together 15 *bigha*s 5 *katha*s 2 *chittack*s, formed the import warehouse premises (see Fig. 45), the ground being bought by the Government from Gopimohun Tagore. Further north was the shipbuilding yard of Messrs Smith and Company, in possession of Messrs Alexander and Company, and Breen's shipyard.[28] The report said that without a new official measurement and 'local enquiry' it would be difficult to state the exact amount of ground apportioned to each of these occupants. According to the 1789 (1196 BS) measurement, the entire area covered 4 *bigha*s 9 *katha*s 8 *chittack*s, but the river's subsequent withdrawal to the west had increased it to 18 or 20 *bigha*s. North of this area was Jackson's Ghat.

What this indicates is that there was sufficient ground reclaimed from the river on which a road could be built. But who was the owner of the reclaimed land? Citing the fact that the area of the two shipyards had increased by more than four times because of the river's shifting course, the committee asserted the claim of the Government 'to alluvial land not included in the pottahs of the occupants, whether the same has been formed by the spontaneous desertion of the stream or by artificial measures'. This arose from the nature of land tenure in the town which, in the committee's view, stipulated that 'tenants or pottah holders have no right to a single yard of ground beyond that specified in their pottahs, and that persons holding...tenures thus limited cannot claim any accretions arising from the retiring of the river'. The point was then made that the East India Company was the 'general zemindar, and as such any new land must...be considered to be at its disposal'. But what if some person had been 'in undisturbed occupancy' of such land for a long time? In that case, according to the committee, a title to the land in question could perhaps be established unless – and this is of some interest – 'shaken...by proceedings to which Government would not probably wish to resort'.

Secondly, the Riverbank Committee focussed on the Government's role, as 'trustee for the public', to 'dispose and control the appropriation of the bank of the river, and especially the space lying between high and low watermark', with the objective of securing 'for the public an open road and quay through the whole or a large portion of the extent of the city'. In cases where the occupancy of land between the high and low watermarks was 'of no very long standing or has (as in many cases, we believe it has) been contested by the magistrates', the Government would be within its rights to assert ownership of such land which would enable it to complete 'at a comparatively small expense the great work of opening a public wharf along the banks of the city'. One of the advantages of having such a quay along the river would be its utility in increasing 'the security of the Customs and the river police of the town'. The committee said that 'by taking measures for gradually raising the ground between [the] high and low watermarks, sufficient ground for a road along the banks of the river could be obtained with little or no interference with private rights'.

Discussing the public's right of access to the river, it was argued that persons who occupied land on the riverbank, even if 'full proprietors' or even the Government itself 'as zemindar', did not have the legal right to 'shut out the public from the benefit of a free access to the bank of the river where it has been long enjoyed by them'. The report said that, barring 'trifling exceptions', no individual had till then 'asserted an exclusive right to the low land in question by enclosing it and excluding the public'. In some cases, landowners on the riverbank were 'in the habit of levying a trifling wharfage on boats loading or unloading on front of their property'. However, since such cargo-related activity at these places would be 'of little value without the right of passage of passing through the adjoining property', the cess probably rested 'on the undisputed title to close such a passage than any right to prevent access to the bank'. The cess also did not indicate any title to the land lying between the high and low watermarks, access to which was the public's 'indisputable' right 'even where the bank may be possessed in full proprietary right'. In any case, the report felt that the 'convenience and advantage' of having a road along the riverbank 'would probably more than compensate to the parties the loss of their irregular exactions which, from commanding the access to the city, they now levy'.[29]

Attention was drawn to the point that, even if it was accepted that individuals did not have the right to prevent the public from having unfettered access to the riverbank 'where it has long been open', the Government's right

> ...to raise the land lying between [the] high and low watermarks for the accommodation of the public could, independently of any peculiar rights belonging to the

> Company as zemindar, be successfully resisted…by showing that the operation would deprive the party of some rightful privilege long enjoyed by them.

One example of this was the shipyards to the north of William Johnson's ground where the Government 'could not probably construct any work in front of them calculated to render those yards inapplicable to that purpose'. However, the chance of serious differences cropping up between the Government and the private parties involved was probably reduced by the fact that not only would the authorities 'naturally be very reluctant to enforce a right destructive of a long-enjoyed privilege', the parties themselves would be ready to back 'any arrangement connected with objects of public improvement'. In other stretches of the bank, the report said that the only issue which could crop up was the right of access to the river with which, however, the projected public road and quay 'would in no degree interfere'. Further, even where the ground had to be raised and godowns built on a part of it, 'the buildings might be so arranged as to leave the right substantially unimpaired'.

As regards financing of the road project along the strand, the Riverbank Committee felt that no 'serious expense' would be involved 'even supposing it necessary to construct at the place where dockyards have been constructed [a] drawbridge such as to allow a free passage for vessels built or repaired in them'. This would also cover cases of indemnification for ground long in the occupation of individuals or where substantial capital expenditure had been effected. Income would also be generated by sale to 'a considerable extent' of the raised land which would not be used for the construction of warehouses. Such proceeds would be 'sufficient to cover the whole or a great part of the expense of forming the road'.

Coming to the operational part of the plan, the report proposed that the Collector of Calcutta be asked to take possession of the ground north of the Old Fort Ghat and that, 'in concert with the magistrates and with the committee of improvement', immediate measures be taken to raise it. When raised,

> ...such part as appears necessary for an open road along the river sufficiently spacious to admit of the convenient landing and shipment of goods should be set apart, the rest to be disposed of to the best advantage, the price obtained for this last portion to be reserved as a fund for the further prosecution of the work or other similar purposes connected with the improvement of the city.

The Riverbank Committee felt that such a representation of the project would reduce 'any unpopularity which might otherwise attach to the assertion of the right of Government' and that the 'public voice [would] be listed on the side of Government and the danger of litigious opposition [would] be much reduced'. If it was found that the work of raising the ground as suggested was implemented smoothly and that sufficient funds were generated for the further improvement of the area, the same course could be followed with regard to 'other portions of the banks of the river and soon, progressively'. If, on the other hand, problems arose (for example, cases where the legal difficulties were 'insuperable'), the report felt that 'little harm' would be done 'by...limitedly agitating the question'. Apart from the investment being under control, if it was found that a road along the entire stretch of the riverbank was not 'practicable' the benefit would still be 'great in opening even one additional means of free and convenient access'.

The Riverbank Committee had submitted its report to the Government on 1 March 1820. Three weeks later, Holt Mackenzie,

Secretary to the Government, informed the committee that the Governor-General in Council had 'entirely' approved of 'the manner in which you have fulfilled the object of your appointment'.[30] It was now time to act. The committee had said that it would be 'desirable to adopt measures' to raise the land to the west of the ground in the possession of William Johnson 'with a view to the appropriation of it to public purposes'. Accordingly, the Collector of Calcutta was asked to take possession of the land in question and transfer it to the Lottery Committee. In fact, it was made clear that the Lottery Committee would be the body to 'consider and suggest the most advantageous mode of disposing of the ground in question' following its raising and levelling 'with a view to the improvement of the city'. The committee would also 'consider in what manner the general scheme suggested...[can] best be prosecuted and to what extent [it] may be practicable to carry it [out]'. Extending the scope of the work on the riverside road further, the Government asked the Riverbank Committee to study the ground disposition 'to the northward of Jackson's Ghat' and report back to it.

On 20 April the Lottery Committee asked John Trotter, Jr, the Acting Collector of Calcutta, when he would be able to hand over the land in question to the committee. Eight days later, Trotter wrote back to say that, 'conformably to instructions received from the Board of Revenue', he was handing over the land in question, namely, 'the low *khamar* lands belonging to Government lying to the north of the Custom House'. Along with his letter, he enclosed a communication he had sent to Messrs Fergusson, Clarke and Company – agents of Henry Smith of London, the late Rev. Johnson's 'personal representative' and 'heir'[31] – 'requiring them to cause the immediate removal of the property now deposited upon the said lands'. The 'property' referred to was 'the timbers now lying there' which the Acting Collector had been led to understand had been 'placed [there] by your permission'. The agents pleaded inability to carry out the suggestion because the ground in question had been 'long in our possession as the agents of the late Reverend William Johnson to whom the same, as we have been informed, rightfully belonged', and that, therefore, no action could be taken 'without authority from our constituents'.

Here was a case of a private party's direct confrontation with the Government regarding acquirement of land for a public project. At the Lottery Committee's meeting of 4 May a subcommittee – 'the subcommittee for the improvement of the Government khamar lands at Old Fort Ghaut' – comprising H. Shakespear, G.J. Gordon and Lt Paton was appointed to 'take immediate measures for raising and levelling the ground in the manner directed by the Government' and to prosecute the work as expeditiously as possible in view of 'the commencement of the approaching rainy season'.[32] It was asked to set up

> …a fence of bamboos along the whole southern line of the spot of ground (in question) leaving a gate or entrance for the access of the workmen and labourers who are to be employed by the committee in raising and levelling the ground in question, and that they be further requested to entertain as many peons or *khulassees* as may be necessary for the purpose of preventing any person not authorised by them from entering into or depositing upon the premises any rubbish or other articles of that description.

Clearly, the apprehension was that Fergusson, Clarke and Company could force the issue by continuing to use the ground in question. This is underscored by the subcommittee being asked to approach the magistrates to instruct the officers who were to be stationed on the premises in question 'to give their assistance in preventing any unauthorised persons from entering the premises and in guarding against the deposit upon the premises of any rubbish or other articles by individuals not acting under the authority of the Lottery Committee'. As regards the removal of material under the control of the agents being kept on the premises, the committee wrote to the agents asking them to remove the articles 'with as little delay as practicable'. The iron fist was shown when 15 May was set as the deadline after which any material remaining on the ground 'belonging to you or to other individuals' would be removed and would be 'deposited either on the side of the road or in some more convenient place, if such can be found in the neighbourhood, at the risk of the respective owner of such articles'.

The committee's hard line was met by a stern riposte. Fergusson, Clarke and Company did not wait till the deadline (15 May) to respond. On 5 May (the day after it received the Lottery Committee's ultimatum), the agents reiterated what was already known, namely, that 'the piece of ground alluded to in your letter has long been in our possession as agents of the late Reverend William Johnson to whom we have been informed it rightfully belonged' and that it 'is now held by us as the agents of his legal personal representation'. This being the case, they could not, 'without the authority of our constituents, comply with the requisitions of your [May 4] letter'. Fergusson and Clarke picked up the gauntlet when it wrote:

> …we are under the necessity of giving notice…to the Lottery Committee that if they do not forthwith order the railing to be removed and the persons employed in filling up the ground to desist [and] leave the premises, we shall consider ourselves obliged in duty to our constituents to apply to the police magistrates to aid in removing the railing put up and the persons employed on the ground in question.[33]

On the following day (6 May), the committee replied that the police magistrates had 'no jurisdiction to determine a question of property' the inference being that the agents would have to have recourse to the law. It was reiterated that the right of the Government to the ground in question was 'incontestable' and that the law officer concerned had already been instructed to defend any action which the agents may bring in a court of law.

A shifting of gears took place when, on receiving the committee's letter turning down its request to vacate the land in question, Fergusson, Clarke and Company approached the Governor-General in Council and informed him of the entire matter, thus taking the matter to the highest level of the Government. The specific request to the Government was that the legal issue 'in respect to this ground may be decided, and in the meantime…the Lottery Committee be desired to desist from further operations'. The agents underscored the point that they had 'positive instructions…not to relinquish the property alluded to unless compelled to do so by virtue of a legal decision'. However, by making a reference to Henry Smith's right to 'negotiate for the purchase of the ground if wanted for public purposes', the agents left the door ajar to a resolution of the dispute without having to take recourse to the law.[34]

Four days later, on 10 May, the attorney of Fergusson, Clarke and Company sent an official communication on the subject to the Lottery Committee thus taking the issue into the legal realm. On its part, the committee had informed the police magistrates of the latest development as also the Old Fort Ghat subcommittee, the latter being asked for its views on how the committee should handle the matter. That the authorities were taking the move by the agents of Johnson's heir seriously was indicated by the induction of Bayley, the Chief Secretary to the Government who was also a member of the Lottery Committee, into the subcommittee. The letter to the police magistrates had been despatched on 6 May, but that to the subcommittee took another 12 days the inference being that consultations had preceded it.

At its level, the Government took two months to respond to the 6 May letter from Fergusson, Clarke and Company during which time the legal aspect of the case was studied in detail. At its meeting of 2 June, the Territorial Department resolved to send the matter to the East India Company's attorney, Robert Poe, the Riverbank Committee being asked to furnish him with 'the papers and every necessary information' relevant to the subject so that, in consultation with the committee, he could prepare a comprehensive statement for the Advocate-General, Robert Spankie. The Board of Revenue, the Lottery Committee and the Acting Collector of Calcutta were also asked to provide inputs. The process took about a month. In early July Poe informed Holt Mackenzie, the Secretary in the Territorial Department, that the Riverbank Committee – of which Mackenzie was himself a member – had (on 24 June) sent him its views on the legal status of the land in question which he had sent on to the Advocate-General.[35]

The first point which the Riverbank Committee made in its representation was that it was not aware of the 'precise form of the grant [to Johnson]...further than what may be inferred from the order passed by Government' on 4 April 1777 (see above).[36] It said that ever since it had espoused the cause of Government ownership of the 'low land' lying to the west of the range of godowns on Johnson's land, 'we have understood, and it may be assumed by the advocate-general as a fact', that the 'western boundary of the land granted is stated in the grant to have been the river Hoogly'. However, it left to the Advocate-General 'to determine how far the force of those terms is restricted by the specification of extent and by the other conditions specified in Mr Johnson's [11 March 1777] letter and in the orders of Government, *which we presume will be found in the grant* [emphasis added]', which was missing. In other words, the committee was drawing pointed attention to the language used by Johnson in his letter which indicated that the range of godowns, which had been built since, was located 'next to the river', the inference being that 'the rest of the ground defined in the orders of Government' should be retained by the Government. The committee also pointed out that the grant included the actual measurement of the ground given to Johnson (120 yards from north to south and 108 yards from east to west) and that no reference had been made 'to the share of the river'.

Applying all this to Johnson's ground, the Riverbank Committee held that there was nothing 'in the orders of Government' relative to the ground to be made over to Johnson which could be construed as conveying to him 'a right of property in the river or in any way (affecting) the property which the sovereign would appear, according to English law, to have in the… alluvion in question'. The proof of the fact that the land claimed by Johnson's agents had been 'thrown up on the bed of the river' lay in 'oral evidence' as also in 'an inspection of the *pucka* ghaut' built by Johnson himself. The further point was made that the ghat and the range of godowns 'appear to afford a clear limit by which the increase may be known', the increase – which the committee described as 'very extensive compared with the quantity granted' – taking place since as recently as 1777 when the grant was made, that is, within the period fixed for 'limitation of public suits'. On the description of the western boundary of the land granted to Johnson being the Hooghly itself, the committee held that it could not 'affect the question'. According to it:

> It can convey…no right to the thing bounding any more than the description of the eastern boundary can be taken to give a right to the high road, and it would seem preposterous to assume that a grant conveying a parcel of land 120 yards by 108 could entitle Johnson to follow the river to whatever extent it might recede.

The Company's Attorney, Poe, had sent the views of the Riverbank Committee to the Advocate-General on 24 June 1820, the latter taking a couple of weeks to formulate his stand on the case.[37] As Spankie saw it, in the eyes of the law (English, civil and the custom of the country), the Government stood little chance of claiming successfully the alluvion which had been added to Johnson's land. He, therefore, asked the authorities to explore the path of negotiation the door to which had been left open by Fergusson, Clarke and Company in its 6 May 1820 letter to the Governor-General in Council (see above). The Government adopted this line without much ado the Lottery Committee being instructed on 1 August to adopt a more tempered stance, which, in fact, had already been communicated to Johnson's agents through a missive sent by Holt Mackenzie on 7 July.[38] In that letter Fergusson, Clarke and Company had been told that the Government was agreeable to negotiate on the matter and that the Chief Secretary, William Bayley, and Mackenzie himself had been deputed to hold talks 'with a view to the adjustment of the conflicting claims of the public and the representatives of the late Mr Johnson'. The agents were informed that the Lottery Committee had 'suspended all operations connected with the land in question', which was a signal that the Government was serious in its intention to forge a settlement. The 1 August resolution instructed the Lottery Committee that it should, 'in any further measure taken by them in the prosecution of the proposed work [the road along the riverbank], proceed on the principle of compromise and adjustment recently followed in the negotiations concluded with Messrs Clarke and Company' for the alluvial ground in front of the property of the late Reverend Johnson.[39] As for the contentious legal debate on the claim of Johnson's heirs to the adjoining alluvion, the Government followed the Advocate-General's advice, namely, that the entire issue be sent home to the Court of Directors.

The Governor-General in Council's decision to adopt a soft stand should be seen against the background of the hard line adopted earlier by the Lottery Committee. The story had, indeed, begun on an altogether different note. On 6 May the committee had stated in no uncertain terms that the right of the Government to the ground in question was 'incontestable' and that the law officer had already been told to contest any legal action which the agents might take on the matter (see above). The change in tack was probably necessitated by the realisation that legal action would take an unconscionably long time to play itself out which would delay the building of Strand Road. Underscoring the seriousness of the Government's intention to solve the issue amicably and quickly, Mackenzie had told Fergusson, Clarke and Company in his 7 July letter that the Government had '(engaged) to confirm any settlement in which we may agree'. In other words, the officials concerned had been given a *carte blanche* to work out a settlement of the issue.

The negotiations took nearly three months to bear fruit. On 30 September 1820 the Government apprised the Governor-General in Council that the parleys had resulted in two-thirds of the alluvion being granted to 'Mr and Mrs Smith', the 'representatives of the late Mr Johnson', the remaining third going to the Government for the construction of 'a public road and wharf on the side of the river'. In return, the Smiths were to withdraw all opposition to the construction of the public works and also 'all claim to the road and wharf when constructed'. This apart, all restrictions imposed by the 1777 grant on William Johnson regarding building on the land concerned were to be withdrawn as also the stipulation that the grantee was to keep the ghat in repair. A *patta* would have to be granted to Johnson's representatives 'for the ground lying between the intended road and wharf and the godowns to which free ingress and egress from the river were to be allowed by two or more gates'. The Government would have to bear half the cost of filling up the land between the road and the godowns, and the road between the old fort and the premises of Johnson (now belonging to the Smiths) to the north would have to remain a public road 'of the same breadth' to the river.[40] Clearly, what all this meant was that both the Riverbank and Lottery Committees had lost out in the contest with Johnson's representatives.

The records do not indicate when the 'personal conference'[41] between Bayley and Mackenzie, on the one hand, and Fergusson, Clarke and Company, on the other, was held in the course of which the above points were hammered out, but on 18 September the agents were communicating to the Government their approval of the 'compromise'. It was, however, made clear that the settlement would become binding on the Smiths only after their concurrence was got and that this would take some time because both of them were, presumably, in England. Till such time the Government could decide whether or not to proceed with the projected improvements. At the end of September, the Governor-General in Council confirmed the deal, Bayley and Mackenzie writing to the agents that it would be implemented subject to the execution of the 'requisite deeds…with the authority of Mr and Mrs Smith'. Work on 'gradually raising and levelling the ground' would, however, commence, the point being made that it would be helpful if 'the cannon and other articles lying on the ground near the old ghaut' were removed, 'as soon as may be convenient to you'. The distance travelled by the authorities along the road of compromise and accommodation can be gauged from the shift in language on this last point, the Acting Collector of Calcutta, John Trotter, Jr, having written with some firmness to the agents five months earlier 'requiring them to cause the immediate removal of the property now deposited upon the said lands'.

The Government had confirmed the agreement with the heirs of Reverend William Johnson at the end of September 1820 thus clearing the way for construction of the new road north of the Old Fort Ghat. Nine weeks later, in the first week of December, the Lottery Committee appointed a subcommittee (comprising W.B. Bayley, H. Shakespear, G.J. Gordon, A. Colvin and Lt Paton) to superintend 'the construction of the road and quay proposed to be carried along the banks of the river Hooghly from Chaundpaul ghaut in a northerly direction towards Chitpore', the subcommittee being asked to prepare a detailed estimate of the project.[42]

During the time the acquiescence of the Smiths was being procured, the Lottery Committee turned its attention to the prospect of developing a ghat on the river which would communicate freely with Clive Street, which had by that time emerged as an arterial road particularly as regards the city's rapidly expanding commerce.[43] The issue had been raised following the 'inconvenience' resulting specifically from the absence of a 'commodious access to the river between the Old Fort ghaut and Meerbuha [Mirbahar] ghaut'.

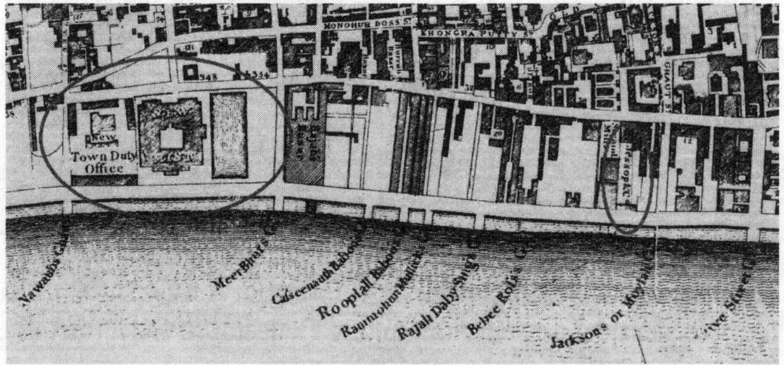

Fig. 50. Schalch's map showing the area south of the new Customs (Town Duty) office which belonged to the Nawab of Murshidabad; also the location of Jessop and Co.

Letters and articles had been appearing in contemporary journals for some time which must have put pressure on the authorities to focus attention on the subject. Thus, on 3 August 1819 a correspondent, who called himself 'A Reformer', complained in *The Calcutta Journal* that if someone from the city had to go on board a ship moored on the river the 'greatest thoroughfare' to use would have to be 'the Aramean [Armenian] or Beebee Ross's Ghat'[44] (see Fig. 43), which was not a pleasant experience. He wrote that the ghat

> …has been encroached upon, as it would seem, by natives, who have built huts, all along, on either side, which project so far out, that only one hackney can pass at a time, and about two persons go abreast go together. Most of these native houses are blacksmith's shops where, at night, large blazing fires are continually kept up, and it seems to me a miracle they are not all entirely consumed; that they are very liable to be so no one can deny, and how dreadful would be the conflagration in that neighbourhood, in such an event.[45]

'Reformer' then wrote that it was surprising that the mercantile population of a growing city like Calcutta had 'so few facilities, or conveniences' afforded them by way of a good, spacious ghat on the river. The Cutchagoody and Koila Ghats were useful establishments no doubt but there were drawbacks which were pointed out by the correspondent. 'With the exception of the Custom-house Ghaut [Old Fort Ghat]', (see Fig. 45) he wrote that 'there is not a commodious Ghaut where any goods can be landed without damage, although there are many places advantageously situated for that purpose'.

A year later, in July 1820, *The Calcutta Journal* itself wrote that wharfage facilities on the river's east bank were very unsatisfactory, the delays 'in the shipment and discharge of goods, which are now taken to the single wharf of the Custom House, (being) felt as a serious evil by all those interested in the safety and dispatch of their export and import transactions'. The paper suggested spreading out the landing of goods as a step to remedy the situation. It said that 'certain situations should be selected along the banks of the river…and small wharfs, planned and constructed for the purpose, be built there, with steps, crane, and shed, each under the superintendence of a Custom House officer'.

These small wharfs would cater to trade in goods 'of every description not subject to duty or drawback' while those goods which attracted these imposts would have to be serviced, as was being done, by 'the regular Custom House wharfs'. This would 'divide the labour, space and risk in such a way as greatly to facilitate dispatch of business in general'.[46]

The journal even suggested a couple of spots where 'small wharfs' could be set up, one of these being Jackson's Ghat (located 'between the premises of Messrs Kyd and Company and those of Messrs Breen and Company in Clive street'), to the south of Jessop and Company's offices (see Fig. 50). This ghat sported a reputation of its own both amongst the native population and the sahibs. Also known as 'Moylah Ghat', it was described as 'that intolerable nuisance', being for 'years past an annoyance to all classes of people whose occupations oblige them to reside within its neighbourhood, as well as to persons crossing the water or living on board ships anchored in the river abreast of it'.[47] It was the point of discharge into the river of all the city's filth, the situation being made even worse by the fact (as claimed by the Hindus who were especially affected) that

> What is there discharged…has not time to be carried to a sufficient distance from the town, even by the whole ebb tide, to ensure it not being floated back again by the

> next flood, which, dispersing it all over the river, renders it unwholesome and offensive to drink.[48]

An important point which *The Calcutta Journal* made was that a new spot was being considered as the depository of all the city's rubbish, which was 'a distant spot to the eastward of the town', adding that the details of the plan

> …are so likely to meet every objection that it is actually before the proper authorities and will very probably be adopted by them as the most effectual method of relieving the metropolis in general from an evil that now infests one part of it grievously, and extends its influence far and wide.

In all probability, the spot was Dhapa (to the east of today's Eastern Metropolitan Bypass) which, in fact, has carried out this specific function for the city ever since.

The second ghat suggested by the journal could be located 'immediately to the southward of the house occupied by John Elliot, Esq', the specific location of which is not known beyond the fact that it was in Clive Street. At both these spots the ingress and egress of goods 'to any part of the town (could be effected) with equal ease and convenience'. *The Calcutta Journal* went further and suggested that the new wharfs suggested could double up as landing spots on the riverbank, 'to be accessible from the River or from the shore at all hours of the day or night'. This would be of great help because 'it appears there is no public landing place between Beebee Ross's, or Armenian, Ghaut, and the Old Fort Ghaut, a distance of a quarter of a mile'.[49] In the absence of such public landing places, people going to and from ships on the river used the landing places in the private shipyards in the area which were closest to the vessels concerned. This indulgence extended by the shipyard owners to the general public during the daytime was restricted at nightfall because of security reasons, which led to altercations and even violent incidents involving the guards employed at the private shipyards.

'Reformer' had written his note on 3 August 1819. The very next day (4 August) the Lottery Committee underscored once again what its functions were compared to those of the city magistrates, the annoyance that it was having to do so again showing clearly. *The Calcutta Journal* carried a note saying that the committee had nothing to do with the nuisances described, and that it was the 'duty' of the Committee for the Improvement of the City to suggest to the Government measures 'for the removal of obstacles to the health, safety, and convenience, of the inhabitants'. The 'preservation of streets, wharves, etc, from *encroachment*' was the job of the police magistrates. The point was laboured that the committee 'makes *new* roads, widens avenues, constructs ditches, etc, but it is the duty of the police to see all these *preserved* to their *proper uses*, and kept in repair' (emphasis in original). This distinction had to be kept in mind for 'it is important to be clear in the facts on which complaints are grounded; it is equally so to know distinctly which branch of the municipal authority is culpable for the neglect, and to whom the application for redress should be made'.

As far as the Lottery Committee was concerned, it had already begun to look into the problem of the absence of easy access to the river from Clive Street, Henry Shakespear informing it that he had requested Lackersteen, the owner of Armenian Ghat, to sell the place to the Government 'for the purpose of throwing it open to the public' the response being that only a price of Rs 50,000 would make the owner part with his property, a 'ghaut of fifty feet in width'.[50] In late September 1820 Shakespear reported[51] that the ghat 'was called Armenian Ghaut, and in the maps Baretto's', which was confusing because both Wood's map of 1784-85 (Fig. 43) and Upjohn's (Fig. 49) showed Bibi Ross's Ghat and Baretto's Ghat as being two different ghats. Shakespear said that Lackersteen had bought the ghat for Rs 25,000 and had spent Rs 10,000 to Rs 12,000 on it, his total investment being a maximum of Rs 37,000. Since his monthly income from the ghat was Rs 375, Lackersteen's objective in any deal was to 'obtain an equivalent for the sum in Government securities'. Shakespear was referred to Palmer[52] 'for further negotiations' who gave him the impression that a price of Rs 50,000 would satisfy Lackersteen which, however, would exclude the 'tiled huts and other temporary buildings' at the ghat.

The tenor of his report makes it clear that Shakespear wanted Armenian Ghat to be acquired by the Government for the benefit of the public. He argued that the ghat was located halfway between the Old Fort Ghat and Mirbahar Ghat between which 'there is at present no *public* [emphasis added] access to the town', the consequence of which was that tolls were 'exacted at the intermediate ghauts by the proprietors of them and the expence of landing goods proportionately enhanced'. This was a reason important enough for the Government to acquire Lackersteen's ghat. There was also another pressing reason to turn the ghat into a public facility, namely, that the blacksmiths' huts at the ghat were made of highly combustible material which posed a 'great danger (to) the houses and property in the neighbourhood', a point which had been made in the August 1819 letter of 'Reformer' (see above). Shakespear said the magistrates had no power 'to remove these huts, or to cause them to be constructed of less inflammable materials', and that the purchase of the ghat by the Lottery Committee would be able to remove 'this very serious nuisance'.

The Lottery Committee turned down Lackersteen's offer as being 'very immoderate for a ghaut of the dimension described in your letter'.[53] In fact, the committee had already begun the process of acquiring a different plot of land 'in the vicinity' which would provide access to Clive Street from the riverside. In the second week of November 1820, it had written to the Government that, trying to 'combine as far as might be possible economy with utility', it had discovered that a 60-foot-wide road could be built on ground 'lately belonging to Dr Lycke'[54] at an expence of Rs 30,000. Such a 'safe, straight and broad' road would provide easy access from the river to Clive Street, 'where it is much wanted', and, at the same time, a 'commodious' ghat would also be built to support the project. Since the cost of making the road and the ghat would be around Rs 3,000, the Government was asked to sanction an investment of Rs 33,000 for the entire project, which came through a fortnight later.[55] No problems were foreseen in the purchase of the ground because it belonged to two Company employees Larkins and Trotter who had bought the property 'recently' from George Lycke and had given the Government to understand that they had no objection to transferring the ground to the Lottery Committee.[56]

STRAND ROAD – STEP BY STEP

A year had passed since 1 March 1820 when the Riverbank Committee had submitted its report to the Government on the Strand Road project. During the time a number of discrete issues had cropped up – such as the legal status of the late William Johnson's ground north of the old fort, among others – which were handled piecemeal by the Government and settled. On 8 March 1821, for the first time, the Lottery Committee wrote to the Government treating the road project along the river as an integrated scheme with a separate and dedicated cost estimate.[1] The subject figured in the last paragraph of a long letter written by the committee on the proposed extension further north of the new road from Baparitala to Bowbazar, which was later to become College Street.[2] Discussing the funds available with it and the demands on them, the committee said that, of the Rs 2 lakhs expected to accrue annually as the lottery proceeds, about Rs 1,20,000 would remain unspent after meeting regular, pre-determined expenses. The committee wanted to use this entire amount 'for some time to come' for the construction of the new Strand project, 'a work which we consider as of essential importance to the navigation of the river, the interests of the mercantile community and the salubrity of the town'. Nothing more was said on the subject, the Lottery Committee intimating the Government that it would 'write more fully' on it 'at an early period', a function it performed five weeks later.[3]

Giving a short history of the birth of the idea of a road along the riverbank,[4] the committee referred to the suggestion of one of its members, George Gordon, made 'at an early period' following the committee's appointment, which was not taken up at the time because of 'the heavy expense likely to attend it and other obstacles to its successful accomplishment'. However, by 1821, the table had been cleared one of the tough obstacles removed being the right to ownership of ground recovered from the river owing to a shift in its main channel westward.[5] In fact, the case involving ownership of alluvion had been resolved in such a way that it would no longer be necessary to purchase such ground for the project. The Lottery Committee acknowledged the contribution of the 1819 Riverbank Committee in establishing the formula, adding that it had 'forcibly urged the importance of constructing the proposed road along the banks of the river'.

The Lottery Committee then listed six benefits which 'the construction of a commodious street or quay along the riverside from the southern to the northern extremity of the city' would generate. These were: it would 'effectually put a stop to those gradual but frequent encroachments which no vigilance on the part of the magistracy has been able effectually to guard against, and which are calculated seriously to injure and obstruct the navigation of the river'; the salubrity of the city would be materially promoted by 'diminishing the extent of alluvion ground and by preventing the formation of pools of stagnant water on the riverside'; an 'easy and commodious line of communication from one extremity of the city to the other' would be provided, 'affording facilities to the conveyance of goods to and fro in the numerous vessels and boats employed in the commerce of the port, and to the loading and unloading of such vessels'; the 'most effectual means' would be afforded of 'putting a stop to the system of smuggling which cannot be...prevented so long as numerous passages and ghats leading to the river shall remain the private property of individuals and not open to the inspection of the Custom House officers'; it would 'greatly increase the difficulty and hazard of introducing stolen property into the city or of conveying stolen property out of the city' apart from facilitating 'the maintenance of an efficient police…in other respects'; and, finally, it would 'add to the embellishment of the city'.

The Lottery Committee felt, with good reason, that work on the project should commence in that part of the city where 'the principal public offices and establishments connected with the shipping and commerce of the port' were located so that 'the influence of opulent British merchants [could] most beneficially be brought to our aid, where the transit of goods by land is the greatest, and where the want of the means of easy communication is more particularly felt'. It was suggested that the part of the road from Cutchagoody Ghat (Colvin's Ghat) in the south to 'the new Town Duty Office in Clive Street' in the north should be taken up first, the public offices located in this stretch being (from the south)

> …the mint, the marine registry office, the master attendant's office, the marine storekeeper's yard, the marine paymaster's office, the intended office and godowns for the Board of Customs, Salt and Opium, the export warehouse, the new Custom House, the import warehouse, and lastly the new Town Duty Office and godowns.

Providing an idea of where precisely the cargo congestion on the river took place at the time, the committee wrote that it was in this stretch of the river that 'the greatest portion of the shipping of the port [is] usually anchored or moored' the 'principal warehouses and

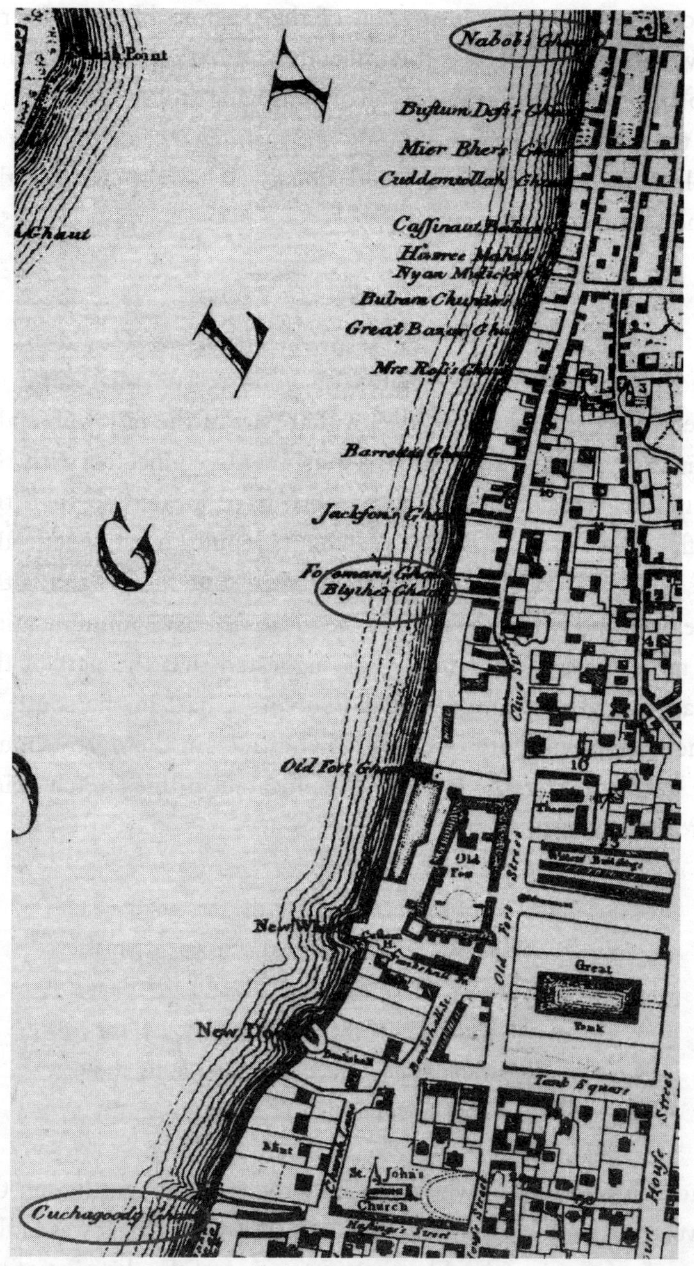

Fig. 51. Upjohn's map of 1793 shows the riverbank where the first stretch of Strand Road was built - from Cutchgoody to Clive Street (Blythe's) Ghats

establishments for the equipment of ships, and for the preparation and supply of marine stores of every description, [being] situated [in] the immediate vicinity'.

The construction of the road would begin from both ends, from Cutchagoody Ghat to 'the new ghat in Clive Street to the north of the import warehouse' (3,100 feet) and, on the other side, from the northwest boundary of the new Customs office southward to Mirbahar Ghat (900 feet), the distance from the Customs office to Cutchagoody Ghat being calculated at 6,300 feet. The remaining part of the road in the middle, from Mirbahar Ghat to Clive Street Ghat would be taken up after the southern and northern parts of the road had been completed.[6] Of the two sections in the south and the north, the committee decided that work on the northern part would not begin till some knots were untied involving the Nawab of Murshidabad who held property in the area. The committee wrote that the 'greatest portion' of the property lying between Clive Street and the river, along the stretch from the new Customs office to Mirbahar Ghat, belonged to the nawab (see Fig. 50), adding that 'his people (derived) some profit from allowing vessels and sloops to be docked and repaired in the excavations [there]'. However, the ground was otherwise unproductive there being 'no buildings of any value situated upon it'. Clearly, it was only the Government which could handle the negotiations with the nawab's agents regarding the property 'adjoining the new Town Duty Office and lying between the river and Clive Street' and this would require some time.

Acquiring the nawab's property adjoining the new office would enable the construction of a 'broad communication from Clive Street on the south side of the Town Duty Office to the river'. Not only would this allow 'abundant space' for the hackeries which would be frequenting the area near the office, but once this was accomplished it would enable the committee to begin making the riverside road towards Mirbahar Ghat. However, till such time the property was taken over from the nawab no work would commence on the project in this sector.

The alluvion in front of the nawab's premises as well as the new Customs office could be raised and levelled, the committee reiterating the oft-repeated point that any space thus acquired and if not needed for the 'public purpose' could, after completion of the project, 'be sold on terms which would probably defray the whole of the expense'. If the nawab was not agreeable to the idea of selling his property, the Government was urged to prevail on him to allow the construction of the new road, his agents in Calcutta being instructed to 'forward this great public improvement by cordially aiding in the measures which may be adopted by the Lottery Committee'. There were other proprietors owning ground 'between the nawab's property and Meer Buhur Ghaut' and, as the committee reported, one of them had already agreed to the proposed plan on condition that the alluvion not required by the project and raised at the expense of the committee would be granted to him by *patta*. The cost of making the road from the north-western extremity of the Customs office to Mirbahar Ghat, including the filling up and levelling of the alluvion lying between the new road and the office and between the new road and the premises of the nawab and other individuals, was estimated at around Rs 22,000. If, however, the nawab agreed to sell his property 'on the same terms' as those on which the ground for the new Customs office was sold, the committee estimated that 'the whole of the projected improvements may be effected at little or no ultimate expense' to the Government.

Since the Lottery Committee had decided that no work would begin immediately south of the Town Duty Office till a decision was taken on purchase of the nawab's ground, the focus of implementation inevitably shifted to the southern section of the road and quay project. The Government was informed that since the stretch 'seemed to involve the greatest difficulties and consequently to require the most attentive consideration', it had deputed different members of the committee to look after the problems in different stretches of the proposed road and submit their reports which would include cost estimates. On 10 April 1821, Bayley and Colvin, who were asked to look after the part of the road from Cutchagoody Ghat to Hare Street Ghat (later Police Ghat, at the foot of Hare Street), submitted two variants of the implementation plan, one costing Rs 78,000 and the other 'either Rs 58,000 or Rs 64,000'. Under the costlier plan, the principal advantage would be that the road would be carried 'in a straight line from ghaut to ghaut, and that it would admit of a sloping bank being formed from the edge of the road to [the] low watermark'. Its disadvantage would be – apart from the 'considerably' higher cost – that it would involve use of a part of the ground attached to the mint though no buildings of value belonging to the establishment would need to be demolished. The common problem faced by both the plans would be that posed by the property of Gabriel Vrignon which would have to be acquired for the road and for which the price sought was an unreasonably high Rs 1,03,000, a good Rs 30,000 more than what was considered to be 'just value'.[7]

Bayley and Colvin had reported that for a long time Vrignon had refused to sell a part of his ground 'under any conditions' and that, in an effort to remove the objections 'arising from want of room to rebuild his out-offices', they had suggested that the Government might be induced to give him

> ...in exchange for an equal quantity of his ground [a space in the mint premises]...extending forty feet beyond his present boundary to the north, proposing to pay him at the rate of Rs 1,500 per cottah for whatever was wanting in excess,

> and allow half as much again as the estimated expense of rebuilding his out-offices might amount to in consideration of his yielding to our wishes.

But the only terms Vrignon would agree to 'were the extension of his northern boundary [to a point marked by Bayley and Colvin in a plan they had submitted, which is not included in the records] and to receive in cash the sum of Rs 15,000', which was considered 'utterly inadmissible'. In view of this situation, the subcommittee wanted a jury to be summoned to determine 'the value of the whole or the portion of Mr Vrignon's property as may be necessary'.

As regards the second variant of the plan, Bayley and Colvin held that even if Vrignon decided eventually to sell his entire property and not just the part of it that would be required for the road and quay project, they would select the first, and costlier, variant. The subcommittee wrote that

> ...the only other mode that presents itself to us is to carry out a strong *puckah postah* (wall) the whole length of the space between the two ghauts, a few feet within low watermark, by which means we should, at the expense of a curve at each end of the road, require only a very small portion of Mr Vrignon's premises, and so far from interfering with the mint it would not be necessary to appropriate the whole of what is already outside of the boundary wall.

Building the *postah* would itself cost Rs 30,000 and 'filling up within the *postah* and making the road' another Rs 10,000. In its letter to the Government, the Lottery Committee asked to be allowed to opt for one of these plans but only after the jury 'assessed the value of the whole or a portion of the premises in question'.

The next part of the proposed Strand Road (from Hare Street Ghat to Koila Ghat) was the responsibility of Gordon who estimated the cost at Rs 15,000 of which Rs 3,824-3-8 had already been spent by the subcommittee in charge of the Bankshall improvements. The plan for the road here would involve the use of 'an inconsiderable portion of ground' attached to the premises of the master-attendant which would not in any way affect adversely the interests of the department. The item of interest in the expenditure estimate was the Rs 2,433-14-2 which would have to be spent on 'extending the tunnel from Tank Square beyond its present limits to (the) low watermark' (this tunnel was made by Richard Blechynden in earlier times to fill the BBD Bagh tank with river water).[8] The next section of the road, from Koila Ghat to the Old Fort Ghat, running along the western face of the Customs House godowns (the location of old Fort William), would cost Rs 8,000, the records indicating that for this stretch of the riverside no member of the committee was given the responsibility to draw up an estimate, in all probability because no cost uncertainty was foreseen involving owners of private property.

Further north, Henry Shakespear was given the job to build the new road from the Customs House godowns to the 'south corner of Mr Watson's premises in Clive Street', his estimate for the work being Rs 13,334. The 60-ft road here would traverse a distance of 800 ft and would have to be raised 9 ft with earth from the river. Shakespear felt that the rate quoted for the job (Rs 5-6 per *choukah* resulting in a total cost of Rs 3,200) was reasonable considering the difficulty involved in getting earth: as he wrote, it was 'generally necessary to remove it in a liquid state and… is procurable only during a few hours of the day when the tide is low'. In fact, the construction of the road along the river was a substantial project, the supply of material to raise the level of the ground and make a firm bed for it being a major issue. At its 21 December 1820 meeting the committee decided to use the 'large supply of shingle gravel or stones' brought as ballast by ships visiting Calcutta for the construction of the quay and road, the expense of landing such supplies being met by the committee itself provided the vessels were anchored 'at the Hon'ble Company's moorings or in the stream between Chaundpaul Ghaut and the new Town Duty Office in Clive Street'. Consequently, a notice was issued which asked ship commanders to bring such ballast to the city, 'when its importation may be found consistent with their own convenience', to 'forward the objects of the committee' in the improvement of the city.[9]

The Riverbank Committee's report had been submitted to the Government on 1 March 1820. In November of that year the Government wrote to the Lottery Committee to get on with the 'preliminary measures' for constructing the proposed road 'from the master-attendant's premises towards the Customs House and import warehouse'[10] one of which was the fixing of the precise alignment of the new road. Alex Burn (of Burn, Currie and Company), who was approached for his ideas on the subject, said that he was all for the new road – from Chandpal Ghat to 'mud-point above Neemtolla' – following

> ...a uniform indented curve, encroaching on private property in some places but, in general, on the river so as ultimately to obtain an uninterrupted and uniform passage for the water along the bank at all places, which would... tend more than any other way to keep the river of an equal depth the whole extent.[11]

Burn's plan was different from the one suggested by the Riverbank Committee, the latter's proposal opting for a road represented by a 'straight line forming angles' instead of a 'uniform curve'. Burn said that such an alignment, if proposed with a view to reducing cost, would have the opposite effect. He said he had 'always found that, to begin with, a plan, well digested, however expensive, and carrying that plan slowly but steadily into effect, is the way to save expence and to give general satisfaction'. If such a plan was drawn up, the inhabitants would, 'for their own advantage, adhere to it in erecting any building instead of the present mode of every proprietor building as he pleases'. Burn said that if such a plan had been followed for the building of the Customs House, 'the line could have been followed at the same expense, and the city improved in appearance'. Burn offered to mark out his line of the road with the help of 'bamboos', which was accepted by the Lottery Committee.

The Burn exercise was necessary because the new road would not just disturb the lay of the land on the riverbank but would also interfere with the use the ground was being put to. An example of this was the wharf opposite the Bankshall which had to be extended further into the river because of the new road. The jetty performed an important function and any interference with it would have disrupted trade operations raising a howl of protest. This is precisely what happened, the protagonists in this case being different Government departments. The opening shot was fired in early January 1821 when George Udny, president of the Marine Board, and Commodore Hayes, the Master-Attendant, told the Government that the new road would 'render the present jetty useless' and that the immediate need was to extend the wharf 20 ft farther out into the river, 'raising the present one four feet, completing the platform for the capstan to the same level, and putting a new crane at the outer end'. Two 'anchor carts' would also have to be installed which were 'much wanted to facilitate the moving of anchors'.[12]

Hayes had kicked off correspondence on the subject in late December when he wrote to the Marine Board that, in view of the plan to build the new road, he had asked the 'master builders'

Kyd and Company of Khidirpur to furnish an estimate for the new wharf (Rs 5,079-7-5) 'certified' by Marmaduke Stalkartt, the Surveyor in the Master-Attendant's office, which had been provided on 20 December.[13] Hayes recommended that Kyd and Company be allowed to execute the work as it was this company which had erected 'the original wharf and crane which has been in use these ten years past, and proved of great advantage to the service and the public interest'. He did not foresee any obstacle because the proposal had been submitted to the Government 'sometime ago' by a committee appointed to look into the subject (of which he was also a member), the proposal being approved 'by such high authority (that) I should imagine it is merely requisite for the board to solicit his Lordship-in-Council to authorise the execution of the said work' for implementation to begin. In a note appended to his 26 December letter, the Master-Attendant said that since the projected new wharf was 'nearly double the extent' of the old one, the cost of making it would also be nearly twice that of the existing wharf.

In early February the Lottery Committee was asked to '(explain) the effects represented by the Marine Board and the Master Attendant as likely to result from the construction of the proposed new road along the banks of the river near the Bankshall premises', and also throw light on the 'proportion of the expense referred to in the correspondence…originating exclusively in the measures now carrying on by the Lottery Committee'. A month later, the committee put its surveyor, Arthur Blechynden, on the job asking him to ascertain 'whether and in what respect the construction of the new road has rendered the jettee and crane less serviceable than before', and the cost of removing them and putting them up 'as far out from the new bank which will be found on the completion of the proposed quay as they were from the old when the jettee were originally constructed'.

Blechynden got back to the committee within a week, shooting down the principal premise of the Marine Board and the Master

Attendant that the need to shift the jetty had been necessitated by the new road being built by the Lottery Committee.[14] His finding was that the new road would not affect the operations of 'the jettee and crane' because it 'does not proceed beyond them'. If indeed the jetty and crane had become 'less serviceable than before' this was because the river had receded from the bank. At the time the jetty was made 'boats were enabled at all hours of the tide to remain alongside', but now the low watermark was 'about 60 feet distant therefrom'. Blechynden, Jr, wrote that if the jetty and wharf were to be shifted they would have to be constructed 25 ft beyond their present position and raised to the height of the new road. The cost of these alterations, along with others such as shifting of the crane, etc., would total about Rs 4,500, which was about Rs 580 less than the estimate provided by Kyd and Company. Armed with this letter, the committee informed the Government that the question of its footing the bill, or any aspect of it, regarding the changes suggested by the Marine Board and the Master-Attendant did not arise because the cause of the problems listed was 'wholly unconnected' with the improvement undertaken by the Lottery Committee.

In its 8 March 1821 letter, the Lottery Committee had said that after meeting planned expenses it would be left with Rs 1,20,000 annually which could be devoted to the Strand Road project (see above). A month later, in April, it asked the Government to disburse Rs 1,14,000, for the construction of the road from Cutchagoody Ghat 'to the new ghaut [Clive Street Ghat] beyond the import warehouse', which would leave Rs 6,000 as a 'surplus'.[15] The Government was also asked to give up 'such portion of the ground attached to the mint and to the master-attendant's premises' which would be needed for the project and also summon a jury 'to ascertain the value of Mr Vrignon's premises or such portion of them as may be necessary'. The Government replied in early May extending full support to the project generally and approving the preliminary measures the Lottery Committee had already taken.[16] As a matter of routine (this stipulation was applied to most major projects), the committee was invested with 'discretionary authority to deviate from the precise plan pointed out in your report whenever any modifications in that plan, not involving heavy additional expense or compromising any important interests either of Government or of individuals, may appear to you expedient'.

Regarding the stretch of the new road from Cutchagoody Ghat to Hare Street Ghat, the Government made two points. Responding to the committee's request, it agreed to set up a jury to help ascertain the value of Vrignon's property required for the project. Secondly, the committee had suggested two variants of the plan of progress the Lottery Committee's view being that the costlier alternative, which would involve using a part of the mint's grounds, would not affect significantly the mint's operation in any way. The Government differed on this point. While giving the committee a free hand to choose between the two implementation plans (a flexibility which the committee had sought specifically), it wrote that the adoption of the first plan would

> …probably be found to involve the surrender of a larger portion of the premises belonging to the mint than can be conveniently spared until the new buildings for the mint shall be completed, and the delay arising from the circumstance may perhaps prove so serious an objection to the plan in question as to recommend the adoption of the other plan proposed in preference.

Alternatively, the committee had asked for a transfer of ground from the premises of the Master-Attendant and the Marine

Storekeeper, which was agreed to by the Government but with a proviso. The committee, it said, was aware that 'some public buildings' were coming up on the premises of the Master-Attendant and that Captain Phipps and Lt Paton, both of whom were members of the Lottery Committee, were 'acquainted with the intentions of Government as to the plan of the new buildings'. The Government suggested that both Phipps and Paton ascertain whether the ground required for the road would interfere with those plans and that if it did they would 'endeavour to apportion the ground in such manner as may seem to them best calculated to facilitate the measures in progress' keeping in mind the 'objects for which the new buildings are required'. They were also asked 'to arrange the scite (scite) of the new buildings (so) as to make their western front correspond with the direction of the new road'.

In the middle of June 1821 Bayley and Colvin, who were looking after the work on this stretch of the new road, asked the mint authorities about the proposal to transfer ground to Vrignon, the Mint Master, J.M. Macnabb, replying a week later, saying that handing over the land in question to Vrignon 'could be productive of no impediment to the actual operations of the mint'. Secondly, the idea that the destruction of 'the regularity of form and cutting off a portion of the mint premises from immediate access to the river' would 'tend in some degree to depreciate the value of the remaining property in the event of its future sale', would not be strong enough 'to constitute in the opinion of Government…a sufficient ground of objection to the transfer'.

However, Macnabb pointed out specifically that the first plan submitted by the Lottery Committee – providing land to Vrignon – 'would not only involve a much greater diminution of the value of the premises but would require the surrender of ground which, I believe, could not be spared without detriment to the operations of this establishment'.[17]

On 26 June, the committee approached the Government for a decision on the issue.[18] It said that Vrignon had demanded, in exchange for the land needed for the road, 'an equal quantity of ground from the mint and the sum of Rs 10,000 for rebuilding his offices' (the mint adjoined his premises in the north). The committee referred to the Mint Master's view to buttress its stand that the ground taken would not affect the mint's operations, and also that the proposed improvement would 'increase the value of the whole property [the mint] in a much greater portion than it will be diminished by the alienation of the part in question'. As for the compensation sought by Vrignon in cash, the committee said that it was Rs 5,000 less than what had been demanded earlier although it was perhaps 'still somewhat more' than what a jury may have awarded. The committee urged the acceptance of Vrignon's position because it had already faced much 'opposition' in the case and would face much more if the issue was allowed to drag further. Three days later the Government approved of both the transfer of mint land to Vrignon as well as paying him Rs 10,000.[19]

In its letter to the Government of 19 April 1821 the Lottery Committee had underscored the pivotal position of the Nawab of Murshidabad in the building of the northern section of Strand Road, specifically his acceptance of the proposal to sell land south of the new Town Duty Office till Mirbahar Ghat, a point with which the Government agreed. The 4 May letter from the Chief Secretary indicates that the authorities were uncertain about the nawab's response.[20] The least that could be expected of him was to sell the ground on the same terms on which he had sold the site on which the new Customs facility had come up. That transaction had recognised the right of the nawab to the alluvial ground in front of the Town Duty Office, which implied that, in the event of the intended transaction going through, it would only be 'proper that some addition should be made to the purchase money in consideration of the cession of His Highness of the right thus acquired'.[21] If the nawab declined to sell his land, the Government hoped that he would 'not, at all events, object to the construction of the new quay on the riverside in front of his premises'. The Governor-General in Council reasoned that since the new project would add to the value of his property, the nawab would agree 'to the occupation by the Lottery Committee of such portion of the alluvion ground belonging to him as may be requisite for the new road and quay'. The nawab's response was important from the point of view of funding of the project because the committee had planned that the alluvion, filled up and levelled, could be resold later at an enhanced price which would 'probably defray the whole of the expense'.

The Government agreed with the Lottery Committee that no steps were to be taken regarding construction of the stretch of the new road south of the Town Duty Office till Mirbahar Ghat until the nawab's stand on the proposal to sell his ground was known. This process took five months, the Chief Secretary, William Bayley, informing the Lottery Committee on 12 October that the matter had been taken up with the nawab's people and that Charles Paton, Assistant Superintendent of Public Buildings in the Lower Provinces, was to make a valuation of the spot of ground and report back to the Government so that the matter could be taken forward.[22]

In the middle of September that year, the Persian Secretary, Henry Thoby Prinsep, was asked to take up the matter with F.W. Russell, the Acting Agent of the Governor-General at Murshidabad. Prinsep's letter of 15 September to the agent is a good example of how persuasive language was to be used in a situation where the Company controlled all the effective levers of power. Prinsep told Russell that the object of the exercise was the Government's taking over 'the ground belonging to His Highness which lies on the bank of the river immediately to the south of the new Custom House in Clive Street'. The agent was told that when the nawab was made 'to comprehend the nature of the improvement that is in agitation', he would 'the more easily be induced to give up the prejudice and scruples ordinarily entertained by natives of rank to dispose of land which has descended to them by right of inheritance'. Apart from the road and quay that were to be built along the riverside in the area, it was to be impressed on the nawab that there were 'other public objects which make it very desirable that Government should obtain possession of the whole of the ground belonging to the Nawab lying between Clive Street and the river'. Russell was told that the house in which Mir Jafar once stayed was 'entirely destroyed' and that the 'rubbish (that) is now lying on the ground' would be useful to the Government for the construction of the '*pooshtu* [*postah*] and ghaut which (is) to run along the river's edge'. The agent was told to communicate early with the nawab so that orders could be issued 'to his people at this city to prevent the removal of the materials in question' for which the Government was prepared to pay the 'usual price'.

Prinsep then provided a description of the state of the nawab's ground at the time. He wrote:

> There is no building of any value on any part of the ground which it is proposed to take for Government. There are indeed a few shops and ryots' houses of *chopper* materials which yield a rent to His Highness, but it may be well to apprise you that the *gunj* and valuable property of the *nizamut* lie on the eastern, or opposite, side of Clive street, and is wholly distinct from these buildings. A rent has occasionally been derived from the *chur* towards the river by allowing boats to be hauled up and repaired there. The

present state, however, of the *chur* is such as to render it a public nuisance, for it is a mere collection of mud and filth.

The Persian Secretary said that remedying the evil would cost a lot of money and the Government could not 'think of suggesting that His Highness should make the necessary outlay in aid of the projected improvement; and yet until the whole shall be raised and levelled the ground must remain an unseemly exception to the generally improved state of that part of the town'. The agent was told that he should endeavour 'to obtain the transfer of the whole of the ground to Government, at a fair price to be assessed by a committee, or in any other manner that His Highness may prefer'.

Russell was also told that it was the intention of the Governor-General in Council to leave to the nawab the naming of the ghat, which was to be built on the riverbank 'in front' of his ground. This additional bait, though entirely unnecessary, proved successful for the agent wrote back on 24 September that he had 'reason to believe' that the nawab 'would feel flattered if the ghaut was named after himself'. Both Wood's map of 1784 and that of Upjohn (1793) show a 'Nabob's Ghat' to the north of Mirbahar Ghat but to the south of the Town Duty Office (see Figs 43 and 51), both maps predating the new ghat referred to in the correspondence. Perhaps the old ghat with the same name testifies to the fact that Mir Jafar had stayed in the old house – now in ruins, as pointed out by Prinsep – next to the Customs office more than half a century earlier. However, Schalch's map of 1824 (see Fig. 50) shows a 'Nawab's Ghat' to the north of the Town Duty Office, which was the new ghat built after September 1821. Prinsep concluded his letter to Russell with the remark that he was 'not [to] fail to impress upon him [the nawab] how much it will tend to his personal credit to forward an improvement of this kind'.

In the event, the new nawab played out his (dictated) role with apparent aplomb. He wrote to the agent that it would 'give me the greatest pleasure in being able to meet the wishes of the Government on the present occasion. I, therefore, make it my earnest request that the Government will accept of the land in question.'[23]

Cremation ghats dotted the riverbank, having being built by affluent Hindus wherever it suited their interest. This being the case, the effort to develop the area in the north would necessarily have had to include measures to put these facilities into proper shape especially where they disturbed the alignment of the new road. The trigger for focussing the Lottery Committee's attention on the subject appears to have been a letter written on 20 December 1821 by Radhamadhab Banerjee, the owner of Nimtala Ghat, the objective of which apparently was to spruce up his property.[24] Banerjee wrote that the width of the ghat ranged from 14 to 19 ft (depending on the 'manner' of measurement) and that it was his intention to widen it to 21 ft 'with a slope to the water's edge'. He said that he wanted to erect 'buildings…for the accommodation of my family or friends either at bathing time or when it may be necessary to perform funeral rites at the riverside, or to perform my daily religious poojah of the idols and Caully Thakarany (Kali Thakurani)', the inference being that the ghat would be used for private purposes (although Banerjee did not say so explicitly). A police outpost, or *thana*, was located within the precincts of the ghat which Banerjee wanted 'removed' so as to make the place 'more uniform'. However, he offered to drop the idea if the committee had any hesitation in doing so.

The committee wrote back to Banerjee a week later telling him that, on the face of it, it had no objection either to the proposed widening of the ghat or to the construction of buildings on it. He would, however, have to give an undertaking that he would not object 'to the construction of a road by the banks of the river similar to that which is now in progress from the Custom House to Meerbhur (Mirbahar) ghaut' (the new Strand Road). Since Banerjee had given the impression that the ghat, after improvement, would continue to be a private one meant for himself, his family and friends, he was told in no uncertain terms that it would 'at all times be left open for persons passing to and from the river side'. Further, since the ghat was one of two (the other being Kashi Mitra Ghat) where the police had allowed cremation of the dead, it was not in the power of the committee 'to direct a discontinuance of this usage'.[25] Further, as the 'buildings proposed by you would appear as likely to interfere with the performance of these offices in future', Banerjee would have to approach the magistrates on the subject. As for the removal of the *thana*, he was told that the committee would 'request' the magistrates to allow him to rebuild it at some other spot 'should no objection appear to the adoption of the contemplated arrangement'.

The committee had taken a week to reply to Banerjee's 20 December letter. During this period it had discussed the subject with those of its members who were engaged in supervising the building of the new road along the riverbank. On 26 December, a day before the committee wrote back to Banerjee, Henry Shakespear, a committee member who had been appointed Chief Magistrate in February that year,[26] drew attention to the fact that the two principal cremation spots, at Nimtala Ghat and Kashi Mitra's Ghat, needed redevelopment because of the increasing pressure on them owing to a steady increase in the Hindu population of the city. The Chief Magistrate wrote:

> It is unnecessary that I should dwell on the inconvenience to which the Hindoos must be put for want of a proper place to perform this funeral rite. The spots appropriated to the purpose at the above-mentioned ghauts are extremely

> confined, and in the height of the rains scarcely admit of its being performed at all. Bodies are kept at the ghaut and the families are obstructed for hours together in paying the last tribute of affection and respect to their deceased relatives.

He felt that 'a considerable portion of the Calcutta community' was interested in the improvement of the ghats, and that unless the Lottery Committee stepped in there was no way in which the work could be carried out.

Shakespear's specific suggestion was that two ten-*katha* plots on the riverbank near the two ghats in question be bought and set aside for the burning of the dead of the Hindu community. These plots were to be enclosed 'on three sides with a wall to prevent encroachment as well as for privacy', and that after the new burning ghats were completed they were to be looked after by the city magistrates. These facilities would cost an estimated Rs 8,000 to Rs 10,000, which would include a gradual sloping of the ground towards the river to drain out water during the rains. The committee asked Shakespear to select two spots of ground for the purpose mentioned. He was also asked to ensure that the two plots selected caused no problems for the new road along the strand. It is only after this firm arrangement had been sewed up that the Lottery Committee replied to Radhamadhab Banerjee's letter of 20 December.

The problem with the Nawab Nazim regarding the area south of the Town Duty Office was settled in October 1821. The nawab had had no choice but to accept the wishes of his English masters which, however, was not the case with other, lesser, mortals. Around the time the Company was having its way with the nawab, another native, Rammohun Dutt, threw down the gauntlet. The substance of his complaint was that the new riverside road was being constructed through his property in Clive Street 'without his sanction and consent'. Dutt's lawyer, W.A. Abbott, wrote to the Lottery Committee on 17 October that no proposals were made regarding compensation for the land in question and that he (Dutt) 'respectfully trusts' that the committee would not 'deprive him of any portion of his estate without in the first instance paying him such a fair price for what is required as a jury or other tribunal may award', such compensation having been paid to others 'for the same purpose'.[27] In case the Government refused to compensate him fairly, he was willing – in order to 'meet the wishes of the party [that is, the Government] for this alleged public improvement' – to sell 'the whole of his premises' for Rs 1,10,000. The concluding paragraph of Abbott's letter, which must have raised the hackles of the committee, read: 'After this notice and communication, any further trespass on the property of my client will, if persisted in, be resisted, and I have his instructions in such case to take such legal measures as may effectually secure his property and rights.'

Others who had complained to the committee at different times regarding improvement projects affecting their proprietorial rights had appealed to the humanity of the 'worshipful' members of the committee, sometimes even claiming that their very livelihood was at stake. Rammohun Dutt adopted a different stand altogether, addressing the committee as an equal and threatening legal action in case the authorities chose to ignore his protestation (see later for Gopimohun Deb's case). The committee wrote back the next day (18 October) challenging Dutt's contention that he had not been approached by the authorities before the construction of the road and quay had begun. Dutt was told that, as regards getting his 'sanction' or permission to make use of the ground concerned, he was 'mistaken in considering it to be his right as the adjoining proprietor'. Secondly, Gordon, a member of the committee, had been in touch with him and from 'the result of a communication which Mr Gordon personally held with him at the request of the Lottery Committee in explanation of their plans for the construction of the proposed road', it had appeared that Dutt had approved of the committee's course of action.[28]

The committee told his lawyer that

> ...several of the proprietors, in front of whose properties the road is already in progress and who supposed themselves to possess the right which your client so erroneously assumes, spontaneously tendered to the committee a sufficiency of land on the condition that Government consent to their being granted a pottah for the remainder.

Not only was Dutt offered similar terms, he was also informed by Gordon that, in the event of his cooperating with the authorities,

> ...the remainder of his ground would be raised at the public expense to the level of high watermark, that the title thereto would be confirmed by a pottah from Government and, further, that he would be remunerated for any land which might be taken above high watermark provided compensation should be allowed to other proprietors similarly situated in consideration for any benefit they might forego from being no longer able to appropriate their premises to marine purposes.

It was emphasised that the ground required for the road project in front of Dutt's property was below the high watermark and the Government's proprietorial right to such land was 'incontestable'. As regards Dutt's offer to sell his entire property to the Government, the committee did not have 'the most remote intention under any circumstance of (entering into) negotiations for the purchase of these premises'. If, even after the 18 October letter, Dutt chose to continue opposing the building of the road and quay in front of this property, Abbott was asked to continue the correspondence with the company's attorney.

Rammohun Dutt could have let the matter rest there, but he did not. His attorney wrote back a week later that while Dutt was not against the riverside road project he was keen on an 'assurance in writing' from the committee that he would 'receive as a compensation for his land what others may [get] from theirs'.[29] Twisting the knife, he also wanted the committee to state in writing that 'in the event of the improvement in question not being completed within a reasonable period of time, or being relinquished [altogether], that he shall receive back so much of his land as shall be taken from him with the same free and uninterrupted communication with the river as he now enjoyed'. If these assurances were forthcoming in the manner suggested, Dutt said that he was ready to accept the terms proposed. The committee had asked Dutt to approach the court in the event of his not agreeing to the proposal made by the Government. Abbott's letter made it clear that Dutt did not accept the committee's view on his proprietorial right to the land below the high watermark, and that since he had 'no fears upon the point himself' he was ready to go to the Supreme Court if urged to do so. In its wisdom, the committee treated this response as 'no distinct reply conveying either acceptance or refusal' of the conditions offered by it,[30] the letter being allowed to 'lie for present consideration'.

Work on the new road did not stop because of the problem with Dutt. The subcommittee continued with its construction 'between his premises and the river without interruption from anyone, and to clear and raise agreeably to the terms of the proposed adjustment the ground situated between the strand and the godowns at their own expense (Rs 800)'. The committee had, perhaps, expected that Dutt would eventually agree with its stand in view of the fact that he continued to receive rent from the committee 'for several months' during which he allowed the levelling and clearing of his ground to be effected 'at the expense of the committee'. This is also perhaps why resort to a jury was not had, which was considered not only to be 'needless' but also 'productive only of unprofitable trouble and expense'.

Dutt's strategy appears to have been to dissuade the committee from appointing a jury, all the while building up his case to take the matter to court, which he did in January 1824. After slapping a demand for Rs 48,262-8-0 from the committee, which was rejected by the latter, he filed a suit for ejectment in which, however, not much headway was made. Dutt then threatened proceedings in equity at which point the Lottery Committee, being 'desirous of finally disposing of this vexatious contest', agreed to send the matter to arbitration the award being unfavourable to the committee. The Advocate-General took the matter to the Supreme Court which passed an order on 12 July 1827 under which the committee would have to pay to Dutt Rs 33,000 'on account of land appropriated to the construction of the Strand Road'. The Government sanctioned the amount on 30 August but not before asking the Lottery Committee to draw the lesson that there are 'advantages…in cases of this nature by an early recourse being had to the assessment of a jury…whenever [an] individual may throw [obstructions] in the way of public improvements or contest the value set upon their premises'.

The October 1821 settlement of the land problem between the nawab and the Government had removed the last major hurdle in the way of building the riverside road till the new Town Duty Office. The Lottery Committee now turned its attention to continuing the road south beyond Cutchagoody Ghat, to Chandpal Ghat. The timing of the extension of Strand Road in this direction was determined by extraneous circumstances. On 21 February 1822 the Government was informed that the family of the Mullicks which had property in the area intended to build on 'the slip of ground…situated in King's Bench Walk'[31] (see Fig. 34), the walk falling 'within the line of the riverside road on its continuation from Cutcha Goody Ghaut to the Esplanade at Chandpaul Ghaut'.[32] At the time, the committee had no plans to send the proposal to the Government, but if action was delayed on this front it would lead to 'additional expense' for the project later. The only other property apart from that of the Mullicks which would be needed for the proposed road was the house at Chandpal Ghat occupied by George Tyler, which belonged to the estate of Claude Martin.[33] The committee had ascertained that, in accordance with Martin's will, the house could only be purchased 'by the intervention of a jury', the assistance of which would probably also be required to settle with the Mullicks although the committee had been informed that 'the managing brothers of the family' were willing to sell the property.[34]

The committee's view was that the success of the project in terms of cost would depend on the resale of the surplus ground that would remain 'between the present houses and the east side of the proposed road'. To start with, a lakh of rupees would be required, which was sanctioned on 26 February, the final cost not exceeding Rs 50,000. In the event, however, the final cost overshot the estimate because only Rs 26,033-3-2 was paid back to the Government. An important offshoot of making this part of Strand Road would be the removal of 'the only serious objection that could be urged to the neighbourhood of the steam engine, Mr Tyler's house being the only one situated immediately to the northward of it'. In the middle of November 1823, the subcommittee (G.J. Gordon and A. Colvin) looking after the project informed the Government that, among other things, 'all the surplus ground' in King's Bench Walk had been disposed of.[35] This involved the 'whole quantity of ground up to the line of the new street [Hastings Street]', the buyers being the proprietors of the 'several adjoining' properties who paid Rs 1,500 a *katha* which was the price fixed by the jury set up for the ground to be bought on the riverbank.

Today, Strand Road extends beyond Chandpal Ghat; to the west of Fort William, past the watergate, but two centuries ago plans to continue the road in this direction were scrapped because of objections from the military authorities of the time. On 12 April 1823, Henry Shakespear wrote to the Government that in the preceding July he had submitted a plan and an estimate 'for opening a more direct road of communication between Garden Reach and the Town' and also 'for the construction of an iron suspension bridge near the mouth of Tolly's Nullah'.[36] He said that he was informed by H.T. Prinsep, the Acting Secretary to the Government, that his suggestion would be kept in abeyance till Schalch's experiment regarding the building of an iron bridge was concluded.[37] Shakespear wrote that as the experiment had been completed and had 'fully answered the expectations formed of it', he was taking the opportunity of approaching the Government again with his road proposal. Five days later, Shakespear's letter was sent to the Lottery Committee which, in early July, sent a report on the *julkur* issue to the Government with the remark that the proceeds from the sale of such land could be appropriated for the construction of the road and bridge proposed by the Superintendent of Police (Shakespear).

A week later, on 10 July, the Government wrote to the Lottery Committee that both the issues relating to the *julkur* land, namely, its public sale and use of the proceeds to construct the road, would be 'further considered' in the Territorial Department. But, as far as Shakespear's plan was concerned, especially after the successful experiment conducted by Schalch, the Governor-General in Council wanted the committee 'to take into their early consideration the most expedient means of carrying [it] into effect'.

The committee was asked to involve Schalch in determining the 'position best suited for the proposed suspension bridge and the line of road to be adopted'. It was also asked to find out whether 'the proprietors of estates at Garden Reach' would contribute towards the cost of the project.

The committee took five long months to draw up the report, Wood, Shakespear, Barwell and Ballard being entrusted with the task. Two reports were submitted, on 9 December 1823 and on the next day,[38] Wood writing a dissent note dated 16 December. While the majority accepted the site of the bridge chosen by Schalch, Wood selected another which was closer to the mouth of the nullah. In their 9 December report, Shakespear, Ballard and Barwell had selected a line of road from the Hospital Sortie, 'across the plain', over Schalch's bridge 'to the corner of Mr Kyd's premises at Kidderpore' across the nullah, the great advantage of which would be that the crowded Khidirpur Bazar would be avoided. Wood, however, had settled for a line of road which would, effectively, be *a continuation of Strand Road* (from Chandpal Ghat) along the river, an alternative which appeared attractive enough for his colleagues to mention as an option in their 10 December report provided it was cleared by the military authorities. The Lottery Committee wanted the Government to consider the majority report which would cost Rs 64,000 as opposed to an estimated Rs 83,395 for Wood's variant.

The military authorities did not approve of the project the 'special committee' set up to examine it pronouncing in early April 1824 that it would not be expedient to interfere 'in any way...with the grand and principal defences of Fort William'. It was concluded that the construction of 'a permanent road of whatever width or however well-constructed passing the sluice or weakest face of the fort' would be objectionable 'in every point of view'.[39] Basing itself on the report of the 'special committee', the Government informed the Lottery Committee in May that the project under consideration could not be sanctioned, which meant abandoning Wood's scheme to extend Strand Road to Garden Reach. The records, however, do not say anything on whether the alternative suggested by the majority of the committee members was accepted and implemented. In all probability it failed to see the light of day because there is today no such road 'across the plain' as suggested by the committee majority. But it would seem that, subsequently, Wood had the last word (perhaps posthumously), for Schalch's map (see Fig. 46) shows a 'new road' along the riverbank past the fort to Garden Reach along the precise alignment suggested by him.[40]

Meanwhile, the Lottery Committee, in its 10 September 1823 report to the Government had said that Shakespear, Colvin and Paton had been asked at the end of May that year to report on 'the best means' of continuing the road 'to the north of the new Town Duty Office, the extent to which it might be carried, and the probable expense attending the work'.[41] The committee had expected

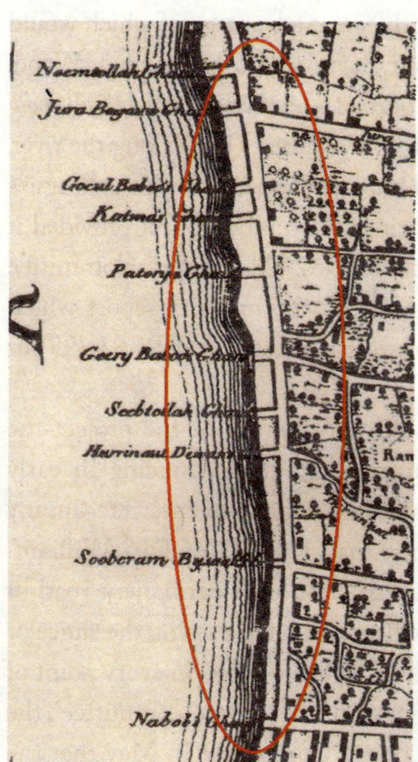

Fig. 52. Upjohn's map showing the riverbank from the Town Duty Office (Nawab's Ghat) to Nimtala Ghat

that the details of the exercise would be communicated 'in the course of a month or six weeks'. In the event, the report was submitted on 22 November its authors, Shakespear and Colvin, offering to superintend the work.[42] Their report indicates that the alluvion issue had once more assumed importance in the construction of the stretch of the new road north of the Town Duty Office. From this establishment to Nimtala Ghat the road would have to be built 'below the high water-mark' an advantage of which would be that no ground would have to be bought for its construction. With the exception of 'one or two sloping ghauts', the road would be built entirely on ground formed by the 'earth excavated from the bed of the river or brought from the opposite side'. The experience gained in making the first part of Strand Road had induced the subcommittee 'to allow one half more than the actual calculation of the earth required for the road', the probability being that much of it would have to be brought from the other (western) side of the river. In any event, the earth deposited for the new road would have to be allowed 'to settle during the next rains when a considerable portion of [it] will be unavoidably washed away'. To prevent this from happening on the 'inner side of the road', the building of a *postah* had been provided for which would be 10 feet high, including the foundation, stretching all along the new road from the Town Duty Office to Nimtala Ghat 'similar to that which Mr Paton has built southward from the Town Duty Office to Meerbuhr Ghaut'.

It was proposed that this part of the road be built 'quite clear of the premises on the riverside and as nearly as possible in a direct line' which, it was hoped, would 'obviate all objections on the part of the proprietors'. The subcommittee said that the owners were 'now fully sensible' of the advantage which they would reap from the construction of the new road and that many of them would gain 'a very considerable accession to their premises if allowed to take possession of the alluvion which will be left between the road and the high land'. However, in case there was any opposition to the building of the road by any proprietor, it was felt that the 'right of Government to the alluvion' should be 'asserted and maintained'. But where there was no such opposition, it would be 'more conformable to the principles on which we have hitherto acted' to hand over the low ground to the adjoining proprietors 'on condition of their filling it up within a given period' which, the subcommittee felt, would entail a 'very heavy expense upon them'. The ground of Gopimohun Deb would form an exception to this scheme of things in view of the fact that it was used as a timber yard and he would 'perhaps wish to retain it in its present shape' (see below).

Shakespear and Colvin then wrote that 'From Meerbuhr Ghaut to Hautcolah Ghaut the strand will be formed by *adding to the old road* [emphasis added] the slip on the west side of it now occupied by huts, by widening it wherever required and constructing a sloping bank'. What this indicates is that, in this part of the town on the east bank of the river, there already existed an old road on the riverbank and that the new road was essentially a widening of that passage.[43] The cost of implementing the project, sanctioned by the Government on 11 December 1823, was put at Rs 1,90,000.[44] In its January 1825 review report, the Lottery

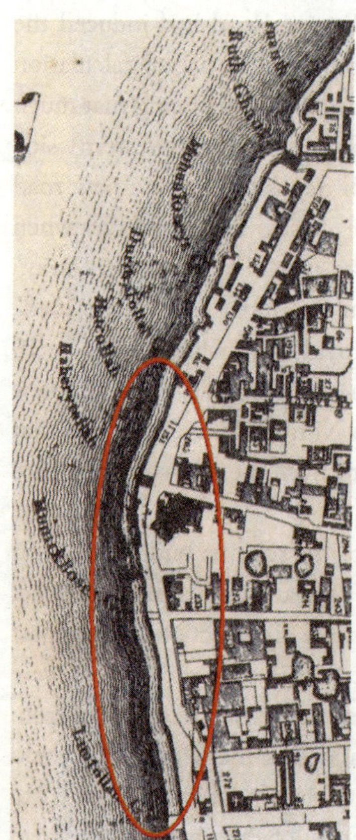

Fig. 53. Schalch's map showing the stretch of the riverbank from Nimtala Ghat to Hatkhola Ghat

Committee wrote that 'considerable progress' had been made in constructing 'the bund on which the roadway is to be constructed' but, in the face of Gopimohun Deb's opposition (subcommittee's letter of 18 March 1824), 'the whole line of the bund could not be completed'. The magistrates were asked to set up a jury to assess the damages due to Deb

> ...for any injury he might sustain by the road being carried in front of premises actually in his possession, but that person having subsequently commenced an action [law suit] against the Lottery Committee in which he laid claim to the whole of the alluvion and other ground over which the bund had been carried, the summoning of the jury has... been suspended.

Deb had, in fact, 'failed in his first application to the Supreme Court for an injunction to stop the proceedings of the Committee', the report stating that he had lately filed an amended petition 'which is now pending'.[45] Apart from Deb's opposition, the Lottery Committee met with no problems 'in carrying the new road in front of the several premises lying between the Town Duty Office and Nimtala Ghat', the hope being that a part of the road would be completed 'during the present working season'.

In the same January 1825 report, the committee reported that the part of the road 'to the south of the new Town Duty Office' which had remained 'unfinished' had been completed, the 'paving of the bank with *jammah* and *koah* at those parts where it was not turfed' (costing Rs 6,864-14-6) being 'in a state of forwardness'. As regards the part of the road to the 'northern extremity' of the Customs office, an 'additional disbursement' of Rs 1,36,853-5-2 had been allowed on 1 August 1822, the project being originally sanctioned on 4 May 1821.[46] Different parts of the work were given to Shakespear, Colvin and Paton who had submitted reports on the progress of the work entrusted to them, respectively together with accounts of their disbursements. The volume of funds still needed was Rs 33,125-15-2 to complete the works pending in each section for which a fresh infusion of credit was required, the funds being sanctioned on 9 October 1823.[47]

In the middle of January 1826 the Lottery Committee informed the Government that the Strand Road, 'from the new Town Duty Office to the premises of Gopeemohun Deb, south of Neemtullah Ghaut', a distance of around 2,000 ft, had been completed on 31 October 1825.[48] The total cost of making the stretch 'up to that date' was Rs 77,400. Since then a jury had assessed the damages payable to Deb 'for carrying the road in front of, and partly over, alluvial ground which he had been allowed by the magistrates to occupy' at Rs 4,000. Some other 'slight obstructions' to the work had also been tackled by the intervention of a jury the sums awarded being generally less than what had been offered previously to other claimants. The committee said that 'almost all difficulties being now removed', work would proceed rapidly and 'be substantially finished before the ensuing rains when we shall be able to finish final accounts to the expenditure'. The original cost estimate had, however, been breached. In March that year the committee informed the Government of the reasons which had led to the estimate of Rs 1,90,000 being exceeded.[49] These were: difficulty in getting the material required for building the embankment which had forced the committee to get it from the 'Sulkeea side of the river'; unexpected purchase of ground from Ramakant Thakur (Rs 3,300) and Gopimohun Deb (Rs 4,336); an abortive experiment with dredging to get earth from the river (Rs 3,000); and making the embankment with costlier *jammah* and *koah* instead of 'being turfed as was first intended', a method used

Fig. 54. A watercolour of the new Mint on the new Strand Road, by Thomas Prinsep, 1829. The view shows old cannon being used as the base of lamp posts

for the southern portion of the road with success. The committee sought an additional credit of Rs 15,000 to bridge the resources gap, which was sanctioned. Incidentally, a number of old guns were bought to serve as lamp posts the cost of which for purchase and installation was Rs 2,888.[50]

Six months later, in late September 1826, the subcommittee was writing that the Town Duty Office-Hatkhola Ghat section of the road had been completed, the recommendation being made that it be continued northward 'at a future period' to 'unite with the old road at Chitpore Bridge…thus connecting it with the

Barrackpore and Circular Roads'. The report described the terrain which would have to be covered for the last projected stretch, from Rath Ghat (at the foot of Sobhabazar Street, see Fig. 40) till 'the road near Chitpore Bridge', the last 1,000 feet being 'in general very steep' most of it being required to be secured by a wall, and that it was 'at this point that the river makes its only encroachments in Calcutta'. The subcommittee said that this, in fact, was 'an additional public reason for carrying the strand along the bank at this point and thus securing the city against the action of the river'. The Government said that it was ready to sanction the extension of the road to Chitpur 'whenever the lottery funds should be in a state to admit of the necessary expenditure,' a point which had been made by the committee itself initially. Being impatient to complete the work, the Lottery Committee hoped that it would be in a position to do so 'during the next ensuing dry season', that is, the early months of 1827.[51]

THE *MAIDAN*, TANK SQUARE, CLIVE STREET…

THE ESPLANADE, OR *MAIDAN*

James Ranald Martin wrote in 1836: 'It has justly been said that the esplanade of Fort William forms the *lungs of Calcutta* [emphasis in original], and certain am I that we should breathe but thickly without them'.[1] Nearly two centuries later the city is literally gasping for its breath, such has been the nature of its expansion since Martin's time. Without the *maidan* Calcutta would have become unlivable today. Thanks to the national defence establishment, under the jurisdiction of which the *maidan* falls (for historical reasons), the 'lungs' are still working – but just about, and no one knows for how much longer. The

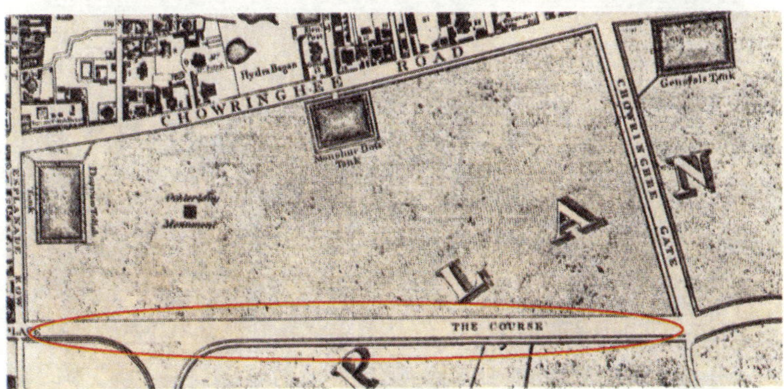

Fig. 55. The Course (Red Road) in Schalch's map (post-1828 version), which also shows 'Chowringhee Gate' Road and Manohar Das's tank

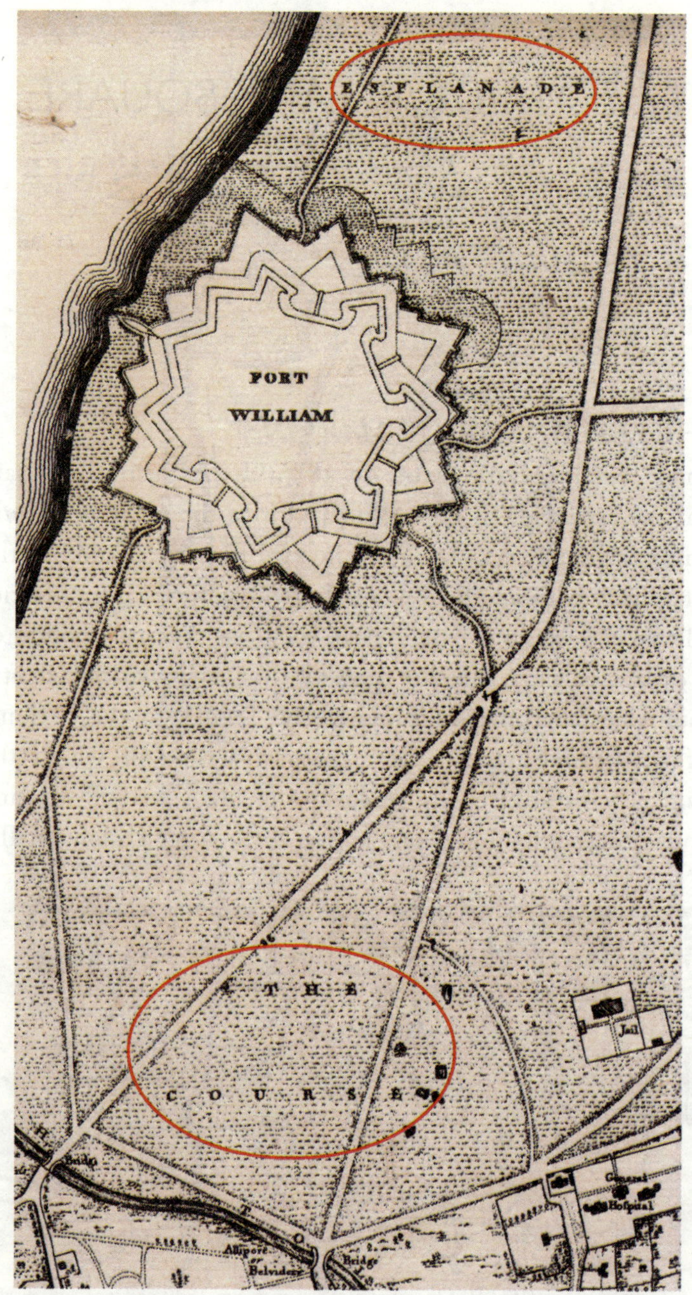

Fig. 56. The Course and Esplanade in Upjohn's map of 1793

history of this 'open space' is around 250 years old, coinciding with the construction of the second Fort William following the destruction of the first fort when Shiraj-ud-Daula wrested the town from the East India Company for six months in June 1756. One of the most-written-about spots in this great open space, especially in its early years, has been the Course,[2] or the wide road or promenade, stretching southward from Government House. It was there that, two centuries ago, the pick of Calcutta's genteel society went for their evening, and moonlit, stroll, the scene often being described as a fashion pageant of the times.

Since the *maidan* today is the remnant of the new fort's esplanade, it is reasonable to assume that the Course emerged after the esplanade was formed, that is, sometime in the 1770s, which is precisely why, as Reverend James Long mentions in his essay 'Calcutta in the Olden Times – Its Localities',[3] Captain Alexander Hamilton made no mention of it in his work in the 1740s.[4] At the end of 1780, Eliza Fay was writing to her friend: 'To the Course everyone goes, though sure of being suffocated with dust.'[5] About four decades later, when the evening drive on the Course had become something of an institution and was probably on the decline, the fictitious Tom Raw, the civilian just arrived from England, wrote:[6]

> The sun now sinking in fair Hoogly's stream,
> His parting beams resplendently displays,
> On Calvin's Ghaut; - and famed Bankshall the gleam
> Reflects, - and on the buildings [Writers'] slant his rays;
> The Custom House, and Clive Street's in a blaze,
> And all the river's bank to Chitpore Ghaut;
> And, as the rosy tint delightful plays
> On every western front, - though monstrous hot
> The evening drive approaches, which is – ne'er forgot.

> The tired civilian, from his daily toil
> Released, hails relaxation, and his chariot;
> The soldier, doomed within the fort to broil,
> Mounts his gay charger, anxious to hurry out,
> The plodding cit'zen with his *palkeegarry* out,
> Enjoys his jaunt as fully as the best,
> All hastening to the well-known course, and tarry out
> As long as light prolongs the driving zest;
> In short, till hunger calls, and savoury meals are drest.

Today, the Course has a brick-and-plaster balustrade on both sides which lends an ornamental touch to the scene, but just barely so. The balustrade has survived the times, the late 1970s in particular and the early eighties, when a virulent form of 'political and cultural cleansing' was practised in the state of West Bengal in India to which, regrettably, some remarkably well-sculpted statuary representing the British-Indian past fell victim. A number of these statues adorned both sides of Red Road along the entire length of the balustrade.[7] Mercifully, the balustrade itself was spared then but it had a closer brush with oblivion some decades later when an effort was made by the political masters of West Bengal to repair and refurbish it. Quite unnecessarily, the original balustrade was removed and replaced in its entirety with a modern version, which, thankfully, is an acceptable copy but so very *different* in the tactile sense, not being a direct 'witness' to the inexorable unfolding of the city's past (including the fashion parades of the early 19th century and, among other things, the landing and taking-off of military aircraft on the road during World War II).

The balustrade which was constructed anew in the 21st century may, in fact, have been first to be built in the *maidan* area in the second decade of the 19th century, replacing the old wooden railings[8] put up in the 1770s and later to separate the fort's esplanade under the control of the military authorities from areas under the jurisdiction of the civil Government. However, not all the fencing installed on the esplanade was meant to separate the civil from the military. As the metropolis was expanding, more space, apart from the Course, was needed for the recreation of its inhabitants, and steps were being taken to mark out such places. On 30 January 1808, the Calcutta magistrates Charles F. Martyn and W.C. Blaquiere wrote to the Government:

> ...we beg leave to suggest that the space between the walk [Respondentia] and the road leading to the Calcutta Fort Gate [to the east of the All-India Radio offices and the Eden Gardens] be enclosed with a railing so as to prevent carriages (with particular exceptions) from traversing it in all directions in the way that is now done, as well as horsemen in squadrons galloping up and down to the great annoyance and terror of every one.

The magistrates said that gates would, of course, be made at 'convenient distances...to admit persons on foot and in *palanqueens* to proceed to the walk'. The proposal was accepted by the Government.[9]

Seventeen years later, in January 1825, the Lottery Committee once more focussed its attention on the Respondentia Walk 'between Chandpal Ghaut and the Water Gate of the Fort', writing to the Government that the officer in charge of the fort's glacis be asked 'to repair the walk and also the railing on the west side of the road leading to the Calcutta Gate' so that horses and carriages 'may be prevented from driving over the grass plot on the side of the walk which is used by children and others for their morning and evening recreations'.[10] The riverside sentries would also have to ensure that horses and carriages were prevented from frequenting the railed grass plot and walk, 'a rule which formerly existed but is now infringed upon to the great inconvenience of

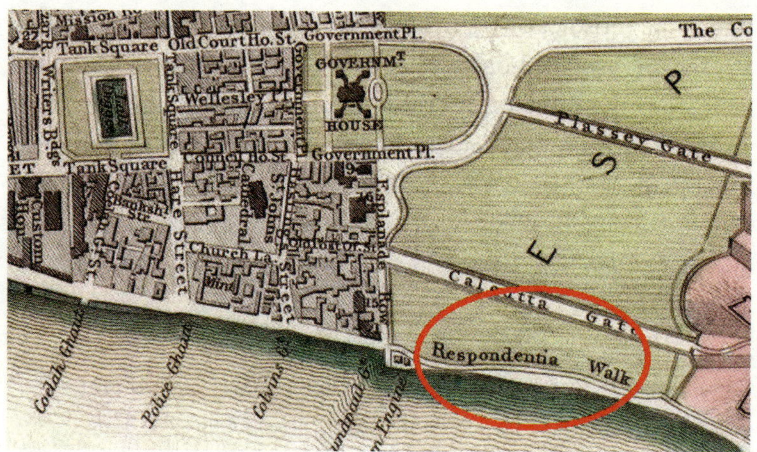

Fig. 57. Respondentia Walk, shown in the 1842 map published by the Society for the Diffusion of Useful Knowledge

the public'. The committee said that the trees which lined the walk should be 'thinned with advantage and other improvements made in it conducive to the comfort and convenience of the public'. The committee wanted to supervise the walk and grass plot 'as far as regards the general appearance and cleanliness of that part of the glacis' was concerned, a proposal which was not accepted by the Government. Two weeks later, J.H. Amherst, the Governor-General's son who was also his Military Secretary, wrote back to say that the Lottery Committee's recommendations had been 'anticipated' and that steps were being taken 'for carrying the improvements and alterations into effect'.

To the east of the Respondentia Walk was the Course. On 16 July 1818, or just about nine months after it was formed, the committee wrote that it had come to its notice that the Military Board was considering 'the expediency of removing the wooden railing on the road between the Government House and the Chowringhee gateway of the fort' and replacing it with 'an iron railing'.[11] The committee wanted the new railing to be 'erected eight or ten feet behind the present railing' so that 'a path for foot passengers *behind the aqueduct* [emphasis added]' could be constructed so as to 'obviate the danger to which they are so frequently exposed proceeding along the Course'. What is clear from this is that the committee was referring not just to the Red Road of today but to the entire stretch of road from Chandpal Ghat to Government House, skirting the latter to the south and then turning south into the Red Road at the point once known as the 'cocked hat'.[12] Two weeks later, the Government told the committee that the Military Board's project had been dropped on account of the 'heavy expense' it would entail. However, since the committee's objective appeared 'to be of importance to the public convenience', it was prepared to consider any suggestion which the committee could possibly have on the subject.[13]

The Lottery Committee got down to work and asked Henry Wood to find out how much a new balustrade 'similar to that erected by him along the Chowringhee Road' with a footpath inside it (see Fig. 21) would cost. It said that the wooden railing 'extending from Chandpaul Ghaut to the Gateway of the Fort towards Chowringhee' was generally in bad condition and that it would in all probability be necessary 'to renew a considerable portion of it at an early period'. The committee wanted a balustrade in place of a railing because of two reasons. First, importance was attached 'to making a separate footpath on the side of some of the principal roads and streets in which foot-passengers are peculiarly exposed to accidents from horses and carriages'. Secondly, an added benefit of the project would flow from the fact that the balustrade would be 'ornamental' in place of a bare railing. Wood's estimate showed that the 4 ½ ft-high balustrade would be 6,000 ft in length and, free labour being provided by convicts, would cost Rs 4,950 to which would have to be added the cost of the 12-ft-wide walk (Rs 1,620) the total cost coming to Rs 6,570.[14]

Since the esplanade fell under the fort's administrative jurisdiction, the committee urged the Government to allow it to go ahead with implementation 'provided no solid objection should arise to its adoption from considerations of a military nature'. The clearance given by the Military Board came through a month later,[15] following which a subcommittee comprising Bayley, Barwell and Wood was formed to get on with the construction of the balustrade and footpath. Nearly two years later, on the last day of August 1820, the Lottery Committee sent a detailed expenditure account of the project drawn up by George Hays, superintendent, which not only declared formally that the project had been completed but that work on it had begun on 23 February 1819, or four months after the project had been approved by the Government. The statement also said that the project was implemented 'in part' by Azimuddin *mistry*, one of the numerous ignored and forgotten players of history.[16]

A CHILDREN'S WALK, AND RED ROAD

Henry Wood had made the balustrade on the western side of Chowringhee Road, from Dharamtala to Park Street. In late July 1820, Henry Shakespear wrote, that 'the paling on the side of the Chowringhee Road, from the corner of Park Street to the extent of the tank [Eliot's Tank opposite the Tata Centre], is gradually rotting away' with the result that it had 'a very shabby and unseemly appearance'. In view of this, he suggested continuing southward, Wood's balustrade already in place on the northern stretch of Chowringhee Road.[17]

In the same letter, Shakespear wrote that, at the 20 July committee meeting, Bayley, who was also Chief Secretary to the Government, had suggested that a walk be made 'on the south side of the road leading from Park Street to the Chowringhee Sortie [today's Outram Road] as a safe and dry place for the exercise of children' (the road is named 'Chowringhee Gate' in Schalch's map: see Fig. 55).[18] A visit to the area had revealed the existence of a 'large ditch between it [the proposed walk] and the plain', the filling up of which and cutting another ditch farther to the south would add to costs unless done by convicts. Shakespear wanted to shift the walk to the northern side of the road, his view being that since 'no cattle or horses (were) allowed to go there' the expence of an inner railing would be saved. Of interest is Shakespear's comment that people regularly walked across the esplanade, or *maidan,* to go to places like Khidirpur, etc.[19] In view of this, he proposed that a 20-ft bridge be built 'over the cut made from the tank to the ditch above-mentioned which intersects a general thoroughfare for foot passengers from Chowringhee, and that part of Calcutta, to Keddorepore,[20] Allipore, etc'. The committee circulated Shakespear's letter among its members for comment but, in an effort to save time, Lt Paton was asked to keep a cost estimate ready. That figure, produced on 19 August 1820, was Rs 2,366-6-2¾.[21]

Shakespear's proposal had led to alternative suggestions being made by some committee members. Gordon, for example, wrote in a minute that

> As no part of the road leading (to) Kidderpore is watered to the southward of the place where it bends to the west and little beyond the Chowringhee Gate Sortie of the fort, there are always copious clouds of dust in dry windy weather reaching and even crossing the road leading to Park Street from that sortie.[22]

In view of this, Gordon suggested a new location for the walk – 'along Chouringhee Road from Dhurrumtollah towards Park Street where there is already a *puckah* railing, where the watering of the high road from the aqueduct will prevent the annoyance of dust'. Another reason for shifting the location was that, owing to the distance involved, children from the northern part of Chowringhee Road, Esplanade Row, Cossitollah and Dharamtala would find it strenuous to walk down to the new walk built for them to the west of Park Street.

Bayley, who had made the original proposal for a walk on the south side of Outram Road, agreed to the change of plan as suggested by Gordon. Along with Colvin and Gordon, he then proposed that the aqueduct along the road from Park Street be connected 'to the Chouringhee Sortie'. Trower, the Collector of 24-Parganas and Bayley's senior in the service by appointment as a writer, declared that, if implemented, both Bayley's proposal and that of Gordon's would be 'a great comfort to the Chouringhee residents'. Shakespear and Barwell, both civilians, seconded Trower's stand their additional suggestion being that there should be both a 20-ft-wide walk from the corner of Dharamtala to Park Street as well as one from Park Street to the Chowringhee Sortie 'and an aqueduct alongside if the levels will permit'. They also wrote that 'a balustrade to [Eliot's] Tank in lieu of the railing falling to decay and the bridge for passages 10 feet wide (were) highly desirable'.[23]

In course of the discussion on Bayley's suggestion on the walk for children down Outram Road, no member had mentioned the construction of a balustrade. No doubt after discussions within the committee, it was left to John Trotter, the committee's Secretary, to ask Paton to draw up an estimate of the cost of making

> …a *puckah* walk from the corner of Dhurrumtollah to Park Street of the same description as the one referred to in my letter of the 3rd instant as also of the expense which would be likely to attend a continuation of the present aqueduct *and* balustrade from Park Street to the Chouringhee Sortie *at the end of the Course* [emphasis added].[24]

Fig. 58. A painting of the tank on Chowringhee opposite Park Street – known as the General's Tank – by William Wood, 1833

The revised cost estimate (Rs 8,588-0-4¾) submitted in the middle of September,[25] included the *pucka* walk 'from the south end of Monohur Doss's Tank[26] (see Fig. 55) to the end of Park Street and from thence to the Chowringhee Sortie', the continuation of the aqueduct and balustrade to the Chowringhee Sortie, the making of a '*puckha* balustrade from the corner of Park Street to the bridge at the south end of the General's Tank,[27] and the construction of a bridge 'over the cut leading from the tank to the ditch on the Chowringhee Sortie Road'. In early October 1820 the committee sought approval for the project, which was granted a fortnight later the letter of approval stating specifically that the funds were being released for, among other things, 'continuing...the balustrade and aqueduct from the end of Park Street *to the Chowringhee Sortie* [emphasis added]'.[28] However, a walk down Outram Road today will show that the balustrade does not extend the whole length of the road till Red Road but covers only a part of it from the road's junction with Chowringhee Road suggesting that the curtailment of the balustrade to the south of Outram Road took place at a later point in time.

By August 1821, work on the balustrade and aqueduct 'with the exception of the plastering', from 'the corner of Park Street to the bridge opposite the [Chowringhee] Sortie', that is, along Outram Road, had been completed and the Lottery Committee turned its attention to Red Road itself. On 4 August Shakespear proposed to the committee the continuation north of 'the balustrade on the east side of the Course from the Chowringhee Sortie Road to the corner of Esplanade Row' (in the estimate prepared by Lt Paton this point is described as 'the crossroad opposite the south-east entrance of Government House').[29] Three reasons were given to justify the proposal, namely, that 'the present wooden railing is completely decayed and is constantly requiring repairs', that since the 'the whole length of the western side of the Course' had a new balustrade it had become 'indispensably necessary for the sake of uniformity and appearance that it should be continued on the eastern side also',[30] and, lastly, that a new wooden railing would incur a 'heavy expence' compared to a brick-and-mortar balustrade. The proposal was approved by the Government in September.[31]

OLD COURT HOUSE STREET

In the middle of July 1818 – that is, nine months after the setting up of the Lottery Committee – the Board of Revenue informed the Government that the firm Stewart and Robertson was keen on buying 2 *katha*s 2 *chittack*s of Government land 'adjoining their premises in Court House Street'[32] at Rs 500 a *katha*, the point being made that in view of its location the spot of ground concerned would be of use only to the firm concerned. The Board felt that, in view of the low marketability of the plot, the price offered by the firm was reasonable. This apart, the purchase would also prevent the plot from being turned into 'a receptacle of filth as it is now'.

The matter being referred to the Lottery Committee, the latter wrote to the Government in the first week of August that it would get back to it on the subject of the interest shown by Stewart and Robertson in buying the ground 'lying between the aqueduct in Court House Street and the premises' only after it had found out from the owners of the houses 'now occupied by Mr Adam and Messrs Tulloh and Co.'[33] whether they were willing to purchase the ground which 'adjoined' their respective houses and which lay behind the aqueduct 'and eventually the price they would give for it'.[34] Arthur Blechynden, the Surveyor to the committee who had been put on the job, reported a couple of weeks later that, despite his best efforts, he could not get any 'definitive answer' from Palmer and Company, the attorneys for the owner of the house occupied by Tulloh and Co. – 'near the Loll Dhiggy' – to his enquiries relating to the purchase of the small piece of ground in front of the house, 'which is the property of the Government'. He was also not able to communicate with the proprietor of the house occupied by John Adam regarding the purchase of the plot lying between the house and the aqueduct.[35] Charles Trower, the Collector of 24-Parganas, then came forward and offered his services to take up the issue of purchase of the two plots of land with their respective proprietors (a suggestion accepted by the committee) 'in the same manner as he has already done with Messrs Stewart and Robertson regarding the ground in front of their premises'.

Nothing happened for nearly seven months. Then, on 1 March the following year, we find Stewart and Robertson writing to the committee that it had been in touch with Trower regarding the 'slip of ground between our premises and the drain in Old Court House Street' which had turned into 'a perfect nuisance, to ourselves, and neighbours, from the impracticability of preventing its being a sink of filth'.[36] The firm said that it proposed building a 'verandah, in a line with the house next to us, the property of Mr Edmonstone,[37] and the cooking house lately built by Government', which 'may be made an ornament to the street'.[38] The committee backed the proposal and recommended that the plot be sold to the firm, which the Government accepted.[39] Meanwhile, Trower had been working on the owners of the premises occupied by Tulloh and Company, and on the last day of 1819 he asked the committee for permission to sell 'the slip of ground immediately before (the) premises (of Messrs Tulloh and Company) on [Old Court House Street] at the same rate purchased by Messrs Stewart and Robertson', Benjamin Turner, 'the manager of the estate to which belongs the shop of Messrs Tulloh and Company', agreeing to the purchase proposal. Two weeks later the committee cleared the sale at the price agreed upon, imposing the condition that 'the spot would be built upon immediately according to a plan to be submitted and approved of by the Lottery Committee'.[40]

Five months later, in June 1820, Nillmanny (Nilmoni) Mullick and Bustomdoss Mullick, owners of No. 22 Old Court House Street, which was next to the godowns of Stewart and Robertson, wrote to the committee that the 'slip of ground' on Old Court House Street attached to their house, which was 'at present waste and of no use to Government, but on the contrary is in its present state rather a nuisance to the public and particularly to our house', be given to them '*gratis* [emphasis in original] and free of all expense'. The Mullicks said that their intention was to build a verandah 'with a wall and railings thereon at our own expence similar to that which has been recently added by Messrs Stewart Robertson and Company to their godowns', and that they would 'derive no particular advantage further than in improving the external appearance of our house whilst the work would be ornamental to the public road'.[41] It is not a little strange that the

Mullicks should have asked for the ground to be given to them free at a time when other similar plots in the same line of the road in question had been sold by the Government. This apart, they were being disingenuous when they claimed that they would derive no pecuniary benefit from the transfer because it is clear that the value of their property would increase after the alteration, which would be tantamount to private gain for the Mullicks. In fact, if the committee agreed to transfer the ground free of cost as proposed by the Mullicks, the net increase in the value of the property would be greater than that of their neighbours who had had to buy the ground in question.

Making the Mullicks' suggestion to be given the land free of cost becomes even curiouser when it is known that the Lottery Committee not only accepted the proposal but did so, seemingly, in a tearing hurry. The very next day after the proposal was received the Mullicks were informed that the plot would be handed over to them 'free of cost on the condition of your adopting immediate measures for completing the engagement proposed in your letter'. There is no doubt that the vacant plot in front of No. 22 was spoiling the entire frontage of the line of houses in that part of Old Court House Street, especially after Stewart and Robertson had completed its 'ornamental addition' in keeping with the frontage of the house of Edmonstone and the 'cooking house'. But was this reason enough for revenue to be sacrificed by the Lottery Committee? It is entirely possible that the Mullicks were not prepared to buy the plot in front of their house as Stewart and Robertson and the others had done, and that the committee, after having come to know of this, had advised the owners to put in a request for acquisition without cost, which was then acceded to with alacrity if only to impart to the street in question a better appearance than previously without any further delay.

TANK SQUARE GARDEN, GHATS, SOUTH GATE

During the time of Lord Hastings, Writers' Buildings shed its original 'workhouse' character when it was given a decorative façade in 1820-21.[42] The effort to beautify Tank Square – the area around Laldighi (BBD Bagh tank) – to the south of Writers' Buildings had begun earlier, in 1804, when Lord Wellesley's special committees had begun their work to suggest ways of improving the town.[43] These efforts were continuing during the Lottery Committee years the early measures involving the simple induction of new chairs at the right places.[44]

There is something indefinably permanent about human behaviour when it comes to exploiting an opportunity to make private gain on the sidelines, as it were. There were allegations that not all of the new chairs placed in Tank Square were being put to the right use. *The Calcutta Journal* of 23 March 1820 carried a letter signed 'An Inhabitant of Calcutta' which said that 'An iron couch, which was intended no doubt for the accommodation of the public who walk in this square, has been…taken to [the gardeners'] huts for them to sit on'. The letter also sought to bring to the notice of the authorities that the gates of the square were 'shut at about 6 or 7 o'clock every evening so that in this sultry weather the benefits of [the] open air is thus denied to the peaceable inhabitants and their families'. The correspondent said that, according to 'the *mollys*, or gardeners, of this public walk', the gates were shut early because cows entered the square at night and also because the flowers were 'plucked by visitors and taken away'. However, as he saw it, the truth lay elsewhere. The flowers were picked and sold in the market by the gardeners themselves and they, therefore, had 'an interest in preventing visitors from seeing their depredations' which they ensured by shutting the gates early.

More substantive was the communication from Charles Trower on 24 July 1818 that, as he had run out of funds, there

Fig. 59. James Baillie Fraser's painting of the west side of the Laldighi (BBD Bagh tank) depicting a scene before 1821

was a possibility of the ghat on the eastern (Old Court House Street) side of Tank Square not being improved in the way the ghat on the western side had been developed.[45] He said that the improvements on the western side had made access to the tank 'clean and dry, the dirty water from the street and ghaut [being] prevented [from] going into the tank, cattle and dogs excluded from the garden on that side, and the appearance of the ghaut very much beautified' (see Fig. 59). Hitherto, the expenditure had been made 'from savings in the establishment for *mallies*' which had been accumulating 'for two or three years'. But just Rs 452-8-0 was left in the kitty 'which was barely sufficient to complete the work'.

Trower wrote that since the development on the western side, particularly the exclusion of cattle from the area, would not be fully effective till the eastern side had been developed in a similar fashion, he asked the committee 'to recommend to Government my being authorised to disburse the sum of 900 rupees' to develop the eastern side. The work to be done included 'raising the ghaut two steps to make the water run off towards the drain, pave the whole with large tiles, and put a teakwood railing from the water's edge to the outside wall of the garden'. The Collector said the ghat on the western side of the square covered 1,818 sq. ft and required 134 ft of railing but that on the eastern side being much larger would require 5,600 sq. ft to be covered and would need 252 ft of railing. Trower wrote that the garden had

> …lately become a place of considerable resort of an afternoon for recreation to all classes of people and particularly for children, and is of itself so pretty an object the committee will not, I trust, consider the trifling disbursement I request as any misappropriation of the funds entrusted to our charge.[46]

The committee sought sanction for the project and asked Trower for a detailed estimate of the work to be done, the approval coming through in early September.[47]

A lot of effort went into the sprucing up of the Tank Square garden which involved the use of manual labour. This was reflected in the increase in the number of people engaged in looking after the tank and its garden. In the second week of February 1820, Trower asked for Rs 400 to put up two buildings – 30 ft long and 10 ft wide – 'on the northeast corner of the Loll Diggee gardens for the accommodation of the gardeners and the convicts employed in the garden'.[48] The buildings, the Collector assured, would be made of 'the best *pucka* materials', the bricks used being supplied by 'the committee at Beparry Tullah'. Trower was a senior civilian and it is surprising that his letter was not enough for the

Fig. 60. The crowd at the eastern gate of Laldighi at Tank Square (BBD Bagh), etching by Thomas Daniell, 1786

sanction to come through. On 24 February the committee asked him to submit 'a detailed estimate' of the project (which was sent nearly three weeks later) the total expenditure adding up to Rs 405-6-8.[49] The approval came through on 23 March the project being implemented in five weeks.[50]

Early in February the following year (1821), the Collector was active once again in trying to improve further the facilities at Tank Square. This time his focus was on improving access to the square from the south, that is, the side which today has been grossly interfered with by the presence of the rather unimpressive Calcutta Telephones building. Trower's point was that the eastern and western gates to the tank and square were nearly always crowded with *bheesties* drawing water from the tank (see Fig. 20), which interfered with easy egress and ingress by 'residents' of the neighbourhood out on an evening's stroll in the garden. The

Fig. 61. The iron gate of the ghat to the south of the Tank Square (BBD Bagh) tank as it is today, hidden away behind the Calcutta Telephones building

Collector said that he had received 'numerous applications' on the subject from such people his proposed remedy being to instal an iron gate on the southern side of the square, the Collector adding that a suitable gate of the sort required being available for Rs 1,300 at Tulloh and Company. Trower wrote that, apart from the new gate being one of great convenience for visitors to the square, it would also be 'a great ornament to that part of the city'. It probably was in its time, but over the past two centuries the gate has lost its utility totally and, what is worse, is now hidden from public view completely. Along with this letter, an estimate for Rs 480 (prepared by Osborne, the Surveyor in the Collector's office) was sent, the total cost of the gate 'complete with the exception of the lamps' being Rs 1,780.[51] The committee lost no time in seeking the Government's approval (given on 20 February) to instal the gate the detail being added that it would be put up 'immediately in front of the Government House'.[52] Seven years later, in 1828, the specific locational attribute of the gate was lost when the statue of Lord Hastings (see Fig. 2) was erected 'near the irongate in the enclosure of Tank-square, facing the Government House', thus blocking forever the unimpeded view from the square of the seat of the East India's Company's ruler in India, which was contrary to the earlier plans for beautification of the area.[53]

Later, in May 1821, Trower devised a scheme to repair and clean 'the walls and balustrade round the garden of Tank Square' (see Fig. 20) since a 'considerable time' had elapsed since any refurbishment work had been done on them. The detailed estimate (computed by Azimuddin *mistry*) appended to the Collector's 18 May letter showed that the work would cost Rs 743-8-0. Trower told the committee that he had pruned the initial estimate drawn up by Azimuddin and that he was satisfied that it was 'as reasonable as any other person would undertake the work for'.[54] But what appeared to be 'reasonable' to Trower was not so to his colleagues on the committee. In fact, the episode once more throws light on the standing of Trower – who was senior in the service even to William Bayley, the Chief Secretary to Government – amongst the committee members and, by extension, the Government itself. Briefly, the committee did not accept Trower's estimate as submitted and sent it to Charles Paton, the assistant to the Superintendent of Public Buildings in the Lower Provinces and a committee member himself, to report upon its 'correctness and reasonableness'. Paton reported at the end of May that the work would cost an estimated Rs 610-14-7¾, which was around 18 per cent lower than Trower's computation.

The committee's seeking another opinion on an inconsiderable cost estimate was tantamount to questioning Trower's ability to supervise and evaluate a project which, given his substantive position as Collector of 24-Parganas and his seniority in the service, could hardly be described as a trifling matter. In early June the committee sought approval for Paton's estimate without alluding to Trower's figures, the approval coming through a week later. On the same day (7 June) Trower was informed by the committee that his estimate had been sent 'for the examination and report of the Superintendent of Public Buildings, Lower Provinces, *conformably to the established usage of the Lottery Committee*' (emphasis added).[55] This may have been so but the fact remains that in a large number of other cases project estimates had been dealt with at the level of the committee itself without involving the Superintendent of Public Buildings. The committee had the discretion to accept the Collector's estimate, a course it chose not to adopt which indicated a lack of trust in Trower which, at the very least, was damning for the officer concerned.

WEST OF TANK SQUARE

In 1804, the first Committee for the Improvement of the Town had called for steps to do away with the ruins of the old fort, an eyesore in the area, which stood to the west of Laldighi (BBD Bagh tank). The special committee on 'nuisances' within the town had written:

> The decayed and ruinous state of that building has attracted the attention of your committee who are of opinion that those high walls, equally useless to the proprietors and disfiguring to the appearance of a principal quarter of the town, serve to obstruct a free circulation of air, and also from their being strongly impregnated with saltpetre and extremely damp, occasion noxious and unwholesome vapours.[56]

It was not only the old fort and the hulk of its ruins that was disfiguring the area. The monument put up by John Zephaniah

Fig. 62. James Baillie Fraser's painting of Holwell's Monument just before it was demolished in 1821

Holwell immediately after the expulsion of Shiraj-ud-Daula from Calcutta, in an effort to perpetuate the memory of the victims of the 'Black Hole', was also, to put it mildly, in bad shape.

Aware of the poor condition the monument was in, the Government removed it in 1821 from the spot just east of the old fort and at the north-west corner of Tank Square. Writing on 16 March 1821 Bayley, the Chief Secretary to the Government, told Henry Shakespear and the magistrates: 'The building of the new Customs House being now nearly completed…you will take early measures for the removal of the old monument situated in the road which leads from the new Customs House in front of the Writers' Buildings towards the Lal Bazar (Lal Bazar)'. He wrote that, 'In its present position, it materially contracts the roadway and interferes with the free and open approach which it is so essential to maintain to the Custom House premises'. Just about 60 years had passed since its installation, and Bayley was already writing that from

> ...the enquiries which have been made it does not appear that the monument in question was erected over the remains of those individuals who perished on the occasion of the capture of Calcutta by Surajud Dowlah; nor does the inscription now upon it record the names of any of those individuals.[57]

The Calcutta Journal cited a different reason backing the demolition of the monument when it wrote that 'we can see no benefit whatever likely to arise by keeping alive in the minds of anyone, but particularly the Natives, the recollection of the horrors suffered by Englishmen, and the cruel tortures under which they then expired, as sacrifices to the caprice of a Mahomeddan Despot'.[58] In view of all this, the Government saw no reason 'which should render the preservation of the monument desirable, while its removal will undoubtedly add to the embellishment of that part of the city, and will be of essential convenience to the mercantile community and to the public at large'. Nearly a century later, Lord Curzon had a replica of the monument installed in the same spot which was subsequently moved to the churchyard of St John's Church to the east of Church Lane, where it still stands forlorn.

In the meantime, nearly four years before the removal of Holwell's Monument, the ruins of the fort had been demolished and on its site had come up 'some extensive warehouses for the Company'.[59] Within two years, the warehouses themselves had to be moved the need arising for an alternative site where the employees of the department could be accommodated (see below). The maps of Mark Wood and Upjohn show that immediately to the south of the old fort, between Council House Street to the east and Bankshall Street on the west, there was a large area containing just a couple of houses. In the early years of the English settlement, it was open ground affording a clear view of the river from the houses to the east of the Laldighi tank across Old Court House Street. The Company's House, where the Governor of the settlement resided for some years, was located on the riverside to the west of the ground, to the south of which was the site of the settlement's first hospital (see Fig. 31).[60] Of passing interest is the fact that in January 1780 Warren Hastings gifted the ground to Captain Joseph Price 'for the services which he had rendered to the public'.[61] The precise location of the spot – known by the name Timber Yard – was then described as 'the intire Property…situated to the South-West of the great Tank'.

SOUTH OF OLD FORT WILLIAM

In 1819, when the need arose to remove the export warehouse from the site of the old fort, what better ground could there be but the vacant land lying in the heart of Tank Square just south of the fort ruins? On 29 January of that year Charles Chicheley Hyde, the Acting Sub-Export Warehouse Keeper, wrote to George Udny, the Export Warehouse Keeper and Acting President of the Board of Trade, that he had 'fixed upon' the spot of ground 'to the south of the export warehouse and adjoining the premises at present in the occupation of Messrs Mackillop and Thomas' for 'the erection of the offices required by this department' because he had found it to be 'the best and most convenient place' for the buildings in question.[62] However, and thankfully for the future of the city, the proposal was opposed by Charles Trower, Collector of 24-Parganas, who refused 'to give up the ground in question without the orders of Government', adding that the ground was 'very valuable and an offer to purchase it has been made which is now under the consideration of the revenue authorities' (see below). Hyde wrote that the reasons cited by Trower probably still existed as no instructions had reached his department 'authorising delivery of the ground for the stated purpose' even though approval for the construction of the new buildings had been obtained. The Board of Trade was urged to take steps to transfer the ground for implementation of the building project. In early February, Udny asked the Government to expedite the transfer of the ground ('long since occupied by the servants of the export warehouse and very necessary to its convenience') to his department on the ground that it could be 'much more profitably occupied by the Commercial Department than by any other appropriation of it'.

Providing us with an idea of how the Company's bureaucracy worked, Holt Mackenzie, Secretary of the Territorial Department, asked the Board of Revenue in early April for 'copies of a letter' written on the subject by Alexander F. Lind, the Acting Collector of Calcutta.[63] While providing the information (on 25 June) sought by Mackenzie, the Board said that the correspondence generated by 'Mr [J.B.] Birch's supposed claims to the grounds required for the additional office of the export warehouse' indicated that Lind 'had misapprehended the nature of that gentleman's communication, by which it now appears that he [Birch] did not intend to prefer any claim founded on a proprietary right in the land'. On 23 June Lind had told the Board that since Birch was 'not quite certain whether the ground is included in his estates', he was 'desirous not of claiming it as his right but of being permitted to purchase it at an equitable valuation'. Lind had added that four years earlier, on 16 March 1815, Birch had made an application to the Board of Revenue 'requesting permission to purchase the spot [measuring 14 *cottah*s 12 *chittack*s] at the rate of sicca rupees 400 per cotta'. The Board had recommended on the very next day sale of the land to Birch at Rs 400 a *katha* Lind, however, adding that 'it does not appear what orders were passed in consequence of that reference'.[64]

The Acting Collector further wrote that, as pointed out by Trower, the Collector of 24-Parganas on 3 March 1818, Birch also wanted to buy another spot of ground measuring 1 *bigha* 11 *katha*s and 1 *chittack* (no details are provided on the precise location of this bit of ground). According to Lind, immediately following Hyde's formal move on the spot of ground and Udny's taking up the issue with the Government on 26 April 1819, Birch had written that 'the erection of the proposed buildings would deprive him of his "right of road" and that the buildings themselves would be considered a public nuisance'.[65] In that letter, Birch had given the precise location of the ground under contention describing it as that 'immediately to the northward of Mr Mackillop's and Mr Mactier's houses' both of which were owned by him. He wrote that there was no access to Mackillop's coach house and stables but over the ground which 'has been always considered as belonging to the estate I have in Tank Square', and that, if the Government were to acquire it for the purpose of erecting buildings on it, 'not only my right of road would be taken from me but the value of my premises very much injured …'[66]

The Board of Revenue had sent Lind's letter to the Territorial Department on 25 June. A fortnight later, Mackenzie had written to the Riverbank Committee[67] seeking its views on the 'appropriation of the grounds' south of the old fort for use as an export warehouse as suggested by the Board of Trade and, if it agreed with the suggestion, 'the manner it would…be advisable to appropriate it'. The tables were turned on the Board of Trade when, on 17 August, the Riverbank Committee wrote to say that its objections to the plan were two-fold: 'the injury which would thereby result to the property of an individual, and the unsightly appearance which such buildings would have in one of the handsomest parts of the town'.[68] It said that the house 'immediately adjoining the spot where it is proposed to erect the offices for the export warehouse servants' belonged to Birch 'who is stated... to have represented that they would deprive him of his right of road and would be considered a public nuisance'. The committee agreed with Hyde who had written in his 9 January letter that the proposed warehouse buildings 'would not interfere' with the coach house door of Birch's premises, adding that, perhaps, they would not also 'amount to a public nuisance'. But Birch had a point in his favour, namely, that the

> ...number of public servants such as are to inhabit them [the proposed premises], being immediately under the windows of Mr Birch's house, and in no wise subject to the control of the person residing there, would be a private annoyance likely to depreciate the value of his property, a consequence which Government would doubtless be unwilling to induce without some more urgent necessity than appears to exist in the present case.

The Riverbank Committee concluded that the ground in question 'should not be appropriated for the purpose proposed by the Board of Trade'. As for an alternative location of the export warehouse premises, the committee suggested that they could be built 'on the piece of ground on the north side of Coila Ghaut, which appears to be already partly occupied by huts inhabited by persons of that description'.

The decision having been taken at the committee level, the time had now come for formal orders to be issued regarding implementation. The Riverbank Committee had given its opinion on 17 August 1819. On the same day the Government resolved that the buildings needed for the export warehouse staff would be erected 'on the site indicated' in the committee's letter, to the north of Koila Ghat.[69] As for the ground adjoining Birch's premises, the Government would be 'guided' by the view of the Lottery Committee 'to whom a reference will accordingly be made from the Judicial Department'. The reference was made in early September, the point made being, first, that the huts, etc., existing on the plot 'adjoining to Birch's premises in Tank Square' would have to be 'immediately removed' under orders already issued from the Judicial Department on 18 June,[70] and, secondly – reflecting the holistic approach adopted by the government of Lord Hastings for the improvement of the rapidly expanding town – that the plot of ground thus cleared would be placed at the disposal of the Lottery Committee 'who will determine [whether] the whole or any of the ground should be sold to Mr Birch on the condition of his constructing upon it suitable buildings on a plan, so far as relates to their external appearance, [which] should be previously seen and approved by the committee'. Needless to say, the committee was given a free hand: if it felt that the ground in question was not to be sold and that, 'for the public convenience', it would be better to be 'annexed to the streets to which it is adjacent', it was free to do so.[71]

In the middle of October, the Lottery Committee apprised Birch of its decision to sell the plot to him 'at a fair price' subject to the condition regarding appearance imposed by the Government. He was also told that the export warehouse servants would be 'permitted to continue in the undisturbed possession of the present huts until another place can be provided for their accommodation'. Birch wasted no time. He accepted the arrangement on the same day offering a price of Rs 600 a *katha* which he justified as being 'as high as any valuation before the master [auctioneer, or vendue master] on the 13th instant (October)'.[72] He, however, hoped that 'the great nuisance of the warehouse huts' would be removed 'with the least practicable delay'. His price was accepted by the committee which reassured him that the huts 'now occupied by the servants of the export warehouse' would be removed 'as soon as other accommodation can be provided for them'. The extent of the plot – described as lying in Tank Square 'southward of the Honourable Company's export warehouse' and 'north of Mr Birch's house' – was measured as 12 *kathas*, the total sale proceeds being Rs 7,200.

Implementation of the scheme was delayed because of inter-departmental wrangling over the removal of the huts. The resolution to vacate the ground had been adopted on 17 August. Nearly two months later, on 13 October, Udny asked for more time to remove the huts till the new buildings for the accommodation of the export warehouse employees were completed. John Forsyth, the Sub-Export Warehouse Keeper, had informed him a day earlier that the huts were 'constantly occupied by the servants dependent upon the warehouse, and by *bhurdars*, peons and sepoys who accompany dispatches from the several commercial residencies'. Forsyth said it would be difficult to find accommodation for these people 'should they be immediately removed' from the huts where they stayed and proposed instead that the plan to shift the employees be put on hold till the new buildings north of Koila Ghat were ready. The Government accepted the plea and suspended the evacuation of the huts until the new ones were ready.

The Board of Trade had got its way, but John Brereton Birch was having to shoulder the financial cross. By the middle of January 1820 he was complaining to the Lottery Committee of being greatly inconvenienced by the fact that despite having paid Rs 7,200 for the ground in question on 25 October the previous year he had 'not yet been able to benefit' from the acquisition as the land was still occupied by the employees of the export warehouse 'whom I have in vain endeavoured to remove'. Birch said that he had already lost Rs 200 in interest, which would carry weight if the matter were to go to court. He held out a veiled threat of taking legal steps unless the 'servants' were 'speedily removed', particularly in view of the fact that he was entitled to rent from the ground which belonged to him.[73]

The committee was stirred into action and on 24 February John Trotter, the Secretary to the Lottery Committee, wrote to Walter Nisbet, his counterpart at the Board of Trade, that the committee was finding itself in an embarrassing situation for having created problems for Birch, its specific suggestion being that, till the new premises of the export warehouse north of Koila Ghat were completed, 'some temporary accommodation' be found for them 'within the premises of the export warehouse' itself.[74] Replying a week later, the Board of Trade turned down the request on the ground that 'there is no place within the premises of the export warehouse or godown...that can be given up as a temporary accommodation' for the people mentioned, adding that even if such accommodation was possible the possibility of fires breaking out and endangering 'the valuable goods stored in the export warehouse' would be 'an insuperable bar to the adoption of the measure'. The Board suggested that the only alternative before it was the erection of temporary accommodation 'westward of the spot on which the permanent buildings are to be constructed'. The Lottery Committee did not accept the suggestion and on 9 March resolved that a 'godown' be engaged from Birch himself, at Rs 50 a month, for the accommodation of the employees concerned.[75]

At last, things had begun to move for Birch. Within three months of the committee resolving to rent his godown to accommodate the export warehouse employees, he submitted to the committee a sketch of the building which he proposed to put up 'in front of the export warehouse' with the objective of getting its approval as stipulated under the arrangement with the committee.[76] He was in a bit of a hurry because the sketch submitted by him was wanting in some respects. As he wrote, 'I am sorry I could not get the elevation properly finished' but he promised that the arches would be 'filled up with (venetian) windows and the whole will, I hope, form a very ornamental building'. In the same letter, Birch told the committee that he had got possession of the land on 1 May 1820 (about seven weeks after the committee had decided to hire a godown where the export warehouse staff could be shifted) while he had paid for it in October the previous year. Since he was paying an interest of 12 per cent on the funds he had used to purchase the ground, he hoped he would be compensated for the 'loss' from the lottery funds. The committee agreed with the design for the house, but, as regards the second point, it said that since the value of the ground bought by Birch had undergone a change following the disposal of surplus land on the road leading from Koilaghat Street to the Bankshall, it would have to consider the 'adjustment' before it took into its 'favourable consideration the circumstance of the loss' alluded to by Birch in his letter.[77]

ACCESS TO THE NEW TOWN DUTY OFFICE, CLIVE STREET

To the north-west of Tank Square was Clive Street, a very old road on the east bank of the river (see Fig. 43). It had become congested even before the construction of the Town Duty Office on Strand Road in 1819 because of the increasing flow of commerce. With the completion of the new inland Customs facility the situation was threatening to turn critical, and it was inevitable that the focus of attention would turn to widening the road.[78] On 29 November 1820, with construction 'nearly finished', the Board of Customs apprised the Government that a couple of issues needed to be attended to in order to prevent bottlenecks developing in the future. One of the officials who intimated the Board regarding 'certain points which are absolutely necessary to be attended to' before the office could be moved to its new location was Henry James Chippendale, Acting First Deputy Collector of Government Customs and Town Duties at Calcutta.[79]

Chippendale focussed attention on two broad points, the first of which related to the space between the street and the river which was to be filled up and which the Board of Customs wanted to be turned into a sloping beach. The Acting Deputy Collector said that the space to be filled up was 360 feet 'in a direct line' but the rubbish lying around – obtained from the demolition of the old building standing in the ground – was just enough to fill up 270 feet. As the 'least expensive plan', he proposed that the remaining 90 feet be filled up 'from the banks of the river'. The step was necessary because if the 90 feet was allowed to remain untreated 'it would afford a just ground of complaint of incapability of accommodating the internal trade of the country'. As Chippendale saw it, even if the ground was filled up according to plan it would still be found to be 'very confined', which is why he thought it would be 'highly advantageous to recover as much ground as possible from the river'. 'Upwards of 100 feet in length' could be recovered, the consequent accretion in the value of ground easily looking after the cost of filling it up.

The Board of Customs was opposed to the proposal because it went against its plans to construct a 'sloping beach…to the water's edge'. While the Board had argued that there was enough space for the Town Duty Office to conduct its business efficiently (which is why it had suggested the making of a sloping beach), Chippendale felt that the new Customs facility would face a shortage of space. The Board had written that 'a very considerable piece of levelled ground of sufficient scope for every object of utility is already allotted to the use of the Town Duty Office, and that no immediate necessity can…exist for appropriating a more extended space to that purpose'. However, within six months the view had changed. On 8 June 1821, the Government informed the Lottery Committee that the Board had put in a request that, in the event of the nawab agreeing to sell his property adjoining the new Customs office, an 'arrangement' could be firmed up with the committee under which the Board would be allotted whatever ground was not required for the project. As the Board said, since the 'public warehouses hitherto sanctioned' would by no means be sufficient to cope with the volume of merchandise generated by river trade, allocation of the extra space near the new office would be very helpful.[80]

Chippendale's second point related to the transport ramifications of the improvements being effected in the area along the riverbank, specifically the easy evacuation of goods entering the town after having passed through the Customs checkpoint. The Board of Customs' attention was drawn to the state of the road between the new Town Duty Office and the river which, the Acting Deputy Collector felt, had to be remedied or else the merchants 'whose goods have been deposited at the Customs House will not be able to remove them'. In fact, some parts of the road were so narrow 'as barely to allow one hackery to pass another, and altogether far from being sufficiently wide for such a thoroughfare as it will of necessity become'. The only substantive solution to the problem would be to open a street 'eastward of the new building', to Chitpur Road.[81]

There was a suggestion for Clive Street as well, the north-south road running to the east of the new inland Customs office. Chippendale wrote that in places where Clive Street was the narrowest, as much of the contiguous buildings and ground required for widening the road should be bought by the Government. Covering up of drains and removing encroachments on the road could also provide 'some little relief to that portion of the trade which must of necessity pass into the merchants' godowns through Clive Street'. The demolition of the ruins of the house belonging to the nawab, lying to the east of the Customs facility, could be of some help to native merchants who would then be able 'to proceed

Fig. 63. A pencil drawing of Clive Street, by Charles D'Oyly, 1840

through any...gully into some one of the small roads leading into the Burra Bazar instead of going down a part of Clive Street'. The Acting Deputy Collector also suggested that the 'straw bazar' to the north of the Town Duty Office be removed to another spot to prevent fires breaking out in the new establishment.

In its comments on Chippendale's letter, the Board of Customs readily agreed that the advantages to be reaped from the erection of the new Town Duty Office would be '[in] great measure be lost to the native merchants if...ready means are not afforded them of carrying away their goods – after they shall have passed through the Customs House – into the interior of the city'.[82] The Board said that there was no alternative to increasing the porosity of the road network in the area concerned. Echoing Chippendale's suggestions, it said that in view of the 'extreme narrowness of Clive Street and the other streets in its neighbourhood' the roads (particularly some parts of Clive Street) had to be widened and a new road opened 'in a direction due east from the ghaut to the Chitpur Road'. However, the Board added that since it did not feel itself to be 'sufficiently acquainted with the subject to suggest any specific arrangement' it would be better if Chippendale's proposals were referred to the Lottery Committee. In the middle of December 1820 the Government asked the committee for its views on the subject, the latter in turn asking the subcommittee for improvements on the banks of the river to send in an 'early communication' on what it thought 'most desirable for improving the access to the Town Duty Office in Clive Street'. The subcommittee failed to produce the report even after ten months, both the Government and the Lottery Committee having to send reminders in October the following year.[83]

Three months later, at the end of January 1822, the committee declared that the choice lay between 'widening and improving the lanes in the vicinity of the Town Duty Office which lie between Clive Street and the Chitpore Road' (Cotton Street, Banstala Lane and Burtala Lane) and constructing a new street 'in an easterly direction from the vicinity of the new Town Duty Office to Chitpore Road'.[84] A survey had shown that it was 'impracticable' to widen the 'very confined' lanes named above and that all that could be done 'to render them useful had been already effected by narrowing the drains and by renewing the roadway with *coah*, but they are still very uncommodious and little calculated for the transit of hackeries'. As regards the alternative of making a new street, 'from the Town Duty Office to the centre of the town', the committee felt that although the investment required 'might not exceed that necessary for

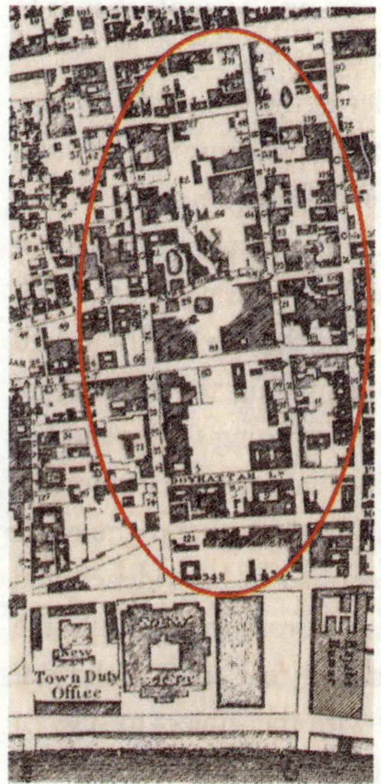

Fig. 64. Schalch's map showing the east-west Banstala, Burtala and Cotton Streets linking Clive Street and Chitpur Road

widening any one of the lanes...noticed', it would still be larger than what the Government would be prepared to incur.

Providing an idea of what the area was like in terms of human habitation, the committee said its survey had indicated that the ground in question was 'covered with valuable buildings closely adjoining each other, being the dwelling houses of many of the most opulent Hindoo inhabitants of Calcutta or houses of business belonging to rich native merchants'. Further, the entire stretch of ground was priced 'very high', fetching a price per *katha* of between Rs 700 and Rs 1,200. Considering this, the committee said that a road of the sort required through the area would cost at least Rs 3,30,000 (Rs 1,57,500 for the ground, 'probably' an equal sum as compensation for buildings to be wholly or partially destroyed, and the rest for drains, etc.). As regards the application of the principle of buying up surplus land to be resold later at a higher price in order to reduce the net investment, the committee said that it was uncertain of being able 'to purchase any considerable quantity of ground in a continued line for the purpose of resale or of building ...warehouses' which could be 'subsequently sold or let on account of Government'.[85]

Importantly, the committee said that if the Government was agreeable to building a new road despite its cost, it harboured the hope of a new major east-west link between the river and Circular Road in the east being opened up sometime in the future. But in case the idea did not find favour, the best way of improving access from the Town Duty Office to the centre of the city would be through Clive Street. The new Strand Road being built was another option but it would only help in transporting goods from that office 'towards the south or European portion of the town and thence (though, of course, by a very circuitous route) into the central parts of the city'. This apart, the committee could not 'safely anticipate' that the road would be ready 'before the end of year 1823'. Till that time, there was no other option but to improve access to the Town Duty Office through Clive Street.

But Clive Street could not be widened easily because of the 'great value of the houses' on either side of it. Even so, the committee felt that it could be 'rendered much more safe and commodious than at present' and could be widened 'generally so as to give it an average breadth of nearly 35 feet by the adoption of...partial improvements'. A specific suggestion was 'lowering the centre of the road which is now in many parts unnecessarily high by altering the form and construction of the drains which sometimes occupy a considerable space'. Another was by removing 'steps, abutments and other inconvenient projections from the houses by which the passage-way is now contracted' as also by 'purchasing and removing portions of houses, godowns and premises which project into the street and form sharp and narrow angles'. South of Mirbahar Ghat, the committee had reached an agreement with some natives such as Kashinath Mullick and Jagannath Das which would involve their relinquishing ground needed to widen Clive Street 'so as to give it a breadth of 35 feet' and to enable the new Strand Road 'being carried on in front of their ground, receiving in lieu a new pottah including all the alluvion ground which will remain attached to their premises, respectively'. The total investment required to improve Clive Street was put at Rs 28,840.[86]

Following receipt of the Lottery Committee's letter in late January, the Territorial Department was asked a week later to raise 'the low ground attached to the premises' of the nawab so as to enable the committee 'to carry on the quay or street on the riverside in front of those premises'.[87] As regards improved access to the Town Duty Office, the Governor-General in Council made clear its unhappiness that the committee had not been able to improve 'the lanes leading from Clive Street in the neighbourhood of the [Town Duty] office to the Chitpore Road' rendering them 'sufficiently commodious for the transit of the merchandise usually passing into the central parts of the town', and also for suggesting that the only solution would be to open a new street 'in the proposed direction'. The Government ruled this out for the time being, the Territorial Department being asked to look into the issue. It was also dismayed that a 'considerable period' would be required before the Strand Road could be completed and used for the transit of goods. Borrowing a suggestion made by the committee itself, the Government said that till such time as Strand Road could be made fully operational, Clive Street could be improved 'at a moderate expence', the committee being asked to get on with the job according to the plan submitted by it.

There was, however, a twist in the unfolding story when, within a month, the Government felt that, after all, a possible 'solution' to the issue did lie in the construction of 'a broad street from the vicinity of the Town Duty Office to Chitpore Road'. In early March 1822 the point was made at a meeting of the Territorial Department that such a street 'would be extraordinarily beneficial' and that the Lottery Committee should

> ...select the line of road which may seem best suited for the purpose, and after ascertaining the chief obstacles to the measure...submit detailed...estimates of the probable expence together with an accurate survey of the whole space between the new Town Duty Office and Chitpore Road.[88]

It is clear that the economic utility of the proposed road had become an important consideration which is why the Board of Customs, Salt and Opium was asked to extend all possible assistance to the Lottery Committee which would be useful in gauging 'the extent of the advantages which the trade of the city and the revenue of Government would derive from the completion of the work and the extensive erection of commodious warehouses in that quarter'.

Six months later, in the second week of September, a subcommittee comprising Shakespear, Ballard and Paton produced a report on 'the best plan for opening a new road from the Town Duty Office to the Chitpore Road', the Lottery Committee fully backing the conclusions.[89] A survey had been conducted of the area 'lying to the north and south of the Town Duty Office between the riverside and the Chitpore Road', a finding being that 'Banstollah Gully (see Fig. 64) would be in many points of view the best line that could be selected'. Three reasons were cited for the choice of the road: first, that it opened 'nearly opposite the Town Duty Office premises, centrically between that office and Meerbuhr Ghaut, much used for the landing of goods and the principal ghaut in that quarter of the city'; secondly, because it was 'nearly straight and has few very large houses in it compared with the two streets (Burtollah and Cotton Streets) further to the southward'; and thirdly, because the subcommittee 'preferred widening an existing road to opening an entirely new one, as one-third of the road would be readymade to our hands free of expence'.

Having located the line of the proposed road, the subcommittee tried to find out which side of it could be widened with the least disturbance to the inhabitants. While this work was continuing, a number of residents lodged petitions on the subject: 'those on one side wishing to preserve their own premises entire and to benefit by the demolition of their neighbours' property on the opposite side'. The battle soon became one of '*thakoorbaries*'. The subcommittee calculated that the cost of widening the road on the southern side would be Rs 1,76,479-1-13 while that for the northern side would be Rs 1,91,729-13-18, that is, a difference of Rs 15,250-12-5. Faced with this situation, the subcommittee decided to choose the alternative which would least interfere with '...religious prejudices, either by the destruction of the *thakoorbaries* or by the removal of the idols placed in them: *the only obstacle that in our judgement ought to be allowed to interrupt a work of such great public benefit and convenience as that contemplated on the present occasion* [emphasis added]'.

In the subcommittee's wisdom, it was the northern side of the road which could be more 'easily' demolished for its widening to the extent of 60 ft throughout its length.[90] As regards the project's total cost estimate, the subcommittee said that, relying on past experience of financing similar projects, it would not recommend the plan unless an outlay of Rs 2,00,000 was sanctioned to which would have to be added Rs 20,000 for the cost of making drains 'on both sides of the street'.

The Government resolved that the estimate of Rs 1,91,729-13-18 submitted for widening Banstala Lane on its northern side was 'considerably' less than what was expected. Another encouraging point was that 'a considerable profit' could be made by purchasing the low ground immediately to the south of the land procured from the nawab after it had been appropriately raised with the rubbish generated by the demolition of buildings for the widening of Banstala Lane. However, the critical point is that the green signal was not given because, as the Government saw it, the poor state of the lottery funds would not permit the improvements to be made 'for some time to come'. The door was left open also because there was another side to the entire issue which the Government could not ignore, namely, 'the several benefits of a territorial nature connected with the increased facility to be afforded to the officers of the Customs Department and to the community interested in the clearance of goods from the new Town Duty Office'. These subjects were not within the domain of the Lottery Committee and would have to be studied by the Territorial Department before a final decision could be taken.[91]

By late November 1822 a firm decision was taken, the Government shooting down both the widening of Banstala Lane and the suggestion of making a new road from Chitpur Road to Clive Street. The rationale behind the decision to scrap the widening of the lane is of interest because it underscores the point that the Government of the day was not averse to considering the convenience of native society as a critical input before taking such decisions. At a meeting of the Territorial Department, the Governor-General in Council resolved that it was not prepared to determine on the measure of widening the Banstala Lane, as proposed by the Lottery Committee, not only because the cost of the project was more than the funds at the disposal of the committee but also because, 'the arrangement involving an extensive interference in the private property in the most ancient part of the city requires a peculiarly full and careful enquiry into all particulars'.[92]

On the construction of 'a broad commodious road of communication' between Clive Street and Chitpur Road, the Governor-General in Council said it had no doubt that the step would improve the 'public advantage and convenience' but it was 'not entirely satisfied of the necessity of the work for the purposes of that office [the Town Duty Office]'.[93] Strand Road would 'at no distant period be extended to that vicinity' and Clive Street had been 'already considerably improved' by the committee. The point was made that when the site of the Town Duty Office was selected by the committee, 'of which the senior member of the Customs Board and Mr Chippendale [Chippendale] were members', neither the widening of Banstala Lane nor the building of a new road had been contemplated. The Government felt that the construction of Strand Road would 'enable the officers of Customs, without risk of fraud, to permit a freer use of the different ghauts both below and above the office'.

The further point was made that if the location of the Town Duty Office in Clive Street was to create difficulties for the merchants regarding 'in carrying their goods, which they would preferably land elsewhere, it might be a question how far it would be expedient to continue the office on its present situation, especially if the approach to the city from the eastward should be facilitated by the adoption of the plans of Lt Schalch'.[94] The Government extended the line of argument further by pointing out that the price of land in the area had already 'risen greatly' following the improvements made, and that it would increase even further when Strand Road was completed.

This being so, the new premises forming the new Town Duty Office establishment could be disposed of 'at a considerable profit – if such a measure [sale] should ever be deemed advantageous'. The same reasoning could be applied to the purchase of ground referred to in the subcommittee's 10 September report (see above), namely, that lying between the premises recently purchased by Government from the nawab and Mirbahar Ghat. With the Town Duty Office being located where it was, Government possession of the ground would 'be highly advantageous, and at all events it appears to be quite certain that at a moderate charge the value of the property may be greatly raised'. In view of this, the Lottery Committee was asked to buy the ground in question, adding that whether it would be transferred to the committee wholly or in part would be 'a matter of future consideration'.

The Nawab of Murshidabad had property to the east side of Clive Street opposite to the Town Duty office, the purchase of which the Government considered to be 'likewise very expedient'. It said that 'at present, [it is] for the most part covered with the ruins of an old building of little value to the Nazim', and that the 'demolition of these [ruins], which in their present state and immediately abutting on the street are a kind of public nuisance, would afford materials that could be usefully employed in filling up the low ground next [to] the river'. The 'properly raised and levelled' ground could generate 'sufficient accommodation for the Town Duty office', the Government cautioning the Board of Customs to be 'careful' that the public interest was 'in no degree [sacrificed] to the personal convenience of the Collector'. The purchase of the property was, therefore, 'advisable', the resale being effected safely 'without loss'. In consultation with the Lottery Committee, Paton, the Assistant Superintendent of Public Buildings, Lower Provinces, was asked to draw up a plan of the premises with an estimate of its value following which the nawab would be approached with a request to sell the property 'who will otherwise be requested to cause the ruinous buildings, with which the ground is now partly covered, to be removed'.[95]

In the next few years the records tell us that the only obstacle which remained to be overcome with regard to the improvement of Clive Street was that posed by the offending part of the premises of Edward Brightman.[96] In fact, it had become some sort of a fixture, for the annual reports of the Lottery Committee for the years 1823-1824 and 1824-1825[97] repeated the refrain that the Brightman issue continued to hold up effective implementation of the Clive Street improvement project. On 30 December 1823 the subcommittee looking after Clive Street (Shakespear, Paton and Ballard) said pointedly that in all other respects the work had been completed except for 'widening a part of the road in front of Mr Brightman's house'.[98] The balance in the hands of the subcommittee was Rs 4,414-4-0 which it wanted to retain to meet the expense of purchasing Brightman's house 'and also for completing the widening of the street as far as the Town Duty Office when huts and *golahs* shall have been cleared away from the ground lately purchased by Government between the office and Meerbhur Ghaut'. The request was sanctioned in early January 1824.[99]

The effective completion of the improvements was reported by the subcommittee in 1827 when it said that what had increased the 'sense of achievement' was their being able to widen Bonfield's Lane, 'the only communication within a considerable space between the most populous part of the town and the river' (see Fig. 43: road No. 65, to the east of Ross's Ghat, is Bonfield's Lane). The annual report for 1825-1826 said that the building owned by Brightman, 'which formed the northwest angle of Clive Street and Bonfield's Lane', had at long last been removed allowing the committee to carry into effect 'the improvement of both streets… at the moderate expence of Rs 3,600 in addition to the sum before sanctioned for Clive Street only, making the expence altogether sicca Rs 6,634-10-5'.[100]

COSSITALA, COLOOTALA, GARDEN REACH...

COSSITALA, WATERLOO STREET

Before Charnock's arrival in August 1690, Bentinck Street formed a part of the north-south Pilgrims' Road which linked Kalighat in the south with the Chitreswari temple in the north following the alignment of Chitpur Road.[1] Reverend Long wrote in 1852 the area was a 'mass of *jangal*' at the time of the fall of Calcutta to Shiraj-ud-Daula 'and, even as late as 1780, it was almost impassable from mud in the rains'.[2] Being an ancient road, it had over time become crowded and congested underscoring the need for improvement.

In early March 1819 a subcommittee comprising G.J. Gordon and A. Colvin drew the Lottery Committee's attention to an 'opportunity' which had arisen to improve a part of 'one of the principal thoroughfares of the town', namely, a spot

> ...nearly at the north end of Cossitollah Street [which terminated at Lalbazar] where some houses have been lately cleared away that formed a sudden projection into the street narrowing the road at once by nearly half its width, at the same time that it had a considerable bend towards the opposite side.[3]

The committee was urged to take 'immediate advantage' of the situation by buying up 'as much of the site of the old buildings as is necessary to render the road commodious and safe'. Early action was needed because 'Mr Johnson',[4] the proprietor, intended 'to erect new buildings on the same spot which will, for a great number of years, preclude the possibility of effecting this improvement except at an enormous expence'. Further, the houses to the south of the spot in question, 'where the street is the narrowest', were so old that there was every possibility of their demolition 'in the course of a few years'. Keeping the future in mind, it was suggested that the 'new line of the widened part [of the street] should, at its southern extremity, be thrown back ten feet from the front of the adjoining premises so that when they shall be taken down the street may there also be widened to that extent'. For this the Government would have to buy 3 *katha*s 1 ½ *chittack*s from the owner (Johnson) which the latter was willing to part with for Rs 3,092-12-0 (at Rs 1,000 a *katha*).

The committee wrote to the Government on 4 March that the suggested improvement was 'highly expedient with a view of affording the access into Cossitollah Street more commodious as well as towards contributing to the general improvement of that part of Calcutta'. A week later the scheme was sanctioned and the funds released.[5] Four months later in the middle of July, Gordon and Colvin submitted a bill for Rs 271-9-3 being 'expenses for making a new piece of road in Cossitollah Street on the ground lately purchased from Mr Johnson for the purpose of widening the north end of that street'. From the details of the bill (submitted by Junmajoy Ruckitt [Janmojoy Rakhit]), it appears that the new stretch of road was 150 ft long and 20 ft wide, the amount spent on *coolies* and *khoah* being nearly 86 per cent (Rs 233-5-9) of the total expenditure.[6]

A year later a second instalment of improvement work was carried out in the Cossitala area, which has left its footprint on city life two centuries later. On 23 November 1820, Colvin wrote that he had drawn up a scheme which would effect a junction of the east end of Weston's Lane (to the east of Bentinck Street) with the western end of Merajanee Gully (later known as Zig-Zag Lane)[7] a project 'the accomplishment of (which) has been long deemed very desirable by the committee'.[8] The junction would effect a free passage from Cossitala in the west through Weston's Lane to Bowbazar Lane in the east and beyond. Wood's map shows the unbridged gap between the two lanes in the 1780s (see Fig. 43) while Schalch's map shows the area after the implementation of the project. Colvin wrote that a large part of the intervening ground had come into his possession and that by purchasing 'a spot in the vicinity' he had been enabled to obtain the remainder 'by an exchange' with the owner, Imambaksh, of the ground he had bought. Colvin said that he would present to the committee two *kathas* of his own ground free of cost and that if the Government agreed to buy from him the ground which formerly belonged to Imambaksh (3 *katha*s 3 *chittack*s) at around Rs 400 a *katha*, a 20-ft-wide road could be built which would join the two existing lanes to the west and east. The total cost of the project would not exceed Rs 1,600. The proposal was sent to the Government on the same day, the approval being given after a week.[9] Nearly six months later, Colvin, who had been asked to implement the project, reported that the road had been completed at a cost of Rs 1,591-5-3 of which 82 per cent (Rs 1,312-8-0) had been spent on land which was bought at Rs 350 a *katha*.[10]

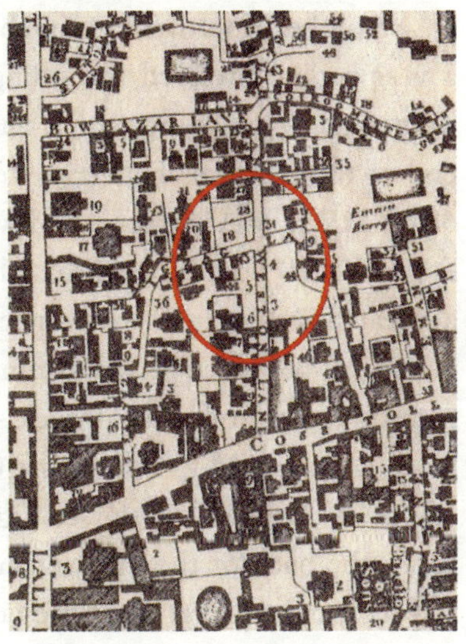

Fig. 65. Schalch's map showing the linking up of Zigzag Lane and Weston's Lane to the east of Bentinck Street

Another improvement in the area, which was implemented a year earlier, involved the filling up of a 'small and dirty tank immediately to the west of a number of tiled huts at the south end of the Cossitala belonging to a baboo (between Nos 66 and 68)'.[11] A Mr McClintock[12] had written to the committee in early August 1818 pointing out that the tank in question had become a 'great nuisance in many respects' and that the neighbourhood would be benefited if the committee ordered its filling up. As regards access to it, McClintock said that there did not appear to be a 'hackery road to it from the Cossitollah Street' but there was one from Crooked Lane[13] (see Fig. 4) on the western side 'running along the back of the undertaker and my premises, where there was formerly a passage into the tank'. However, for some years the passage had been 'stopped up by way of reserving the tank for the dirty uses of the native tenants in the tiled huts'. McClintock felt that the passage could be re-opened easily 'as there is only a kind of gateway built up at the place I have mentioned'.

The committee was aware of the problems posed by the tank and felt that the only way to tackle them was by filling it up. The tank was the property of Raja Rajkrishna but this would not be a hurdle because Trower, the Collector of 24-Parganas, had found out that the raja also wanted to fill up the offending waterbody. Barwell was given the job to implement the scheme, the tank being filled up with rubbish generated by the development of Hastings Street and its vicinity.[14] This rather insignificant episode in the story of the city's early development – one of its countless building blocks, so to speak – is useful in the sense that it provides an idea of how little the layout of some places have changed over the past couple of centuries, which is specially true of the area today at the 'back of the Esplanade Row where it joins Cossitollah' (the corner of Esplanade Row East [Sido-Kanho Dahar] and Bentinck street).

Immediately to the north of this area is Waterloo Street[15] the construction of which was the handiwork of the Lottery

Committee. The project was proposed in May 1826 the justification being that such a road would provide 'a new and more direct communication' between the part of the town 'lying to the east of Cossitullah Street and the western part towards the river'.[16] Cotton writes that Waterloo Street 'has no existence in Upjohn's map of 1794', which is correct. But he adds that the period of its construction 'is indicated with sufficient clearness by its name', which is misleading since the battle was fought in 1815.[17]

The opportunity for making the new road was provided by the demolition of 'the large, old building known by the name of Waterloo Hotel' which lay 'on a direct line with the street which runs eastward from the northeast corner of Government Place'. This road was, in effect, a continuation of the line of road eastward from Colvin's Ghat through Hastings Street. Wood's 1784 map shows clearly that this short road was, in fact, a part of Dacre's Lane (see Fig. 30), renamed today James Hickey Sarani.[18] The committee felt that such an opportunity 'might never again occur' which led the Government to approve the project at an estimated cost of Rs 65,000. Work began in 1826 the road being completed by the end of March 1828.[19]

COLOOTALA STREET, MIRZAPUR STREET

Three years before the construction of Waterloo Street was proposed, an important road (in fact, twin roads) was developed a bit further to the north, beyond Bowbazar, which facilitated the movement of traffic greatly along an east-west alignment. The two roads were Colootala and Mirzapur Streets located between the two important thoroughfares of the time, Bowbazar Street in the south and Mechuabazar Street in the north, a project which stood out in the eyes of the Lottery Committee because of its cost effectiveness. The two roads were proposed almost simultaneously,

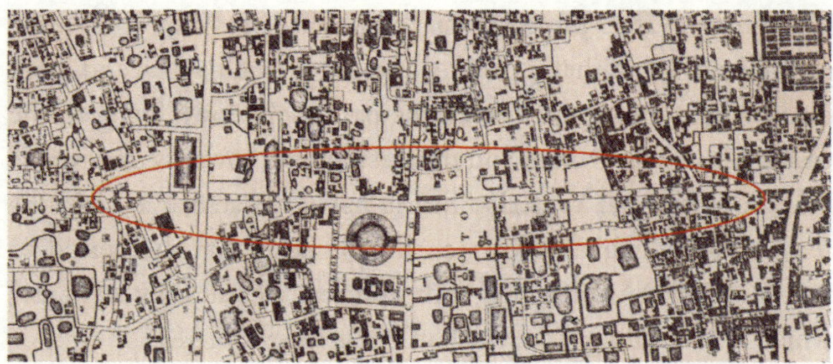

Fig. 66. Schalch's map showing the east-west Mirzapur and Colootala Streets after they were constructed

the extension of the project eastward to Circular Road from the south-west corner of College Square being planned when it had become almost certain that the Government would approve of the road from Chitpur Road to College Square (Colootala Street).

The first shot was fired in early September 1823 when Alexander Colvin wrote to the Lottery Committee on the possibility of building a 45-ft-wide road 'from Chitpore Road to the new tank in the Central Road' (College Square) utilising the financial good offices of a native, Madhab Dutt, who had 'extensive' property in the area.[20] The plan entailed that, at the end of the entire process, the Lottery Committee would have to spend just Rs 25,000 of which as much as Rs 17,000 would go towards 'excavation of a tank to supply the wants of the neighbouring population'. Colvin wrote that, initially, Dutt was interested in offering Rs 10,000 towards the expense of making the proposed road 'in consideration of the benefit his property would derive from it'. The road would commence from the Foujdar's house on Chitpur Road and, 'skirting the northern boundary of the jail of the Court of Requests', would terminate at 'the south side of the new square'. Adding to the advantages of the new road would be the fact that it would be located 'exactly at equal distances between the Bow Bazar and the Mutchua Bazar, and in the line that has lately been recommended by the magistrates for the construction of a tunnel to drain all that quarter of the city'.[21] It was Colvin who took the initiative and proposed to Dutt the precise nature of his financial involvement in the project. Colvin said that after 'a great deal of negotiation occasioned by the usual doubts and difficulties of a native', Dutt agreed to take up the project the end result of which would be that the Government would have

> …the whole course of the road (with the exception of about two cottahs of the Fouzdar's premises to be given up for it) to be also cleared and levelled, at no other cost to the lottery ſunds than the expense of paving and draining and without any outlay of money.

Colvin's estimate for the project was as follows:[22] buildings to be bought – Rs 25,000; ground to be bought – from Chitpur Road to Colootala, 16 *katha*s at Rs 800 a *katha*, Rs 12,800; ground from Colootala to Narain Thakur, 3 *bigha*s at Rs 400 a *katha*, Rs 24,000; from Narain Thakur to Madhab Dutt, 1 *bigha* 16 *katha*s at Rs 200 a *katha*, Rs 7,200; from Madhab Dutt to the new square, 13 *katha*s at Rs 320 a *katha*, Rs 4,160 (total 6 *bigha*s 5 *katha*s, cost Rs 48,160); expense of clearing, levelling, filling up of old tanks, drains, etc., Rs 7,000 (Rs 12,000 less Rs 5,000 worth of old materials). The surplus ground to be bought would be 7 *bigha*s 5 *katha*s at Rs 400 a *katha*, Rs 58,000; 8 *bigha*s 5 *katha*s at Rs 200 a *katha*, Rs 33,000; 2 *bigha*s at Rs 300 a *katha*, Rs 12,000 (total Rs 1,03,000). (Dutt agreed to purchase the surplus ground at Rs 575 a *katha*.) The interest paid on the funds used would be Rs 8,090. The cost to the Lottery Committee would comprise Rs 8,000 for paving and draining (exclusive of the tunnel), and Rs 17,000 for a small public tank (cost of 1 *bigha* 10 *katha*s at Rs 400 a *katha*, Rs 12,000, plus Rs 5,000 for digging, ghats, railing, etc.,). A sum of Rs 1,91,250 would be advanced by Dutt as needed, the interest on it being 6 per cent per annum 'till the expiration of one year' within which period it was expected the road would be completed and the ground made over to Dutt. If the ground was not handed over to him within this time, the interest for any further period of time would be a separate charge on the lottery funds. Colvin wrote that the 'chief inducement' for Dutt was that about two *bigha*s of surplus ground could be got from 'the many large ditches which will become unnecessary' which would be sold at the enhanced rates, and that around 'two or three bighas more' could be purchased at favourable rates thereby reducing 'in some degree the average cost', all of which would have the effect of 'materially' reducing the expense.

Clearly, this was a novel arrangement as far as development work undertaken by the Lottery Committee was concerned, which led Colvin to conclude his letter to the committee by saying that 'such arrangements' for developing an area should be backed 'wherever the situation is favourable'.

On 9 September the committee sent Colvin's proposal to the Government explaining why Madhab Dutt was advancing money and not the committee itself when the investment was expected to lead to a profit. The first point made in favour of the project was, of course, that the location of the proposed street would be 'of essential advantage to the public'. Secondly, a reference was made to the letter sent to the committee by the conservancy magistrates which had pointed out that the location of the new road was one 'peculiarly calculated for the course of the new [drainage] tunnel'. The new road would be 45 ft wide, its length from Chitpur Road in the west to College Street in the east being about 870 yards. The committee said that, in the event of official sanction coming through, it would 'suggest the most expedient measures for continuing it from the south-eastern angle of College Square to the Circular Road, being a further distance of about 700 yards'.

Having underscored the importance of the project, the committee spelt out the details of the financial arrangement with

Dutt the salient feature of which was that, while the committee's total expenditure on the project would not exceed Rs 25,000, the advances required for the purchase of the ground needed for the street itself or of the buildings 'lying on the site of the street' as well as for the purchase of 'the surplus ground and all other incidental expenses', totalling Rs 1,91,250, would be made by Madhab Dutt. The committee added that 'some other conditions' favourable to Dutt were included in the scheme such as the 'surrender' of about two *katha*s of the Foujdar's premises on Chitpur Road but since it was expected that the new street would 'far improve the value of those premises' the concession of the two *katha*s would not be more than 'a nominal sacrifice'.

The Lottery Committee's explanation as to why Dutt was involved financially in the project lays bare the point that the principal reason was the shortage of resources faced by the committee. It was, in fact, stated rather bluntly that the funds with the committee would not admit of the 'requisite outlay of nearly two lacks (lacks) of rupees' and that it would not, 'except under very particular circumstances', wish to enter into further loan arrangements with the Government until it had repaid the amount 'due to the public treasury on account of the purchase of Mr Camac's estate in Chowringhee'.[23] The committee backed the arrangement on the ground that, if Dutt's investment proved profitable, it would 'probably lead to similar financial overtures from other natives possessing landed property in this city, and that important improvements may thus be accomplished with much greater celerity and less risk than could be effected by means of the funds at the disposal of the Lottery Committee'. The project would, therefore, open a new vista of public-private cooperation which would, among other things, solve to a great extent the resource problem.

On its part, the Government accepted fully the contention that the new road would be helpful to the 'native inhabitants of a populous portion of the city' and agreed that it should be extended eastward to Circular Road provided the work could be accomplished 'without incurring an expence disproportionate to the value of the improvement'. Its location would also be helpful for the 'course of the new tunnel', which had already been approved (see below), which would 'facilitate the draining [of the area] and improve the salubrity of the ground in the vicinity of the jail of the Court of Requests' apart from '[shortening and improving] the communication between the jail and the court house of the commissioners'. As regards the arrangement with Dutt, the Government wrote that there was no 'material objection' to 'the conditions of the arrangement and the principle of the plan itself', but a special effort would have to be made to ensure that, in the process of the sale of surplus ground, no influence would be used by Dutt 'to induce the proprietors of the additional ground...to sell their property contrary to their own inclination, and that the sale [would] be on their part entirely voluntary'. The Rs 25,000 sought by the committee was sanctioned, the Government making it clear that the scheme was being tried out as an experiment the result of which would 'afford sufficient grounds to show whether it can be extensively adopted in other situations with advantage to the public'.

In its 9 September letter to the Government, the committee had laid stress on the old theme of buying up surplus ground and selling it after completion of a project at a higher price to reduce net investment. It wrote that should the Government grant to it 'considerable advances or loans of money' to buy up surplus ground to be sold later for pecuniary gain, or should allow the committee to borrow funds 'from other quarters' for the same purpose, opportunities would 'doubtless occur of purchasing considerable portions of ground in situations where it is desirable to construct new streets, and which ground could be so advantageously resold after the improvement was completed as to render the expense of making such new streets comparatively trifling'. In view of the fact that over the past five years the principle had been implemented with profit, the Government readily agreed with the committee's view. It said that such funding was to be supported because of reasons of 'economy and...the advantage the public would derive from the improvements which could thus be effected more rapidly and more extensively than by the gradual application of the ordinary resources at the disposal of the Lottery Committee'. It concluded with the happy tidings that the committee had 'actually disposed of the whole of property purchased from Mr Camac in Chouringhee' and that the transaction had confirmed 'the anticipation which led the Government to advance the sum of three lacs (lacs) of rupees for the purchase of the property in question'. The committee was told that on its submitting to the Government a 'full report' on the Camac transaction showing full repayment of the advance given along with the interest, any application made for a further advance for 'similar undertakings' would be treated favourably.[24]

Within two years, however, the arrangement with Madhab Dutt had stalled, the records indicating an uncertain future for the project. On 15 January 1825 the committee reported to the Government that 'it was yet impossible to state with accuracy the probable result of the experiment in opening the road through Colootullah to College Square'. Even so, 'great progress' had been made on it and it was hoped that the road would be opened to the public 'in the course of a few months'. The committee reported that there had been 'much difficulty' in obtaining the ground on which the original calculation was based, a problem which had not yet been 'entirely overcome' the delay itself leading to 'an addition to the anticipated cost'. However, putting on a brave face, the hope was expressed that the result would show 'the benefit of proceeding on the same system when practicable in other situations'.[25] A year later, in the middle of 1826, the committee reported that, along with Mirzapur Street, Colootala Street had been opened to the public. But the point was made that 'the experimental arrangement under which this improvement was conducted has, in this instance, ended in disappointment both to ourselves and to the person with whom it was entered into'. Crucially, the failure of the arrangement working out held out the threat of incurring an excess expenditure of around Rs 55,000 to 60,000.[26]

The construction of the 45-ft-wide Mirzapur Street was sanctioned on 9 October 1823, that is, a month after approval was given to build Colootala Street, the proposal being submitted by Shakespear and Colvin in the last week of September.[27] The cost estimate totalled Rs 90,000 (to be sought as a credit from the Government) the break-up being as follows: 'probable expense of land and house', Rs 40,600;[28] 10 *bigha*s of surplus land to be resold later at an average price of, say, Rs 175 a *katha*, Rs 35,000; paving of the road, Rs 6,750; constructing surface drains on both sides, Rs 17,500; levelling and clearing, Rs 2,250; and contingencies, Rs 3,650. Deducting the sale proceeds of the surplus 10 *bigha*s at an estimated price of Rs 262-8-0 a *katha* (Rs 52,500) would result in a final net cost of Rs 36,500. The subcommittee said that some of the estimates could be altered 'when we come to ascertain the exactly straight line of the road which at present we are unable to do'.

The estimated final cost of Rs 36,500 would exclude 'the great object' of providing for the tunnel which had been strongly recommended by the magistrates to be carried along the line of the road, the road itself forming 'a most acceptable and convenient access from the Circular Road to a very populous quarter of the native part of the city'. The tunnel would extend 'throughout the whole length' of the new road from Chitpur Road to Circular Road its importance being gauged by the fact that it would, in fact, be 'the first full experiment of effectual draining that has been attempted in that direction and will serve as a guide to further similar efforts throughout the city'. A cost estimate prepared by Arthur Blechynden in late September 1823 indicated that the construction of the tunnel would cost Rs 33,996-14-0.

The building of Colootala Street had entailed excess expenditure. It now fell to the lot of this stretch of road to help find a way to reduce the burden of the excess spending, the subcommittee's hope being that the 'solution would work out [and] lead to the surplus expenditure being limited to Rs 25,000'. The hope was based on the fact that the whole of the surplus ground had been sold at the rate of Rs 380 per *katha* (against an anticipated Rs 262-8-0) which would lead to the final cost being considerably less than the original estimate. Even at this point when things were not going well for the project, the Lottery Committee was feeling confident enough to write to the Government that the two new roads stretching for more than 5,000 ft would 'prove one of the least expensive [projects] which the committee have ever undertaken'. A year later, the committee wrote[29] that, despite the 'many difficulties' regarding the completion of Colootala Street, the total expenditure on the entire line of the two roads 'conjointly forming a new and most useful communication through the heart of the city…very nearly equal to Bowbazar Street in length' amounted to Rs 1,35,454-6-15, including a tank valued at Rs 17,250 'which may be hereafter appropriated to forming part of a new line of road through that part of the city'. There was a balance in the accounts of Rs 20,454-6-5 which the committee asked the Government to sanction, which was duly allowed.

ROAD FROM THE FREE SCHOOL TO PARK STREET

Nearly three years earlier, developments were taking place south of Dharamtala Street which would eventually lead to a link-up with Park Street with the help of a road which, today, is one of the most important north-south thoroughfares in the area. At the time, the road (Janbazar 4th Lane) going south from Janbazar

Fig. 67. Schalch's map showing Free School Street after completion

Street (S N Banerjee Road) – terminating roughly at the point where the Fire Brigade facility is located on Free School Street[30] (renamed Mirza Ghalib Street) – was already in place and it was only a matter of time before an effort would be made to extend it futher south and link it up with Park Street. The linkage was necessary not least because, at the time, Dharamtala Street and Park Street were the two important east-west roads between the 'great road' in Chowringhee and Circular Road in the east.

Describing the topography of the area, Kathleen Blechynden, a great grand-daughter of Richard Blechynden,[31] the Surveyor of Roads, wrote:

> When the school first moved into the Jaun Bazar house, the lands surrounding it were mostly open fields among which were scattered villages, with here and there a garden house, standing in wide grounds.[32] The road leading to it from Jaun Bazar was called Jaun Bazar Fourth Lane, and another lane to the south led to Park Street. It was on the lines of these two lanes that Free School Street was made, about 1810.[33]

The trigger for the linking of Dharamtala Street and Park Street was provided by Henry Shakespear's new road between

Dharamtala in the north and Janbazar in the south[34] the Lottery Committee asking the Acting Chief Magistrate to submit a report on the feasibility of such a link ('the practicability of opening a communication between the Jaun Bazar and Park Street in the direction of the new road constructing from the Durrumtullah to Jaun Bazar').[35] In its 18 January 1821 letter seeking approval for Shakespear's plan, the Lottery Committee wrote that the road

> ...lately authorised by Government from the Durrumtullah to the Jaun Bazar, opening into a street which though not quite straight, extends of a sufficient width nearly to the northern boundary of the Free School, naturally led the committee to ascertain whether they could not conveniently complete the communication with Park Street in this direction *through Free School Street* [emphasis added], the want of which had already been frequently brought to their observation.[36]

Shakespear's plan had shown that a 40-ft-wide road could easily be made 'with very few obstructions from *puckah* buildings, nearly in a straight line', the estimate indicating that the cost of the ground required and the houses to be bought would total Rs 47,166-13-10. Having recourse to the stratagem of raising funds for a project by selling off surplus land, Shakespear had proposed that some extra ground be bought which could later be sold to foot the cost of making the road 'and of filling up the tanks through which it will have to pass'.

Providing an idea of what the area was like two centuries ago, the committee said that most of the tanks were 'excessively filthy', and one particular tank would have to be deepened and enlarged 'sufficiently to fill up the rest'. The total cost would not exceed Rs 50,000 but as the surplus ground could not be sold to advantage till the road was nearly complete, the Government was asked to provide Rs 60,000. The approval came through in early February a subcommittee comprising Bayley, Shakespear and Colvin being set up to implement the project.[37] Eighteen months later, at the end of July 1822, Shakespear and Colvin reported completion of the work at a total cost of Rs 59,664-14-6, which was Rs 335-1-6 less than the estimate.[38] The subcommittee said that, in view of 'the favourable opportunities that presented themselves of purchasing ground for resale', the effective project cost could have been restricted to a maximum of Rs 50,000 'had we succeeded in our wishes for further purchases' of surplus ground in the neighbourhood.[39]

The Lottery Committee had only praise for the members of the subcommittee, the Government being informed of 'the high satisfaction' which the committee felt 'in observing the complete efficiency with which these improvements have answered the views which directed their original expediency'.[40] In fact, the committee wanted the subcommittee to take a break from continuing with their good work the Government being told that

> ...however sensible the committee may be of the additional [advantages] likely to be derived from continuing their operations in the above quarter of the city, they still refrain from immediately submitting for the consideration of Government the points to which Mr Shakespear and Mr Colvin [Bayley was also a member of the subcommittee] have further directed the attention of the committee, on account of their contiguity to the works in which they have recently been engaged.

WELLESLEY STREET AND ELIOT ROAD

While work was in progress on Free School Street, moves were afoot to implement another north-south connexion which would link the new square at Baparitala with Park Street in the south. In 1821, the construction of two new roads was suggested in the area east of Free School Street and north of Park Street which today bear a heavy load of vehicular traffic. On 4 July Shakespear and Colvin, the subcommittee looking after the developments, wrote to the committee proposing 'the opening of a road from Park Street northward to Colinga Bazar Street...and for continuing the road from Free School Street...[to] the road [today's Elliot Road] commenced by the late Mr Eliot opening on the Circular Road'.[41] Clearly, the north-south road (from Park Street) was part of a much larger scheme which today extends from Theatre Road (Shakespeare Sarani) in the south to the Shyambazar five-point crossing in the north, another arterial thoroughfare. As a first step, the new 60-ft-wide road of Shakespear and Colvin would extend from Park Street in the south to the Colinga Bazar Street in the north, its direction being 'nearly in a straight line to Wellington Street' – the new road further to the north which had just been

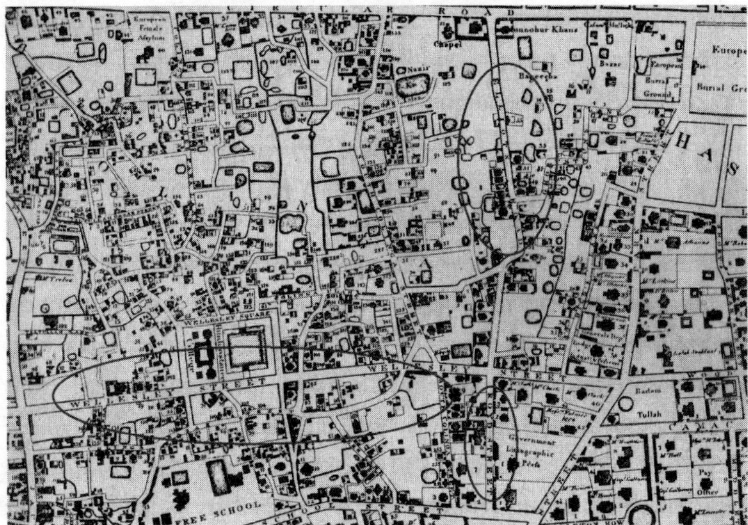

Fig. 68. The extension of Wellesley Street south to Park Street; also Eliot Road and Royds Street, in Schalch's map of 1824

completed – 'with which it will be a future object to connect it'. In other words, the proposed road would be the first section of the future Wellesley Street (Rafi Ahmed Kidwai Road) extending from Park Street in the south all the way to Dharamtala Street (Lenin Sarani) in the north. As Shakespear and Colvin put it, the new road southward would be a continuation 'of the road leading from Theatre Street (Shakespeare Sarani) northwards, which is *now* [emphasis added] named Wood Street [renamed Martin Luther King Sarani]'.[42] As regards the east-west road, it would, 'through Colingah', link Free School Street (the part of it renamed Mirza Ghalib Street) to Circular Road in the east through the road begun by Eliot.[43] The section of the road linking Free School Street and Eliot Road was named Royds Street, named after Sir John Royds, a judge of the Supreme Court (1787-1816).

Shakespear and Colvin pointed out a number of physical advantages which would result from the construction of the two roads.[44] The link between Free School Street and Eliot Road, they said, could 'at present be completed with scarcely any interference from brick buildings, and at much less expense than can be expected at any future period', a point which also applied to the north-south road the alignment of which was determined by the fact 'it interferes with few buildings of much value and because the ground can be obtained without difficulty'. The section towards Circular Road would pass 'almost entirely through huts' (giving an idea of what sort of people resided in the area), which led the authors of the plan to propose that, for the time being, it would be appropriate 'to do no more than finish the road in earth with a ditch on one side sufficient to drain the whole [area] from Free School Street'. In fact, it was felt that the plan as a whole would enable the '(effective) draining (of) a large portion of the city which at present stands greatly in need of it', underscoring once again the important link between the building of roads and improved drainage.[45]

These advantages apart, there was also a strategic need to provide the road linkages proposed. The Lottery Committee was told that the

> …want of access to Colinga, and particularly from Colinga Road [see Fig. 68] to the southward, has long been felt as a very serious inconvenience by the rapidly increasing population of that part of the town, which is becoming a favourite residence for the middle and lower classes of British subjects.

The letter referred to a petition 'numerously signed' by the inhabitants of the area 'sometime ago' which had drawn attention to the facilities needed, the point being made that the road project could 'well provide for one main object of their wishes'.[46] The allusion here is probably to the October 1820 petition signed by A. Fleming, Ramjohn Barber (who signed in 'native writing'), C.W. Hutchins, J. Edmond and C. Krorge which, among other things, tells us something about the lay of the land south of Colinga Street which was sought to be improved and developed in 1821.[47] The specific request of the petitioners was the paving of the road on which they resided, which joined South Colinga Street on the north with 'the street of Sir John Royds, Beebee Hamilton, Kyd and others on the southern end', both the roads being *pucka* (see Fig. 68). The point made was that the 270-ft-long, 15-ft-wide road was 'much frequented by buggies, carriages and foot passengers' and that 'after every fall of rain [it became] very muddy and too dirty to admit any decent person to pass clean through it'. The revenue side of the proposal was also pointed out, namely, that once the road was paved it would induce people to build houses in the locality, which 'in a short time will greatly increase the assessment of Government'.

The Lottery Committee sent the request of the petitioners to the 'subcommittee for rendering roads *pucka*' asking it to use its own discretion whether 'eventually' to render *pucka* the lane referred to.[48] The subject was revisited on 20 November 1820, the committee telling the petitioners that the paving work would be done only if the house and landowners concerned agreed 'to give up two-feet-and-a-half of ground on each side for the purpose of widening the road'.[49] The cost estimate of the two projects, which included paving the north-south road in its entirety and the part of the west to east link from Free School Street till the new north-south road and making drains, was put at Rs 67,342-4-5.[50]

The proposal for opening the two roads had been submitted to the Lottery Committee on 4 July 1821. The committee wrote to the Government the next day backing the project and stating that the 'upwards of 60,000 rupees' saved from the Bankshall improvements could not be ' appropriated in a more useful manner than in that now suggested'.[51] Underscoring the expedition with which major decisions of this sort were taken by the Government, the project was approved on 6 July the point being specifically mentioned that its implementation would lead to the 'draining and improving that part of the town which lies between Free School Street and the Circular Road'. In another two weeks' time a subcommittee was formed, comprising Shakespear and Colvin, to implement the project.[52] The Lottery Committee kept up the pressure of developing the area to the east of Free School Street such as widening Colinga Street, Shakespear writing in early 1822 that he had received such requests 'several times' in the past which had now become important 'since the grand road has been opened connecting it with Park Street'.[53]

To the west of Free School Street lay Kyd Street (renamed Dr M Ishaque Road),[54] and it was during this time that some work was done to improve the road, alterations which have left their footprint till today. In June 1821 Shakespear and Colvin brought up the subject of widening the road which, at the time, though being one of 'very general resort', had a width where two carriages could pass 'but with great difficulty'. The estimate of Rs 2,500 for widening the road 'throughout' to 27 feet was approved by the Government in early August, a subcommittee being formed comprising Colvin and Lt Paton to oversee the work.[55]

PARK STREET, MIDDLETON ROW

In the early years of the 19th century the road we know as Park Street today was not an important thoroughfare. Both Wood's map and Upjohn's indicate that (till the early 1790s) the area was, in a manner of speaking, out of bounds for even those sahibs who were adventurous in selecting residences 'out of town'. Till this time, the main purpose of the road was to serve as a passage to the European burial ground at its eastern end (set up in 1767) a function which, however, had begun weakening after the closure of the ground at the end of the 18th century, the last interment taking place around 1830.[56] The Lottery Committee records do not contain much on improvements effected in Park Street proper: the earliest reference to such activity (at the end of 1821) relates to an effort to widen the road at a particular point. That year, on 13 December, the committee prepared an estimate for the purchase of a spot of ground from Lala Suklal for Rs 2,000 which would 'render the road in question as nearly as possible of a uniform breadth'. The point of contention was the projection into the road of a building occupied by the Adjutant-General and owned by Lala Suklal which led to an 'inconvenient' constriction of the roadway. The Government, which allowed the purchase on 28 December, was told that Suklal was agreeable to the sale for Rs 1,913-6-10 and that the work would also lead to better drainage 'of that part of Calcutta'.[57] Schalch's map (see Fig. 69) does not tell us where the Adjutant-General's office was located on Park Street at the time but it does point out Lala Suklal's ground which is today

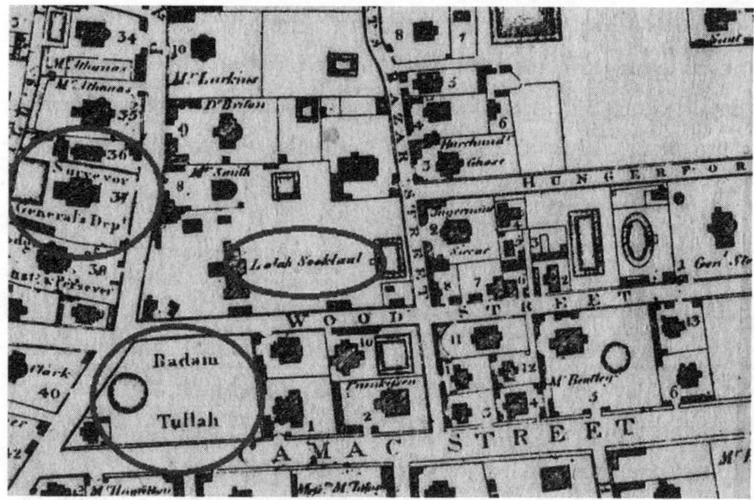

Fig. 69. Schalch's map showing Lala Suklal's ground in Park Street, where the Survey of India's offices are located today; also Badamtala (Allen Garden) and the location of the Surveyor-General's department at the time

occupied by the Surveyor-General's office at the south-eastern corner of the Park Street-Wood Street crossing opposite Allen Garden (marked Badamtala in the 1824 map).[58] (In the 1820s the Surveyor-General's department was located on the opposite side of the road.)

A second improvement effected in Park Street was that suggested by the Lottery Committee in February 1823 the objective of which was to remedy the offending 'south corner' of the street at its western end which was jutting out into Chowringhee Road and proving to be 'very inconvenient and even dangerous' to road traffic. The problem was an old one having its genesis in the unplanned nature of the junction of Chowringhee Road and Burial Ground Road which had, in fact, been noticed in the late 18th century.[59] In 1823 Alexander Colvin, Jr, who had brought the subject to the notice of the committee, suggested that the corner be 'removed' the total cost coming to Rs 2,250 (Rs 2,000 for purchase of the buildings 'which must be destroyed' and Rs 250 for 'making the road on the new line').[60] A third improvement was made the following year when the magistrates submitted a Rs 1,320-plan to cover 'a large and dangerous drain on the north side of Park Street between Free School Street and the north end of Camac Street'. The Lottery Committee was to have implemented the work but it was given to the magistrates because such expenses were 'now chargeable to the fund [the collection of Town Duties] the disposal of which has been placed under our [magistrates'] superintendence'.[61]

In 1822 steps were taken to spruce up the area which involved a road leading southward from Park Street to the 'park' – where the Loreto Convent is located today – which, in fact, gave Park Street its name.[62] There is sketchy cartographical evidence to indicate that before Charnock's arrival there existed a road or passage through field and jungle and scattered huts (there was no 'town' at the time), following a tortuous path, from the north of Tiretta Bazar off Chitpur Road to the area north of Park Street leading into Middleton Row, a link which was important enough to be listed in official proceedings in 1749.[63] Since the Pilgrim's Road (the alignment of which ran along the present-day Jawaharlal Nehru Road) was located to the west of this point, and since (as the name indicates) the road was used by pilgrims making their way to the Kali temple then located on the *maidan* it is reasonable to assume that there must have been some human traffic from the interior areas along the old road joining the Pilgrim's Road from the east at the point where Park Street links up with Jawaharlal Nehru Road. What is also probable is that the eastern part of what is today Park Street, from the point where the old, pre-Charnock road met it from the north, came into existence as a direct result of the opening of the burial ground to the east. The entrance to the park (directly opposite the point where Free School Street meets Park Street today; see Fig. 70) was a private drive used only by those who lived in it who, over the decades, included people like Governor Henry Vansittart, Judge Elijah Impey and Bishop Reginald Heber. The drive was named Middleton Row (renamed Sir William Jones Sarani) after the first Bishop of Calcutta, Thomas Fanshawe Middleton who died in 1822, the grounds on both sides of it being bereft of buildings in the early years of the 19th century.[64]

But, inevitably, with time the topography of the area would change. One of the earliest efforts at improving the state of the road was made by the Lottery Committee in response to a petition made in January 1822 by three owners of 'a considerable portion of ground lying on each side of Middleton Street (sic)'.[65] The timing of the letter, written by Major Duncan McLeod, J. Jameson and Captain A. Galloway, was determined by the road 'leading from Park Street in a southerly direction towards the oval tank in front of Mr Leycester's[66] house having been recently declared to be the property of the public' (previously it was a private drive), the inference being that the magistrates would now be in a position to make '*pucka* drains on each side of it' for the purpose of better

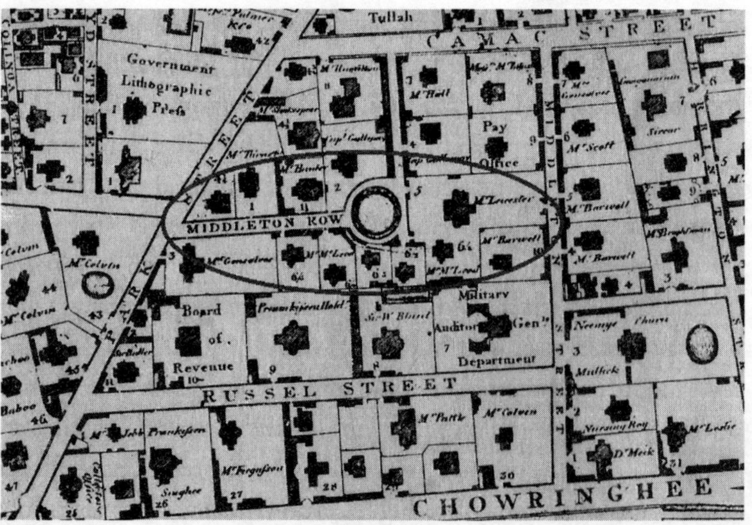

Fig. 70. Schalch's map showing Middleton Row to the south of Park Street

drainage which in turn would allow the owners of ground on either side of the road to develop the entrances to their property. A request was also made to take down the 'present hedge fence around the oval tank' and replace it with a balustrade, the hedge being 'very insufficient protection against such accidents as may occur from the oversetting of carriages during dark and foggy nights or falling in of children at play'.

The Lottery Committee formed a subcommittee comprising Shakespear and Gordon to look into the issue, which submitted a scheme in March the funds being sanctioned a month later.[67]

GARDEN REACH

Very early in the life of the Lottery Committee, Henry Wood, the Civil Auditor who had been made a member of the committee, took on the responsibility of 'cleaning up' the Khidirpur area by turning *cutcha* roads into pucka ones.[68] By this time, Garden Reach (the east-west reach of the river below Calcutta which was dotted with gardens and 'elegant mansions' giving the area its name) had developed into a residential area for some of the senior sahibs of the city, the garden houses along the south bank of the river below Khidirpur forming a visual ornament for Englishmen and others sailing up the river to Calcutta. To take an example, Eliza Fay wrote to her friends on 22 May 1780:

> Calcutta, you know, is on the Hooghly, a branch of the Ganges; and, as you enter, Garden Reach, which extends about nine miles below the town, the most interesting views that can possibly be imagined greet the eye. The banks of the river are, as one may say, absolutely studded with elegant mansions called here, as at Madras, garden houses. These houses are surrounded by groves and lawns, which descend

> to the water's edge, and present a constant succession of whatever can delight the eye or bespeak wealth and elegance in the owners.[69]

Thirty-two years later, Maria Nugent wrote in her diary on 22 March 1812:

> In the evening drove again to Garden-reach…The road, though flat, is extremely pretty, and many of the houses look like villas in the neighbourhood of London, only they are without chimneys, and the roofs are all terraces, where the inhabitants take the air early in the morning, or late in the evening.[70]

Two maps – one of 1817 and Schalch's – show in some detail the extent of the garden houses along the reach. Much before Lord Wellesley landed in Calcutta in 1798, Garden Reach had taken shape with luminaries like Sir William Jones choosing to stay there. The Judge is said to have walked daily to 'his apartments in town…at the first appearance of the dawn', a distance of 'five miles from the court' opposite Chandpal Ghat, probably along the banks of the river which would then have been the shortest route to the town.[71] Jones's neighbour was Sir John Shore (later Lord Teignmouth)

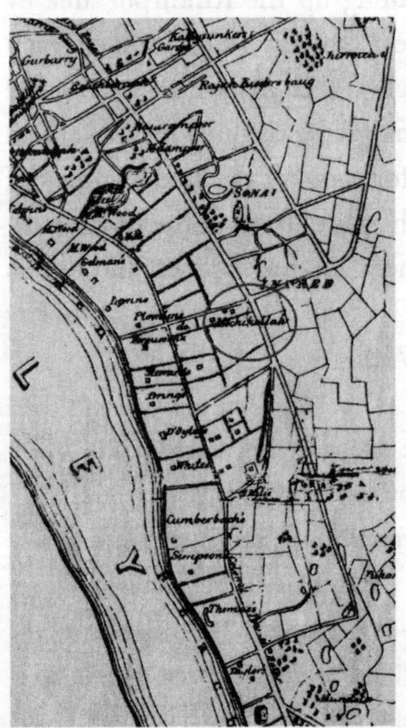

Fig. 71. An 1817 map of Garden Reach showing Muchikhola

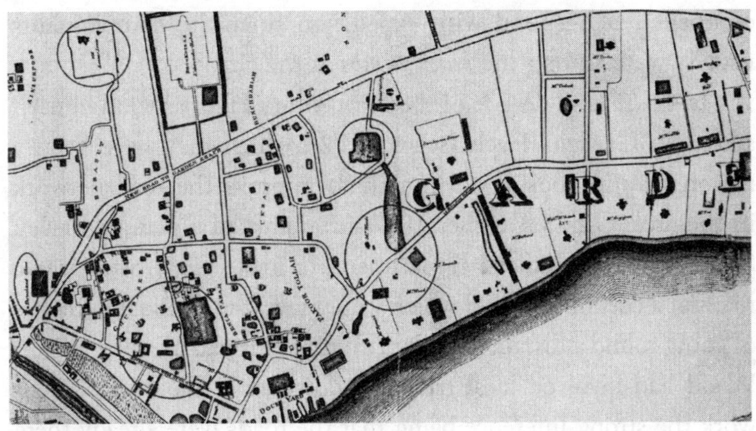

Fig 72 Garden Reach in Schalch's map showing the old road, Paddopukur, Wood's houses, Meeta Pukur, the location of Tarachand Ghose's property, and the Old Laskar Lines

who became Governor-General in 1793, succeeding Lord Cornwallis. In the 18th century, there was no continuous road along the eastern bank of the river which went down south from Chandpal Ghat (located north of the new Fort William) to Khidirpur and beyond. This meant that the sahibs who had made the reach their home had to use what is known as the Old Garden Reach Road to get to work and return home. The maps show that the road (route) originated from Tank Square, ran through Council House Street/Court House Street and traversed the *maidan* following the alignment of Red Road and Khidirpur Road. After crossing Tolly's Nullah at Surman's (Khidirpur) Bridge, it turned right into Watgunje Street (Kabitirtha Sarani) and then went down to Garden Reach along the river (the docks had not come up then; see Fig. 72). The stretch of road in Khidirpur passed through a number of bazars with the result that it was not the best of passages in the best of seasons. Not surprisingly, in the late 18th century, those who lived along the reach had cause for complaint regarding its condition, petitions being submitted with regularity to the authorities who were compelled to respond with expedition since the complainants usually were among the *burra sahibs* of the city.[72]

In the second decade of the 19th century Henry Wood himself stayed in Garden Reach (see Fig. 72), which may have been a reason why he took it on himself to improve the road network in the area. On 25 October 1817 he submitted a plan to Bayley, Secretary in the Judicial Department, to make *pucka* two specific roads at a cost of Rs 2,600 which would save 'the public the trouble of going round a distance of near two miles instead of half a mile'.[73] Wood had involved local native landowners in the development work the strong inference being that the roads were already there in a *cutcha* state. He said that 'in the past year' they had given up on their own ground required for the construction of two roads, and '*puckah* bridges' – costly propositions – had been made to draw off water free of charge to the Government. Wood said that the Government's gesture of making the two roads *pucka* would persuade the natives to 'readily agree to give up any ground which may be required for other roads without demanding pecuniary remuneration'. He had already persuaded the proprietors to build some other roads in the area free of cost to the Government, setting an example himself by giving a part of his own land for building one road. Wood wrote that the development of the road network would 'considerably add to the healthiness of the reach' by opening up 'space for the free circulation of air, clearing away the jungle, and draining the ground' which had assumed importance 'now that so many native inhabitants are crowding into the bazaar of Kidderpore and occupying the whole space between the old and new roads.'

Each of the two roads to be made *pucka* was 30 feet wide and 2,600 feet long. Throwing light on the mode of construction, he said that the *pucka* part of the roads would comprise 'one flat brick and one brick on edge without any *koah*, the breadth to be 15 feet on being finished'. The bricklaying would be done by convicts free of cost to the Government. The technology was new for the times but, in fact, had been used by native road-builders of the past, going back centuries.

The plan to develop the road network in Garden Reach was, in fact, one of the earliest projects to have been taken up by the Lottery Committee along with the Baparitala tank and square and the Dharamtala Street aqueduct, Wood, as we have seen, being closely involved with the latter project. On 25 October 1817, that is, just four days after the Lottery Committee was set up, the Civil Auditor sent his Garden Reach proposal directly to the Government instead of routing it through the committee of which he had been made a member. The Government shifted the project to the new committee seamlessly when, three days later Bayley wrote to Wood complimenting him for the scheme and telling him that, since the Rs 2,600 to be spent on the project would have to come from the lottery funds, the Government was '(suspending) passing any final orders on the subject' till the newly appointed committee's views on it were known.[74] Nearly two months later, on 18 December, the committee wrote to Bayley approving of Wood's project, in the process highlighting the fact that natives should be encouraged 'when they come forward, as in the present instance, in aid of undertakings for the general good'.[75] As regards the new road-laying technique suggested by Wood, the committee said it was not in a position 'to judge accurately how far it would answer in the principal streets and roads in and near Calcutta' although 'the experiment' would probably enable them 'to form conclusions on the subject which may hereafter prove highly useful'. The Government's approval for the project came through in the New Year (6 January).[76]

The records are silent on the subject for nearly three years, which is probably explained by the fact that Wood was absent from Calcutta for most of the time.[77] On 12 October 1820 Wood wrote that the paving of the two existing *cutcha* roads which he had taken up three years earlier had been completed in 1818 at a cost which was a trifle higher (by Rs 13-7-0) than the estimate of Rs 2,600 because of problems created by Raghunath, a bricklayer. Wood had initiated legal proceedings against him at the 24-Parganas civil court to recover Rs 600, in which he had succeeded but the bricklayer had appealed against the award and Wood had 'not yet been able to realise the money'.[78]

The important part of Wood's 12 October letter, however, related to the rapid pace of road development in Garden Reach over the preceding two years. The two roads he had had paved had 'perfectly answered the ends I held out for recommending (their) construction' and the only repair work they 'were ever likely to require' was 'a new covering of earth after the expiration of every rainy season, which will prevent the bricks from being worn by the carriages and render it less injurious to the feet of the horses and bullocks passing on it'. He said he 'had already finished some miles of roads through the jungles' all of which were 30 feet wide and 'clear of the ditches'. Considering that just about Rs 2,600 had been spent on making the two roads *pucka*, he hoped the committee would see 'the propriety of going on with the works till such time as the whole of Kidderpore and Garden Reach is well-drained, and every part of it made accessible to carriages'. Wood offered to superintend the work but said he would need about 100 convicts and that he should be allowed to spend 'such trifling sums as may be required to pay for the removal of houses and for such portions of ground as may belong to poor individuals who may be unable to afford giving up the same to the publick'. The total expenditure on this count, including the making of bridges, would not exceed Rs 2,000.

Wood then referred to certain measures he had taken to improve the drainage of Garden Reach. As he saw it, the effective drainage of the whole of Alipur and Garden Reach depended on the proper functioning of 'sluices at Mr Compton's[79] garden' which needed thorough repair. The work was, in fact, completed at the end of December 1820, Wood writing on 27 December that he had ordered the construction of the sluice gate 'for the purpose of keeping out the tide, [a step which] was essentially necessary owing to the gate having given way'.[80] The sluice gate, made of *sal* wood and being '10 ft high 8 ft broad and 5 inches thick covered throughout with 18-ounce copper hung with strong iron hinges', was installed 'at Moochee Colah at the head of Mr Compton's garden', an 1817 map providing an idea of the rough location of the garden (see Fig. 71). The cost of installing the new gate by Simpson and Hayes, contractors, was Rs 1,096-8-0, which Wood considered to be 'moderate'. During the period Wood was away, the cost incurred on the project, as well as for a 'new teakwood platform' (measuring 13 ft by 11 ft 8 inches) covering the sluice, totalled Rs 1,339, which was sent to the committee by Barwell in April 1821 the expenditure being approved of in due course.[81]

In his 27 December 1820 letter, Wood had also asked the committee to consider whether the roads which had been completed already and which lay between the old and new roads to Garden Reach, 'and between the bridge at Kidderpore and the new *pucka* crossroad opposite Mr Reese's house',[82] could be made *pucka*, the cost of the project not exceeding Rs 6,435 if the roads were constructed 'in the same way and on the same principles as the new experimental road'. Providing an idea of the lay of the land in the area, Wood told the committee that 'throughout this extent' the ground was 'fully occupied by houses and the natives are building in every direction' thus suggesting that this was a period when Garden Reach was filling up rapidly.

The proposal was important enough to invite comment from other members of the committee, the consensus being that the ongoing plans to build *cutcha* roads should be pursued instead of the focus being shifted to building paved roads. Bayley said that he would like to see such roads 'opened in every direction', the conversion to paved roads ('they should ultimately be almost all made *pucka*') being put off till such time 'when Mr Wood joins the committee again'. Colvin and Barwell agreed with Bayley that the plan to build paved roads could be taken up later, Barwell (who was Magistrate of the Suburbs) adding that even for the building of *cutcha* roads there would be a problem given the shortage of guards looking after the convicts at work (Wood had asked for 100 convicts in his 12 October 1820 letter). His suggestion was that if *coolies* were inducted to construct the *cutcha* roads – which would add to the cost – and if the superintendence of the work was given to Wood, every assistance would be provided by 'the establishment of the magistrate's office of the suburbs as well as (by) the magistrate himself'.[83]

Shakespear had suggested that if Wood was unavailable to carry out the work at Garden Reach Barwell could step in, which is precisely what the committee ordered. In early December 1820 Barwell was asked to look after the projects keeping in mind 'the furtherance of the objects stated in Mr Wood's letter'.[84] Six months later, in June 1821, Barwell drew the committee's attention to the work being done on the large *jheel* known as Meeta (Meta) Pooker (see Fig. 72) which had been interrupted by a shortage of labourers but which had to be completed before the rains got under way in the weeks ahead. The Magistrate of the Suburbs wrote that at the close of the monsoon in the previous year the waterbody had become 'so intolerably offensive that the necessity of the immediate adoption of some measures for the removal of a nuisance so injurious to salubrity' had been represented to him by people residing in the neighbourhood most of whom, needless to say, were personages in Calcutta society. The only way in which the situation could be tackled was by 'excavating the centre of the *jheel* and employing the earth thus obtained in embanking the sides in such a manner as to form a capacious tank'. Only one side of the *jheel* remained to be firmed up, work on the three other sides having been completed by convicts. As a seasoned administrator,

Barwell's point was that unless 200 'hired labourers' were drafted for the work immediately 'the further advance of the monsoon' would not only halt the progress of a work really essential, but that 'considerable injury will ensue to those parts which have been finished'. The cost of employing 200 labourers for a month would be Rs 800 in view of the fact that the wages of 'this class of men have risen in consequence of the advanced season from 3 Rs 8 as to 4 Rs'. The Lottery Committee allowed the expenditure in view of the progress already made and the 'great' public advantage likely to result from it.[85]

Wood was back in the saddle in the middle of 1822, for he was writing to the committee on 14 July that he wanted to 'finish the road laying between the old and new road to Garden Reach' – 'from Tarachand Baboo's Gardens corner to be joined with the old *puckah* road, with one brick laid flat and a brick laid on an edge above it' – the estimated expenditure of which would be Rs 1,921-8-0[86] (for the location of Tarachand Ghose's property, see Fig. 72). He said that the road had been constructed three years earlier and was now 'sufficiently solid to admit of bricks being laid on it'. This apart, the labour of convicts could be better spared 'at this period than at any other season'. Further, the earth 'by being converted into mud with the rain' would admit of bricks being regularly laid 'as in a *kutcha* or *puckah* wall'. Again, like so many other works undertaken by him in the area, the natives of the area were to be involved in the making of the road. Wood wrote that if the project was sanctioned it would be 'pleasing to the people' who had in the first place 'permitted the earthen road to be constructed at little or no cost to the Government'. He added that the 'experimental road originally made by me has now stood for three years without costing the Government anything in repairing, and has never had anything else done to it but that...annually in the dry season a little earth thrown on it'. The project was sanctioned and was to be implemented 'under the immediate superintendence of Mr Wood'.

Wood was one of those officers of the East India Company who were prepared to spend from their own pocket to get a project through obstacles. Thus, at the beginning of 1824 he informed the Lottery Committee that he had made bridges and roads in Garden Reach 'during the past year' paying from his 'private account', the amount due to him on this count being Rs 303-12-11. That the work had not been sanctioned officially prior to commencement is indicated by his informing the committee that he would 'have the pleasure in pointing out to the committee the works performed whenever they may be pleased to appoint any member to accompany me round the Reach'. In the July 1822 letter he had asked for an advance of Rs 2,000 to enable him 'to complete the draining of the Reach', offering to superintend the projects himself which included the construction of bridges. Wood said that he would be able to complete the works within the funds sought by him along with the help of '2 or 3 *mistrees*, convicts'. The projects involved were 'emptying the Puddoo Pookah (Paddopukur)' (see Fig. 72) and 'making a road round it 100 feet wide and finishing the square'. Since Barwell had told the committee that he would not be able to spare convicts for the work, the Lottery Committee sought Rs 2,392-5-0 from the Government for Wood to implement it, which was sanctioned.[87]

Two years later, in May 1826, the committee wrote that in its previous 'general report' it had submitted to the Government the estimated cost of the projects formulated for development of the area and had also received official sanction to begin work.[88] Among the projects being implemented 'under the charge of Mr H Wood', which would entail an estimated expenditure of Rs 3,055 (sanctioned in November 1825), was the conversion of the Paddopukur 'into a fine square with 4 puckah ghauts', a 30-ft-wide road parallel to the new Garden Reach Road 'with crossroads leading to it of the same breadth', and another road 'to the mouth of [Tolly's] nullah and two crossroads [paved] with brick'. The details were provided by Wood himself in his 26 October 1825 letter to the committee in which he had asked for an advance of Rs 1,200 to pave two *cutcha* roads, both of which led from the old road to Garden Reach to the new one in the east.[89] The first of these was that 'by the side of the Puddoo Pokar, the other from the middle of Mr Kyd's dockyard,[90] the former 2,540 feet in length and the latter 2,690 feet'. The roads were already in general use and their paving would 'greatly add to the convenience and comfort of the inhabitants'. The interesting part of Wood's letter was his finding that the new method of road-paving which he had carried out earlier in the area (and which he was using for the two roads in question) had been successful. He wrote that if all the *cutcha* roads in Garden Reach were paved in the same way, it would 'be a great inducement to the landed proprietors to permit new roads to be constructed free of all charge for the ground'.

Reflecting this spate of activity on the part of Wood, the Lottery Committee's annual report for the period 1 November 1825 to 31 October 1826[91] reported that a lot of work had been done in Garden Reach. The road from Kyd's dock to the new road to Garden Reach 'by the north of the Puddo Pooker'[92] (see Fig. 72) had been paved with a brick on edge and a flat brick. A 'new *cutcha* road leading from Raj Kishore's tank by the south of the Bhookoilas to Bunneah Pooker in the Allipore Road, upwards of a mile in length and 30 feet in breadth', had been completed 'and a crossroad uniting the above with the new road to Garden Reach along the west side of Bhookoilas has been nearly finished'. A 24-ft 'straight crossroad' to the river from the old road to Garden Reach had been completed by Manuel de Lauruleta and opened to the public 'on condition of Mr Lauruleta's being allowed in exchange an inconvenient, circuitous road to the river which ran to the east of his property, and the further condition of the new road being paved with brick at the public expence, which is now in progress'.

The report also said that all the

> ...old *cutcha* roads have been raised and put in order, and the road in the vicinity of the old Lascar Lines [see Fig. 72], and between it and Allipore, are now raising, and improvements making to the drains in that direction, which, when finished, must greatly add to the health and convenience of the population.

All this makes it clear that, during 1825-26, Garden Reach was given a major facelift, the report stating that 'crossroads of inferior importance have been finished, all the old roads thoroughly repaired and not less than twenty new substantial *pucka* bridges... built during the past season'. The committee took note of the work done by Barwell, Magistrate of the Suburbs, pointing specifically to a 'new road' being made from 'old Tolly Gunje to the banks of a nullah at Cowrapooker 30 feet broad and a-mile-and-a-half in length'. Of significance is the report's description of the road's utility being great, 'the principal supplies of rice, fish, etc from the lower parts of the 24 Pergunnahs being landed at Cowrapooker (the east end of a water communication with Channel Creek and the Sunderbunds) and forwarded from thence by land to the several markets and *hauts* in the vicinity'.[93] Taking note of an act of native munificence, the committee referred to the 'liberal and public spirited conduct of a respectable native named Oodaynarrain Mundul [Udaynarain Mandal] who consented to make *puckah* at his own expence the road leading from Allipore to Russapuglah, being a distance of one-mile-and- ¾, and which, with the assistance of the magistrate, he has almost completed'.[94]

❦

THE LAND OF WILLIAM CAMAC

Widespread sickness in Calcutta after the rains was an annual visitation, and the year 1819 was no exception. At the end of the year the part of Chowringhee situated 'to the east of the theatre' – towards Camac Street (renamed Abanindranath Sarani) and beyond – was in the grip of such sickness which was severe enough to have become the talk of the town. The extent of the illness had probably turned into an epidemic (not an uncommon occurrence at the time, if the records are any indication) which led a correspondent in *The Calcutta Journal*[1] to say that the natives 'were never before so alarmed as at present'. The writer added that this was not a surprising development 'when there are such filthy and offensive drains, and dirty lanes, numerous *mater's totties*, all situated between the habitations of the people, and as many livery stables in the centre, all of which must tend to corrupt the air in a great degree'.

It is at such a time that Henry Shakespear wrote that there was a 'prevailing opinion of the unhealthiness' in the part of the town east of the theatre (see Fig. 73), which he had visited.[2] The Acting Chief Magistrate of Calcutta said that he had found the area – between Theatre Road in the north and Circular Road (AJC Bose Road) in the south – to be 'extremely low, having a marsh of considerable extent in the centre of it'. Those who lived there attributed the sickness to the marsh and 'the general lowness of the ground'. The magistrate suggested that the entire ground be bought from 'the proprietor' (Charles Short)[3] and a tank dug in the centre of it with the surrounding ground raised two or three feet, all of which could be resold afterwards. The ground 'in its improved state, would doubtless be purchased for the erection of substantial dwelling houses, and would repay the committee at least the principal laid out in the improvement'. With this in mind, Shakespear wanted the Surveyor to the committee, Arthur Blechynden, to prepare a plan of the ground and to report how much it would have to be raised 'to put it on a proper level, the size of the tank that it would be necessary to dig for that purpose, and the probable expence of digging it'.

Before responding to Shakespear's specific proposal, the committee wanted to have a look at 'a plan of the ground' and asked Schalch (on 13 January 1820) to prepare one with the help of Arthur Blechynden and also provide the technical details sought by Shakespear which would provide an idea of the overall expenditure to be incurred on the 'improvement'. In his report submitted at the end of February, Blechynden gave the names of the individual landowners within the large tract in question 'with the quantity of ground possessed by each, and have likewise delineated all such tanks, pools, swamps and drains as the scale would admit'.[4] The surveyor wrote that there were 'numerous holes which have been dug to furnish earth for the floors of huts scattered over the different spots, as also small drains cut in all directions by the occupiers of the huts, which holes and drains from their minuteness preclude the possibility of measurement'.[5] The survey concluded that the ground mentioned by Shakespear was four feet 'lower than its proper level' and that the tank which was to be dug would occupy 'the whole of the marshy ground'. In order to raise the spot of ground 'to a proper level calculated on an average of 4 feet' it would need 3,000,000 cubic feet of earth, to generate which the proposed tank would have to be '500 ft long,

Fig. 73. A view of the Chowringhee Theatre at the corner of Chowringhee and Theatre Road, by William Wood, 1833

300 broad and 25 deep'. The cost of digging such a tank would be Rs 11,000 and Rs 5,500 would be required to spread the earth excavated from it.

In the couple of weeks following submission of Shakespear's proposal the subject was discussed at the highest levels of Government, vesting the subject with additional importance. In the second week of January 1820, William Bayley, Chief Secretary to the Government, wrote to the committee that there 'being reason to believe that an extraordinary degree of sickness has for sometime past prevailed in and about that part of Chowringhee which is situated to the eastward of the theatre and to the northward of the Circular Road, and more especially in the immediate vicinity of the Birjee Talao', the Governor-General in Council wanted the Lottery Committee to 'ascertain the ostensible cause of the sickness in question' and suggest 'such remedies for the evil as may appear to them practicable and expedient'. The letter spurred the committee into action and, at its meeting on 13 January, a subcommittee was formed comprising Shakespear, Ballard,[6] Paton and Barwell (the first three of whom resided in Chowringhee), its brief being to investigate the causes of the sickness and also to consider the 'expediency' of Shakespear's suggestion to purchase the ground 'in the vicinity of the theatre with a view to its improvement and ultimate resale on the public account'.[7]

During the next two months the 'subcommittee at Brijeetulah'[8] was busy with its investigations Shakespear and Ballard reporting to the committee at the beginning of March that, following their visits to 'the suburbs lying south of the Circular Road to the Ballygunge Lines, and the Russapuglah Road', they were of the view that 'the unhealthiness of Brijeetollah and its neighbourhood' was 'in great measure' the result of the 'thick jungle and stagnant pools in that quarter'. They suggested that a detailed survey of the area be done by someone familiar with the area and Captain Rainey,[9] 'who is intimately acquainted with that neighbourhood' and who had accompanied the subcommittee on its visits to the area, had suggested the name of W. Schoop, who was then surveying 'the immediate vicinity of the Body Guard lines', as someone who could conduct the survey 'in a short time at the moderate expense of from two to three hundred rupees'. The suggestion was accepted and Schoop was asked to draw up a map of the area 'upon a large scale in order clearly to elucidate the defects and remedy' referred to by the subcommittee.

The subcommittee's letter was discussed at the committee's 9 March meeting which deputed Alexander Colvin, Jr, to consider the scale of investment which would be required 'to level and raise it [the ground in question] sufficiently to prevent its continuing a nuisance to the neighbourhood'.[10] Four days later, he wrote that Arthur Blechynden had proposed the digging of a tank which was 'nearly twice the area of the new tank at Bepareetollah', which

Fig. 74. Schalch's map showing the ground belonging to Charles Short and William Camac bounded by Circular Road in the east and south; it also shows the location of Colvin's Bazar and Brahmin Bustee

was 'much larger than necessary for the attainment of all useful purposes'. Colvin said that the cost of making the tank, based on 'an estimate given me by the natives', seemed to be 'nearly as much below the mark as his [Blechynden's] are beyond it'. The main objective in digging the tank was to raise the ground in the area so that it did not become a receptacle for water and rubbish, especially during the rains. Colvin wrote to the committee that, 'after personal inspection and calculation', he was satisfied that the ground could be raised 'to the level of a line from Theatre Road to the Circular Road for about the sum of sicca Rupees 7,000'. Apart from his own firm, Colvins, Bazett and Company, being Short's agent, Colvin took a special interest in improving the drainage of the area because he also had personal business interests there. Schalch's map of the mid-1820s shows a 'Mr Colvin's bazar' to the west of Camac Street, bounded on the south by Circular Road with a tank in the middle of it (see Fig. 74).

Colvin's letter was circulated in the Lottery Committee and on 18 March the Secretary, John Trotter, wrote that while the committee was 'fully sensible' of the need to begin work early it wanted to know the 'principles' on which the estimate of Rs 7,000 was based. The data produced by Colvin two days later[11] was accepted but of more interest was his view on the subject of the proprietors being benefitted by the raising of the ground in the area. The Lottery Committee had laid emphasis on the point that the rights of the proprietors should 'be found (to be) reconciliable with the convenience of the public'. While Colvin had no difficulty in agreeing with this, being a landowner himself he drew attention to the point that the projected improvement was 'not a gratuitous benefit to the owner of the ground'. This was because the *pattas* would show that 'since the last measurement by the collector, upwards of two bigahs have been taken into the roads'. This 'deficiency', Colvin wrote, would not be found 'to exist in the pottahs for the remainder of what was formerly Mr Short's estate'. In other words, Colvin's argument was that the Government owed the planned improvement to the owners of land in the area in view of the sacrifice they had made by parting with their property for the building of public roads.

First and last, Colvin was a man of commerce. In his 20 March 1820 letter he had referred to the fact that he had begun digging a tank in his own ground, a decision which he said he now regretted as having been too 'hasty' in view of the Lottery Committee's policy to improve the drainage of the area generally. He wanted the committee to bear the expenses of his own tank project, a request which the committee does not appear to have responded to. Instead, yet another subcommittee comprising Shakespear, Barwell, Colvin and Lt Paton was set up to get on with the digging of the projected tank and to submit to the committee 'a detailed estimate of the expence for the information of Government'.

The Birjeetala subcommittee had been set up on 13 January 1820. Its report, submitted in April, contained suggestions to render the part of the town extending towards the east of the theatre and northward of the Circular Road 'more salubrious in future'.[12] The subcommittee said that it had been informed by people residing in the area, presumably Europeans, that during the rains, and particularly towards the end of the season, the natives living there suffered from 'intermittent fevers'. The situation, in fact, had turned so bad that 'an unusual mortality' had been reported among the people 'during that period in the past year of late'. Echoing Shakespear's comment made in January, the subcommittee felt that 'the cause of so much sickness may in a great measure be traced to the low, and in many parts, marshy nature of the soil'.

The existing drains were also responsible for the poor state of affairs. As a result of these imperfections, the drains emptied themselves 'very slowly and imperfectly leaving a deposit of putrifying matter to be acted on by the sun and producing the noxious exhalation in which diseases are known to originate'. The state of the country to the south of Circular Road, 'lying between Russapuglah and Ballygunge roads', was also a 'very material cause' of the unhealthiness prevailing to the north of Circular Road, and that it was because of this linkage that it had sought sanction from the Lottery Committee to have the area surveyed. If the sanction was forthcoming, the subcommittee would only then offer its views 'more decidedly on the subject'. However, it added that it had written to Mr Schoop for his views which would be sent to the committee once they were received.

Towards the end of its report, the subcommittee referred to a 20 January 1820 letter from Richard Blechynden in which the state of the drains 'in the vicinity of the theatre and Birjeetollah' had been discussed.[13] The burden of the surveyor's finding was that the drainage of the area in question from north to south was being impeded by the level of Circular Road 'south of the city', which was 'one foot and half an inch higher than the Burial Ground Road taken through Camac Street'. Further, while the fall of the ground 'southerly' was 3 ft 2 ½ inches, the ditch on the south side of Circular Road was from five to nine inches higher than that to the north resulting in 'stagnation of the water in the latter'. The obvious solution was a 'cleaning and deepening' of the southern ditch.

This apart, the east-west drainage into Tolly's Nullah was defective. Blechynden wrote that no water found 'its way to the Mahomedan Burial Ground [at Kassiabagan]' from Tolly's Nullah. When the sluice was shut, 'the large ditch that is on the west side of it merely receives the waste water in the rains from a large tank in the south-west corner of it [marked in Schalch's map as "Mr Wilford's"]'[14] (see Fig. 75). The *mullah* who was in charge of the burial ground[15] reported that the water 'formerly flowed west, i.e. towards Tolly's Nullah, but for the last 4 has flowed east or into the town'. Blechynden wrote that this was to be expected because 'a bed of dried mud to a depth of 2 feet has been allowed to accumulate under the bridge on the entrance of the road to Russapuglah [what is known today as the Exide Crossing]'.

Blechynden's considered remedy was a 'scouring out' of the south ditch of Circular Road which would allow the stagnant water to be drained out. Further, the convicts, who formed an impressive reservoir of free labour for the authorities, could be employed to clean the ditch from the Russapaglah Road 'to the

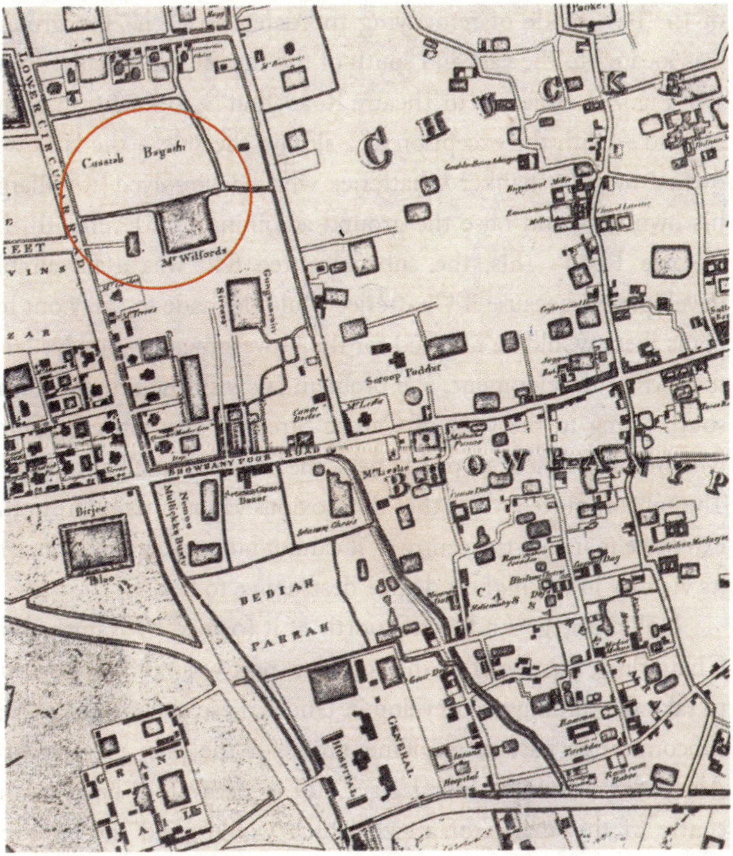

Fig. 75. Kassiabagan, Wilford's tank and the drainage channels to Tolly's Nullah, in Schalch's map of 1824

sluice-gate opposite the Allypore Jail' not forgetting to slope the sides properly which 'At present…are cut so steep as to crumble down continually and check the current of the water'.

Commenting on the state of the ground in question, the subcommittee said that it would focus separately on each plot making up the entire ground so that the committee could 'judge of the best mode of remedying the defect in each'. The ground was located to the east and south of the theatre till Circular Road (see Fig. 74). Adjacent to Theatre Road, that is, to the north of the ground – 'with the exception of a slip on the side' – the land was owned by Ramshanker Chatterjee who had resolved 'to enlarge his own tank and raise the ground adjoining to a level with the Theatre Road'. This, the subcommittee felt, was a favourable development because if Chatterjee could be made to carry out his plans there would be no need for the Government to buy his land for further development. The problem lay with the ground to the south (lying to the west of Camac Street) – the native name of which was *dhankhet*, or paddy field, the property of Charles Short. The subcommittee wrote that the 'noxious vapours rising from the extensive marsh in the centre of it cannot but render a residence in its vicinity in the highest degree destructive to health'.

Unlike the ground to the north of it (owned by Ramshankar Chatterjee), the owner of the southern part was not in a position to take the initiative to develop it. Under these circumstances, the subcommittee backed implementation of the plan proposed by Alexander Colvin to invest Rs 7,000 to excavate a tank 'in the centre of this marsh' of a size which would yield the required quantity of earth to fill the remaining part of it and raise the adjoining ground. To the south and east of the marshy land were two wide drains which, the Birjeetala subcommittee felt, could be partly filled up and narrowed. These drains were cut not to drain the ground but to provide earth for 'raising the roads'[16] with the result that during the rains they were 'for the most part filled with weeds, and grass, which must add to the baneful effects we have already described'. It was proposed that the ditches be reduced to 'a due width with good earth some of which can be procured from the (Circular Road) south ditch' thus deepening the latter.

Filling up of the drains would, however, lead to the problem of an increase in the quantity of ground for private landowners which, the subcommittee held, would have to be paid for by them to the extent their holdings exceeded their *patta* figures. If they were not agreeable to do so, the public roads adjoining the drains could be widened which would not affect the holdings of the private landowners. In order to make the proposed tank useful to the natives living nearby, it was suggested that the agents of Short, Colvins, Bazett and Company, be asked to construct 'a good *puckah* ghaut on one side of the tank' and 'give up a sufficient space for a public way to it', which was agreed to by Short's representatives. The subcommittee laid stress on the point by saying that 'Good water is so essential to health among the natives that the improvement will lose half its value' unless the ghat and road was made. To the east of this plot, across what is today Camac Street, was a big plot of ground known as 'Brahmin [Brahmin] bustee' (see Fig. 74 where it is named 'Bhamun Bustee') owned by Ramshankar Chatterjee who had already carried out the improvements suggested by the subcommittee for the land to the west. The only point which had to be communicated to Chatterjee was the bit about the extra land which would be generated following the reduction of the width of the two drains to the south and west of the plot (adjacent to the Circular Road and Camac Street) which were 'in an equally bad, if not worse, state' than those associated with the plot to the west.

The remaining part of the ground south of Theatre Road and stretching away to the east covered 250 *bighas* (broken up into four discrete sections)[17] and was the property of William Camac under the management of Palmer and Company. Separating the first section and that owned by Chatterjee was the ditch measuring at some places 46 ft in width (see above) which was 'the receptacle of all sorts of filth and in the rains choked up with grass and jungle'. The Birjeetala subcommittee lamented: 'We cannot conceive anything more injurious than such a place as this must be to the health of those residing (and the residents are numerous) immediately on the edges of it'. Clearly, the residents in this case were natives. Parts of this spot of ground were 'very low' which triggered the application of the subcommittee's set formula for a remedy to this sort of problem, namely, digging a tank and using the earth generated from the excavation to raise the level of the ground. The subcommittee suggested that the large ditch to the west of it be turned into a road[18] 'by which means a wholesome current of air would flow through it instead of the most destructive exhalations'.

The subcommittee described the next parcel of ground to the east as being 'not quite so low'. Even so, it suffered from the same defects which could only be remedied 'by enlarging the tank in the centre of it'. This tank was an old one and is seen clearly in Wood's, Upjohn's, and Schalch's maps spanning a period of nearly 40 years. The next section of Camac's ground required the same treatment, namely, enlargement of an existing tank to raise the ground. However, the waterbody in it was more of a *jheel* rather than a tank which needed to be excavated. The last and easternmost section, described as being densely populated, had a 'broad ditch running north and south' which the subcommittee suggested could be turned into a road. The land was 'full of holes and receptacles for filth, though too minute to be particularly inserted in the survey'; and it needed 'ventilation'. The tank located in this section needed to be enlarged considerably. A point of interest is, where did the natives who were displaced from the area go? F.P. Strong, Surgeon to 24-Parganas, throws some light on this when he wrote in 1830:[19]

> A few years back a great number of poor were turned out of grounds [Short's Bazar] purchased by the Lottery Committee, and they built their huts in a particular part of the eastern suburbs [today's Karaya] on the other side of Circular Road, surrounded by *jangal*, and badly drained. So great a number died of cholera, that it was found difficult to dispose of the dead bodies…

In March 1820, the subcommittee had asked Palmer and Company whether it was in a position to sell any part of the Camac premises which figured in its report, and at what price.[20] In case the land could not be sold or if the price asked was too high for the Lottery Committee to accept, the agents were asked whether they would allow tanks to be dug 'in the centre' of three of the four sections 'for the purpose of raising the ground and otherwise rendering them more salubrious'. They were also asked whether they would be willing to share the expense of the development work which would not exceed Rs 10,000 in each of the three sections (the fourth section was left out because it did not 'demand the remedies' proposed). The request to Palmer and Company was hung on the peg of the social benefits which would flow from the completion of the improvements involving 'a large population'.

Replying three weeks later the subcommittee was informed that Camac had allowed them to sell the 'ground near Short's bazaar'[21] at the 'moderate' rate of Rs 50 a *katha* but they were not to '(take) any part in the expense' for developing the area as proposed by the subcommittee. If purchase of the ground was not feasible, the agents had no objection to tanks being dug at the centre of three of the four sections pointed out by the subcommittee without bearing any part of the cost incurred for the work. The subcommittee urged the Lottery Committee to accept the price offered 'immediately' because of its 'manifest advantage', a stand which the committee backed when it sought the Government's approval for the deal. The purchase of the entire Camac estate was urged, the plan being to resell the land

> ...when improved, or let out on building leases, some ground however (being) reserved for an experiment (on) how far sickness amongst the native population can be corrected by

> (an) improved situation – better water and better ventilation – than is to be found about their habitations at present.

The expectation was that the developed land would be bought mainly by Europeans. If, however, the committee did not consider it sensible to buy the Camac land, the subcommittee 'strongly recommended' that permission be granted for the three tanks to be dug and that a proposal be made to Palmer and Company regarding the 'construction of a *puckah ghaut* to each of the tanks'. In case such action on the part of the Government was construed to be improvement of the property of a private individual with public funds, the subcommittee made the point that such improvements would have to be allowed to take place in 'whatever part of the town the committee may disburse their funds' because 'the health and comfort of thousands' were at stake.

The subcommittee had submitted its report to the Lottery Committee on 20 April. Eight days later the committee sent the report to the Government with its comments, among which was the reiteration of the basic principle hitherto applied to all development projects.

As far as the project in hand was concerned, the committee felt confident that the investment laid out by the Government would be 'entirely' recovered from the sale proceeds of the ground. However, since there was not enough funds with the committee to finance the scheme, Government assistance was necessary. Further, since the funds would be used for a cause 'connected... with the health, safety and convenience of a populous part of the city of Calcutta' the committee suggested that such assistance be extended interest-free. However, even if an interest was charged, it 'would not consider that charge as materially diminishing the general expediency of the measures proposed'.

The committee laid out the scale of investment required as follows: Rs 8,500 to dig the tank in Short's ground (which Colvin was to superintend) and defray 'the expenses as may attend the construction of the proposed ghaut and roadway to the tank', Rs 2,50,000 to buy Camac's ground at the price offered by Palmer and Company (nearly 250 *bigha*s at Rs 1,000 per *bigha*), and about Rs 50,000 for the construction of four large tanks with *pucka* ghats, making of new roads, levelling the ground and filling up drains and pools mentioned in the subcommittee's report, 'making altogether an outlay in the first instance of about 3 lacks of rupees'. In terms of the final agreement, the price was fixed at Rs 2,63,900.[22]

The Government took a week to respond to the Lottery Committee's letter.[23] There was no problem with Short's ground, the investment of Rs 8,500 being cleared easily. For Camac's ground the investment of around Rs 3 lakhs sought by the Lottery Committee was also approved but not before the familiar homily was delivered on who was to foot the bill for such city improvements (see below). Since the earliest days of the presence of the East India Company in Calcutta, the subject had cropped up with clockwork regularity in correspondence between the Court of Directors and the Bengal Government, Leadenhall Street unfailingly laying emphasis on the precept that the people should bear the burden of expenditure on city improvement rather than the coffers of the Company.[24]

The specific issue involved here was the purchase of Camac's property on the assumption that the investment laid out for the purpose and other improvements of the ground concerned would be recovered from the eventual sale of the property at an enhanced price. The investment was to be made from funds made available to the Lottery Committee by the Government in the shape of a loan, interest-free or otherwise. As the committee had suggested, in the case of any shortfall in the eventual sale proceeds of the land compared to the investment made, the deficiency was to be covered by the proceeds of future lotteries. The Government was apprehensive 'that a precedent might be established tending to charge the general resources of the Government with the expense attendant on improvements in the city'.

Having said all this, the Governor-General in Council saw

> ...little cause to doubt that, by judicious management, the sums disbursed for the proposed improvement may be recovered by the resale of the ground in its improved state, or that, at all events, the improvements will be ultimately effected in the manner proposed at a less expense than by any other plan.

The loan, extended to the Lottery Committee, carried an annual interest of six per cent and was to have a term of three years (till 1 May 1823) for full repayment. If the loan remained unpaid at the end of the period, 'further appropriation of the proceeds of the lotteries to general purposes connected with the improvement of the city (would) be suspended until the sums advanced from the treasury under the present instructions with the interest due upon them shall have been entirely repaid'.[25]

Ten months later, in March 1821, the committee felt comfortable enough to reassure the Government that it was confident of repaying the loan with interest, adding that 'the important objects to which that sum was intended to be applied will be accomplished not only without any ultimate expense but with an actual pecuniary advantage to the lottery funds'.[26] The committee's mood was upbeat even though the tank dug on Short's land was one of those rare projects which had overshot the budgeted investment by a tidy sum and at a time when the Government had underscored the efficient use of the funds allocated for it. In October the previous year (1820), while reporting the completion of the work of digging the tank in Short's ground, the Birjeetala subcommittee had informed the committee with 'great regret' that the original estimate for constructing it (Rs 7,000) had been exceeded by the 'very considerable' amount of Rs 3,840-10-0 because of circumstances 'which it would have been extremely difficult, if not impossible, for us to have anticipated'.[27]

In the case of the tank at Baparitala, there was a problem in digging it in view of the water that was constantly issuing from springs in its bed.[28] No such problem had disrupted work on the new tank in Short's ground, which had turned out to be much larger in area than planned. Initially, the area covered by the tank was to have been 60,000 sq. ft (200 by 300 sq. ft) but, in fact, it was increased to 75,350 sq. ft (275 by 274 sq. ft) resulting in the proprietor losing 'more than 1 bigha of available ground for building on, in excess [of] for what he originally calculated upon appropriating to the tank'.[29] Not only were there no unexpected springs on the floor of the tank, it had been filled up easily 'to within four feet perpendicular of the present surface' with water got from Tolly's Nullah 'by opening the flood gates during the last spring tide… through the adjoining drain'. This is yet another example showing how the network of drains in this part of the rapidly expanding city was linked to Tolly's Nullah and the use to which such water was put to in flushing out the water channels. For natives living in these parts, the easy availability of water from the *Adi Ganga* must have been of great social significance for obvious reasons, which may explain partly why, in the first place, one finds an agglomeration of old *bustees* along water channels linked to the nullah.

A point of interest relates to the composition of the subsoil which was revealed in the course of digging the tank on Short's ground. The Birjeetala subcommittee had written in its October 1820 letter to the committee that

> A considerable portion of the tank was excavated 32 feet below the former level of the swamp in which it was chiefly

> situated. At that depth we had still a strong blue clay without any appearance of water…At the depth of about 26 feet we found many trees, chiefly sundry [*sundari*] and generally upright, cut off about 6 ft above the roots, bedded in blue clay over which, about 16 feet from the surface, was a layer 18 inches thick of a black vegetable substance resembling peat.

The discovery of *sundari* trees *in situ* around 30 ft below ground level – indicating that in primeval times the area was an extended mangrove swamp – was not a first-time event in Calcutta, for a similar discovery had been reported in the early years of the 18th century at the time of the excavation of a tank to the southeast of the BBD Bagh tank.[30] About a fortnight after receiving the subcommittee's report on the excess expenditure relating to the digging of the tank in Short's ground, the committee asked the Government to sanction the additional investment, which was allowed.[31]

The Government had approved of the purchase of the Camac land, but progress was disrupted by complications regarding the title of the property. In its 5 May 1820 letter to the Lottery Committee sanctioning the project the Government had said that 'proper precautions' were to be taken 'to have (Camac's) property legally and regularly transferred' to the Company.[32] On the same day, after writing to the committee, the Government had asked Robert Poe, the Company Attorney, to look into the legal details of the issue. Nearly six weeks later, in late June, Poe forwarded to the committee the Advocate-General, Robert Spankie's opinion on the validity of Camac's title to the land in question, which was far from favourable.[33] Spankie minced no words in pointing out that the title was 'so clearly defective' that there could be 'no difficulty in a professional man declaring that it is not good or marketable'.[34] However, the Advocate-General held that it would be for the purchaser (in this case the Government) 'to consider whether, notwithstanding such defect, the purchase with all faults may not be desirable'. Amplifying, he said that the length of time which had elapsed during which Camac appeared to have had possession of the ground 'affords a presumption in favour of his right'. Spankie felt that Camac would perhaps

> ...have no objection to covenant in the usual way...and this, according to all practice, he is bound to do as the purchase is not accompanied by such covenants as would afford the purchaser a right of action against any other person whatever, and even these covenants,

adding that even such instruments were 'not considered a good security'.

Throwing some light on the complexity of the ownership issue, the Advocate-General said that from the papers sent to him his conclusion was that Camac had bought the property from Luckenarain (Lakhinarain) Chund who was himself a 'sub-lessee or assignee of another person, a Portuguese' whose name he could not remember. In any case, if the deal was to be pursued, it had to be ascertained that Camac had the right to evict the actual occupiers of the ground. This apart, Camac's agents, Palmer and Company, would have 'to make arrangements with the farmer of the bazaar as to his giving up his lease'. The further point was made that it had to be 'well-ascertained' that Camac would be able to give the Government possession of the entire property. To start with, Palmer and Company would have to enter into an agreement with the Company for the sale of the land in question 'engaging to produce within a given time a regular power to sell under the *stipulated terms and covenants* [emphasis in original] specified in the agreement or conveyances executed by Mr Camac himself'. Since there was bound to be some uncertainty on whether conveyances drawn up in England could be smoothly executed in Calcutta, the Advocate-General suggested that 'a power of attorney to sell and to execute the conveyances would be preferable'.[35]

Following procedure, the Lottery Committee sent the Advocate-General's opinion to the Birjeetala subcommittee for its comments. But this was not the end of the story as far as Spankie was concerned. In course of the following weeks, he was provided with 'further deeds relating to Mr Camac's title to the ground' which led the Advocate-General to soften his stand on the deal. In a supplementary note sent to the Government in the last week of July, he reassured the Government that, 'under all the circumstances of the case', there was 'no such title in any other person that renders it dangerous for the Company to complete the purchase', which should nevertheless contain a reference to 'their own paramount title'. Spankie focussed on George Vansittart's title to the land when he wrote that 'the legal title to this property appears still outstanding in that Gentleman or his Heirs, but every condition of the Grant has, as may be expected in all such cases, been utterly neglected by the Grantee'.[36] However, the Advocate-General felt it was 'too late to think of reverting to the original title of the Government against the Grant under which so many new rights have been acquired'. As regards the conveyance under which 311 *bigha*s was transferred to Charles Short, he said it was 'very extraordinary' that the actual document had gone missing.[37]

The Advocate-General's supplementary opinion was sent to the Birjeetala subcommittee in early August with the suggestion that 'a covenant should be introduced into the conveyance effectually to protect the public interests against the consequences of any defect which may exist in the title of the present proprietor'. This is precisely what the subcommittee recommended when it suggested that the agents of Camac in India furnish a 'covenant of indemnity' protecting the Lottery Committee from any unforeseen complications flowing from 'any defect which may exist in the present title', which could arise after the sale of the plot had been completed. The point was then made that, with this legal protection, there could be little objection to the Lottery Committee going ahead with the purchase of the Camac plot 'upon the terms proposed by Messrs Palmer and Company' on 17 April (see above).[38] In the middle of August the committee asked Poe to arrange for a covenant of indemnity and also to go ahead with the purchase of the ground in question as suggested by the subcommittee. Under Spankie's tutelage, the Company Attorney drafted an agreement on behalf of Palmer and Company for sale of the property and also a bond of indemnity, which was accepted by Camac's agents.[39]

Spankie, however, was not finished with the deal as yet. A further twist to the tale was added when, on reading the draft, the Advocate-General wrote that the agreement being worked on was 'certainly a species of transaction to which more risk is attached than I should wish to advise being incurred, particularly as the Company is to take possession and perhaps incur a large expense on improvements, and Mr Camac or his heirs may refuse to confirm the bargain'. He wondered whether Palmer and Company could be persuaded to indemnify against such a contingency. If Camac was willing to send a power of attorney to convey, 'it must refer to the agreement and empower the attorneys to convey agreeably thereto and must be very full and particular'. As suggested by the Lottery Committee, Poe asked the Advocate-General whether 'the contract might not be carried into effect provisionally under the indemnity of Messr Palmer and Co.'. Once again, Spankie's response was a cautious one. Poe reported that the Advocate-General chose to sound the warning that it was for the Government to determine 'the propriety of purchasing a title not strictly regular' but that, 'at all events', it would be proper that the agents 'should engage to repay the moiety (advance) of the purchase money paid and to indemnify Government for improvements in case the sale was not completed'. The agents would also have to give up possession of the land once the funds were 'laid out' on the property the point being emphasised that Palmer and Company would have to commit itself to procuring 'regular conveyances' within two years of the contract being signed.

In the middle of September, the Company Attorney wrote that it had been suggested (by whom the records do not make clear) that the guaranteed funds should be Rs 50,000 'in the event of the contract not being finally completed', a figure which the Advocate-General thought was reasonable and which Palmer and Company had accepted. Poe sought the Government's sanction for the move, Bayley, the Chief Secretary, writing to him a couple of days later saying that there appeared to be 'little or no risk of any serious loss' to the Government provided the Lottery Committee did not disburse a sum larger than Rs 50,000 on the projected improvements 'during the interval which may elapse between the payment of the 1st moiety of the purchase money and the date fixed upon for the receipt from Mr Camac of legal powers for the completion of the contract and for the execution of the regular conveyances'. This apart, since 'the public benefit likely to result from the purchase and improvement of the ground [would greatly] outweigh any risk arising from the defect of title', the Government had no hesitation to authorise 'the completion of the purchase in the manner and with the securities proposed'.

The purchase was formally completed with Poe informing the Lottery Committee on 20 September that an agreement had been clinched with Palmer and Company to 'procure within two years from the 18th instant [September] a conveyance of the land appertaining to the estate of Mr Camac in Chouringhee and a bond for the due performance of that agreement'.[40] The committee wrote to the agents the next day to take the measures necessary (involving the farmer of the bazar concerned) to clear the ground of 'the present occupiers' so that the committee could take possession of the land in a vacant state as quickly as possible (which was effected on 2 October). The agents were also told that after payment of the first advance, amounting to Rs 1,31,950,[41] the remaining part of the land price would be paid 'upon production by you of conveyances from Mr Camac himself or of adequate legal powers to enable you to complete the contract under the stipulated terms and covenant specified in the agreement…'

The agreement had stipulated two years as the period within which it would have to be fully implemented. The Government did not have to wait this long. A year later, on 2 October 1821 the agents informed the committee that they had received from William Camac 'the necessary powers to enable us to complete the conveyance of the purchase of his bazaar and ground by the Government'.[42] Reiterating that the deal was 'quite final', Palmer and Company, however, wanted a re-measurement of the ground because Camac felt that 'a larger quantity' would be found 'than at present estimated' for the purpose of the sale. In fact, the re-measurement led to a small problem involving the *cutcha* road which led from Short's Bazar to Circular Road in the south.[43] The agents wrote to the committee that this road was not included in Camac's ground although it should have been because it was 'a private road which led only to the bazaar', adding that it 'might… have been taken by Mr Camac at any time on the abolition of the bazaar'. The committee differed with the view and said that it had consulted 'the best maps and authorities' on the issue and had found that, 'so far back as the last 20 years, it appears from Upjohn's plan [see Fig. 38] to have been in every respect a "public way" and (referred) to as such by the proper authorities'. In fact, in his 13 January 1820 minute,[44] Shakespear had suggested that 'the fine broad road from Short's bazaar should be made *puckka*', the inference being that it was not so much a private road as a public one. Palmer and Company accepted this interpretation of the road's status and, on 13 December 1821 let the Lottery Committee know that the original measurement of Camac's ground was acceptable to it for drawing up the conveyance.[45]

As a financial venture, the project turned out to be a success. In the middle of November 1823, the Lottery Committee informed the Government that the 'extensive improvements' connected with Camac's estate ('now Hastings Place') were 'nearly complete' and that, despite some 'trifling works' which remained to be done, 'including the construction of a balustrade round the several tanks and a *pucka* walk within the enclosures of the tanks', the committee was 'likely to realise about two lacks of rupees…*after* [emphasis added] providing for the repayment of the loan from the Government and for every expense connected with the improvement in question'.[46] Not much work had to be done to resell the ground for, at the end of October, the subcommittee concerned had reported that the entire ground (153 *bigha*s 16 *katha*s 7 13/45 *chittack*s) had been sold to Manuel de Lauruleta (agent for the Philippine Company) at a public auction held at the Town Hall on 18 August at a price of Rs 154-11-0 a *katha*. Of the total sum yielded by the transaction (Rs 4,75,889-3-6), Rs 2,80,000 (reduced to Rs 2,79,568-5-4 because of prompt payment) was realised immediately which was paid into the general treasury as repayment of the loan. The subcommittee said that Rs 32,407-4-0 was realised from J. Llewellyn (of the firm Simpson and Llewellyn) for ground sold to him, Rs 36,288-1-6 as 'the remaining moiety of Mr Spankie's purchase', and Rs 15,004-0-0 from 'Captain Henderson' as payment for ground bought by him. Among other things, Rs 18,544-0-10 was repaid to the treasury 'in full [payment] of the balance of principal and interest due to Government on account of the original loan made to the committee for the purchase of Mr Camac's estate'.

The Government was satisfied with the results of the entire exercise. On 20 November it wrote back to say that the Governor-General in Council had been 'much gratified by the stated results of this useful and important undertaking' noting that the loan sanctioned by the Government along with the six per cent interest on it had been repaid and that, despite the fact that the development had been executed on 'a very liberal scale', at the end of the transaction the Lottery Committee stood to gain Rs 2 lakhs which could be used for the other projects in which it was engaged. Taking advantage of hindsight, it can be said that this was the precise starting point of the journey of this particular part of the city into the 'modern' period.

EPILOGUE

The foregoing pages suggest that the city of Calcutta gained immensely from the development work carried out by the Lottery Committee since its setting up in October 1817. The Strand Road had spruced up the eastern bank of the river Hooghly beyond recognition; the western side of Tank Square (today's BBD Bagh), down to the *maidan* till the West Bengal Legislative Assembly, had been given its modern shape with its grid of streets; *pucka* drains had been built and upgraded all over the city; the major north-south arterial road extending from Park Street in the south to Shyambazar in the north with four squares along it had been constructed; Free School Street had been made; the entire area south of Park Street up to Circular Road had been transformed into 'virgin' land ready to be settled in by the genteel (for the most part, sahib) population of Calcutta; and the 'modernisation' of the Garden Reach area, reaching up to Khidirpur in the north, had been begun. In its 13 years of effective functioning (till 1830), the committee had been successful in providing the critical push necessary to transform Calcutta from the topographical shape it had inherited since the years immediately following the landing of Job Charnock at Sutanati in August 1690 into one which, in a manner of speaking, would make the city ready to be launched into the 20th century and beyond.

The beneficial impact of the committee's work affected everyone, native and European alike, and there was nothing

Fig. 76. A watercolour of East India House in Leadenhall Street, London, in 1817 where the Court of Directors of the East India Company had their offices, by Thomas Hosmer Shepherd

remotely furtive about it. Yet, the Directors of the East India Company in London were not happy with what was happening in distant Calcutta on the city-development front, choosing to view the evolving picture in a different light. What, then, was the reason behind this gulf of difference in appreciating the Lottery Committee's work? Throughout the 18th century, the Company had focussed on the virtues of economy in expenditure, particularly where the beneficiaries of such investment were the city people, irrespective of whether they were natives or Europeans. A point of principle was involved here: in 1752 the Company was writing to its Government in Bengal that whenever there was any activity relating to 'general and Publick Utility, some part of the Charges *ought* [emphasis added] to be borne by the Inhabitants'. Further, the Lottery Committee was handling large sums of money and there was – perhaps inevitably given the Company's deep-seated scepticism about the sensibility of such expenditure in general

– a tendency to conclude that the money was not being spent efficiently. Seen in this light, it is hardly surprising that, prior to the Lottery Committee, the magistrates were in the line of fire from the Company's guns because of the same reason (see below).

The committee had begun work in late 1817. By early 1819 the Court was already complaining that 'Most of the statements of charges on the lottery funds for the construction and repair of various works in and about Calcutta are wholly unsatisfactory', adding, 'We know no reason why these disbursements should not be submitted to at least as severe checks and control as any other disbursements under the Government.'[1] By the end of 1820 the Directors had formed a strong enough view of the Lottery Committee's work in Calcutta to send a scathing critique to the Government of Lord Hastings. Four basic points were made which were not to the Court's liking.[2] The first was the nature of the information sent to London by the Government in Calcutta on the work done by the committee. Citing the example of the expenditure on 'the continuance of the aqueduct…and a drain recommended by Mr [Henry] Wood' which added up to Rs 28,186 in two tranches, the Court wrote in February 1818 that it desired 'more exact information' respecting the receipts and disbursements of the lottery funds. In the absence of such information, 'we have only to state that, although we approve of the application of those [funds] to the improvement of Calcutta, we must object to your anticipating them by drafts on the general treasury'. The very direct allegation was made that 'the estimates for the works above referred to appear to us to be founded on very questionable data; and great as the probable expense is stated to be, we have no doubt that the actual cost will be much greater' (see below).

The Directors had not developed this view of the financial operations of its officials in Calcutta in a vacuum, so to speak. The comment was linked to the performance of the magistrates in the Conservancy Department the Court observing: 'We do not observe that you have ordered any enquiry into the abuses referred to in the Department of Conservancy and the application of the lottery funds; nor can we see in your new plan any prospect of future good management'. The reorganisation of responsibilities following the establishment of the new Lottery Committee had led to a reduction in the pressure of work on the magistrates.[3] Referring to this reduction, the Directors wrote that the Government had asked them 'to report whether some new arrangement of their duties could not be made in a manner likely to secure the more prompt discharge of some branches of their business'[4] the point being made that the magistrates did not seem to have paid any attention to this. Further, the Court said that on 25 September 1817 it was reported that 'the balance of money from the lottery funds' in the hands of the magistrates was Rs 6,177-13-3. It wrote that this sum,

> ...with any other actual surplus, is the sum which might have been considered as applicable to the purpose of improvement. But when the committee goes back to past times and discovers that disbursements have been made from the lottery funds which, in their opinion, might more properly have been made from other funds, they open a door *for the admission of a principle which it would be extremely inconvenient to admit* [emphasis added].[5]

Fourthly, the Directors doubted the ability of the Lottery Committee members to devote enough time to the work demanded of them in view of the fact that each of them had his own work to do, private and public. Listing the officials who were members of the committee along with the positions they held in the Government, the Court wrote that it was sceptical that the Lottery Committee would be 'likely to fulfil the various purposes for which it is constituted, and whether the members of it will be able, consistently with their more immediate professional vocations, to devote the requisite time and attention to the duties of the committee'.[6]

In its 13 December 1820 despatch, the Court had provided details about the implementation of improvement projects in Calcutta which had upset it. Replying to the Government's letter of 29 October 1817,[7] the Directors said that on 12 March 1817, Henry Wood, 'to whom you had entrusted the construction of an aqueduct', had suggested that 'the direction of that work should be changed'.[8] He had also proposed the making of a drain and had referred to a letter of 29 August 1814 'suggesting other works'. The Court's point was that the letter was not to be found in its records implying that it was not sent by the Government;[9] neither did it have a copy of a map 'which Mr Wood refers to where the suggested improvements are marked'. It was because of these reasons that the Directors were unable 'to understand fully the original plans' of the Civil Auditor. Further, the Government had written to the magistrates on 28 March 1817 – that is, a good seven months before the Lottery Committee had been appointed – approving of Wood's plan to alter the direction of the aqueduct and make a new drain and seeking the views of the magistrates before going ahead with the project. But the magistrates had not responded to that request, nor had the Government taken any notice of their omission.[10]

On the same day (28 March 1817) the Government had appointed a committee[11] of several persons of whom Wood was one (the others being Eliot, Trower and J.W. Hogg), an extract being sent to them of the Civil Auditor's letter which dwelt mainly with the construction of tanks. The Directors then quoted the following Government instruction sent to the committee:

'You are authorised to exercise your discretion in commencing arrangements for the excavation of one or more tanks in that part of the town where they may appear to be most urgently required'. On 6 June that year the committee submitted its report in which it said that 'it had fixed on the centre of the Dhurm Tullah as the spot where a tank was most urgently required'. The Court's point of contention was that the report contained no details but merely said that 'the probable expense' of purchasing ground buildings, etc., and excavating the tank 'will not exceed 1,80,000 rupees'. The Court then said that, faced with such a report, the Government 'very naturally' asked for more information regarding the project – objects of the plan, its extent, and cost. The committee was asked to procure from the magistrates as well as the Government's Sub-Treasurer 'a statement of the funds realised from the lotteries for the improvement of Calcutta, the purposes to which those funds had been appropriated and the balance available for public purposes'. On 25 September the committee submitted to the Government a second report which contained a map and a plan of the proposed improvements with an explanatory letter.[12] The Court's point was that 'no copy of the map and plan having accompanied your proceedings, we are unable perfectly to understand the references'. Since the detailed estimates were not sent to London, the Directors said they could 'judge of them but partially' from the committee's letter which was sent to them.[13]

Five years later, the Court returned to the theme with its ire directed against the Lottery Committee undiminished. In fact, by this time (1822-23) there were unmistakable signs that the importance of the Lottery Committee in the Government's scheme of governance was declining. A new Governor-General, Lord Amherst, had taken over and it was to be expected that the Lottery Committee's work would be viewed through a new set of glasses. It is also likely that the constant pressure of the critical view taken by the Court of Directors of the committee's work may have contributed to the metamorphosis. An important signal that the Lottery Committee was being 'demoted', in a manner of speaking, was the decision taken at the end of 1825 to reduce the salary of its Secretary from Rs 800 to Rs 500.[14] A 'trifling' reduction of Rs 50 a month was also made in the budget for the Secretary's office.[15] At the same time, the weightage of the office of the Assistant Secretary, A.C. Seymour, was increased with Rs 200 per month being sanctioned 'for office rent for the records and officers of the establishment'.[16] In other words, from now on an assistant secretary would be enough to run the affairs of the Lottery Committee which had changed the face of certain areas of the city radically over the preceding eight years.

In April 1826 Leadenhall Street wrote that it had seen the Governor-General in Council's despatch of 7 December 1821 in which a memorandum had been furnished of 'the most important works' sanctioned by the Government at the recommendation of the Lottery Committee.[17] The first project referred to in the memorandum was Shakespear's letter regarding sickness prevailing in Chowringhee.[18] The Court wrote that, basing itself on the report of the subcommittee concerned, the Lottery Committee 'expected that the whole of this expense (Rs 3 lakhs) would be reimbursed by the sale of the land in its improved state', the Government being told by the committee that the general improvement of Calcutta 'could in no way be so effectually or so cheaply secured as by the purchase of large tracts of land with the object of excavating tanks, opening roads, drawing and levelling the ground and making other improvements, and of selling the ground so improved'. The Court pointed out that despite the Advocate-General's view that the title to William Camac's land 'was not good or marketable', the Governor-General went ahead with the project on the ground that the 'public benefit likely to result from the purchase and improvement of the ground' would 'greatly...outweigh any risk from the defect of title'.[19]

The Court felt that before doing so the Government should have consulted 'some experienced engineers and the Medical Board rather than the Lottery Committee'. Its considered view was that such projects, involving so large an expenditure and where the title to the land to be bought was questionable, 'ought not to have been undertaken without the fullest examination of their necessity'. Repeating the point made in its 13 December 1820 letter, the Directors said that they were not happy with the incomplete nature of the information sent by the Government in Calcutta regarding projects being undertaken by the committee. It wrote, scathingly, that 'a considerable part of the correspondence relating to improvements in Calcutta' was 'unintelligible' to it 'from want of plans, maps and illustrations', the Camac land project – which was one of the major works implemented by the committee – being brought to its notice 'by a short memorandum indicating generally the local situation of the works, unaccompanied by any other information whatever'.

In the same letter, the Court was critical of the surface-draining project undertaken in Calcutta. It wrote that the project had been sanctioned based on the result of 'some experiments made by Mr Shakespear'[20] and that no estimate had been formed of the final expense. The Court regretted the fact that it could form 'no notion' of the final expense; neither did it have 'any assurance of the correctness of the principles on which the new mode of draining is founded'. The subject of the sale of land by 'Messrs Trotter and Larkins of the civil service' for providing 'a commodious access to the river at some particular spot' was also commented on, the Court's view being that it had 'no information in regard to the utility of the work in question'.[21] Even a measure meant to facilitate children having fun on the *maidan* did not escape the Court's notice as a point of criticism. It wrote that the expenditure on making a 'safe and dry walk for children' down Chowringhee appeared to be 'wholly unreasonable' on the ground that 'places of exercise for the children of the inhabitants of Chowringhee are not to be provided at the public expense'.[22]

The Court referred to the huge cost of constructing Wellington Square (the Baparitala tank and square) – which it described as 'a great structure' – and the Central and Strand Roads. Regarding the riverside project, it said that no prior estimate had been prepared for the entire project the cost of which was bound to be 'very great' considering the fact that 'the line of operation must have included many extensive premises of value, among which there is said to be a space of 2,300 feet comprehending several yards for ship-building'. The Directors concluded their 11 April 1826 letter by saying:

> When under your authority large sums of money are thus expended, and the interests of the Government, of many private individuals, and of the community of Calcutta are at stake, we expect to be furnished with full explanations as to the propriety of the various projects undertaken, and the ability and economy with which they are executed. Such explanations we have not yet received in regard to the proceedings of the lottery committee.

Harping on the decades-old refrain, the Government was asked to observe the 'strictest economy' with regard to 'the construction and repair of public works', a caution which was applicable equally to investment on the improvement of Calcutta.

On receiving the Court's 13 December 1820 despatch, the Government had written to the Lottery Committee (28 July 1821) that London had raised a number of issues regarding its work since its inception in 1817 and that it was to submit 'a general report or statement of the chief improvements effected under their superintendence since their appointment as well as of those now in progress showing the expense attending these works'.[23] The committee took five months to prepare the report which was submitted on the last day of 1821 and was described as a 'general report of the improvements on which we had been engaged since the appointment of the committee in 1817, specifying the expenses incurred on each separate work'.[24] It did not give the reasons 'which originally led to each improvement', but it did provide 'as short a summary of them as possible, pointing out in the margin the dates of the reports submitted to Government and of the instructions under which we acted so as to facilitate a reference to the documents requisite for the full explanation of each particular subject'. A sketch was also provided by the committee (which is not included in the records) 'of that part of the city to which our attention has hitherto been chiefly directed', the report commencing with those projects which had already been planned or were being implemented at the time of the committee's appointment. The report referred to 31 specific projects beginning with the Baparitala scheme and ending with 'surface drains'.[25] The letter listed three principal areas on which the committee's attention was focussed at the time (the end of 1821). These were: opening wide communications throughout the city, chiefly in a direction from south to north; completing the quay and road on the riverbank from Chandpal Ghat to Chitpur Bridge (Strand Road); and 'improving the draining of the city wherever we may have an opportunity without interfering with general measures of which further information may suggest the expediency'.

On its part, the committee was disappointed with the Directors for having taken the view they had of its work since October 1817. It is easy to imagine that the members must have been smarting at the thought that the Court, in faraway London, had run them down when the usefulness of their work was there for all to see in the rapidly expanding city of Calcutta itself. They wrote:

> It is unnecessary to insist on the advantages of all these measures at much length. They will readily occur to everyone acquainted with Calcutta where, from the heat of the climate, the lowness of the situation, and the dirty habits of natives, the benefits of free ventilation and good draining are so much the more wanted as they have hitherto been little attended to. The facilities already afforded of communication between the different portions of so thickly inhabited a place are very apparent, and in preventing the spread of destructive fires as well as for the general purposes of police, there can be no doubt of the benefits already conferred on the inhabitants of Calcutta.

The town was full of holes and ditches in which water gathered and which ultimately became the breeding ground for widespread pestilence, a problem which had been noticed by the authorities as early as 1709.[26] The committee went out of its way to draw attention to this point when it wrote:

> We may here notice one important benefit resulting from our operations [which] has not been before specifically adverted to. We allude to the numerous small ponds, swamps and holes which we have been enabled to fill up and level in the course of our operations. The number of these noxious receptacles of filth which are still to be found in the interior and most populous parts of the city, and their injurious effects on the health of the inhabitants, cannot be justly appreciated by those who are in the habit of passing only the wide and commodious streets in that part of the city occupied by Europeans

– or, perhaps, what the committee left unsaid, by people sitting in faraway Leadenhall Street waiting for the next despatch from India.

The committee could implement effectively its work by following one of two routes, or both: cooperation extended by individuals whose property was affected by its work and/or by using the stick (laws) to force people to part with their property. The committee wrote that 'on many occasions' it had received 'cordial assistance and cooperation both from Europeans and natives'; at other times it had 'encountered prejudices and opposition'. Even so, the committee felt that both the Government and the Court would be '[satisfied] to learn that we have yet been obliged to appeal to a jury only on two occasions'.[27]

This indicated the committee's penchant 'to avoid coercive measures as long as others can be found available'. It was also suggested that the law could not be had recourse to easily because of certain structural issues. Once more the opportunity was taken to point 'to the defects of the bye-law under which juries can at present be summoned', in particular 'the absence of any provision…for clearing spots for tanks', which (as we have seen) was mainly responsible for 'the unreasonable expense' of constructing Wellington Square.[28]

Another point which the committee underscored was the growing ineffectiveness of the method of paying for projects through the sale of surplus land, which had paid rich dividends in the early stages of its work. It wrote that most of its estimates had hitherto been based

> …on the expectation of reselling at an advanced price the surplus ground purchased in effecting our improvements. But this source of advantage, we fear, will not last long, for the advance of price has been so uniform on these occasions (from 25 to 75 per cent) that the proprietors are now become

> exceedingly unwilling to dispose of more than is actually required for the use of the roads.

The committee noted the invaluable service provided by natives during implementation of projects, especially when land purchase was involved. In fact, it went out of its way to emphasise that such purchases had '...almost entirely been effected through a respectable native whose information, derived from his situation in the office of the Collector of the Ground Rents', had been found to be 'of the most essential benefit to us', adding that this person acted 'under the direction of subcommittees into which we have found it expedient to divide ourselves for each separate work'. The native here referred to is, of course, Rupnarayan Ghoshal whose work, as the preceding pages indicate, the Lottery Committee found invaluable, even indispensable.[29]

The last paragraph of the committee's letter to the Government shows that it had taken to heart the insinuations the Directors had made in their despatches regarding the quality of work put in by members. It wrote that the Government was aware that all the members of the committee had 'other public or private invocations to pursue' and that, 'with the exception of a meeting for a few hours twice a month, their duty is performed in the usual hours of exercise and relaxation in the morning and evening'. The members hoped that the report would indicate that they 'have not been idle and that while we have not hitherto been unprofitably employed, the experience we have obtained will enable us to continue our operations with greater facilities and less chance of error than has hitherto existed'.

The Government's response to the committee's report is a clear vindication of the Governor-General's support for the work done by the Lottery Committee since 1817 as opposed to the strictures passed on the committee by the Court of Directors. In his 29 March 1822 letter, H.T. Prinsep, the Acting Secretary to the Government, made it clear that it was the intention of the Governor-General in Council to send the report to the Court, the hope being that when it was read the Directors would have 'become sensible of the extent and utility of the operations' the committee was engaged in and would appreciate better the 'success [which] has attended your vigilance in restricting the expence of every separate undertaking so as to increase to the public the benefit capable of being conferred by the funds at your disposal'. In particular, the Directors had said that what the committee was doing could have been done better by a single officer 'whose whole time and attention could be devoted to its superintendence', the members of the committee 'scarcely (having) the leisure to attend sufficiently to the duty'. One of the principal objects of the Governor-General in Council seeking an exhaustive report from the committee was to 'satisfy' the Court that 'howsoever much engaged personally in other arduous employments of a public or private nature, inattention to the objects for which you were incorporated in a committee was not in any way to be laid to your charge'. On the other hand, the Government went out of its way to aver that the performance-record presented by the committee underscored the point that

> ...the services of a single individual, howsoever zealous or intelligent, could never have comprehended so wide a field or constituted such facilities of execution as the present system has yielded in the combination [of] personal influence, intelligence and the zeal of your several members directed towards the same general object.

Extending further this line of the argument, special mention was made of the fact that, in the four years since October 1817, there were only two occasions when a jury had to be summoned to sort out a problem, which was nothing short of an 'achievement' considering the scale of the work implemented and the diverse types of people the committee had to deal with. The Government wrote that the need to refer to a jury on just two occasions to value land and building required for the purposes of public improvement was 'strongly illustrative of the extent of your influence' apart from throwing light on 'a degree of consideration for private rights that must deservedly have given popularity to your exertions'. It added:

> When, however, the multitude of persons of every character and persuasion with whom your various works have brought you into contact is taken into the account, the inference seems unavoidable that the structure of your committee must have given you advantages in combating rooted prejudices, and in leading individuals to submit voluntarily to temporary inconvenience in furtherance of your plans for the public good, such as no single person could have hoped to possess.

The second reason why the committee's 31 December 1821 report was important to Lord Hastings was a personal one. Since his Governor-Generalship was coming to a close, he could now reflect with satisfaction on the fact that the Lottery Committee, set up under his aegis in 1817, had done sterling work as far as the city's improvement was concerned. In a different vein, Prinsep wrote:

> His Lordship in Council desires me to offer to your committee his own grateful acknowledgement of your very beneficial services which are, in his opinion, calculated to reflect great credit upon you, while the result fully justified the policy of Government in resolving to avail itself of your gratuitous exertions. These acknowledgements will, he trusts,

> be acceptable in proportion to your own conviction of their being sincerely and deservedly applied.

The despatch of the Lottery Committee's report to London was left to his successor, Lord Amherst, which was effected as late as on 29 September 1825.[30] Writing to Calcutta two years later (on 22 August 1827),[31] the Directors had altered their tone. They told the Government that had the information contained in the September 1825 letter 'been communicated to us at an earlier period' it would have prevented the Court from making 'some of the remarks' it had made in the earlier despatches respecting the improvement of Calcutta. However, this was as far as the Court would go in diluting its views on the Lottery Committee; it had travelled too far down the road of opposition to the committee to reverse gear, as it were. And so it wrote:

> There can be no doubt that many of the great works effected by the lottery committee, especially the excavation of tanks, the construction of drains, the widening of old streets, and the opening of new ones, must have been of essential benefit to the public. It is nevertheless important that the most approved principles should be applied in the planning and execution of such works; and that funds so extensive as those at the disposal of the committee, amounting to several lacs of rupees a year, should be employed in the most economical manner and under the best system of check and control.

Even after being informed in the 29 September letter about the projects undertaken by the committee till the end of 1821, the Court wanted the Government to send to it 'full information on these points in regard to all works undertaken by the lottery committee'.

The stick was then applied the Court expressing its 'surprise and regret at the enormous advances from the public treasury which you have made to the committee in anticipation of their ordinary funds, amounting on one occasion to no less than 6,00,000 rupees'.[32] The Court reminded the Government that the advance was made despite the clear message in its 13 December 1820 letter in which 'we objected to any such advances being made', adding, 'We hope we shall not have occasion to notice any repetition of such inattention to our clear and precise orders.' The Directors said it was even considering the appointment of an officer to do the work of the committee but was abstaining from taking the step 'in consideration of the high opinion you entertain of the fitness of the lottery committee'.

Three years later, in its despatch of 20 July 1830, the Directors returned to the subject of the financial arrangement for the Cornwallis Street-Amherst Street project and passed even more severe strictures on the Government in Calcutta and the Lottery Committee.[33] A finger was pointed directly at Henry Shakespear and Alexander Colvin, Jr, who were in charge of the project, the Court stating in paragraph 25 of its letter:

> We think it very objectionable that the conduct of such extensive works, and the disposal of such large sums of money, should be left to individuals who are without any official responsibility [sic], who are not appointed on account of any qualifications which they possess for the duties entrusted to them, whose labours are unpaid, and whose proceedings, instead of being subjected to a strict superintendence and control, are scarcely limited but by their own discretion.

The Court added that it was 'especially improper that such an employment as that of the subcommittee of the lottery committee should be held by the Secretary to Government, and we direct that it be immediately discontinued'.[34]

In an attempt to soften the blow on the two members of the committee who along with their colleagues (as this book shows) had toiled without respite to make Calcutta a better place to live in, the Directors said: 'At the same time, we must apprise you that whatever we may think of skill, regularity and economy in Mr Shakespear and Mr Colvin, the above remarks are not intended to call in question their good intention and zeal'.

In this letter the Court laid down proper audit mechanisms, one of these being the inclusion in 'the general account all the receipts from the Town Duties and the Lottery funds'. When works of 'urgent necessity' were undertaken, the Government was to order disbursement from the treasury 'under those safeguards of check and control which ought to be universally established on the expenditure of public money'. The Court ordered that 'large sums may no longer be placed at the disposal of individuals or members of committees for *supposed* [emphasis added] improvement of Calcutta or other towns'. It wrote: 'In furtherance of our orders,[35] we trust that you will have *abolished* [emphasis added] the Lottery Committee, and in this expectation we shall refrain from making any detailed remarks on such of the proceedings for the committee as you have lately brought to our notice'. After this, the Government had no choice but to bring down the curtain on the Lottery Committee. The Wheel of History had turned one more notch and the time had arrived for setting up another committee for the improvement of Calcutta, the Fever Hospital Committee.

ENDNOTES

INTRODUCTION

1 This part of the Census (Volume 7, Part 1), entitled 'A Short History of Calcutta' and written by A.K. Ray of the Provincial Civil Service, Bengal, was published as a separate book (by Riddhi-India) in 1982 under the same name. The quoted passage appears on p. 73 of the Census document and on p. 159 of the book.

2 Published by Niyogi Books, New Delhi, 2016.

3 See 'Epilogue'. The East India Company's instruction to 'abolish' the Lottery Committee was issued in February 1829 but, going by the index to the volumes of the Judicial Criminal Proceedings at the West Bengal State Archives (WBSA), the committee continued to function as a separate entity till the early 1840s. Among other things, it continued to hold the two lotteries every year. In 1840 the Court of Directors ordered the discontinuance 'of Rs 200 per mensem [given] to him [the secretary of the committee] on account of office rent' and removal of the committee's office 'to the General Treasury buildings'. The last year for which the index has a separate listing of the Lottery Committee's activities is 1843.

4 For the new names of streets, see P.T. Nair, *A History of Calcutta's Streets* (Calcutta: Firma KLM, 1987).

5 Calcutta, 1837. The monograph launched effectively the move to set up the Fever Hospital Committee in 1835 (Judicial Criminal Proceedings, 16 June 1835, West Bengal State Archives). At the time, Martin was Presidency Surgeon and Surgeon to the Native Hospital.

6 *Extracts from the Topography and Vital Statistics of Calcutta* (Calcutta, 1849). Strong was Surgeon of 24-Parganas.

7 See Ray Choudhury, *A City in the Making*.

8 A.K. Ray writes that 'the practice of raising money for public improvements by means of lotteries first came into fashion' in 1793 (*A Short History of Calcutta*, p. 158). W.S. Seton-Karr edited, *Selections from Calcutta Gazettes*, vol. 2 (Calcutta, 1865), p. 563, carries a lottery advertisement inserted by the Commissioners of the Bengal Lottery for 1793 on 8 August 1793. The lottery was to be held for the setting up of a hospital for natives (ibid., p. 542). See chapter 'A Committee is Set Up', note 4.

9 See chapter 'River Water for the Town'.

10 Lord Amherst brought back the magistrates on to centre stage when he arrived in August 1823 their responsibility being limited to the 'operation of the magistrates in the Conservancy Department'. These were 'more effectual and systematic draining of the town', extension of the aqueducts to the principal streets, watering of the main streets and roads during the dry season, lighting of the streets, and paving of streets or lanes which 'are at present made of earth only'. The shift in responsibility

has to be seen against the background of the arrival of the new Governor-General who had probably been briefed before he left home by the Court of Directors on the work of the Lottery Committee, specifically the need to reduce its work burden (Judicial Criminal Proceedings, 25 September 1823). Within two months the magistrates had got down to work, submitting to the Government a list of streets they wanted to water along with the number of *bheesties* required for the job (ibid., 20 November 1823).

11 Peter Robb, *Sentiment and Self: Richard Blechynden's Calcutta Diaries, 1791-1822* (New Delhi: Oxford University Press, 2011), pp 191-192. The three volumes in the series (see Bibliography), based mainly on the voluminous diary kept by the senior Blechynden, are invaluable for the light they throw (at the micro level) on the events of the time and the insights they provide into relationships among the sahibs and between sahibs and natives in course of professional work and the development of personal ties. As of now, there is no comparable source of *first-hand* information on the Calcutta magistracy during the period under study, the magistrates epitomising the basic features of the old system of work.

12 On the Blechyndens, see chapter 'A Committee is Set Up', note 17.

13 See chapter 'The *Maidan*, Tank Square, Clive Street…'

14 See chapter 'A Committee is Set Up'.

15 See 'Epilogue'.

16 W.C. Blaquiere, the city police magistrate, arrived in Calcutta in 1777 (the year is engraved in the epitaph of his tomb) along with his father Jacob, Superintendent of Piece Goods (Peter Robb, *Useful Friendship: Europeans and Indians in Early Calcutta* [New Delhi: Oxford University Press, 2014], p. 7). He died in 1853 and lies buried in the Circular Road cemetery. See also H.E.A. Cotton, *Calcutta Old and New* (Calcutta: W Newman and Co., 1907), p. 583.

17 In its 14th June letter the committee had suggested that Rs 9,045-2-3 due to Blaquiere 'on account of the provision of bricks and *coah* from the 16th February 1811 to the 30th April 1814' be paid to him (Judicial Criminal Proceedings, 12 July 1814).

18 Ibid.

19 *Sentiment and Self*, pp 194-195.

20 Judicial Criminal Proceedings, 24 October 1815. See chapter 'A Committee is Set Up'.

21 See 'Epilogue'.

22 Despatch from the Court of 26 February 1817, paragraph 8 (that is, before the establishment of the Lottery Committee); in Letters from the Court of Directors, Judicial, West Bengal State Archives.

23 A footprint of this confusing practice is to be found in the arrangement of the official records of the Government at Fort William (preserved at the West Bengal State Archives) into Judicial Civil and Judicial Criminal Proceedings.

24 See chapter 'River Water for the Town'.

25 See chapter 'Reforming the Lottery System'.

26 The Cornwallis Street-Amherst Street project. See chapter 'Birth of Three More Squares' and 'Epilogue'.

27 See 'Epilogue'.

28 As Lewis Namier once wrote citing George Meredith, the English novelist, the 'parent question of humanity' is, 'Am I thy master or thou mine?' (Essay on 'Trotsky' in *Skyscrapers and Other Essays* [London: Macmillan, 1931], p. 84).
29 See chapter 'Henry Shakespear's Minutes'.
30 Judicial Criminal Proceedings, 26 July 1804; Lottery Committee (LC) Proceedings, 3 February 1820 (Victoria Memorial Hall). The letter of John Lumsden, Chief Secretary to the Government, and the suggestions for improvement made by Lord Wellesley's Committee for the Improvement of the Town in 1804 are important, first, because they portray in some detail the state of the town before the era of planned development began in Calcutta and, secondly, they underscore the basic similarity between the earlier suggestions and the schemes proposed by the Lottery Committee. See Ray Choudhury, *A City in the Making*, pp 408-417, 419-423.
31 See chapter 'The *Maidan*, Tank Square, Clive Street…'
32 The native involved was Madhab Dutt. See chapter 'Cossitala, Colootala, Garden Reach…'
33 See chapter 'Strand Road – Step by Step'.

A COMMITTEE IS SET UP

1 See Ray Choudhury, *A City in the Making*, pp 16, 22–23, 104 (note 52), 117.
2 His decision to build the Government House in Calcutta (today's Raj Bhavan) is the best manifestation of this streak in him. See Ray Choudhury, *The Lord Sahib's House* (Calcutta: Wild Strawberries Books, 2010), p. 132.
3 Ibid., pp. 121-122 and chapter 9.
4 Lottery funds were already being used to raise money for executing public projects such as putting up the Town Hall and 'for the reception, among other objects, of the statues voted to the late Marquis Cornwallis and Marquis Wellesley' – letter of G. Dowdeswell, in Judicial Criminal Proceedings, 16 October 1807.
5 Ibid., 20 January 1809.
6 See Ray Choudhury, *A City in the Making*, chapters 27 and 28.
7 John Adam had joined the service as a writer in 1791 and had become a member of the Governor-General's Council on 29 January 1819 – E. Dodwell and J.S. Miles edited, *Alphabetical List of the Bengal Civil Servants, 1780-1838* (London: Longman, Orme and Brown, 1839), pp 4–5.
8 The records do not throw any light on what these difficulties were.
9 Dowdeswell and Fombelle had joined as writers in 1783, Thornhill in 1790, the latter becoming a Director of the East India Company in 1815 after resigning from the service in 1812 (Dodwell and Miles, *Bengal Civil Servants,* pp 146–147, 178–179, 510–511).
10 The details of the first Calcutta lottery are to be found in the Judicial Criminal Proceedings of 20 January 1809. The currency denominations were the rupee, anna and pie, 12 pies making an anna and 16 annas a rupee.
11 Registrar.
12 See chapter 'The First Planned Square' for details on the genesis of the Tank-Excavation Committee.
13 Judicial Criminal Proceedings, 14 October 1817.
14 Letters to the Court of Directors, Judicial, 29 October 1817, paragraph 133.

15 Judicial Criminal Proceedings, 21 October 1817; Lottery Committee (LC) Proceedings, 24 November 1817.

16 Colvin, Jr, was one of the directors of the Bank of Bengal (*The East India Register* for 1819, p. 127). His father, Alexander Colvin, Sr, was a leading merchant of Calcutta who was, among other things, a partner of the firm Colvins, Bazett and Company. It was after him that the old Cutchagoody Ghat, at the head of Hastings Street, was renamed Colvin's Ghat. After his death in December 1818 an impressive memorial was installed at St. John's Church which catches the eye even now two centuries later. Strangely, his tomb in the South Park Street Cemetery is nondescript enough to be easily lost among the other monuments.

17 Arthur Blechynden's father, Richard, remained 'Surveyor of Roads' to the magistrates till his death on 4 February 1822, the son ultimately succeeding to the position. See Robb, *Sentiment and Self*, pp 138-139; also his *Sex and Sensibility: Richard Blechynden's Calcutta Diaries, 1791-1822* (New Delhi: Oxford University Press, 2011), p. 5.

18 Judicial Criminal Proceedings of date. 'Baparitala' is not shown in either Mark Wood's map of 1784-85 or Aaron Upjohn's of 1792-93.

19 See chapter 'The First Planned Square'. Also, Judicial Criminal Proceedings, 28 March 1817.

20 See below for the Lottery Committee's recommendation on the subject and the Government's 1819 decision. See also the chapter 'Birth of a Canal' in Ray Choudhury, *A City in the Making*.

21 LC Proceedings, 24 November 1817, *passim*.

22 Eliot passed away on 19 January 1818 (Dodwell and Miles, *Bengal Civil Servants*, pp 158-159) while Bayley went on to become Chief Secretary in early 1819.

23 Ibid., pp 30-31, 158-159, 530-531.

24 LC Proceedings, 18 December 1817.

25 See chapter 'Filthy State of the Drains' for Henry Wood's initiative to clean up the town's drains.

26 See chapter 'Henry Shakespear's Minutes' for Gordon's further views on the subject.

27 *Calcutta Old and New*, p. 183.

28 See chapter 'The *Maidan*, Tank Square, Clive Street...'

29 In the first decade of the 19th century the description '*pucka* pavement' referred to a particular method of road-making and not to what we would call a pavement or footpath today. Thus, the records (Judicial Criminal Proceedings, 22 February 1811) contain an estimate (Rs 12,285-0-0) being submitted by Richard Blechynden in February 1808 for 'a *pucka* pavement' the actual cost incurred being Rs 12,298-7-6.

30 LC Proceedings, 18 December 1817, *passim*.

31 See chapter 'Filthy State of the Drains' for Wood's views on drainage of the city in February 1818.

32 LC Proceedings, 11 December 1817.

33 Judicial Criminal Proceedings, 22 April 1814. Schalch's map calls it Dhobah Pooker. The great jail stood on the present site of the Victoria Memorial Hall.

34 Judicial Criminal Proceedings, 1 April 1814; LC Proceedings, 11 December 1817. The tank was dug in 1790-91 and filled at the turn of the 19th century. The Esplanade 'tram goomty', the well-known Calcutta landmark, was located on

the tank's site the structure being pulled down in the 1970s when the city's first metro railway line was being constructed. See W.S. Seton-Karr, ed., *Selections from Calcutta Gazettes*, vol. 2 (Calcutta, 1865), pp 13-14; Ray, *A Short History of Calcutta*, p. 246; Nair, *Calcutta's Streets*, p. 834.

35 Although the tank was named after John Eliot, who presided over the committee for improving the town of Calcutta in 1813, its digging was first recommended by George Dowdeswell who was at the time, as well as being a member of the committee, Chief Secretary to the Government (Judicial Criminal Proceedings, 23 January 1813).

36 LC Proceedings, 5 February 1818, *passim*.

37 Charles Richard Barwell, the Acting Magistrate of the Suburbs of Calcutta, had just been appointed (on 27 January 1818) a member of the committee in place of Eliot (ibid., 12 February 1818).

38 Ibid., 8 July 1819.

39 Archibald Trotter, who had joined as a writer in 1807, had gone to England on leave in December 1818, returning to India in 1823. He was succeeded by John Trotter as Superintendent of the Lotteries (Dodwell and Miles, *Bengal Civil Servants*, pp 526-527; Judicial Criminal Proceedings, 24 December 1818; LC Proceedings, 26 December 1818, 28 January and 18 March 1819).

40 See 'Epilogue'.

41 LC Proceedings, 5 February 1818.

42 Judicial Criminal Proceedings, 13 May 1819; LC Proceedings, 24 June 1819. In fact, immediately after its formation the Lottery Committee had suggested that 'the balance at the Bank of Bengal on account of unclaimed prizes be paid into the general treasury', a proposal which was accepted (Judicial Criminal Proceedings, 30 December 1817).

43 Ibid., 24 June 1819.

44 LC Proceedings, 18 January 1821.

45 Ibid., 15 February 1821. Incidentally, the estimate was prepared by Azoddey *mistry* (is this Azimuddin who figures later in the works undertaken by the Lottery Committee?), a member of that vast tribe of Calcutta native workmen which played its role diligently in the march of history during the period under study but which has been largely forgotten today, not even finding a place in a passing note.

46 Ibid., 8 March 1821.

47 Ibid., 11 December 1817.

48 Ibid. of date.

49 Ibid., 15 April 1819.

50 See chapter 'The *Maidan*, Tank Square, Clive Street…' for the Lottery Committee not accepting the cost estimate of a project drawn up by Trower in 1821, a rare occurrence in the period under study. Trower arrived in India in February 1797 and was in official harness as Civil Auditor till his death on November 19 1842 (information derived from fibis.org, accessed on 30 December 2018; see also *The Bengal Directory* for 1842, p. 35).

51 The details of the statement can be found in LC Proceedings, 14 October 1819.

52 Ibid. See Judicial Criminal Proceedings, 29 October 1819 for refund of the sums taken from the lottery funds for making the Beliaghata canal; also LC Proceedings, 25 November 1819.

53 LC Proceedings, 15 January 1818.
54 The new rules governing the Lottery Committee's functions came into effect three weeks later, on 21 October 1817, under which only the making of new roads would be the responsibility of the Lottery Committee. The letter from Eliot, Trower and Wood was dated 25 September which means that they were acting under guidelines which existed prior to the appointment of the committee.
55 LC Proceedings, 24 May 1821. See next chapter for more changes suggested on the audit front.
56 The officer concerned was Henry Wood, the project for which the funds were withdrawn being the 'extension of the aqueduct from the corner of Dhurrumtullah as far as the Birjee Tullow', which was not completed (ibid., 17 September 1818). See chapter 'River Water for the Town'.
57 Ibid., 15 January 1818. See 'Epilogue' for the stringent comment made by the Court of Directors on this aspect of the financial performance of the magistrates.
58 See 'Epilogue'.
59 LC Proceedings, 4 May 1820. There was a definite schedule involving the procedure for in early May the following year (1821) the Sub-Treasurer again submitted the receipt-disbursement account of the general treasury relating to the lottery funds, as well as an interest account, from 1 November 1820 to 30 April 1821 (ibid., 10 May 1821).
60 A year later, on 18 May 1821, the committee was asked to submit 'a general statement of the receipts and disbursements of the lottery funds', and a second statement relating to the balance of those funds remaining in the treasury on 30 April 1821 and whether any portion of the balance 'is subject to deduction or of appropriations sanctioned by Government for public works now in progress'. It was in response to these specific demands that the committee set up a standing sub-committee of accounts (ibid., 24 May 1821).
61 Similar instructions were sent to Trower a year later, on 10 May 1821, for a statement of disbursements made from his treasury to the lottery funds between 31 October 1820 and 30 April 1821 (ibid., 10 May 1821).
62 Ibid., 15 June and 4 May 1820.
63 Ibid., 3 August 1820, *passim.*
64 Ibid., 28 January 1819. Robert Leny arrived in India in 1798 and had initially joined the Military Department. In 1799 he was asked to join as surgeon to the civil officers' deputation which had gone to Ramgarh on some work (Judicial Criminal Proceedings, 19 April 1799). By 1812 he was Staff Surgeon to the Commander-in-Chief and Secretary of the Medical Board.
65 LC Proceedings, 7 September 1820. Peter Robb writes that 'Much business was conducted informally, without written orders.' See his *Sentiment and Self*, pp 246-247, note 38.
66 LC Proceedings of date.
67 Ibid., 19 July 1821.
68 Ibid., 7 September 1820.
69 Ibid., 18 May 1820.
70 See 'Epilogue'.
71 See chapter 'Filthy State of the Drains'.

72 LC Proceedings, 24 February 1820.
73 Ibid., 23 March 1820.

REFORMING THE LOTTERY SYSTEM

1 LC Proceedings, 26 March 1818.
2 The contingency expenses of the Calcutta lotteries were under control throughout the life of the Lottery Committee. In 1830, for example, they remained at Rs 2,000 for the second of the two draws held that year (Judicial Criminal Proceedings, 13 April 1830).
3 The LC Proceedings of 23 October 1818 contain a letter from Archibald Trotter dated 5 October which spelt out in detail the structure of the contingency expenditure of the lottery establishment, the Government asking the superintendent to exercise his 'discretion in the gradual adoption of the several suggestions' made by him towards reducing the contingency charges.
4 Ibid., 26 February 1818.
5 Ibid., 21 May 1818, *passim.*
6 Wood was Trotter's senior in the service by three years, the two being appointed writers in 1804 and 1807, respectively (Dodwell and Miles, *Bengal Civil Servants,* pp 526-527, 572-573).
7 LC Proceedings, 4 June 1818.
8 Ibid., 12 March and 9 April 1818; Judicial Criminal Proceedings, 24 March 1818.
9 Judicial Criminal Proceedings, 24 December 1818 and 8 January 1819.
10 LC Proceedings, 4 March 1819, *passim.*
11 This was not a new observation. In December 1817 Archibald Trotter had written to the Government suggesting, among other things, that 'the balance at the Bank of Bengal on account of prizes unclaimed be paid into the general treasury' (Judicial Criminal Proceedings, 30 December 1817).
12 LC Proceedings, 15 April 1819, *passim.*
13 Among the early changes sought by the new committee in December 1817 regarding the release of funds, the Government had been asked to arrange for payments from the treasury of the Collector of 24-Parganas instead of from the general treasury (Judicial Criminal Proceedings, 30 December 1817; LC Proceedings, 11 December 1817).
14 LC Proceedings, 14 October 1819, *passim.*
15 Ibid., 9 March 1820.
16 Ibid.
17 LC Proceedings, 23 March 1820.
18 Ibid.
19 Ibid., 15 June 1820, *passim.*
20 These were times when months elapsed before news of developments in England reached Calcutta. Having ascended the throne of Great Britain and Ireland on 25 October 1760, George III had died on 29 January 1820 and had been succeeded by his son George IV. That the news had not reached Calcutta by the end of May is indicated by the fact that the Superintendent of the Lotteries was referring to the relevant Act as one relating to 'the present reign' (that of George III).
21 LC Proceedings, 15 June 1820, *passim.*

22 Written on 30 May 1820 with a postscript dated 7 June.
23 LC Proceedings, 20 July 1820. Gordon had mentioned the names of John Adam, the civilian, and A.C. Seymour, the Registrar of Lotteries, who had supported the idea as early as 1812 that big prize tickets were far more important than those with a 'middling value' in attracting the notice of serious investors (ibid., 15 June 1820).
24 Ibid., 17 September 1818.
25 Ibid., 7 October 1818.
26 Judicial Criminal Proceedings, 25 September 1823.
27 Ibid., 14 April 1825.
28 Ibid., 29 September 1825, 27 March and 7 September 1826.
29 In 1823, Lord Amherst decided that Rs 1 lakh from the town duties would be set aside for the lottery funds every year, the expectation being the injection of extra funds would enable the Lottery Committee to focus more extensively on improving the conditions prevailing in the suburbs. An additional Rs 75,000 from the town duties was to be used annually by the Conservancy magistrates to help with activities formerly looked after by the committee (Judicial Criminal Proceedings, 25 September 1823).
30 Ibid., 13 April 1830.
31 LC Proceedings, 18 January 1821, *passim.*
32 On account of the 24th Lottery, sold by public auction on 15 September 1820, the Bank of Bengal paid into the Government's coffers Rs 88,500 (up from the usual Rs 72,000) comprising 'the 12 per cent commission and premium'; ibid., 8 March 1821.
33 LC Proceedings, 18 January 1821, *passim.*
34 Ibid., 18 January 1821.
35 Ibid.
36 Ibid., 10 February and 5 April, 1821. For objections to the new scheme, see ibid., 9 August 1821.

THE FIRST PLANNED SQUARE

1 Judicial Criminal Proceedings, 14 March 1815.
2 See chapter 'River Water for the Town'.
3 Judicial Criminal Proceedings, 14 March 1815. See also ibid., 16 June 1835 for J.R. Martin's later view of filling up tanks with 'wholesome water' and keeping them clean, generally.
4 Ibid., 14 March 1815. The Government was, in fact, responding to the stand taken by the Calcutta magistrates (21 February) on certain points made by Wood on 22 December 1814, the details of which are to be found in the chapter 'River Water for the Town'.
5 Ibid., 28 March 1817.
6 See chapter 'River Water for the Town' for details.
7 Judicial Criminal Proceedings, 28 March 1817.
8 Ibid., 6 June 1817.
9 Ibid.
10 LC Proceedings, 15 January 1818; Judicial Criminal Proceedings, 14 October 1817, *passim.*

11 James Weir Hogg's name is missing but this does not mean that he was no longer a part of the proceedings. The records (LC Proceedings, 24 November 1817) indicate that the plan for the Baparitala square, tank and road was recommended by Eliot, Trower, Wood *and* Hogg, the last-named being very much a part of the Tank-Excavation Committee. This apart, the Government's 14 October approval letter to the committee included Hogg's name (LC Proceedings, 15 January 1818). The Baparitala project was transferred to the Lottery Committee (of which Hogg was not a member) after its formation on 21 October (LC Proceedings, 24 November 1817), the latter giving charge of the project to Eliot, Trower and Wood by a resolution passed at its 24 November meeting.

12 Neither the plan of the square and tank nor the cost estimate was sent to London. See 'Epilogue'.

13 Dodwell and Miles, *Bengal Civil Servants*, pp 158-159. He was interred in the North Park Street Cemetery which no longer exists (see *The Bengal Obituary*, p. 200).

14 LC Proceedings, 12 February 1818.

15 Judicial Criminal Proceedings, 3 March 1818 (34); LC Proceedings, 12 February 1818.

16 In 1785 Imambaksh (Emaum Bux) was the 'superintendent officer' of the *thana* set up at the Armenian Church, one of seven established for the 'English Town' by a notification dated 9 June 1785 (Seton-Karr, *Calcutta Gazettes,* vol. 1, pp 115-116). There was also a road named after him in north Calcutta (Nair, *Calcutta's Streets,* p. 418). Conjecturally, if this Imambaksh was the same man who was obstructing the Lottery Committee's plans in 1818, he must have been around 60 years old at the time assuming he was around 30 when he was made a *thanadar* in 1785.

17 For the Jury Act, see Ray Choudhury, *A City in the Making*, pp 525-527.

18 *The East India Register* for 1819 (p. 134) refers to a W. Black who owned at least one ship.

19 Judicial Criminal Proceedings, 3 March 1818; LC Proceedings, 12 March 1818.

20 LC Proceedings, 1 October 1818. Article 8 of the bye-law gave the Justices of the Peace the power 'to treat and agree with the owners of such lands, houses, tenements and other hereditaments…as it shall and may be necessary to purchase for the purposes of cutting any drains or sewers and of making and completing such roads, streets and passages'.

21 LC Proceedings, 12 February 1818.

22 Ibid., 1 October 1818.

23 Ibid., 1 October 1818 and 4 March 1819.

24 Judicial Criminal Proceedings, 9 October 1818; LC Proceedings, 5 November 1818.

25 LC Proceedings, 4 March 1819.

26 LC Proceedings, 24 June 1819.

27 Ibid., 9 December 1819. Article 9 of the bye-law stipulated that in case of any refusal on the part of any person to agree with the Justices of the Peace on 'the sale of any such lands, houses, tenements or hereditaments', the Justices were to 'cause the value of the said premises to be enquired into, and ascertained, by and on the oath of a jury of twelve indifferent men'. Where the property concerned belonged to a native,

the jury would have to include 'natives together with British subjects' 'resident in the same settlement'. The jury was to decide on the damages and compensation to be made to owners and other people involved in the premises concerned.

28 Judicial Criminal Proceedings, 17 December 1819; LC Proceedings, 23 December 1819.

29 LC Proceedings, 13 January and 23 March 1820.

30 Ibid., 23 March 1820.

31 Ibid., 20 April 1820.

32 Ibid., *passim.*

33 Ibid., 1 June 1820.

34 Ibid., 15 June 1820. The description 'Moira Square' is used for the first time in a letter written by Shakespear to the Lottery Committee on 9 March 1820 (ibid., 9 March 1820). Prior to this date, Lt Paton had referred to it as 'Dhurrumtollah Square' (ibid., 3 February 1820).

35 See chapter 'Birth of Three More Squares' for another case where the argument was forwarded that if Hindu families were moved from their ancestral house it would have serious social repercussions.

36 LC Proceedings, 20 July 1820. For the committee's 18 May 1820 request, see chapter 'A Committee is Set Up'.

37 A month later, on 1 August, Trower submitted to the committee a list of 38 people who had executed deeds of conveyance regarding the sale of their houses and premises for the construction of the tank and square (ibid., 7 September 1820). Of interest is the fact that the 'bibees' who figured in the list were prostitutes/courtesans indicating, among other things, their contemporary economic and social status (see S.N. Mukherjee, *Calcutta: Myths and History* [Calcutta, 1977], pp 99, 101-102).

38 LC Proceedings, 20 July 1820.

39 Ibid., 9 March 1820.

40 Shakespear told the committee on 16 August 1821 (ibid., 23 August 1821) that the quality of the spring water was bad. In view of the representations made to him on the subject, he suggested the construction of 'a conduit from the aqueduct' on Dharamtala Road to the tank 'for the purpose of filling it from the river', the cost of the project being 'inconsiderable'.

41 LC Proceedings, 7 September 1820.

42 Ibid., 5 October 1820. See chapter 'The Land of William Camac'.

43 Ibid., 7 September 1820.

44 Ibid., 15 January 1818.

45 Ibid., 7 September 1820.

46 On 17 April 1822, the subcommittee in charge of making the Wellington Square and the road to Bowbazar submitted its final consolidated statement of accounts for the entire project, the total expenditure coming to Rs 2,84,881-4-18 (Judicial Criminal Proceedings, 9 May 1822).

47 LC Proceedings, 20 July 1820.

48 Judicial Criminal Proceedings, 25 August 1820; LC Proceedings, 7 September 1820. See also LC Proceedings, 15 January 1818.

49 LC Proceedings, 9 November 1820.

50 Ibid.
51 Ibid., 26 October 1820.
52 Ibid., 26 October 1820 and 8 March 1821.
53 Ibid., 8 March and 19 April 1821.

BIRTH OF THREE MORE SQUARES

1 LC Proceedings, 8 March 1821, *passim*.
2 Creek Row, the name appearing in Schalch's map of 1824 (see Fig. 9).
3 The *khal* was in all probability a remnant of the ancient creek which ran from the river in the west to the salt lake in the east.
4 This was a debatable point. See previous chapter (notes) for Henry Shakespear's contrary view.
5 LC Proceedings, 21 June 1821.
6 Ibid., 8 March 1821, *passim.*
7 A statement on the general funds position of the Calcutta lotteries till 31 October 1820 is included in ibid.
8 Ibid., 19 April 1821.
9 Ibid.
10 Ibid., 10 May 1821.
11 The Simleah area of Calcutta derived its name originally from a profusion of the '*simuleah*', or cotton, tree which marked the place. It was bound on the north by Beadon Street, on the west by Central Avenue, on the east by Amherst Street, and on the south by Baranoshi Ghosh's Street (*Bengal Past and Present*, vol. 29, p. 101).
12 Judicial Criminal Proceedings, 22 August 1822.
13 Ibid.
14 See previous chapter for details.
15 Judicial Criminal Proceedings, 22 August 1822.
16 Thantania Kalibari.
17 Judicial Criminal Proceedings, 22 August and 1 November 1822.
18 LC Proceedings of date.
19 On 23 December 1823, the Lottery Committee had sent the Government a list of 126 people from whom ground and buildings had been bought for the purpose of making College Street and Square (Judicial Criminal Proceedings of date).
20 LC Proceedings, 27 September 1821.
21 LC Proceedings, 11 October 1821.
22 Judicial Criminal Proceedings, 4 May 1826. On 31 October 1823, the subcommittee looking after the project told the Lottery Committee that, as the Hindu College 'is to be built on the north side of the new square', it wanted the square to be named College Square and the road from Bowbazar to Machua Bazar College Street, names which have, mercifully, stuck for two centuries (ibid., 23 December 1823).
23 On the tunnel, see chapter 'The *Maidan*, Tank Square, Clive Street…'
24 Judicial Criminal Proceedings, 22 March 1827.
25 Ibid., 20 March 1823, *passim*.
26 For the Colinga improvements, see chapter 'The *Maidan*, Tank Square, Clive Street…'
27 See Judicial Criminal Proceedings, 20 March 1823 for details.

28 Appended to the proposal, which was approved by the Government in March, was a list of owners of land and buildings whose property would be required for the project, and the expected expenditure under the separate heads (ibid.).
29 Judicial Criminal Proceedings, 27 January 1825.
30 Was this Henry Wray who was a Lt-Col. in the infantry in 1787 ('The Bengal Calendar for the Year 1787' in *The European Magazine and London Review*, vol. 11 for 1787, London, after p. 296)?
31 Probably John Chew, Senior Pilot (*East India Register* for 1819, p. 118).
32 Judicial Criminal Proceedings, 8 January 1824.
33 Ibid., 27 January 1825, *passim*.
34 Ibid., 4 May 1826.
35 Ibid., 22 March 1827.
36 This was the madrassa which was founded by Warren Hastings and was formerly located in Bowbazar.
37 Judicial Criminal Proceedings, 27 January 1825.
38 Ibid., 23 December 1823.
39 Judicial Criminal Proceedings, 23 December 1823. This advance came in for severe criticism from the Court of Directors in 1827. See the last note of this chapter; also see 'Epilogue' for the Directors' critique of the entire financial arrangement made for the project.
40 Judicial Criminal Proceedings, 17 February 1825. The resale issue became complicated later; see below.
41 The obstacle put up by Gopimohun Deb, the adopted son of Nabakrishna Deb and father of Radhakanta Deb, is of interest because this was perhaps the first time that the Lottery Committee's work in improving Calcutta was challenged by a *talukdar* whose main point was that, in dealing with landowners individually, the committee was violating his *talukdari* rights, which entitled him to certain payments made by the purchasers of such land (Judicial Criminal Proceedings, 24 March 1825). The Lottery Committee recommended the setting up of a jury which was agreed to by the Government on 24 March (Judicial Criminal Proceedings, 25 March and 29 April 1824). Deb went to the Supreme Court and when the latter issued orders 'allowing the pleas filed by the Company and the Lottery Committee', he appealed to His Majesty-in-Council in England (ibid., 24 November 1825). See chapter 'Strand Road – Step by Step' for the final outcome of the action.
42 Judicial Criminal Proceedings, 9 June 1825.
43 Writing in 1830, F.P. Strong says (*Topography and Vital Statistics of Calcutta*, p. 30) that, following the construction of the new square, the area had become 'very healthy' there being now 'an excellent square, a good large tank with iron rails round the grounds…' The Judicial Criminal Proceedings of 31 May 1827 carries the list of people who sold their land and buildings for the making of Cornwallis Street.
44 Judicial Criminal Proceedings, 31 May 1827 and 7 November 1828 provides the list of owners from whom ground was bought for the Amherst Street project.
45 George Money was a barrister and Standing Counsel for the East India Company (*East India Register* for 1819, p. 125).
46 Judicial Criminal Proceedings, 29 May 1829.

47 The details of the transaction with Money are to be found in Judicial Criminal Proceedings, 7 November 1828.

'FILTHY STATE OF THE DRAINS'

1 Judicial Criminal Proceedings, 27 September 1814.

2 Known for decades as Red Road, renamed Indira Gandhi Sarani.

3 See later for Henry Wood's critique of the drainage system existing at the time, and also for the views of Henry Shakespear.

4 Eliot had headed Lord Minto's Committee for the Improvement of the Town in 1813 (Judicial Criminal Proceedings, 14 May 1813). See *A City in the Making*, pp 508-509, for Eliot's 'success' in 1813 of ridding Chitpur Road of the scourge of regular flooding following 'any slight excess of rain'.

5 LC Proceedings, 18 December 1817, *passim.*

6 In the early years of the English settlement, the 'thickness of the trees' was seen by the Bengal Council as an impediment to healthy city life and steps had to be taken to cut it down to improve conditions (in 1711 and 1757). Writing in 1828, F.P. Strong pointed to the 'great quantity of trees and *jangal* to the eastward of Calcutta' urging that it be removed to improve the health of the people of the city (*Topography and Vital Statistics of Calcutta,* pp 2-3). See also Ray Choudhury, *A City in the Making*, p. 126.

7 Judicial Criminal Proceedings, 6 January 1818, *passim.*

8 Ibid., 18 December 1817, *passim.*

9 LC Proceedings of date.

10 Ibid., 15 January 1818. In the event, the total investment for the project overshot the mark by Rs 2,991-11-11 on account of payment for land which had to be made to Ruplal Mullick (ibid., 4 March 1819).

11 He had made his first payment associated with the project on 9 December 1817 (ibid., 4 March 1819). For Eliot's death, see Dodwell and Miles, *Bengal Civil Servants*, pp 158-159.

12 Judicial Criminal Proceedings, 3 February 1818; LC Proceedings, 29 January 1818.

13 LC Proceedings, 4 March 1819.

14 Ibid., 24 November 1817.

15 See Ray Choudhury, *A City in the Making*, pp 419-420.

16 LC Proceedings, 12 March 1818, *passim.*

17 Richard Blechynden records in his voluminous diary at least one specific instance where the cart establishment was milked for pecuniary profit by those who were temporarily in charge of it – the case of constable Hessen, a henchman of the magistrate William Blaquiere (Robb, *Sentiment and Self*, p. 194).

18 LC Proceedings, 29 April 1819.

19 Ibid., 25 November 1819.

20 Ibid., 20 April 1820. Phipps, the Superintendent of Public Buildings in the Lower Provinces, had been appointed a member of the Lottery Committee on 26 February 1819 in place of Captain Montague who was leaving for Europe (Judicial Criminal Proceedings, 26 February 1819; LC Proceedings, 4 March 1819).

21 LC Proceedings, 20 April 1820, *passim.*

22 See 'Epilogue'. For details of the draining of Chitpur Road, see chapter 'Henry Shakespear's Minutes'.
23 LC Proceedings, 29 January 1818.
24 Ibid., 12 February 1818.
25 For the roads mentioned here, see Nair, *Calcutta's Streets*, pp 200, 248-249, 283, 335, 418, 485, 752, 801 and 808.
26 Judicial Criminal Proceedings, 24 December 1819; LC Proceedings, 13 January 1820.
27 LC Proceedings, 4 May 1820.
28 Ibid., 3 August 1820, *passim.*
29 Neither the LC Proceedings nor the Judicial Criminal Proceedings (of 11 May 1821) carry the full Schalch report.
30 See Ray Choudhury, *A City in the Making*, pp 488-489.
31 Brijootollah (Birjeetala) probably refers to the Chowringhee area till Circular Road (further south the area is designated 'Birjee' in Upjohn's map).
32 Judicial Criminal Proceedings, 11 May 1821; LC Proceedings, 21 September 1820 and 10 May 1821. Andrews was to be retained for the job for four months and paid a salary of Rs 800 a month.
33 Judicial Criminal Proceedings, 9 May 1822.
34 LC Proceedings, 21 September 1820.
35 Judicial Criminal Proceedings, 29 October 1819; LC Proceedings, 14 October 1819. The map of Calcutta was entitled the 'Plan of the City of Calcutta and its environs, surveyed by the late Major J A Schalch, for the use of the Lottery Committee, and containing all their improvements with additions from the Surveyor-General's office, and from recent surveys by Captain T Prinsep'. The version of it included in the *Atlas of the City of Calcutta* (the National Atlas and Thematic Mapping Organisation, 2010), was published after 1832 (see *Atlas* contents for the date). The copy of the map at the National Library in Kolkata is dated 1828. That Schalch completed the map in 1824 is suggested by the fact that the Government was writing to the Court of Directors on 3 September 1824 regarding its shipment to London (the relevant volume of Letters to the Court of Directors, Judicial, is missing at the West Bengal State Archives although the index to the letters has the entry concerned). See Robb, *Useful Friendship*, p. 279.
36 LC Proceedings, 14 October 1819.
37 No such sketch is to be found in the LC Proceedings of 14 October 1819 at the West Bengal State Archives.
38 Ibid., 4 November 1819.
39 Ibid., 25 November 1819.
40 Ibid., 6 July 1820.
41 Judicial Criminal Proceedings, 17 February 1825.
42 Territorial Revenue Proceedings, 28 July 1821, *passim.*
43 LC Proceedings, 23 August 1821. The Government set up a committee comprising Bayley, Shakespear, J. Young, Captain D. McLeod, Captain H. Morrieson and Gordon to study the Schalch project in its entirety.
44 Judicial Criminal Proceedings, 9 October 1823. The full report is to be found in Territorial Revenue Proceedings, 20 March 1823.

45 *The East India Register* for 1819 (p. 118) described James and Robert Kyd as 'master builders' and 'assistants' to the Master-Attendant.

46 Richard Blechynden passed away very soon after this, the Judicial Criminal Proceedings of 14 February 1822 recording his death and also the appointment of his son Arthur to the office of Superintendent of Roads. Henry Osborne was made Surveyor to the Lottery Committee.

47 See chapter 'Hare Street and its Vicinity'.

48 Territorial Revenue Proceedings of date, *passim.*

49 This was the Colootala Street-Mirzapur Road project, which has been discussed in some detail in the chapter 'Cossitala, Colootala, Garden Reach…'

50 Territorial Revenue Proceedings, 2 October 1823.

51 Judicial Criminal Proceedings, 9 October 1823.

RIVER WATER FOR THE TOWN

1 Judicial Criminal Proceedings, 14 May 1813. See also Ray Choudhury, *A City in the Making*, pp 498-499.

2 The word 'aqueduct' was not used by the improvement committee in the 1813 letter.

3 Judicial Criminal Proceedings, 28 February, 1815.

4 The *bheesties* were to be seen in Calcutta even in the 1950s not quite watering the roads (although they did that too in selected areas), but carrying water mainly from place to place. At the time Wood's suggestion on the building of aqueducts was being accepted by the Government, Maria Nugent, the wife of George Nugent, the Commander-in-Chief, wrote in her diary (1812): 'We have a good many of these people [*bheesties*] attached to our establishment – they all carry leather bags on their backs, or rather across their loins – the bag has a long neck to it, which they bring out on one side, and run along spouting out the water in the oddest manner – I cannot help laughing when I see them for it appears to be a most ridiculous occupation – yet this business, like all other trades and employments in this country, descends from father to son' (Ashley L. Cohen, ed., *Lady Nugent's East India Journal* [New Delhi: Oxford University Press, 2014], p. 53).

5 Judicial Criminal Proceedings, 14 May 1813.

6 The Chandpal Ghat waterwheel was proposed by the Committee for Improvement of the Town on 28 January 1814 and sanctioned by the Government the next day. (Ibid., 29 January and 15 April 1814.)

7 Ibid., 14 March 1815, *passim.*

8 Judicial Criminal Proceedings, 14 March 1815.

9 It was to the Board of Conservancy, appointed on 14 June 1814, that the duties of the committee for improving the town of Calcutta were transferred, the board being abolished in 1841 (ibid., 14 June 1814 and 27 April 1841).

10 Ibid., 24 October 1815.

11 Ibid. For a subsequent funds accounting problem, see chapter 'A Committee is Set Up'.

12 Judicial Criminal Proceedings, 22 December 1815.

13 For the construction of the balustrade on both sides of Red Road, see chapter 'The *Maidan*, Tank Square, Clive Street…'

14 Judicial Criminal Proceedings, 29 March 1822.
15 LC Proceedings of date.
16 Ibid., 11 December 1817. For the deepening of the Dharamtala tank, see Judicial Criminal Proceedings, 1 April 1814.
17 LC Proceedings, 11 December 1817.
18 Judicial Criminal Proceedings, 24 February 1818; LC Proceedings, 15 January 1818. The views of Wood included in the proceedings constitute partly an extract of his communication to the Government on the subject dated 12 March 1817 (see Judicial Criminal Proceedings, 28 March 1817). It is in the 12 March letter that he informed the Government of the completion of the extension of the aqueduct from the west end of Dharamtala to the west end of Burying Ground Road (Park Street).
19 This provides an idea of the state of the built-up part of the land immediately to the east of the Chowringhee Road in 1817. For the development of this area, see *A City in the Making*, chapter on 'Sprucing Up Chowringhee', p. 221.
20 Judicial Criminal Proceedings, 28 March 1817. There were three such tanks: the one opposite Park Street, Eliot's tank opposite today's Tata Centre, and the Birji *talao* itself which had been deepened and cleaned at a cost of Rs 5,619-4-1 in 1812, the project, incidentally, resulting from a demand for 'pure water' by the 'inhabitants of the southern end of Chowringhee' (ibid., 25 April 1812).
21 LC Proceedings, 15 January 1818. This, therefore, was the reason why the aqueduct was built between the drain and the road, which led to drainage problems later.
22 Judicial Criminal Proceedings, 14 March 1815.
23 Ibid., 24 February, 1818; LC Proceedings, 15 January 1818, *passim.*
24 LC Proceedings, 15 January 1818.
25 Ibid.
26 Ibid., 29 January 1818.
27 On 31 August 1820 Bayley and Colvin wrote to the Lottery Committee that Wood's 'absence' and the death of Arthur J. Macan (a member of the subcommittee at the time) had held up the project greatly (ibid., 13 January and 5 October 1820). Macan had passed away on 19 September 1819 and was buried in the South Park Street Cemetery (*The Bengal Obituary,* p. 142). George Ballard of Alexander and Company was made a member of the committee in place of Macan.
28 LC Proceedings, 5 October 1820. The Court of Directors later said that it had not been supplied with full and adequate information about the Dharamtala drainage project, the excess expenditure of Rs 1,200 on the European overseer's salary being specifically mentioned in this regard (Letters from the Court of Directors, Judicial, 13 December 1820). See 'Epilogue'.
29 LC Proceedings, 5 October 1820.
30 Ibid., 15 February 1821.
31 Ibid., 13 September 1821.
32 Ibid., 5 October 1820.
33 Ibid., 8 July 1819.
34 In fact, mounds of earth, gravel, *koah* and *soorkey* were to be found lying in the middle of the street all over the town where work was being done with the result that there was no dearth of reports of road accidents taking place in the journals

of the day (*The Calcutta Journal*, for example). See Satyajit Das compiled, *Selections from the Indian Journals*, pp 160 (vol. 1); pp 173-174, 199, 272-273 (vol. 2).

35 LC Proceedings, 2 September 1819.

36 Ibid.

37 Ibid.

38 For the technical aspect of the construction work, see the 31 August 1820 letter from the Subcommittee on Drains in Dharamtala to the Lottery Committee, the contract being handled by 'George Hays, Superintendent' (ibid., 5 October 1820).

39 Judicial Criminal Proceedings, 14 December 1819; LC Proceedings, 23 December 1819.

40 LC Proceedings, 7 September 1820.

41 Quoted in *The Calcutta Annual Register* for 1821, 'Bengal Occurrences', pp 25-26.

42 LC Proceedings, 4 March 1819.

43 Ibid.

44 Ibid., 1 April 1819, *passim.*

45 Ibid., 29 April 1819.

46 See Ray Choudhury, *A City in the Making*, pp 400-401, 502-504.

47 LC Proceedings, 13 January 1820.

48 Ibid.

49 Ibid., 3 February 1820, *passim.*

50 On perhaps the earliest proposal to 'convey water through the streets by cast iron pipes instead of brick channels', see Judicial Criminal Proceedings, 29 September, 1835. See also Letters to the Court of Directors, Judicial, 8 September 1836, paragraph 12.

51 On 3 November 1820, the Government was writing to the Court of Directors that it had sanctioned the purchase of a pair of 'sucking pumps' for raising water at Chandpal Ghat in March 1819. The previous reference to such pumps is 'china pumps' (Letters to the Court of Directors, Judicial, 3 November 1820, paragraph 147).

52 Judicial Criminal Proceedings, 30 December 1817, and 24 March, 9 and 16 June 1818; Letters to the Court of Directors, Judicial, 22 July 1818. On their part, the Directors felt generally that money spent on *bheesties* was not a sensible proposition. Commenting on the Government's establishment of *bheesties* to water the roads near Government House (amounting to Rs 414 a month), the Directors wrote that the employment of *bheesties* appeared to them 'to be very uneconomical', the Government being asked to ascertain 'whether the same object cannot be effected at a cheaper rate' (Letters from the Court of Directors, Judicial, 27 June 1821).

53 See Ray Choudhury, *A City in the Making*, pp 489-491, for a method proposed by Richard Blechynden to get river water into the town using the drains. See LC Proceedings, 6 August and 26 December 1818 for two other proposals made by J.R. Douglass and John Foster for the introduction of alternative technology to raise water, both of which were rejected by the Lottery Committee.

54 LC Proceedings, 16 July 1818.

55 Ibid., 6 August 1818.

56 Ibid., 26 December 1818.

57 See chapter 'Strand Road – Clearing the Table' for more on Jackson's Ghat.

58 LC Proceedings, 3 February 1820.
59 Ibid., 15 April 1819, 25 October and 13 December 1821.
60 Throwing some light on the transport and insurance charges of the time, the cost-sheet indicated that 'Freight to London by canal, wharfage [would cost] pound sterling 88-10-0, ditto to Calcutta 95-3-0, insurance to Calcutta, policy duty, etc, 23-10-0'.
61 An increase in the power of the steam engine and an expansion of reservoir capacity did occur over a period of time but not before the mid-1830s (Judicial Criminal Proceedings, 27 January and 7 March 1835).
62 LC Proceedings, 15 April 1819, *passim.*
63 Judicial Criminal Proceedings, 30 April 1819 (1, 3); LC Proceedings, 27 May 1819. Lt Forbes was then engaged in work at 'Titty Ghur' (Titagarh, to the north of Calcutta) which required 'much personal attendance'. On 24 September the Government agreed to the establishment charges proposed by Forbes, which came to Rs 229 per month. Additionally, an expenditure of Rs 429, incurred by Forbes on the city survey work during the months of June and July 1819, was to be paid to him by the committee (LC Proceedings, 14 October 1819). See chapter 'Filthy State of the Drains'.
64 LC Proceedings, 27 May 1819. Arthur Macan, who had introduced Jones to the Lottery Committee, was associated with the firm of Alexander and Company from which Jones had borrowed funds (*East India Register* for 1819, p. 158).
65 LC Proceedings, 9 December 1819.
66 Ibid., 23 December 1819.
67 Ibid., 21 September 1820.
68 For the town's air being vitiated by brick-making in 1778, see Ray Choudhury, *A City in the Making*, p. 374.
69 LC Proceedings, 7 December 1820.
70 This letter is incomplete in the LC Proceedings of 7 December 1820. It would appear from subsequent correspondence (see later) that the committee also wrote to Kyd and Company of Khidirpur on 15 December 1820 for its views on the subject.
71 See Nair, *Calcutta's Streets*, pp 852-853, for an informative note on Shobha Bazar Street.
72 LC Proceedings, 19 April 1821.
73 College Street, the plans for which had just been sanctioned by the Government. See chapter 'Birth of Three More Squares'.
74 LC Proceedings, 19 April, 1821.
75 Judicial Criminal Proceedings, 11 May 1821; LC Proceedings, 19 April and 10 May 1821.
76 A complete list of these items is to be found in the LC Proceedings of 25 October 1821.
77 Ibid., 10 May 1821.
78 Ibid., 27 September 1821. Jones died on 23 September and was buried in the North Park Street Cemetery (*The Bengal Obituary*, p. 203).
79 Ibid.
80 Judicial Criminal Proceedings, 8 February 1822.

HARE STREET AND ITS VICINITY

1 The native name of Church Lane is given as *pathuriagirjah-ka-paschim-rastah* (Nair, *Calcutta's Streets*, pp 262-263) the inference being that the name was given *after* the church was consecrated in 1787. Assuming that the road existed before this time, it ought to have had a different native name, if any at all. Whether it formed the western boundary of the settlement's first graveyard on the east bank of the river is not known. Today, the churchyard is bounded by Church Lane on the west.

2 The mint was set up in 1757. See H.N. Sinha, ed., *Fort William-India House Correspondence* (Delhi: Government of India, 1957), vol. 2, pp 274-275, paragraphs 76-78. See also chapter 'Strand Road – Clearing the Table'.

3 The 1753 plan shows a passage to the river south of the fort but there is no confirmation whatever that it had already been designated a street. H.E.A. Cotton's reasonable explanation of the name is that the Dutch word *tackshall*, meaning a Customs house (which then stood at the south-west corner of the old fort), had been misspelt and converted into 'Tankshall' (*Calcutta Old and New*, p. 327).

4 The editor of *Bengal Past and Present* (Vol. 2, Part 1, p. 216) wrote in 1908: 'The house in the corner formed by the junction of Hastings Street and Church Street was at the time the residence of Mrs [Eliza] Fay, and before her day it was the old Post Office and has thus given its name to Old Post Office Street.'

5 See S.C. Grier, *The Letters of Warren Hastings to his Wife* (London: William Blackwood, 1905), p. 94; Cotton, *Calcutta Old and New*, pp 319-320, for a description of the Governor-General's house at the turn of the 19th century. While the street had not yet got its name in 1784-85 (Hastings left India in February 1785), Upjohn's map of 1792-93 shows 'Hastings Street'.

6 Judicial Criminal Proceedings, 25 July 1805.

7 Gabriel Vrignon was described as a 'ship chandler' in *A New Oriental Directory* and *The East India Register* for 1802. In 1825 *The Bengal Directory* (p. 337) was describing Vrignon and Company as shipbuilders based in Howrah. The 1842 map of Calcutta published by the Society for the Diffusion of Useful Knowledge shows clearly Vrignon's Dock in Howrah opposite Mirbahar Ghat.

8 Judicial Criminal Proceedings, 25 July 1805. See also Ray Choudhury, *A City in the Making*, pp 453-457.

9 Board of Revenue Proceedings, 26 August 1796 (West Bengal State Archives).

10 Calcutta Committee of Revenue Proceedings, 20 April 1780 (West Bengal State Archives).

11 See Letters to the Court of Directors, Judicial, 3 November 1820, *passim*.

12 Judicial Criminal Proceedings, 24 February 1818; LC Proceedings, 26 February 1818. This was probably Francis Vrignon if his letter to the committee dated 8 March 1818 is any indication (LC Proceedings, 12 March 1818). *The East India Register* for 1819 (p. 129) described F and G Vrignon as a house of agency.

13 Probably Charles Becher who was at this time salt agent at Cuttack and Collector of Customs at Balasore (Dodwell and Miles, *Bengal Civil Servants*, pp 36-37; *East India Register* for 1819, pp 5, 22).

14 LC Proceedings, 9 April 1818.

15 Ibid.

16 This house was located on King's Bench Walk (ibid., 2 July 1818), its frontage being on Hastings Street, a part of which was required by the committee. Incidentally, in a letter to the Board of Revenue dated 11 July 1818, Charles Trower, Collector of 24-Parganas, refers to King's Bench Walk as King's Bench Walk Street (ibid., 6 August 1818).
17 LC Proceedings, 9 April 1818.
18 Ibid., 23 April 1818.
19 Ibid.
20 Ibid., 23 April and 21 May 1818. The spot of ground offered was located 'to the north of Mr Birch's buildings in Tank Square'. For the location of John Brereton Birch's property, see chapter 'The *Maidan*, Tank Square, Clive Street...'
21 LC Proceedings, 21 May 1818.
22 Ibid., 4 June 1818, *passim*.
23 Ibid., 18 June 1818.
24 Ibid., 2 July 1818.
25 Ibid.
26 Judicial Criminal Proceedings, 14 July 1809.
27 The language used in the 1809 letter suggests that Hare owned the house in which he lived. However, in Peary Chand Mittra's biography (*A Biographical Sketch of David Hare* [Calcutta: W Newman, 1877], pp 80, 121-122), Colesworthy Grant writes that Hare stayed with Earnest Grey, 'his old friend, at Hare street, where Grey's house was located' implying that the house did not belong to Hare. Mittra himself writes that Hare 'lived and died' in Grey's house. Incidentally, according to Grant, it was from this house that Hare walked to Barrackpore and back as part of a wager with a visitor.
28 Judicial Criminal Proceedings, 14 July 1809.
29 Ibid. See also Ray Choudhury, *A City in the Making*, pp 465-466.
30 See Ray Choudhury, ibid., p. 204, note 12.
31 Judicial Criminal Proceedings, 13 November 1810.
32 Ibid., 29 December 1809.
33 Ibid., 13 November 1810.
34 Probably the Police Office Street or Lane.
35 LC Proceedings, 16 July 1818.
36 The LC Proceedings of 6 August 1818 do not throw any light on what the measures were.
37 Ibid., 5 November 1818.
38 The infant's name was, in fact, Rajnarain Roy, his father being 'the late Rajah Cossinot [Kashinath] Roy' (Judicial Criminal Proceedings, 3 December 1819). At the time, the house was rented by one of the magistrates, Robert Fergusson.
39 See Judicial Criminal Proceedings, 15 January 1819 for the Lottery Committee's letter on 'excess of expence incurred for purchase of property in Hastings Street'.
40 LC Proceedings, 5 November 1818.
41 Judicial Criminal Proceedings, 16 October 1818; LC Proceedings, 5 November 1818. The railing was subsequently pushed back and alterations made in the church grounds. Today, the churchyard has been further encroached upon, as a visit to the area will show.

42 LC Proceedings, 26 December 1818.
43 See chapter 'The *Maidan*, Tank Square, Clive Street…' The tank referred to was located at the north-east end of what is today Sido-Kano Dahar (formerly Esplanade East), behind the line of houses fronting the road.
44 LC Proceedings, 26 December 1818. On Wood's footpath and balustrade, see chapter 'The *Maidan*, Tank Square, Clive Street…'
45 LC Proceedings, 26 December 1818 and 18 February 1819.
46 Judicial Criminal Proceedings, 15 January 1819; LC Proceedings, 18 February 1819.
47 Minutes of the 2 December 1818 meeting of St John's Church Vestry.
48 This was Eliza Fay's house, then owned by Madhub Dutt. See note 4 above.
49 Ibid. The letter was signed by Joseph Parson, W. Morton, Robert Campbell and D. Heming.
50 LC Proceedings, 26 December 1818.
51 Ibid., 18 February 1819.
52 LC Proceedings, 24 October 1819.
53 LC Proceedings, 14 October and 25 November 1819. See also Letters to the Court of Directors, Judicial, 3 November 1820.
54 Judicial Criminal Proceedings, 21 May 1819; LC Proceedings, 18 February and 29 April 1819. Schalch's map of 1824 confirms that this ghat was the Police Ghat.
55 LC Proceedings, 29 April 1819.
56 Letters to the Court of Directors, Judicial, 3 November 1820, paragraph 122.
57 LC Proceedings, 29 April 1819.
58 Ibid.
59 The Governor-General had initially given the merchants 'a site in Bankshall Street about where the Court of Small Causes now stands [Judicial Criminal Proceedings, 18 June 1819], but the scheme, on being referred to England, to the Honourable Board of Directors, fell through, perhaps through the jealousy evoked by the increasing influx of European traders not connected with the H E I Co.…The outside merchants were not, however, to be thwarted, and, in 1818 (sic), they secured the premises in Dalhousie Square now occupied by the Bengal Nagpur Railway Company, at the corner of Council House Street and Dalhousie Square' (*Bengal Past and Present*, vol. 1, July-December, 1907, pp 123-124). The year cited (1818) is misleading because the Lottery Committee proceedings show that even in April 1819 the fate of the exchange building was hanging in the balance.
60 Das, compiled, *Selections from the Indian Journals*, vol. 2, p. 84.
61 LC Proceedings, 29 April 1819, *passim.*
62 Judicial Criminal Proceedings, 21 May 1819; LC Proceedings, 27 May 1819.
63 The precise location of the gift to Dey was as follows: 'A piece of ground granted to Ramdoololl Day out of the old Police Lane: length 136 feet, width 20 feet, contains 3 cottahs and 12 ½ chittacks; bounded by Church Lane on the east, by the ground purchased by Dr Hare on the north, by the ground purchased by Mr Palmer for the registry office on the west, and by Ramdoololl Day's own premises on the south' (LC Proceedings, 13 September 1821).
64 LC Proceedings, 5 July 1821. The final cost of the project was Rs 39,350-9-2 against an estimate of Rs 40,000 'after deducting the sums which have been realised

from the resale of the surplus ground and from the disposal of the materials of the old houses purchased' (ibid).

65 Ibid., 9 November 1820.

66 Ibid., 19 April 1821. The tunnel, made by Richard Blechynden (see chapter 'Filthy State of the Drains'), ran from the river to the tank at Tank Square.

67 Ibid., 9 and 23 November 1820.

HENRY SHAKESPEAR'S MINUTES

1 A ready example of this was his suggestion to the committee to circulate a letter he had written on 5 January 1820 on the watering of Chowringhee Road till as far as the new aqueduct extended to the south 'without waiting for the regular committee day' (LC Proceedings, 13 January 1820).

2 Ibid., 3 February 1820, *passim*. For his report on the northern part of the town, see below.

3 For the impact of Tolly's Nullah on the general drainage of the area, see chapter 'The Land of William Camac'. The Chowringhee Theatre, which opened on 25 November 1813 (*The Calcutta Annual Register* for 1821, Historical Sketch, p. 94) and was destroyed in a fire in 1839, was located at the corner of Chowringhee and Theatre Roads. See Nair, *Calcutta's Streets*, p. 820. Also, R. Ray Choudhury, ed., *Glimpses of Old Calcutta* (Bombay: Nachiketa Publications, 1978), p. 42.

4 See Ray Choudhury, *A City in the Making*, pp 16-17, 499-504.

5 Judicial Criminal Proceedings, 26 July 1804. See also LC Proceedings, 3 February 1820. For details, see Ray Choudhury, *A City in the Making*, pp 408-417, 419-423.

6 Judicial Criminal Proceedings, 26 July 1804. See Ray, *A Short History of Calcutta*, pp 161-162, for the impact of fires affecting life in early Calcutta.

7 LC Proceedings, 3 February 1820, *passim*.

8 He rose to become Secretary in the Judicial Department in 1825.

9 The Court of Directors, however, had a different view on the subject. See 'Introduction'.

10 LC Proceedings, 3 February 1820.

11 The drain was a remnant of the creek of ancient times which ran east towards the salt lake from the river. The native name 'Dingabhunga' is said to have had its origin 'in the wrecking at that place of a ship which, during the terrible cyclone of 1737, had been driven up by a storm wave from the river' (Cotton, *Calcutta Old and New*, p. 304). See also chapter 'The First Planned Square'.

12 The Beliaghata canal.

13 LC Proceedings, 3 February 1820.

14 Was this Horace Hayman Wilson, the Assay Master of the Mint, Secretary of the Asiatic Society, afterwards Boden Professor of Sanskrit at Oxford, and for many years Librarian at the India House (Cotton, *Calcutta Old and New*, p. 369)?

15 LC Proceedings, 3 February 1820.

16 See chapter 'Birth of Three More Squares'.

17 See chapter 'The Land of William Camac' for details.

18 Going by Upjohn's 1792-93 map, the *cutcha* road would correspond to today's Loudon Street (Dr U.N. Brahmachari Street) leading southwards, across Circular Road, to Sarat Bose Road (formerly Peepulputty Road and later Lansdowne Road).

19 See chapter 'The Land of William Camac'. There were quite a few other *bustees* in the area not all of which were removed by the Lottery Committee. In 1858-59 efforts were still being made to acquire the remaining *bustees* in the area (see Atis Dasgupta, ed., *Select Documents on Calcutta 1800-1900* [Directorate of State Archives, West Bengal, 2011], pp 45-46).

20 LC Proceedings, 3 February 1820.

21 Perhaps this is why the native name of Creek Row was *Dingabhanga-ka-rustah* (*The Bengal Directory* for 1875).

22 LC Proceedings, 1 June 1820.

23 Beginning his service with the East India Company as a protégé of John Eliot, Ghoshal subsequently became a useful factotum of the Lottery Committee as a whole, especially when it came to negotiating with natives on property prices, etc. See chapter 'The *Maidan*, Tank Square, Clive Street…', notes.

24 LC Proceedings, 1 June and 20 July 1820.

25 Ibid., 20 July and 7 September 1820.

26 The church/chapel, easily located in Schalch's and Heysham's maps, was known to natives as *nyaragirja*, or (loosely translated) the church without a steeple. Nair quotes *Newman's Calcutta Guide* (p. 125) to say that in 1858 the roof of the church fell in reducing the building to a complete ruin and that it was then resolved to rebuild the church at a new location. The foundation stone of the new church and school was laid on 7 June 1862 'opposite the Female European Orphan Asylum', on Circular Road, the church being commonly known today as *joragirja*, or twin churches.

27 LC Proceedings, 5 April 1821.

28 Scavengers Lane was renamed St James's Lane in 1890 and subsequently, in 1940, Ram Kanai Adhikary Lane (Nair, *Calcutta's Streets*, p. 752).

29 More money than just this amount was spent in developing the area, as indicated by Shakespear in his statement of accounts submitted on 14 July 1821 (LC Proceedings, 19 July 1821). Altogether Rs 2,000 had been allotted for the 'Niboo Tollah' Street on 10 November 1820 of which Rs 1,698-15-5 was spent. Further, although no funds were allotted, Rs 1,331-0-10 was spent on 'Saukaurrey Tollah' (Sakharitala) Street to the north-east of Wellington Square (for this road, see Nair, *Calcutta's Streets*, p. 801).

30 LC Proceedings, 13 September 1821.

31 Ibid., 13 September and 11 October 1821.

32 Judicial Criminal Proceedings, 12 July 1822.

33 A detailed financial report on the project is to be found in the Judicial Criminal Proceedings of 16 January 1824.

34 LC Proceedings, 24 February 1820.

35 The road is named Kutooah Street in Wood's (1784) and Upjohn's (1793) maps, but in Schalch's (1824) it is called Sobhabazar Street. In fact, the road had come to be called Sobhabazar Road by February 1820.

36 This ghat is shown in Schalch's map. In Wood's and Upjohn's it is named Ketoah and Keetoah Ghat, respectively.

37 LC Proceedings, 9 March 1820.

38 Ibid., 24 February 1820, *passim*.

39 The 'great' Simleah drain. See chapter 'Filthy State of the Drains'.

40 Originally, the bazar had been named 'Tiretta Bazar' after Edouard Tiretta who was the East India Company's Surveyor of Roads for long years in the late 18th century. Being a sahib, there is no good reason why Shakespear should have used the expression 'Terethee Bazar' in his minute instead of 'Tiretta Bazar'. It can only be a guess that the use of 'Terethee Bazar' in the minute is the handiwork of the native transcribers of the letter for the records who went by the native pronunciation of 'Tiretta'. Incidentally, the bazar is still known as 'Terethee Bazar', generally.

41 LC Proceedings, 24 February 1820.

42 See chapter 'Strand Road - Step by Step'.

43 See chapter 'Filthy State of the Drains' for a tunnel being built from the Foujdar's house eastward to Circular Road. This house – the 'lofty mansion' of the *foujdar* of Hooghly ('military governor') – stood 'at the corner of Lower Chitpore Road and Colootollah' (Cotton, *Calcutta Old and New*, p. 52).

44 A. Lackersteen is described as a shipowner in *East India Register* for 1819, p. 136. See chapter 'Strand Road – Clearing the Table'.

45 LC Proceedings, 24 February 1820.

46 Ibid., 21 September 1820. The 24th lottery was the first to be auctioned on 15 September 1820 resulting in an increase in resources. See chapter 'Reforming the Lottery System' for details.

47 See chapter 'Filthy State of the Drains'.

48 LC Proceedings, 21 September 1820. See Ray Choudhury, *A City in the Making*, p. 485.

49 LC Proceedings, 21 September 1820.

50 Ibid., 5 October 1820.

51 Ibid.

52 Ibid., 26 October 1820.

STRAND ROAD – CLEARING THE TABLE

1 Rev. James Long, *Selections from Unpublished Records of Government*, ed. Mahadevaprasad Saha (Calcutta: Firma K L Mukhopadhaya, 1973), p. 659.

2 Calcutta Committee of Revenue Proceedings, 6 August 1779 (West Bengal State Archives).

3 See chapter 'The *Maidan*, Tank Square, Clive Street…'

4 For details, see Ray Choudhury, *A City in the Making*, pp 197-202.

5 Territorial Revenue Proceedings, 24 March 1820. LC Proceedings, 4 May 1820.

6 LC Proceedings, 4 May 1820, *passim*.

7 Upjohn's map of 1792 does not show Baloo Ghat the location of which was very close to, if not coincidental with, the Prinsep Ghat of today.

8 Inevitably, the removal of the mint to a spot some distance away from the populated areas became necessary in view of the pollution it was generating, even as early as the second decade of the 19th century. At the time, the mint was located on the riverbank to the west of Church Lane.

9 A report prepared in 1797 by Francis Gladwin, Collector of Calcutta, indicated that neither of these two ghats was included in *pattas* granted to individuals. Cutchagoody Ghat had been considerably enlarged by the Lottery Committee two years earlier, in 1818, its width then measuring 80 ft.

and destroyed the property of an individual, in the neighbourhood, would not Mr Lackersteen, or the owner of the place, be liable in an action for damages?'

46 Das, *Selections from the Indian Journals*, vol. 2, pp 242-244.

47 Ibid.

48 See LC Proceedings, 23 April 1818 for a petition dated 9 April 1818 by some leading natives of the city appealing to John Eliot to put a stop to the 'filthy, disgusting and noxious practice' of throwing into the river 'filth of all kinds'. The ghat continued to remain a nuisance for many more years (see Judicial Criminal Proceedings, 9 June 1835; also Letters to the Court of Directors, Judicial, 19 July 1836, paragraphs 39-44).

49 Clive Street Ghat had not yet been built.

50 LC Proceedings, 9 November 1820.

51 Ibid., 23 November 1820.

52 John Palmer, the 'prince of merchants', whose firm Palmer and Company collapsed in 1830 (Cotton, *Calcutta Old and New*, pp. 491-492, 579).

53 LC Proceedings, 23 November 1820.

54 George Lycke was a surgeon and Commissioner of the Court of Requests.

55 LC Proceedings, 9 November 1820 and 4 January 1821.

56 At the time John Pascal Larkins held the position of junior member of the Board of Salt, Customs and Opium (Dodwell and Miles, *Bengal Civil Servants*, pp 264-265). The seniormost Trotter in the Company's service at this time was Archibald who was away in England in 1820 although this does not rule him out as an owner of the plot because he could have bought the ground from Dr Lycke before 1818 when he went on leave. The second seniormost Trotter was John, the Secretary of the Lottery Committee, who was, in fact, writing the letter to the Government. The third Trotter was John, Junior who, in 1820, was Assistant Secretary to the Board of Revenue and in April of that year Acting Collector of Calcutta (ibid., pp 557-560).

STRAND ROAD – STEP BY STEP

1 LC Proceedings, 8 March 1821.

2 See chapter 'Birth of Three More Squares'.

3 LC Proceedings, 19 April 1821, *passim*.

4 Some details are provided in Ray Choudhury, *A City in the Making*, chapter 11.

5 See previous chapter.

6 One of the reasons behind this was to leave undisturbed for a longer period of time the 'several' shipbuilding yards in the intervening space in view of the fact that 'some difficulty' could be encountered in getting the road past them. The advice of the Governor-General in Council to the Lottery Committee was 'not to lose sight of any favourable opportunity which may occur of removing those difficulties by entering into an amiable arrangement with the parties interested'. The Government wanted shipbuilding activity to be moved to 'the other side of the river' its view being that given the slump in shipbuilding at the time, 'opportunities may occur for securing this object at a comparatively trifling expense' (LC Proceedings, 10 May 1821).

7 LC Proceedings, 19 April 1821.

8 See chapter 'Filthy State of the Drains'; also Ray Choudhury, *A City in the Making*, p. 66, note 14 for the potability of BBD Bagh water.

9 LC Proceedings, 21 December 1820 and 8 March 1821.

10 Ibid., 23 November 1820.

11 Letter dated 13 December 1820 in ibid., 21 December 1820.

12 Ibid., 8 March 1821, *passim.*

13 The detailed break-up of the estimate (ibid.) is of some interest because, among other things, it provided details of what exactly was needed to build a river wharf in the early years of the 19th century, in particular the role played by *sal* wood, iron and copper.

14 Ibid., 5 April 1821, *passim.*

15 Ibid., 19 April 1821.

16 Ibid., 10 May 1821, *passim.*

17 LC Proceedings, 5 July 1821. Macnabb's letter is a bit confusing, a confusion which the Lottery Committee employed to its advantage in telling the Government that the Mint Master had no objection to transfer the land concerned to Vrignon (see later).

18 Judicial Criminal Proceedings, 29 June 1821; LC Proceedings, 5 July 1821.

19 Ibid.

20 LC Proceedings, 10 May 1821. The uncertainty was not unwarranted, for three months later, on 6 August, the Nawab, Zain-ud-din Ali Khan, passed away at the age of 29 making way for a new incumbent, Ahmad Ali Khan, who assumed his seat on the *musnud* on 30 October (*Calcutta Journal,* 13 August 1821, quoted in *The Calcutta Annual Register* for 1821, p. 128).

21 See below note 23.

22 LC Proceedings, 25 October 1821, *passim.*

23 On 29 January 1822 the Lottery Committee wrote to the Government (Judicial Criminal Proceedings, 8 February 1822) that the value of the 4 *bigha*s 14 *katha*s of 'high ground or ground above high water mark belonging to the Nazim of Bengal' would be Rs 47,000, the rate per *katha* being 'the same as that fixed by the committee', namely, Rs 500. As regards the low ground measuring 6 *bigha*s, 18 *katha*s 6 *chittack*s, the 'right' of the nawab to 'the low or alluvion ground was recognised when the arrangement for transferring to Government the premises now appropriated to the new Town Duty Office was made', and in view of this the nawab 'seems to be justly entitled to some compensation for the cession of the right thus acquired by him'. The compensation amount was adjudged by the committee to be Rs 10,000 based on a rate per *katha* which was 'somewhat more than the average rate of 70 rupees'. The total price to be paid to the nawab came to Rs 57,000.

24 LC Proceedings, 27 December 1821, *passim.* The ghat was previously the property of Radhakanta Deb who had sold it 'many years' ago to Radhamadhab Banerjee, formerly Dewan of the East India Company's opium factory at Patna (*Bengal Past and Present,* vol. 29, p. 101).

25 The stipulation that any ghat built on the riverside would have to be a public facility was formulated in 1826 (Judicial Criminal Proceedings, 24 October 1826).

26 Dodwell and Miles, *Bengal Civil Servants*, pp 456-457.

27 LC Proceedings, 25 October 1821, *passim.*
28 Going by the Lottery Committee's admission made much later, it would appear that Dutt had *not* been approached personally by the authorities before the work began (Judicial Criminal Proceedings, 30 August 1827).
29 LC Proceedings, 25 October 1821.
30 Judicial Criminal Proceedings, 30 August 1827, *passim.*
31 Apart from Upjohn's 1793 map, the walk is also marked in Wood's earlier map of 1785. From the former map it would appear that between the walk and the river there was a row of trees.
32 Judicial Criminal Proceedings, 26 February 1822.
33 See previous chapter.
34 A jury was set up which awarded Rs 65,000 for Martin's property and Rs 71,500 for that of the Mullicks (Judicial Criminal Proceedings, 27 June and 25 July 1822).
35 Ibid., 20 November 1823. The amount received for surplus ground sold included Rs 16,968-12-0 from the Bank of Bengal (for 11 *katha*s 5 *chittacks*), which perhaps marks the beginning of the presence of the bank's offices on Strand Road, where they are still located in the shape of the offices of the State Bank of India. *The Bengal Directory* of 1824 (p. 458) gives the bank's address as 1, King's Bench Walk. Of the other buyers, Colvins and Company bought 14 *katha*s 6 *chittack*s for Rs 21,562-8-0, and E.A. Roussac 10 *katha*s 11 *chittack*s for Rs 16,031-4-0.
36 Judicial Criminal Proceedings, 10 July 1823.
37 Ibid., 9 May 1822.
38 Judicial Criminal Proceedings, 22 January 1824, *passim.*
39 Ibid., 13 May 1824. The special committee set up by the military authorities comprised C. Mouat (Chief Engineer), T. Wood, J. Vaughan, R.H. Cunliffe and H. Faithful.
40 This road did not exist in the 1824 map which Schalch drew but was included in it later. Heysham's map of 1856 clearly marks the road as Strand Road.
41 Judicial Criminal Proceedings, 9 October 1823.
42 Ibid., 11 December 1823.
43 A 1755 allusion to this riverbank road is cited in Ray Choudhury, *A City in the Making*, p. 140.
44 A detailed estimate was appended to the letter which also included the names of the people from whom ground (at Rs 800 a *katha*) and buildings were bought to build the stretch of the new road extending from Madan Dutt's Ghat (see Fig. 43) to Hatkhola Ghat (Judicial Criminal Proceedings, 11 December 1823).
45 The case in the Supreme Court dragged on for more than 15 years, its prosecution being reluctantly taken over by Gopimohun's son, Radhakanta Deb. Available correspondence suggests that the latter was desperate to conclude the litigation even if it meant a sacrifice on his part of the basic principles involved in the suit launched by his father (Judicial Original Consultations, 1 August 1837; Judicial Criminal Proceedings, 15 August and 17 October 1837, 10 November 1840 and 30 March 1841, Judicial Judicial Proceedings, 18 April 1842).
46 Judicial Criminal Proceedings, 1 August 1822.
47 Ibid., 9 October 1823.

48 Ibid., 4 May 1826.
49 Ibid., 27 March 1826.
50 Ibid., 16 January and 12 November 1824. Two years later, the Government sanctioned a further Rs 1,903-14-0 for 'the purchase and fixing up of old iron guns along the banks of this part of the Strand [by Burn and Company] as had formerly been done in the southern part of [it]' (ibid., 17 August 1826).
51 Ibid., 24 October 1826.

THE *MAIDAN*, TANK SQUARE, CLIVE STREET...

1 J.R. Martin, *Notes on the Medical Topography of Calcutta*, p. 10. An esplanade is 'a level space separating citadel or fortress from town'. The space known as the *maidan* today in Calcutta was the esplanade of the new Fort William (see Ray Choudhury, *A City in the Making*) which is why it is referred to as the 'esplanade' in the Company records. What is known as Esplanade today is merely the north-east corner of this vast area, probably the result of an early tramway station or depot being located at the spot in the closing years of the 19th century.
2 Upjohn's map distinguishes the entire *maidan* south of Fort William as 'the Course', the northern part being called 'esplanade'. Schalch's map, however, designates the Course as a part of the Esplanade.
3 *The Calcutta Review*, July-December, 1852, p. 289.
4 *An Account of the East Indies* (London, 1744), two volumes.
5 Walter Kelly Firminger, ed., *The Original Letters from India of Mrs Eliza Fay* (Calcutta: Thacker, Spink & Co., 1908), p. 148.
6 By a Civilian, *Tom Raw the Griffin, A Burlesque Poem* (London: R Ackermann, 1828), pp 63-64. Canto the Third, Verse 20 and 21.
7 A number of these statues were removed to Flagstaff House at Barrackpore, where they still remain.
8 On the original 'wooden Chinese railing' to the south of Government House and its subsequent replacement with a brick-and-mortar balustrade, see Ray Choudhury, *The Lord Sahib's House*, pp 321-326.
9 Judicial Criminal Proceedings, 5 February 1808.
10 Ibid., 27 January 1825.
11 Ibid., 21 July and 2 October 1818; LC Proceedings, 16 July 1818.
12 On the location of the 'cocked hat', see Cotton, *Calcutta Old and New*, p. 392. The traffic island is still there but not in the shape of a cocked hat. The aqueduct, which had just been built, commenced from the reservoir at Chandpal Ghat, ran along Esplanade Row West (the native name of which was '*Chandpal Ghaut ka samnah rasta*'), then to the south of Government House finally turning north along Old Court House Street till the north-east corner of Tank Square or BBD Bagh.
13 LC Proceedings, 3 September 1818.
14 Judicial Criminal Proceedings, 2 October 1821; LC Proceedings, 3 September 1818.
15 Judicial Criminal Proceedings, 2 October 1818; LC Proceedings, 15 October 1818.
16 LC Proceedings, 5 October 1820.
17 Ibid., 3 August 1820.
18 Bayley's suggestion does not figure in the 20 July 1820 proceedings of the Lottery Committee.

19 There were brick-and-mortar platforms built by the authorities on the *maidan* where people crossing the plain on foot and others could take some rest. On 21 March 1821 Charles Trower was writing to the committee (LC Proceedings, 5 April 1821) seeking Rs 277 for the construction of a 40-ft-square 'chabootah' on the esplanade, the funds being sanctioned on 5 April.

20 Note the spelling and pronunciation of 'Khidirpur' which here appears to be close to 'Kedarpur'. Quoting Henry Yule and A.C. Burnell, *Hobson-Jobson* (1st edition 1886, Rupa and Co, 1986, Calcutta), p. 483, Nair (*Calcutta's Streets*, p. 491) suggests that Kedarpur could possibly have been the original name of the locality.

21 LC Proceedings, 7 September 1820.

22 Ibid. The passage indicates how little the alignment of Red Road has changed over the centuries. In the second decade of the 21st century, the 'bend' in the road westward is still where it was two centuries earlier.

23 Ibid. The Court of Directors was not happy with the children's walk project (see 'Epilogue'). In 1826 the walks for children 'from Chaundpaul Ghaut to the Chowringhee Sortie Gate [of the fort] and from thence all round the Chowringhee Road' were in 'a dilapidated and ruinous state', an effort being made at the time to bring them 'into a good state of repair' (Judicial Criminal Proceedings, 4 May 1826).

24 This is yet another indication that the Course terminated at the point where Outram Road meets Red Road today. In *Tom Raw, the Griffin* (p. 77), Charles D'Oyly confirmed the point when he wrote in the 1820s: 'The Course is the road from the Government-house to that crossing it from the Fort to Chowringhee. It is very broad, the centre only bricked, and about quarter of a mile in length. All the inhabitants of Calcutta are seen congregated here in the evenings. The heat of the climate, and the sedentary lives led in India, render an evening's ride necessary for the health'.

25 LC Proceedings, 5 October 1820. The figure was raised subsequently by Rs 844-11-9 owing to exclusion in the initial estimate of the cost of constructing 'siphon drains' under the walk which, according to Paton (ibid., 19 April 1821), were indispensable to keep the road free from flooding during the rains.

26 The committee describes the location of this tank as being 'opposite to the College of Fort William' (ibid., 5 October 1820) thus indicating where the college was located at the time.

27 This view of the tank opposite Park Street from the *maidan* was disrupted forever when the Calcutta metro railway came to be built 40 years ago.

28 LC Proceedings, 5 and 26 October 1820.

29 Ibid., 23 August 1821.

30 LC Proceedings, 23 August 1821. The records carry a detailed estimate for the project prepared by Lt Paton. See also ibid., 27 September 1821.

31 Ibid., 23 August and 13 September 1821.

32 The firm was located at 13, Old Court House Street (*The Bengal Directory* for 1825, p. 330).

33 Both these houses were located near Larkin's Lane which today connects Old Court House Street with Wellesley Place, the lane being named after William

Larkins, a confidante of Warren Hastings (Cotton, *Calcutta Old and New*, p. 314). John Adam was at the time a member of the Supreme Council.

34 LC Proceedings, 6 August 1818.

35 Ibid., 20 August 1818.

36 Ibid., 4 March 1819.

37 Neil Benjamin Edmonstone had been a member of the Supreme Council and had returned to England in 1818 (Dodwell and Miles, *Bengal Civil Servants*, pp. 154-155).

38 In all probability the 'cooking house', located opposite the Great Eastern Hotel (renamed today the Lalit Great Eastern), was the new kitchen of Government House. Sixty years later, in the 1880s, Lady Dufferin was writing to her mother: 'We have been to our stables. They are across the road and next to the kitchen. Did I ever tell you that the kitchen is somewhere in Calcutta, but not in this house?' A consequence of this arrangement was that the food had to be brought from across the street and warmed in Government House before being served on the table. The second Lord Minto (1905-10) brought the kitchen into the premises of Government House. See Ray Choudhury, *The Lord Sahib's House*, pp 250, 252, 264 note 26.

39 Board of Revenue Proceedings, 2 April 1819.

40 LC Proceedings, 13 January 1820.

41 Ibid., 15 June 1820.

42 The Lottery Committee played no part in this transformation. See Ray Choudhury, *The Lord Sahib's House*, p. 354.

43 For details, see Ray Choudhury, *A City in the Making*, pp 466-468; *The Lord Sahib's House*, pp 338, 354 note 2.

44 LC Proceedings of 5 and 26 February, 1818.

45 Ibid., 6 August 1818.

46 Ibid.

47 Ibid., 20 August and 17 September 1818; Judicial Criminal Proceedings, 4 September 1818.

48 LC Proceedings, 24 February 1820.

49 Ibid., 23 March 1820.

50 Ibid., 4 May 1820.

51 Ibid., 15 February 1821.

52 Ibid., 8 March 1821.

53 See Ray Choudhury, *The Lord Sahib's House,* pp 338-339.

54 LC Proceedings, 7 June 1821.

55 LC Proceedings, 21 June 1821.

56 Judicial Criminal Proceedings, 25 July 1805. For details about the recommendations of Wellesley's special committee on 'nuisances', see Ray Choudhury, *A City in the Making*, pp 464-465.

57 Judicial Criminal Proceedings, 16 March 1821.

58 6 April 1821 (from *The Asiatic Journal* for 1821, Bengal Occurrences for April, p. 64).

59 *The Asiatic Journal* for 1817, p. 104.

60 For more details on the Company's House, see Ray Choudhury, *The Lord Sahib's House*, pp 5-10. On the first hospital of the settlement, see Ray Choudhury, *A City in the Making*, pp 146-148.

9 LC Proceedings, 7 December 1820.
10 LC Proceedings, 10 May 1821.
11 Ibid., 20 August 1818.
12 Possibly Robert McClintock, who is described in *The East India Register* for 1819 (p. 159) as a 'merchant and agent'.
13 An old road, Crooked Lane (which still exists) is marked in Wood's map of 1784-85. See Nair, *Calcutta's Streets*, p. 276.
14 LC Proceedings, 26 December 1818.
15 Although the road is still generally known as Waterloo Street, there is some confusion regarding its official name. Nair (*Calcutta's Streets*, pp 927-928) writes that in 1965 the Calcutta Corporation changed the name to Jogendra Chandra Ghose Street, and again in 1977 to Bande Mataram Sarani.
16 Judicial Criminal Proceedings, 8 June 1826 and 22 March 1827.
17 *Calcutta Old and New*, p. 312.
18 Nair, *Calcutta's Streets*, pp 435-436.
19 Judicial Criminal Proceedings, 8 June 1826; 22 March 1827.
20 Ibid., 18 September 1823.
21 See chapter 'Filthy State of the Drains' for details on the tunnel.
22 Judicial Criminal Proceedings, 18 September 1823, *passim*.
23 See next chapter 'The Land of William Camac'.
24 Judicial Criminal Proceedings, 18 September 1823.
25 Ibid., 17 February 1825.
26 Ibid., 4 May 1826.
27 Ibid., 9 October 1823, *passim*.
28 The Judicial Criminal Proceedings of 9 October 1823 provide the names of the owners of land and buildings needed to construct the road.
29 Judicial Criminal Proceedings, 22 March 1827.
30 Free School Street was named after the Free School which was located at the northern end of the road. Kathleen Blechynden (*Calcutta Past and Present* [London: W Thacker and Co., 1905], pp 211-212) writes: 'Opening into Park Street nearly opposite to Middleton Row is Free School Street, leading to the Free School. This school was established in 1790, in connection with the Mission Church, and in 1800 it was united to the old Charity School, then seventy-one years old. About the time that the two schools were united, a house in Jaun Bazar, in which Justice Le Maistre, one of the judges who tried Nuncomar [Nandakumar], had lived, was purchased for their accommodation, and there they have remained ever since. The present spacious buildings, however, present a very different appearance to the old house, which fell in 1854, through jackals undermining the foundations'.
31 See Robb, *Sentiment and Self*, p. 183, on Kathleen Blechynden and the diaries of Richard Blechynden.
32 Cotton writes that Free School Street 'was a bamboo jungle in 1780, which people were afraid to pass at night' (*Calcutta Old and New*, p. 291).
33 Kathleen Blechynden's timeline is supported by an entry in the Judicial Criminal Proceedings of 24 February 1809 but only to the extent that it mentions a 'Free Scool (sic) Street'. The entire stretch of Free School Street we know today was completed a decade later.

34 This road, to the east of Rani Rashmoni's house on S N Banerjee Road, linking Lenin Sarani with S N Banerjee Road, was proposed by Henry Shakespear in December 1820. His justification was that 'The Jaun Bazar and Dhurrumtollah Streets run parallel with each other the length of a mile, from the Esplanade to the Circular Road, without a single road of connexion sufficiently wide to admit of two carriages passing. [The] intermediate space, therefore, forms a barrier between the northern and southern parts of the town by which carriages proceeding from one to the other are compelled to go nearly a mile out of their way' (LC Proceedings, 7 December 1820).
35 LC Proceedings, 18 January 1821.
36 LC Proceedings, 18 January 1821.
37 Ibid., 15 February 1821.
38 Judicial Criminal Proceedings, 27 August, 1822.
39 A list of property owners from whom land was bought for the construction of Free School Street was appended to the letter (ibid.).
40 Ibid.
41 LC Proceedings, 5 July 1821. On Eliot Road, see Nair, *Calcutta's Streets*, pp 342-343.
42 This makes it clear that Wood Street had got its name by July 1821. But after which Wood was the road named? Cotton (*Calcutta Old and New*, pp 290-291) says that the road was named after Henry Wood, the member of the Lottery Committee who later became the Accountant-General. But in 1821 he was 'Sub-Accountant-General, and Accountant to the Revenue and Judicial Department, and Civil Auditor' which was not a position senior enough for a road to be named after him (Dodwell and Miles, *Bengal Civil Servants*, pp 572-573). Further, having joined as a writer in 1804, Wood had spent just 17 years in the service, and, in the committee itself, there were members who were years senior to him. More plausible appears to be the claim that the road was named after Colonel Mark Wood who produced the map of Calcutta in 1784-85 and who was 'an extensive landholder' in the growing city. He was Chief Engineer in Bengal in 1790 and returned to England in 1793 (*Bengal Past and Present*, vol. 30, p. 101.)
43 LC Proceedings, 19 July 1821.
44 Ibid., 5 July 1821.
45 See Ray Choudhury, *A City in the Making*, p. 129, where an example of this linkage from as early as 1720 is cited.
46 LC Proceedings, 5 July 1821.
47 Ibid., 9 November 1820.
48 Ibid.
49 Ibid., 23 November 1820.
50 Ibid., 5 and 19 July 1821. Of the Rs 67,342-4-5 around Rs 41,292 would be spent on buying ground from 26 landowners and Rs 16,086 on purchasing houses from 13 proprietors (ibid., 5 July 1821).
51 Ibid., 5 July 1821.
52 Ibid., 19 July 1821.
53 Judicial Criminal Proceedings, 8 February 1822.
54 See Nair, *Calcutta's Streets*, pp 311-313 for an informative note on Robert Kyd after whom the road was originally named.

55 LC Proceedings, 5 July and 9 August 1821. In 1809 the Committee for Improving the Town of Calcutta (comprising G. Dowdeswell, G.D. Guthrie, T. Wood, C.F. Martyn and J. Leyden) had taken the initiative of buying up ground at 'the eastern extremity' of the road and linking it with 'Free Scool (sic) Street', a project approved by the Government of Lord Minto on 24 February that year (Judicial Criminal Proceedings, 24 February 1809). On the early history of Kyd Street, see Ray Choudhury, *A City in the Making*, p. 237.

56 *The South Park Street Cemetery* (undated monograph printed in Calcutta) brought out by the British Association for Cemeteries in South Asia in collaboration with the Christian Burial Board, p. 3.

57 Judicial Criminal Proceedings, 28 December 1821; LC Proceedings, 13 December 1821.

58 On Allen Garden, see Nair, *Calcutta's Streets*, p. 140.

59 See Ray Choudhury, *A City in the Making*, p. 26.

60 Judicial Criminal Proceedings, 27 July 1823.

61 Ibid., 13 May 1824.

62 For a brief history of the 'park' and those who resided there, see Ray Choudhury, *The Lord Sahib's House*, pp 34-38.

63 See Ray Choudhury, *A City in the Making*, pp 137-139.

64 See Cotton, *Calcutta Old and New*, p. 283; Nair, *Calcutta's Streets*, p. 843; and Ray Choudhury, *A City in the* Making, pp 498, 504-505.

65 Judicial Criminal Proceedings, 10 April 1822.

66 W. Leycester was Chief Judge at the Nizamut Adalat in 1822.

67 Judicial Criminal Proceedings, 10 April 1822. The elevated resident profile of the area is underscored by the fact that H.T. Prinsep, Acting Secretary to the Government at the time, lived in the house at the northwest corner of the junction of Middleton Row with Park Street, Charles Paton, a member of the Lottery Committee, owning the ground at the northeast corner.

68 On the state of Khidipur around two decades later (1835), J.R. Martin wrote (Judicial Criminal Proceedings, 16 June 1835): 'I thought I had visited the worst of the suburbs in Bhowaneepore, but Khideerpore, which is next in populousness, greatly surpassed it. I think I never saw in any part of Bengal or Orissa a locality so generally bad, and the result corresponds entirely with its condition – fever is general throughout...and the want of good water forms a universal complaint amongst the inhabitants. There is not a...road that is not in a state of surprising neglect and the portion between the bridge and Kyd's Dock [the Watgunje area] is one entire *jheel*'.

69 Firminger, *The Original Letters from India of Mrs Eliza Fay*, p. 131.

70 Cohen, ed., *Lady Nugent's East India Journal*, p. 55.

71 Lord Teignmouth, *Memoirs of the Life, Writings, and Correspondence of Sir William Jones* (Philadelphia: W M Poyntell & Co., 1805), p. 295. See also Ray Choudhury, *The Lord Sahib's House*, pp 86-87.

72 See Ray Choudhury, *A City in the Making*, pp 430-432.

73 Judicial Criminal Proceedings, 6 January, 1818; LC Proceedings, 18 December 1817. Wood had submitted a detailed sketch of the location of the roads, which is not included in the records.

74 LC Proceedings, 18 December 1817.
75 Ibid.
76 LC Proceedings, 15 January 1818. In March 1819 Captain P. Phipps, the Superintendent of Civil and Military Buildings, Lower Provinces, suggested a 'new' method of making roads which, too, was nothing but a revival of the technology used in 'all the large cities under the Moghul Government' (Judicial Criminal Proceedings, 26 February 1819; LC Proceedings, 15 April 1819).
77 LC Proceedings, 5 April 1821. From 24 November 1817 Wood attended nearly every meeting of the Lottery Committee till the one held on 28 December 1818. He was absent for the whole of 1819 and the first eight months of 1820, resuming his committee seat on 7 September of that year. After skipping the meetings held in October and November, he was back on 7 December 1820.
78 Ibid., 7 December 1820.
79 Herbert Compton was 'once a private soldier in the Company's army, and subsequently Advocate-General at Madras and Calcutta' (*Bengal Past and Present*, vol. 27, January-June 1924, p. 222). *The East India Register* for 1819 (p. 146) describes him as a barrister.
80 LC Proceedings, 5 April 1821.
81 Ibid., 5 April and 10 May 1821.
82 As with Compton's garden, this house too is not marked in any contemporary map.
83 LC Proceedings, 7 December 1820.
84 Ibid.
85 Ibid., 5 July 1821.
86 Judicial Criminal Proceedings, 25 July 1822.
87 Judicial Criminal Proceedings, 8 January 1824.
88 Ibid., 28 October and 17 November 1825; 4 May 1826.
89 Ibid., 17 November 1825.
90 Formerly, Watson's dockyard.
91 Judicial Criminal Proceedings, 22 March 1827.
92 Paddopukur Road, renamed Hem Chandra Street. See Nair, *Calcutta's Streets*, pp 405-406.
93 Judicial Criminal Proceedings, 22 March 1827. This road (named Mahatma Gandhi Road) is probably the one which today leads south from Karunamoyee Bridge (beyond the Tollygunje metro railway station) to Haridebpur. Further, since the road was '*from* old Tolly Gunje' the latter would appear to have been located on Tolly's Nullah where the Karunamoyee Bridge is situated now, or at least close to the spot.
94 Did this road follow the alignment of today's Circular Tollygunge Road (often called Tollygunge Circular Road)? See Nair, *Calcutta's Streets*, pp 263, 899-901.

THE LAND OF WILLIAM CAMAC

1 27 April 1820 (Das, *Selections from the Indian Journals*, vol. 2, pp 168-169). Every year the fever struck with ferocity. The Magistrates of Calcutta informed the Government at the end of April 1819 that 'the number of deaths occasioned by the cholera morbus and small pox have been considerable in the town of Calcutta during the two months last past as will appear by the following statements: Cholera Morbus – January 73, February 81, March 203 April 29 inclusive 262; Small Pox

– January 22, February 130, March 390 April 29 inclusive 285' (Judicial Criminal Proceedings, 6 May 1819).

2 LC Proceedings, 13 January 1820.

3 After whom Short Street is named. He died on 2 July 1785 (*The Bengal Obituary*, pp 73-74) at Russapaglah and lies buried in the South Park Street Cemetery. See also Nair, *Calcutta's Streets*, pp 826-827. Short bought this land from George Vansittart, the brother of Henry Vansittart, the Governor (1760-64), and set up a bazar in the area (see Fig. 38). On George Vansittart and his landholding, see Ray Choudhury, *The Lord Sahib's House*, p. 42, note 70.

4 The scale of the plan was rather large following that 'of the map which is forming of Calcutta [Schalch's], and which is nearly five times as large as that of Upjohn's'.

5 For the origin of the scourge of 'numerous holes' in the ground, see Ray Choudhury, *A City in the Making*, p. 125. See also 'Epilogue'.

6 George Ballard had just been appointed a member of the committee (11 January 1820) in place of Macan who had passed away (LC Proceedings, 13 January 1820).

7 Ibid. See 'Epilogue' for the critical view taken by the Board of Directors of the entire project.

8 This is how the subcommittee is named in the LC Proceedings of 9 March 1820.

9 At the time Captain W.H. Rainey was attached to the Governor-General's Bodyguard (*East India Register* for 1819, p. 35).

10 LC Proceedings, 23 March 1820, *passim*. The ground, with the offending marsh in the middle of it, was the property of Charles Short and was looked after by Colvins, Bazett and Company, the agents of Short, 'who, in consequence of a law-suit [pending] in England regarding it, are unable either to dispose of the property or to expend any considerable sums in its improvement' (ibid., 4 May 1820).

11 Ibid., 23 March and 4 May 1820.

12 Ibid., 4 May 1820, *passim*.

13 The letter, sent to the committee as an enclosure by the subcommittee, was written by Blechynden, Sr, in response to one from Shakespear (dated 11 January) which, incidentally, is not to be found in the records.

14 Lt-Col Francis Wilford (*East India Register* for 1819, p. 124).

15 In all probability, Ghulam Rahman who had been in that position for the past 15 years. See Ray Choudhury, *A City in the Making*, p. 460.

16 Were these roads the Circular Road to the south and Camac Street to the east? Upjohn's map of 1793 (see Fig. 38) shows that a road corresponding to Camac Street was already there. Since the 1742 map does not show any such road, it is likely that the road in question was made after the sack of Calcutta by Shiraj-ud-daula at a time when the area was being developed for habitation by the sahibs.

17 In terms of the final agreement made between the East India Company and William Camac (the LC Proceedings of 5 October 1820 contain a copy of the agreement), the total area involved was 263 *bigha*s and 18 *katha*s. Instead of four, the property was spread over five 'certain pieces or parcels of land or ground'.

18 Schalch's 1824 map shows a tank on this ground while Upjohn's of 1793 had none. In all probability, the road built was the Hungerford Street (renamed Picasso Bithi) of later years (see Fig. 74).

19 Strong, *Topography and Vital Statistics of Calcutta*, p. 28.
20 LC Proceedings, 4 May 1820, *passim*.
21 Palmer and Company had been asked specifically by the subcommittee whether William Camac had taken over the ground marked 'the estate of Short' in its plans, to which there was no separate reply. But the fact that the agents had communicated to the subcommittee Camac's price, etc., for the same bit of land indicates that Camac had, in fact, taken over Short's former estate.
22 LC Proceedings, 5 October 1820. In terms of the final agreement, the price was fixed at Rs 2,63,900.
23 Ibid., 18 May 1820.
24 See Ray Choudhury, *A City in the Making*, pp 400-403, for a clearer view of the justification of the stand propagated by Leadenhall Street. See p. 99 (ibid.) for the East India Company's stand as early as 1704 to make the people pay for measures to improve living conditions in the town. See also 'Epilogue'.
25 LC Proceedings, 18 May 1820.
26 Ibid., 8 March 1821.
27 Ibid., 26 October 1820.
28 See chapter 'The First Planned Square'.
29 LC Proceedings, 26 October 1820.
30 See Ray Choudhury, *A City in the Making*, pp 85, 102-103.
31 LC Proceedings, 26 October and 23 November 1820.
32 Ibid., 18 May 1820.
33 Ibid., 6 July and 21 September 1820.
34 The Court of Directors in London attached great importance to this point. See 'Epilogue'.
35 LC Proceedings, 6 July 1820.
36 See note 4 above.
37 LC Proceedings, 3 August 1820. The Company Attorney had got in touch with Colvins, Bazett and Company who had shown him 'some other deeds connected with the same property' which the attorney had passed on to the Advocate-General (LC Proceedings, 21 September 1820).
38 Ibid., 7 September 1820.
39 Ibid., 21 September 1820, *passim*.
40 See Judicial Criminal Proceedings, 22 September 1820 for the two deeds executed by Palmer and Company regarding Camac's ground.
41 LC Proceedings, 5 October 1820. This amount constituted half the price of the land which was Rs 2,63,900.
42 Ibid., 11 October 1821.
43 Ibid., 29 November 1821.
44 See chapter 'Henry Shakespear's Minutes'.
45 LC Proceedings, 13 December 1821.
46 Judicial Criminal Proceedings, 20 November 1823 (24), *passim*.

EPILOGUE

1 Despatch of 2 February 1819, paragraph 77 (Letters from the Court of Directors, Judicial). At this point of time, two-way correspondence between Calcutta and

London took seven to eight months to complete at the earliest, and normally about a year or longer.

2 Ibid. Despatch of 13 December, paragraphs 258-266.

3 See chapter 'A Committee is Set Up'.

4 LC Proceedings, 24 November 1821.

5 The Court of Directors had noted the Lottery Committee's view that 'no rules have as yet been established for checking the estimates in which disbursements from the lottery funds have been authorised (or) for obtaining the usual survey reports on works which have been constructed at the expense of the lottery funds', the point being also made that 'sums are withdrawn from the public treasury and remain in the balance of the Conservancy Department which furnishes no account to any public department'.

6 This was not a new point. George Dowdeswell, who later (1814) became a Member of the Supreme Council, had written in 1807-1808 about the problem 'of the interruption' in the discharge of their official duties faced by some of the 'present commissioners' for improving the town. See Ray Choudhury, *A City in the Making*, pp 481, 486.

7 Letters to the Court of Directors, Judicial, paragraphs 129-139 of letter dated 29 October 1817. Letters from the Court of Director, Judicial, paragraphs 247-248 of letter dated 13 December 1820.

8 See chapter 'River Water for the Town'.

9 The letter is in Judicial Criminal Proceedings, 14 March 1815.

10 See chapter 'The First Planned Square'.

11 The Tank-Excavation Committee. See chapter 'River Water for the Town'.

12 See chapter 'River Water for the Town'.

13 Letter from Court of Directors, Judicial, 13 December 1820, paragraphs 249-254.

14 Judicial Criminal Proceedings, 1 and 8 December, 1825.

15 Ibid., 5 January 1826.

16 Letter to the Court of Directors, Judicial, 12 April 1827, paragraph 35.

17 Despatch of 11 April. Letters from the Court of Directors, Judicial (p. 135 in the relevant volume). The volume of the Court's letters to the Government, comprising despatches from 1821 to 1825, is missing at the West Bengal State Archives.

18 See chapter 'Henry Shakespear's Minutes'.

19 See chapter 'The Land of William Camac'.

20 See chapter 'Filthy State of the Drains'.

21 See chapter 'Strand Road – Clearing the Table'.

22 See chapter 'The *Maidan*, Tank Square, Clive Street…'

23 LC Proceedings, 27 September 1821. In fact, in May 1820, the Lottery Committee had already been asked to furnish a financial statement (ibid., 18 May 1820) which was to include 'such general observations or remarks as may be calculated to make the Honourable the Court of Directors better acquainted with the course of (the) proceedings adopted by the committee, and with the beneficial results of those proceedings'.

24 Judicial Criminal Proceedings, 29 March 1822, *passim*.

25 The 31 December 1822 letter makes it clear that the practice of the Lottery Committee submitting a regular statement of work done over the past six months/

year began that year itself, the first half-yearly report (till 31 October 1822) being submitted along with the 31 December letter.

26 See chapter 'The Land of William Camac'.

27 The letter was written on 31 December 1821. Subsequent to this date, more recourse was had to jury awards than just two.

28 See chapter 'The First Planned Square'.

29 See chapters 'The First Planned Square' and 'Henry Shakespear's Minutes'.

30 This letter is not available in the volumes containing letters to the Court of Directors at the West Bengal State Archives.

31 Letters from the Court of Directors, Judicial. When this despatch was sent from London, Lord Amherst was about to be replaced by Lord Bentinck who took over as Governor-General in 1828.

32 The loan related to the Cornwallis Street-Amherst Street project. See chapter 'Birth of Three More Squares'.

33 Letters from the Court of Directors, Judicial.

34 By this time Shakespear had become Secretary to the Government in the Judicial Department (he died on 20 March 1838 and was buried in the South Park Street Cemetery; see *The Bengal Obituary*, p. 143). Bayley, an important member of the Lottery Committee, had been Secretary to the Judicial Department in 1817 as well as Acting Chief Secretary at the time, being elevated to the post of Chief Secretary subsequently.

35 Paragraph 23 of the letter begins with the words: 'Under the orders contained in our dispatch of the 18th February 1829…' This despatch is not traceable at the West Bengal State Archives.

GLOSSARY

Adi Ganga: the old (original) Ganga

Bheesti: carrier of water for domestic use

Bhurdar: servants

Bigha/begah/bigah: measure of land varying in different places, but usually between half and three-quarters of an acre. In Bengal it was equal to 1,600 square yards

Bustee: a group of native huts crowded together the sanitary state of which has often been found wanting

Byaparitala: area populated by traders and the like; an area known by this name

Chabootah: a paved or plastered platform, often attached to a house, or in a garden

Chur: new land formed in the bed of a river

Chitta: account, memorandum

Chittack: measure of land equal to a sixteenth part of a *katha*

Chopper: thatched roof

Chokeydar: anyone in charge of a police station or any place where a watch is posted

Choukah: a volume measure used for material like sand, earth, etc.

Chunam: the common name of a plaster of which quicklime and sand are the chief ingredients, and which is largely used in building

Cooly: hired labourer

Cutcha/kutcha: unbaked; the opposite of *pucca*

Gunje: market

Ghat/ghaut: a landing-place; a path of descent to a river

Golah: store room, place where grain or salt is kept for a season

Goukhana/gowkhawnah: cowshed

Jalkar/julkur: the right of fishing; revenue derived from lakes and ponds

Jammah: rubbish from construction sites

Jangal: jungle, dense vegetation

Jemedar: chief or leader of a group; a designated rank in the native army, the police and customs

Jheel: swamp, often in the rains becoming a lake

Katha: measure of land equal to a twentieth part of a Bengal *bigha* (see above)

Khal: water channel; creek

Khalashi/clashee: tent-pitcher; someone employed as chain-man or staff man, etc., by a surveyor

Khamar: cultivated land which is not hereditary

Khoah/coah: kind of concrete made of broken brick, lime, etc.

Lack/lakh: one hundred thousand

Laldighi: red tank; a tank known by this name

Maidan: plain, any large open space

Mali/molly: gardener

Maund: standard of weight in British India equal to 40 *ser*s, the standard *ser* being equivalent to 80 *tola*s, a *tola* being equal to the weight of a rupee

Mahter: sweeper or scavenger

Mistree/mistry: artisan, mason, bricklayer, mechanic, blacksmith, etc.

Mohur: the official name of the chief gold coin of British India valued at fifteen rupees

Mullah: a learned Muslim

Moylah: filth

Musnud: large cushion, etc., used by native Indian princes in place of a throne

Mussuck: bag carried by a *bheesti*, which is made of the entire skin of a large goat, stripped of the hair and dressed

Naib: deputy

Nizamut: office of the Nizam

Nizamut Adawlut: the court on the criminal side, set up by the British Government in 1793

Palkeegarry: palanquin

Patta: deed of lease

Postah: wall

Pucca/pucka/puckah/puckha: 'permanent' hence a building, pavement or road made of brick and mortar; the opposite of *kutcha*

Sarkar: someone who keeps the accounts and makes the purchases; also applies to the Government

Soorkee/soorkey/surkey: pounded brick used to mix with lime to form a type of mortar

Sicca: silver coin of the standard value in Bengal under the East India Company's administration till it was changed to the Company's rupee. It was introduced by the Bengal Government in 1793 and abolished in 1836

Taluk: in Bengal the term was applied to tracts of proprietary land, sometimes not easily distinguished from zemindaries

Talukdar: the holder of a *taluk*

Thakoorbari: a house set apart for a family idol; a Hindu place of worship

Thana: police station; the term belongs properly to the times when military force was used to keep the peace and to collect revenue

Thanadar: person in charge of a *thana*

Tindal: the head of a body of men, especially of a gang of labourers or the crew of a ship

Zillah: an administrative district which, in the older provinces of British India, had a Collector, or Collector and Magistrate combined, and a Sessions Judge

BIBLIOGRAPHY

BOOKS

Atlas of the City of Calcutta and its Environs. Kolkata: The National Atlas and Thematic Mapping Organisation, 2010.

Blechynden, Kathleen. *Calcutta Past and Present*. London: W. Thacker and Co., 1905.

Busteed, H. E. *Echoes from Old Calcutta*. Shannon: Irish University Press, 1972. Reprint of fourth edition (first edition 1908).

By a Civilian and an Officer of the Bengal Establishment. *Tom Raw the Griffin, A Burlesque Poem*. London: R. Ackermann, 1828.

Cohen, Ashley L. *Lady Nugent's East India Journal*. New Delhi: Oxford University Press, 2014 (first published: London, 1839).

Cotton, H. E. A. *Calcutta Old and New*. Calcutta: W Newman and Co., 1907.

Das, Satyajit, ed. *Selections from the Indian Journals*. Calcutta: Firma K L Mukhopadhay, 1963, vols 1 and 2.

Dasgupta, Atis, ed. *Select Documents on Calcutta 1800-1900*. Kolkata: Directorate of State Archives, West Bengal, 2011.

Derozario, M., ed. *The Complete Monumental Register*, Calcutta, 1815.

Dodwell, E., and J. S. Miles, ed. *Alphabetical List of the Bengal Civil Servants, 1780-1838*. London: Longman, Orme and Brown, 1839.

Firminger, Walter Kelly, ed. *The Original Letters from India of Mrs Eliza Fay*. Calcutta: Thacker, Spink & Co., 1908.

Graham, Maria. *Journal of a Residence in India*. Edinburgh, 1813.

Grier, S. C. *The Letters of Warren Hastings to his Wife*. London: William Blackwood, 1905.

Hamilton, Alexander. *A New Account of the East Indies*. 2 vols. London, 1744.

Hyde, H. B. *The Parish of Bengal*. Calcutta: Thacker, Spink & Co., 1899.

Lethbridge, Roper. *Ramtanu Lahiri, Brahman and Reformer*. London:

Swan Sonnenschein & Co. Limited, 1907 (a translation of Sibnath Shastri's *Ramtanu Lahiri O Tatkalin Banga Samaj*, 1904).

Long, James. *Selections from Unpublished Records of Government 1748 to 1767*. Edited by Mahadevaprasad Saha. Calcutta: Firma K L Mukhopadhaya, 1973 (first published 1869).

Martin, J. R. *Notes on the Medical Topography of Calcutta.* Calcutta: G H Huttmann, Bengal Military Orphan Press, 1837.

Mittra, Peary Chand. *A Biographical Sketch of David Hare.* Calcutta: W Newman, 1877.

Mukherjee, S. N. *Calcutta: Myths and History.* Calcutta: Subarnarekha, 1977.

Nair, P. T. *A History of Calcutta's Streets.* Calcutta: Firma KLM Pvt Ltd, 1987.

Namier, Lewis. *Skyscrapers and Other Essays.* London: Macmillan, 1931.

Ray, A. K. *A Short History of Calcutta*, Calcutta: Riddhi-India, 1982 (first published in 1902 as part of the 1901 Census).

Ray Choudhury, Ranabir. *A City in the Making: Aspects of Calcutta's Early Growth*. New Delhi: Niyogi Books, 2016.

———, ed. *Glimpses of Old Calcutta*. Bombay: Nachiketa Publications, 1978.

———. *The Lord Sahib's House*. Kolkata: Wild Strawberries Books, 2010.

Robb, Peter. *Sentiment and Self: Richard Blechynden's Calcutta Diaries*, 1791-1822. New Delhi: Oxford University Press, 2011.

———. *Sex and Sensibility: Richard Blechynden's Calcutta Diaries*, 1791-1822. New Delhi: Oxford University Press, 2011.

———. *Useful Friendship: Europeans and Indians in Early Calcutta*. New Delhi: Oxford University Press, 2014.

Seton-Karr, W. S., ed. *Selections from Calcutta Gazettes*, vols 1 and 2. Calcutta: Government of India, 1864 and 1865.

Sinha, H. N., ed. *Fort William-India House Correspondence*, vol. 2. Delhi: Government of India, 1957.

Strong, F. P. *Extracts from the Topography and Vital Statistics of Calcutta.* Calcutta: 1849.

Teignmouth, Lord. *Memoirs of the Life, Writings, and Correspondence of Sir William Jones.* Philadelphia: W. M. Poyntell & Co., 1805.

The Bengal Obituary. Calcutta: Holmes and Co., 1848.

Yule, Henry, and A. C. Burnell, ed. *Hobson-Jobson.* Calcutta: Rupa and Co., 1986. Reprint (first edition 1886).

OFFICIAL PAPERS

Board of Revenue Proceedings, West Bengal State Archives (WBSA).

Board of Trade (Commercial) Proceedings, WBSA.

Calcutta Committee of Revenue Proceedings, WBSA.

Committee of Revenue Proceedings, WBSA.

Judicial Criminal Proceedings, WBSA.

Judicial Original Consultations, WBSA.

Letters from the Court of Directors, Judicial, WBSA.

Letters to the Court of Directors, Judicial, WBSA.

Lottery Committee Proceedings, Victoria Memorial Hall, Kolkata.

Minutes of Vestry Meetings, St John's Church, Kolkata.

Territorial Revenue Proceedings, WBSA.

PERIODICALS

Bengal Past and Present, vols 1, 27, 29 and 30.

The Asiatic Journal for 1817 and 1821.

The Bengal Directory for 1824, 1825, 1842 and 1875.

The Calcutta Annual Register for 1821.

The Calcutta Review, July-December, 1852.

The East India Kalendar, or Asiatic Register for 1792.

The East India Register for 1819.

The European Magazine and London Review, vol. 11 for 1787.

MONOGRAPHS

The South Park Street Cemetery. Brought out by the British Association for Cemeteries in South Asia in collaboration with the Christian Burial Board on the occasion of the founding of the Association for the Preservation of Historical Cemeteries in India, Calcutta, 1978.

PHOTO CREDITS

Christian Burial Board: Figures 1 and 8

C.R. Wilson, *Old Fort William* (1906): Figure 31

H.B. Hyde, *The Parish of Bengal* (1899): Figure 47

Lottery Committee Proceedings 15 January 1818: Figure 10

National Atlas & Thematic Mapping Organisation (NATMO): Figures 4, 5, 7, 9, 11, 12, 14, 15, 16, 17, 25, 27, 29, 30, 32, 34, 36, 37, 38, 39, 40, 41, 42, 43, 44, 45, 46, 49, 50, 51, 52, 53, 55, 56, 64, 65, 66, 67, 68, 69, 70, 71, 72, 74 and 75

Ranadev Ray Choudhury: Figures 33, 35 and 61

St John's Church: Figures 3 and 28

The British Library: Figures 2, 6, 13, 18, 19, 20, 21, 22, 23, 24, 26, 48, 54, 58, 59, 60, 62, 63, 73 and 76

ACKNOWLEDGEMENTS

At the very outset, two former Curators of the Victoria Memorial Hall, the late Nisith Ranjan Ray and Dr Chitto Panda, have to be thanked profusely for allowing the author to consult the volumes of the Lottery Committee Proceedings kept at the Hall during the period they were in office. As usual, Bidisha Chakraborty and Sarmishta De helped out selflessly with relevant material located at the West Bengal State Archives. The permission given by Reverend P.K. Nanda to consult the St John's Church vestry records is much appreciated. Ranojoy Bose, of the Christian Burial Board, enabled the author to locate the tombs of W.C. Blaquiere and Charles Trower at the Circular Road Cemetery, and also that of Charles Short at the South Park Street Cemetery. The National Atlas & Thematic Mapping Organisation needs to be complimented for bringing out the 'Atlas of the City of Calcutta and its Environs' (2010) from which most of the maps have been sourced. The author is thankful for the immaculate and exacting editorial work done by Sucharita Ghosh of Niyogi Books. Finally, the author takes great pleasure in acknowledging the constant support extended by Tultul Niyogi as also the encouragement provided by his wife and the children living in Singapore, not to speak of the occasional push and shove by Aurobindo Roy.

INDEX